WORLD PREHISTORY

WORLD PREHISTORY

A Brief Introduction

FOURTH EDITION

Brian M. Fagan

University of California, Santa Barbara

 **LONGMAN**

An imprint of Addison Wesley Longman, Inc.

New York • Reading, Massachusetts • Menlo Park, California • Harlow, England
Don Mills, Ontario • Sydney • Mexico City • Madrid • Amsterdam

Editor-in-Chief: Priscilla McGeehon
Marketing Manager: Megan Galvin
Project Coordination and Text Design: York Production Services
Cover Designer/Manager: Nancy Danahy
Photo Researcher: Mira Schachne
Full Service Production Manager: Richard Ausburn
Senior Print Buyer: Hugh Crawford
Electronic Page Makeup: York Production Services
Printer and Binder: The Maple-Vail Book Manufacturing Group
Cover Printer: Coral Graphic Services, Inc.

For permission to use copyrighted material, grateful acknowledgment is made to the copyright holders on pp. 337–338, which are hereby made part of this copyright page.

Library of Congress Cataloging-in-Publication Data
Fagan, Brian M.
    World prehistory: a brief introduction/Brian M. Fagan.—4th ed.
      p. cm.
    Includes bibliographical references and index.
    ISBN 0-321-02365-X
    1. Prehistoric peoples. 2. Anthropology, Prehistoric. 3. Human evolution. 4. Antiquities, Prehistoric. I. Title.
    GN740.F34   1998
    930—dc21   98–35076
                                                 CIP

Please visit our website at http://longman.awl.com

ISBN 0-321-02365-X

1 2 3 4 5 6 7 8 9 10 — MA — 01 00 99 98

There is not yet one person, one animal. . . . Only the sky alone is there; the face of the earth is not clear. Only the sea alone is pooled under all the sky; there is nothing whatever gathered together. It is at rest; not a single thing stirs. . . . Whatever there is that might be is simply not there: only the pooled water. . . .

From the Quiche Maya legend of the creation.
Dennis Tedlock, *Popol Vuh* (New York: Doubleday, 1985, p. 127).

Contents

PART 3   THE BIRTH OF THE MODERN WORLD   89

Preface

Golden pharaohs, lost cities, grinning human skeletons: archaeology is the stuff of romance and legend! Many people still think of archaeologists as adventurers and treasure hunters, like Indiana Jones of Hollywood movie fame seeking the elusive Holy Grail. This enduring image goes back to the late nineteenth century, when archaeologists like Heinrich Schliemann fame could still find lost civilizations like Troy and excavate three royal palaces in a week. Today, few, if any, archaeologists behave like Indiana Jones. They are scientists, not adventurers, as comfortable in an air-conditioned laboratory as they are on a remote excavation. The development of scientific archaeology from its Victorian beginnings ranks among the greatest triumphs of 20th-century science. Archaeology has changed our understanding of the human experience in profound ways. A century ago, most scientists believed humans were no more than 100,000 years old. Today we know that our origins go back 5 million years. Our predecessors assumed the Americas were settled in about 8000 B.C. and that farming began around 4000 B.C. New excavations date the first Americans to at least 12,000 B.C. and the beginnings of agriculture to 8500 B.C. Most important of all, archaeology has changed our perceptions of ourselves, our biological and cultural diversity. Welcome to the fascinating world of archaeology!

The fourth edition of *World Prehistory* continues a long tradition of providing an interesting, jargon-free journey through the 5-million-year-old landscape of the human past. I hope you enjoy your sojourn in its pages!

HIGHLIGHTS OF THE FOURTH EDITION

This is an exciting time to be writing about archaeology, for many scientific advances are changing our perceptions about the past. Accordingly, the fourth edition is somewhat longer than its predecessors, with expanded coverage of major theoretical issues and the early civilizations. The fourth edition contains important new discoveries about early human evolution, the late Ice Age, and the origins of agriculture. New and updated coverage of the field appears in every chapter, with an up-to-date Guide to Further Reading at the end of the book along with Glossaries of Technical Terms and Archaeological Sites and Cultural Names.

Updating and Rewriting

- *New perceptions of world prehistory.* Chapter 1 includes new discussion of archaeology and alternative perspectives on the past, reflecting new thinking on this important topic.
- *Early human evolution.* Chapter 2 discusses the latest advances in the study of human origins, including the latest fossil discoveries in Ethiopia and Kenya, among them *Ardipithecus ramidus,* the earliest known human ancestor.
- *Origins of modern humans.* Chapter 3 covers new research into the controversial issue of the earliest modern humans and fresh perceptions of Neanderthal ancestry and behavior.
- *Origins of food production.* In Chapter 6, the fourth edition incorporates much-expanded coverage of the latest theories on the origins of agriculture and animal domestication. Chapter 7, which describes the first farmers, incorporates new dates for early agriculture obtained from accelerator mass spectrometry (AMS) radiocarbon dates.
- *Origins of states and civilization.* Chapter 9 has been expanded to include current theoretical debates on the origins of state-organized societies. Chapters 10 to 14 offer an up-to-date description and analysis of the first civilizations, with expanded coverage of ancient Egyptian civilization and of south and southeast Asian states. Chapters 12 and 13 offer more comprehensive analysis of highland and lowland Mesoamerican civilizations than in previous editions.
- *Revision and updating throughout.* The entire text and Guide to Further Reading have been revised and updated on a page-by-page basis. Over half the book has been completely rewritten for this expanded edition.

Boxes

Two types of in-text boxes enhance the book, designed to amplify the narrative:

- *Discovery.* These boxes include brief accounts of spectacular discoveries that have revolutionized our understanding of the past, such as Grotte de Chauvet, France, the Ice Man of the Alps, and the Lords of Sipán, Peru.
- *Dating the Past.* These boxes introduce key dating methods, such as radiocarbon and AMS dating.

In addition, Chapter 1 includes boxes on ethnographic analogy, classification of ancient societies, and chronological methods.

New and Revised Art Program

The fourth edition's art program has been expanded with new photographs and fresh or revised line art. The new illustrations provide additional background on recent discoveries, amplify the narrative, or replace older art with new pictures. Some expanded captions serve to integrate the illustrations more closely into the text.

ACKNOWLEDGMENTS

The fourth edition has benefited from the expertise of many colleagues, too numerous to list here. I am deeply grateful for their encouragement and assistance. I would like to thank the following reviewers for their help in revising the ninth edition. I appreciate their frank comments:

Anagnosti Agelarakis, *Adelphi Univeristy*
Cliff Boyd, *Radford University*
Charles Ellenbaum, *College of DuPage*
Thomas Foor, *University of Montana*
Alan McPherron, *University of Pittsburgh*
Jane Peterson, *Marquette University*
John Pryor, *CSU-Fresno*
Anne Rogers, *Western Carolina University*

Lastly, my thanks to my editor of many years, Alan McClare, also to photographic researcher Mira Schachne, and the editorial and production staff at York Production Services. They have turned a complex manuscript into an attractive book and done all they can to minimize unexpected difficulties.

As always, I would be most grateful for criticisms, comments, or details of new work, sent to me c/o Department of Anthropology, University of California, Santa Barbara, CA 93108 (e-mail: bfagan@west.net).

Brian M. Fagan

A Note on Chronologies and Measurements

The narrative of prehistory in these pages is organized in as linear a fashion chronologically as is practicable. It is based on radiocarbon, potassium-argon, and tree-ring dates, as well as historical documents. Although every effort has been made to make dates accurate, many of them should be recognized for what they are—statistical approximations. The time scales of prehistory are presented in two ways:

- At the beginning of each chapter (except Chapters 1, 5, 8, and 13), a Timelines column shows the reader the relative position of the developments described in that chapter within the broad time frame of prehistoric times.
- Chronological tables placed at strategic points in the book provide a comparative view of developments in different areas of the world. Each is linked to its predecessors and successors, so that they provide background continuity for the narrative.

The following conventions are used:

- Dates before 10,000 years ago are expressed in years Before Present (B.P.)
- Dates after 10,000 years ago are expressed in years Before Christ (B.C.) or Anno Domini (A.D.).

Another common convention is B.C.E./C.E. (Before Common Era/Common Era), which is not employed in this book. By scientific convention, "present" is A.D. 1950.

Please note that all radiocarbon dates and potassium-argon dates should be understood to have a plus and minus factor that is omitted from this book in the interests of clarity. They are statistical estimates. Where possible, radiocarbon dates have been calibrated with tree-ring chronologies, which adds a substantial element of accuracy (see Chapter 1).

For tree-ring calibration of radiocarbon dates, see *Radiocarbon*, 1993. *Measurements.* All measurements are given in miles, yards, feet, and inches, with metric equivalents.

P A R T

1

PREHISTORY

It is a capital mistake to theorize before one has data. Insensibly, one begins to wish facts to suit theories, instead of theories to suit facts. . . .

SHERLOCK HOLMES
A Scandal in Bohemia

CHAPTER 1

The Study of Human Prehistory

Since time immemorial, humans have been intensely curious about their origins, about the mysterious and sometimes threatening world in which they exist. They know that earlier generations lived before them, that their children, grand-children, and their progeny in turn will, in due course, dwell on earth. But how did this world come about? Who created the familiar landscape of rivers, fields, mountains, plants, and animals? Who fashioned the oceans and sea coasts, deep lakes and fast-flowing streams? Above all, how did the first men and women settle the land? Who created them, how did they come into being? Every society has creation stories to account for human origins. However, archaeology and biological anthropology have replaced legend with an intricate account of human evolution and cultural development that extends back more than 2.5 million years. This chapter describes how archaeologists study and interpret the past.

"IN THE BEGINNING . . ."

> After the Great Fire destroyed the world and before the little bird Icanchu flew away, he roamed the wasteland in search of First Place. The homeland lay beyond recognition, but Icanchu's index finger, of its own accord, pointed to the spot. There he unearthed the charcoal stump that he pounded as his drum. Playing without stopping, he chanted with the dark drum's sounds. . . . At dawn on the new Day, a green shoot sprang from the coal drum and soon flowered as Firstborn Tree. . . . From its branches bloomed the forms of life that flourished in the new World. . . .[1]

We Westerners take the past for granted, accept human evolution as something that extends back many thousands, even millions of years. Science provides us with a long perspective on ancient times. In contrast, the story of Icanchu's drum is a classic origin myth of the cosmic fire told by the Mataco Indians from South America. Like all such accounts, the tale begins with a **primordium** (the very beginning) in which a mythic being, in this case Icanchu, works to create the familiar animals, landscape, and plants of the world, and then the human inhabitants. Icanchu, and his equivalents in a myriad of human cultures throughout the world, create order from primeval chaos, as God does in Genesis, Chapter 1.

---

[1] Lawrence Sullivan, *Icanchu's Drum* (New York: Macmillan, 1988), p. 92.

D I S C O V E R Y

The Tomb of Tutankhamun, Egypt

The two men paused in front of the doorway that bore the seals of the long-dead pharaoh. They had waited six long years, from 1917 to 1922, for this moment. Silently, Howard Carter pried a hole through the ancient plaster. Hot air rushed out of the small cavity and massaged his face. Carter shone a flashlight through the hole and peered into the tomb. Gold objects swam in front of his eyes, and he was struck dumb with amazement.

Lord Carnarvon moved impatiently behind him as Carter remained silent. "What do you see?" he asked, hoarse with excitement.

"Wonderful things," whispered Carter as he stepped back from the doorway.

They soon broke down the door. In a daze of wonderment, Carter and Carnarvon wandered through the antechamber of Tutankhamun's tomb. They fingered golden funerary beds, admired beautifully inlaid chests, and examined the pharaoh's chariots stacked against the wall. Gold was everywhere—on wooden statues, inlaid on thrones and boxes, in jewelry, even on children's stools. Soon Tutankhamun was known as the golden pharaoh, and archaeology as the domain of buried treasure and royal sepulchers. His is the only known undisturbed Egyptian pharaoh's tomb.

Myths, and the rituals and religious rites associated with them, function to create a context for the entire symbolic life of a human society, a symbolic life that is the very cornerstone of human existence. The first human beings establish the sacred order through which life endures from one generation to the next. This kind of history, based on legend and myth, is one of symbolic existence. Creation legends tell of unions between gods and monsters, of people emerging from holes in the earth after having climbed sacred trees that link the layers of the cosmos. They create indissoluble symbolic bonds between humans and other kinds of life, such as plants, animals, and celestial beings.

The vivid and ever-present symbolic world has influenced the course of human life ever since humans first acquired the power of creative thought and reasoning. The Cro-Magnons of late Ice Age Europe depicted mythical animals and the symbolism of their lives in cave paintings more than 20,000 years ago (Figure 1.1) (Chapter 4). They modeled clay bison in dark chambers deep beneath the earth. The sculptures seemed to flicker in the light of fire brands during powerful rituals carried out by **shamans,** tribal priests with the ability to voyage into the mysterious supernatural world. So compelling was the influence of the unknown powers of the cosmos and of the gods that inhabited it that the Maya and other central American civilizations created entire ceremonial centers in the form of symbolic landscapes to commemorate their mythic universe (Chapters 12 and 13).

Today, Western science has chronicled more than 2.5 million years of prehistory, a narrative of human endeavor that extends back through hundreds of thousands of years of unfolding time. This story is one based on scientific research, something quite different from the creation legends that people use

Figure 1.1 MANELESS LIONS Painted by late ice age Cro-Magnon people on the walls of the **Grotte de Chauvet,** South-western France. c. 31,000 to 24,000 years ago.

to define their complex relationships with the natural and spiritual worlds. These legends are deeply felt, important sources of cultural identity. They foster a quite different relationship with the past than that engendered by archaeology, which seeks to understand our common biological and cultural roots, and the great diversity of humanity.

PSEUDOARCHAEOLOGY

Golden pharaohs, lost civilizations, buried treasure—archaeology seems like a romantic world of high adventure and exciting discovery. A century ago, archaeology was indeed a matter of exotic travel to remote places. It was still possible to find a hitherto unknown civilization with a few weeks of digging. Today, archaeology is a highly scientific discipline, concerned more with minute details of ancient life than with spectacular discoveries. But an aura of unsolved mysteries and heroic figures still surrounds the subject in many peoples' eyes—to the point of obsession.

The mysteries of the past attract many people, especially those with a taste for adventure, escapism, and science fiction. These people create elaborate adventure stories about the past—almost invariably epic journeys or voyages based on illusory data.

For example, British journalist Graham Hancock has recently claimed that a great civilization flourished under Antarctic ice 12,000 years ago. (Of course, its magnificent cities are buried under deep ice sheets, so we cannot excavate them!) Colonists spread to all parts of the world from their Antarctic home, colonizing such well-known sites as Tiwanaku in the Bolivian highlands and building the Sphinx by the banks of the Nile. Hancock weaves an ingenious story, by piecing together all manner of controversial geological observations and isolated archaeological finds. He waves aside the obvious archaeologist's reaction, which asks where traces of these ancient colonies and civilizations are to be found in Egypt and other places. Hancock fervently believes in his far-fetched theory, and being a good popular writer, he has managed to piece together a best-selling book that reads like a "whodunit" written by an amateur sleuth.

Flamboyant pseudoarchaeology of the type espoused by Hancock will always appeal to people who are impatient with the deliberate pace of science and to those who believe in faint possibilities. It is as if a scientist tried to reconstruct the contents of an American house using artifacts found in Denmark, New Zealand, South Africa, Spain, and Tahiti.

Nonscientific nonsense like this comes in many forms. There are those who believe that the Lost Continent of Atlantis once lay under the waters of the Bahamas and that Atlanteans fled their sunken homeland and settled the Americas thousands of years ago. Others fantasize about fleets of ancient Egyptian boats or Roman galleys that crossed the Atlantic long before Columbus. All these bizarre manifestations of archaeology have one thing in common: they are overly simple, convenient explanations of complex events in the past, with explanations based on such archaeological data as their author cares to use.

These kinds of pseudoarchaeology belong to the realms of religious faith and science fiction. The real science of the past is based on rigorous procedures and meticulous data collection, its theorizing on constantly modified hypotheses tested against information collected in the field and laboratory—in short, archaeological, biological, and other evidence.

PREHISTORY, ARCHAEOLOGY, AND WORLD PREHISTORY

Human beings are among the only animals that have a skeleton adapted for standing and walking upright, which leaves our hands free for purposes other than moving around. These physical traits are controlled by a powerful brain capable of abstract thought. The same brain allows us to communicate symbolically and orally through language and to develop highly diverse cultures—learned ways of behaving and adapting to our natural environments. The special features that make us human have evolved over hundreds of thousands of years.

The scientific study of the past is a search for answers to fundamental questions about human origins. How long ago did humans appear? When and how did they evolve? How can we account for the remarkable biological and cultural diversity of humankind? How did early humans settle the world and develop so many different societies at such different levels of complexity? Why did some societies cultivate the soil and herd cattle while others remained hunters and gatherers? Why did some peoples like, for example, the San foragers of southern Africa or the Shoshone of the Great Basin in North America live in small family bands, while the ancient Egyptians and the Aztecs of Mexico developed highly elaborate civilizations (Figure 1.2)? When did more complex human societies evolve and why? The answers to these questions are the concern of scientists studying world prehistory.

Prehistory is defined by archaeologists as that portion of human history that extends back some 2.5 million years before the time of written documents and archives. In contrast, **history**, the study of human experience through documents, has a much shorter time span. Written records go back to before 5000 years in western Asia. Writing and written records came into use centuries later elsewhere in the world, in some parts of Africa and Asia only within the past century, when European powers annexed vast new territories and started to rule their new possessions. The study of prehistory is a multidisciplinary enterprise that involves

Figure 1.2   Pyramids of Giza, Egypt

not only archaeologists but scientists from many other disciplines, including biologists, botanists, geographers, geologists, and zoologists—to mention only a few. But archaeology is the primary source of information on human prehistory.

The archaeologist is a special type of anthropologist concerned not with living societies but with ancient cultures. **Archaeology consists of a broad range of scientific methods and techniques for studying the past, used carefully and in a disciplined way.** The archaeologist studies the human societies of the remote and recent past, using the surviving material remains of their cultures to do so. Archaeology is a highly effective way of studying human cultures in the past and the ways in which they have changed over long periods of time. It covers the entire time span of human existence, from over 2.5 million years ago right up to the study of 19th-century railroad stations and the garbage from modern industrial cities.

A century ago, most archaeologists worked in Europe and western Asia. They thought of human prehistory in very provincial terms and were convinced that all significant developments such as agriculture and civilization itself had originated in the area between Mesopotamia and the Nile. Today, archaeologists are at work all over the globe—in Africa, Alaska, and Australia. Thanks to universal dating methods such as radiocarbon dating, we can date and compare prehistoric developments in widely separated parts of the world. We know, for example, that agriculture began in Syria in about 8000 B.C. and in central Africa about 2000 years ago. We can date the first human occupation of Europe to about 500,000 years ago, and that of North America to about 15,000 years before present. This is the study of **world prehistory,** the prehistory of humankind evaluated not just from the perspective of a single region such as western Asia, but from a global viewpoint.

World prehistory developed as a result of two major developments in archaeology. The first was the development of **radiocarbon (¹⁴C) dating** by

University of Chicago physicists Willard Libby and J.R. Arnold in 1949. For the first time, archaeologists had at their disposal a dating method of potential global application that enabled them not only to date sites in all corners of the world, but also to compare the chronology of, say, the first agriculture in southwest Asia with that in the Americas (See "Radiocarbon Dating" box in Chapter 4).

Until then, no one could make easy, direct chronological comparisons between widely separated regions, nor did they have a way of measuring the rate of cultural change through time. Within 15 years of Libby and Arnold's remarkable discovery, radiocarbon dates from hundreds of sites allowed the construction of the first reliable global chronologies, as a population explosion of professional archaeologists occurred worldwide. Today, archaeological expeditions are at work in every corner of the world, and in every environment imaginable: in the remote wilds of Siberia, in tropical rain forests along the Amazon River in South America, on Easter Island in the Pacific, in the middle of the arid Sahara Desert, and under the world's oceans.

In 1961, the Cambridge University archaeologist Grahame Clark published his classic *World Prehistory* (3d ed., 1977), the first synthesis of archaeology that took full account of radiocarbon chronology and global archaeological research. This ground-breaking volume became a modern classic and helped turn archaeology intellectually from a somewhat provincial discipline into the global enterprise it is today.

MAJOR DEVELOPMENTS IN HUMAN PREHISTORY

World prehistory, as described in this book, is concerned with the broad sweep of the human past, more specifically with four major developments (Table 1.1):

- The origins of humankind some 2.5 million years ago. We describe the ancestors of the first humans, the fossil evidence for our origins, and some of the behavioral changes and innovations that accompanied the appearance of our earliest forebears.
- The evolution of archaic *Homo erectus* and the origins of anatomically modern people, ourselves. These developments span a long period between about 1.6 million and 15,000 years before the present. We also describe the spread of fully modern humans through the Old World and into the Americas, a process that ended about 15,000 years ago.
- The origins of more complex forager societies, of agriculture and animal domestication, sometimes called **food production**, after about 10,000 years ago. We evaluate the different theories developed to explain greater cultural and social complexity and why humans took up farming, and describe the early beginnings and spread of agriculture in western Asia, Europe, Asia, and the Americas.
- The origins of urbanized, literate civilization (**state-organized societies**) in about 3100 B.C. in western Asia and the development of similar, complex societies in other parts of the world in later millennia.

These major developments provide us with a broad framework for telling the story of prehistory. And central to this framework are the notions of time

Table 1.1   Major Developments in Human Prehistory

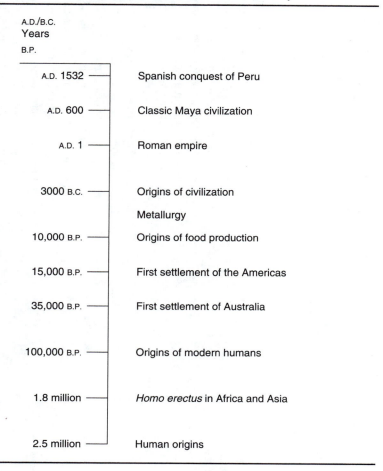

A.D./B.C. Years B.P.	
A.D. 1532	Spanish conquest of Peru
A.D. 600	Classic Maya civilization
A.D. 1	Roman empire
3000 B.C.	Origins of civilization
	Metallurgy
10,000 B.P.	Origins of food production
15,000 B.P.	First settlement of the Americas
35,000 B.P.	First settlement of Australia
100,000 B.P.	Origins of modern humans
1.8 million	*Homo erectus* in Africa and Asia
2.5 million	Human origins

and space—the context of biological and cultural developments in the past. (For a brief summary of how archaeological research proceeds, see Figure 1.3.)

CYCLICAL AND LINEAR TIME

All societies have an interest in the past. It is always around them, haunting, mystifying, tantalizing, sometimes offering potential lessons for the present and future. The past is important because social life unfolds through time, embedded within a framework of cultural expectations and values. In the high Arctic, Inuit preserve their traditional attitudes, skills, and coping mechanisms in some of the harshest environments on earth. They do this by incorporating the lessons of the past into the present. In many societies, the ancestors are the guardians of the land, which symbolizes present, past, and future. Westerners

A. The results of the research, the data, and interpretation are published in a scientific monograph or journal article. The site and research are now on permanent record for posterity.

B. Interpretation of the data is now undertaken, in the context of the research design, which is modified constantly as the research proceeds. This interpretation is based on the results of hypothesis testing during survey, excavation, and laboratory work.

C. The hypothesis generated at the beginning of the research are now tested against the analyzed data, again a process that takes place constantly as research and excavation proceed.

Analysis and data reduction are processes that begin as soon as archaeologists start collecting artifacts and other information in the field. While some of this work takes place in the field, most of it is undertaken back in the laboratory. It is now, too, that specialist data like animal bones, plant remains, or isotopic analysis or radiocarbon dating are sent out for examination by experts.Their reports form part of the analysis process and are critical to later stages of the research.

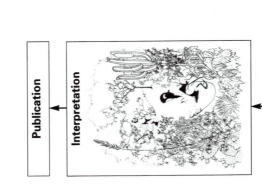

Publication

Interpretation

Analysis

F. Guila Naquitz was published as a monograph edited by Kent Flannery: *Guila Naquitz: Archaic Forging and Early Agriculture in Oaxaca, Mexico* (Academic Press, Orlando, 1986).

G. The core of the interpretation was an elaborate computer-based simulation that used the data from the excavations to test two hypotheses:

- What strategy led the ocuupants to select the mix of plants found on the living floors?
- How did this strategy change during the period of incipient agriculture?

Robert Reynolds developed an "adaptive computer model" for this purpose, incorporating the data from the excavations and laboratory work. His simulations showed that potential domesticates were probably first planted in wet years, and then, after they were proved reliable, in dry and average years. As time went on, plant cultivation assumed more importance in the diet and shifted from the thorn forest where people had originally concentrated their foraging activities into mesquite grassland, better suited for agriculture.

H. The cave was small enough to be excavated in its entirety, using small test trenches to identify the natural stratigraphy, then removing each living surface horizontally and separately. The entire site was excavated with trowels and brushes and the deposit passed through two screens of different sizes. Radiocarbon samples taken during the excavations dated the Guila Naquitz occupations to between 8750 and 6670 B.C.

Back in the laboratory, a team of nearly 20 specialists examined the finds, everything from chipped stone tools to tiny rodent bones. Others analyzed the distributions of artifacts on living surfaces, analyzed the division of labor at the site, and assessed the nutritional value of the food remains.

I. Excavations were undertaken to develop a model to account for the underlying and more universal aspects of early plant domestication. They were also designed to tie this process into what was known about the cultures of the Valley of Oaxaca between 10,000 and 5000 B.C.

J. The site was discovered in January 1966 and excavated between February and May of the same year.

Data Collection

Research Design

Discovery

D. Data collection is a process that begins with initial site survey and continues right through excavations and all fieldwork. The excavation crew may include not only trained archaeologists but specialist experts on such topics as soil chemestry or animal bones. The collection process involves very accurate record keeping and the application of the initial research design. The hypotheses generated as part of this design are tested and modified constantly—as is the design—as data collection proceeds.

E. Archaeological research begins with the discovery of a site, or with a campaign of deliberate survey to find locations for later excavation. All research commences with the formulation of a formal research design, which includes not only background information, but objectives and hypotheses to be tested during the work, and a general theoretical framework for the fieldwork. A research design is the blueprint for survey and excavation, the working document for subsequent research. The best designs are highly flexible, designed to be easily modified as the work proceeds and objectives and hypotheses change.

Figure 1.3 How Archaeology Works   The process of archaeological research, as illustrated by excavations by Kent Flannery at Guilá Naquitz rock shelter, Valley of Oaxaca, Mexico.

have an intense scientific interest in ancient times, partly borne of curiosity, but also out of a need for historical identity. There are many reasons to attempt to preserve an accurate record of earlier times, and no one, least of all an archaeologist, should assume that they are uniquely privileged in their interest.

We may all share an interest in the past, but we think of it, and use it, in different ways, just as we have different perspectives on time.

While it is true that archaeology is the only method Western science has of studying cultural change through time, that does not give archaeologists unique authority over the past. In many societies, history is a valued cultural commodity, in ways that are fundamentally different from those of the archaeologist. The transmission of knowledge about ancient times lies in the hands of respected elders, who take pains to preserve the accuracy of oral traditions. Such traditions are of vital importance, and they are carefully controlled, for they define and preserve a group's identity from one generation to the next. The past is vested not in science, but in household, community, kin groups, and territory. Among the Yolngu Aborigines of Australia's Northern Territory, for example, only the oldest clan members are repositories for the most important historical knowledge. As both Australian Aborigines and Native Americans have pointed out, there is a fundamental incompatibility between Western science and its perspectives on the past and those of other societies. In part, this incompatibility revolves around the notion of linear time.

Westerners think of the passage of the human experience along a straight, if branching, highway of time. The great nineteenth-century German statesman Otto von Bismarck called this the "stream of time," upon which all human societies ride for a time. We have a sense of linear, unraveling history that goes back through 5000 years of recorded history to early Egypt and Mesopotamia. Ancient Egyptian civilization began in 3100 B.C.; Rome was founded in 753 B.C.; Christopher Columbus landed in the Bahamas on October 12, 1492; and the Declaration of Independence dates to July 4, 1776. These are landmarks along the ladder of historical chronology, which continues to unfold inexorably every day, month, and year, as we live our lives.

An unfolding, linear past is not the only way of conceptualizing ancient times. Many non-Western societies, ancient and modern, think of time as a cyclical phenomenon, or sometimes as a combination of the linear and the cyclical. The cyclical perspective stems from the passage of seasons and of heavenly bodies, from the close relationships between foragers and village farmers and their natural environments. It is also based on the eternal verities of human life: fertility and birth, life, growth, and death. The endlessly repeating seasons of planting and harvest, of game movements or salmon runs, and of ripening wild foods govern human existence in deeply significant ways. The ancient Maya developed an elaborate cyclical calendar of interlocking secular and religious calendars to measure the passage of the seasons and to regulate religious ceremonies (Chapter 12).

However, we should not assume that societies with cyclical views of time did not have linear chronologies as well. The celebrated Maya "Long Count" was a linear chronology that formed an integral part of the close relationship between Maya rulers and the cosmos. The ancient Egyptians developed a linear chronology for administrative purposes. But, in general, societies develop linear chronologies only when they need them. For example, Western societies use linear time to regulate times of prayer, to control the working day, and for airline schedules. It is hard to generalize, but societies with centralized political systems tend to use the reigns of chiefs or kings as signposts along a linear time scale. For instance, the history of the rulers of the state of **Benin** in West Africa shows a significant shift in the interpretation of time. Before the fourteenth century A.D., Benin history is essentially mythological, with inaccurate chronology and a variable number of kings. But with the founding of the Yoruba dynasty, the deeds and reigns of every *oba* (king) are remembered in detail with chronological accuracy right down to modern times (Figure 1.4).

Figure 1.4 A Bronze Plaque from Benin City, Nigeria, West Africa, Showing a Seated *Oba* (King) with Kneeling Attendants These artifacts served as important historical records of royal reigns and genealogy and were stored in the royal palace.

Many non-Western societies do not perceive themselves as living in a changeless world. They make a fundamental distinction between the recent past, which lies within living memory, and the more remote past, which came before memory. For instance, the Australian Aborigine groups living in north-east Queensland distinguish between *kuma,* the span of events witnessed by living people, *anthantnama,* a long time ago, and *yilamu,* the period of the creation. Furthermore, many societies also accept that there was cultural change in the past, among them Hindu traditions of history, which speak of early people who lived without domesticated animals and plants, and the Hazda hunter-gatherers of East Africa who speak of their homeland's first inhabitants as being giants without fire or tools. These paradigms of the past take many forms, with mythic creators of culture, usually primordial ancestors, deities, or animals establishing contemporary social customs and the familiar landscape, or a more remote, discontinuous heroic era like that of the Greeks, which allowed writers like the playwright Aeschylus to evaluate contemporary behavior.

WRITTEN RECORDS, ORAL HISTORY, AND ARCHAEOLOGY

Most human societies of the past were nonliterate, meaning that they transmitted knowledge and history orally, by word of mouth. Written records are the most comprehensive source of information about the past, but they usually follow a strictly linear chronology. They also served as educational tools. Apart from anything else, written documents were useful as cues for people to memorize standardized historical, ritual, or mythical information.

The Aztec oral histories, partially set down after the Spanish Conquest of the 15th century A.D., are an excellent example of history transmitted by word of mouth. They were recited according to a well-defined narrative plot, which focused on Great Men, key events (like the dedication of the Sun God Huitzilopochtli's temple in the Aztec capital in 1487), and the histories of favored groups. In these, as in other oral histories, there were formulas and themes, which formed the central ingredients of a story that varied considerably from one speaker to the next, even if the essential content was the same. Many oral histories are mixtures of factual data and parables that communicate moral and political values. But to those who hear them, they are publicly sanctioned history, performed before a critical group, and subject to the critical evaluation of an audience who may have heard the same stories before (Figure 1.5).

Both written records and oral histories are subject to all kinds of bias. Neither can claim to be totally objective, any more than archaeology is. The problem for the archaeologist is to correlate data from excavations with that from oral traditions, to establish critically what is factual history and what is myth or moral exhortation. Oral traditions are hard to use, as their antiquity is very difficult to establish. In some cases, in Australia for exam-

Figure 1.5 MAYA HISTORY Two monkey scribes sit on either side of a thick screen-fold book, discussing a page they have opened. The scribe on the left holds a writing instrument in his hand.

ple, there are instances in which oral histories and archaeology coincide in general terms. For example, the traditions speak of the arrival of the first people from overseas, of flooding of coastal areas, and of the hunting of giant marsupials (pouched animals like the kangaroo). So Australia's past can be said to come from two sources: archaeological data and oral traditions. In some instances, the archaeologists and indigenous people have shared interests and come together in identifying sacred places and historic places, often to ensure they are preserved. Sometimes the two groups differ drastically on the "significance" of a particular location, where the archaeologist finds no buildings or artifacts, yet the local people consider it a "sacred place."

But, all too often, the archaeologist and a local community have different interests in the past. To the archaeologist, the past is scientific data to be studied with all the rigor of modern science. To local people, the past is often highly personalized and the property of the ancestors. Such histories are valid alternative versions of history that deserve respect and understanding because they play a vital role in the creation and reaffirmation of cultural identity.

Archaeologists are not alone in considering the past of value, nor are they immune to the politics that sometimes surround the interpretation of aspects of the past. Many Westerners may consider "world prehistory" written from archaeology and many other sources the most reliable account of the human past. But we should never forget that alternative, and often compelling, accounts of ancient times exist, which play an important role in helping societies to maintain their traditional heritage as it existed before the arrival of the Westerner.

World Prehistory offers an account of 2.5 million years of human history based on the latest scientific archaeological research, but it does so with a profound respect for the cultures and histories of others with different historical perspectives.

STUDYING WORLD PREHISTORY

The study of human prehistory extends back from modern times deep into the remote past. It is as if we are looking back into prehistoric times through the wrong end of a telescope. We can discern relatively recent cultures like those of the Aztecs or the 16th-century Pueblo Indians of the Southwest with relative clarity, even if our knowledge is lamentably incomplete. Further back into the past the images become dimmer, more blurred, the scale smaller. We cannot use the lifeways of, say, modern arctic foragers or Maya farmers from Guatemala to interpret this remoter past. The first Native Americans of 15,000 years ago, the late Ice Age foragers who flourished in Europe 25,000 years ago—these peoples lived in a world that is unimaginably remote from our own. And the world of the archaic humans of earlier prehistory, of a quarter of a million years ago or more, is so far distant that it is hard for us to comprehend in realistic terms. Such, then, is the objective of world prehistory—to understand prehistoric human behavior in a past separated from our own not only by thousands of years, but by environmental and social challenges very different from those we face today.

World prehistory can be likened to a vast, branching chronological tree, whose roots ultimately extend back to the seminal moment some 5 million years ago when the remotest ancestors of humanity split off from the forebears of our closest living ape-like ancestors, chimpanzees. We may think of the human past as linear, but the tree analogy is an apt one, for even the earliest hominids and their cultures diversified rapidly after the first tool-making humans appeared some 2.5 million years ago. Studying the many branches of this hypothetical tree requires use of a fundamental theoretical conception, that of culture.

Culture

As anthropologists, archaeologists study human cultures and how they have changed through time.

Culture is a concept developed by anthropologists to describe the distinctive adaptive system used by human beings. Culture can be called a society's traditional systems of belief and behavior, as understood by individuals and the members of social groups, and manifest in individual or collective behavior. It is also part of our way of adapting to our environment. Our tools and dwellings are also part of our culture. Humans are the only animals to manufacture tools for this purpose.

Ordinarily, when animals die their experience dies with them. However, human beings use the symbolic system of language to transmit ideas and their culture, their feelings and experiences, from one generation to the next. This is why oral traditions are so important in many societies. Culture is learned by intentional teaching as well as by trial and error and simple imitation. People could share ideas, which in turn became behavior patterns that were repeated again and again—witness the long-lived stone hand ax, a multipurpose tool that remained in use for more than 1 million years of early prehistory (Chapter 3). All archaeological research is based on the principle that culture is an ongoing phenomenon that changes gradually over time.

Unlike biological adaptation, culture is nongenetic and provides a much quicker way to share ideas that enable people to cope with their environment. It is the adaptiveness of culture that allows archaeologists to assume that artifacts found in archaeological sites are patterned adaptations to the environment.

A **cultural system** is a complex system comprising a set of interacting variables—tools, burial customs, ways of getting food, religious beliefs, social organization, and so on—that function to maintain a community in a state of equilibrium with its environment. When one element in the system changes, say hunting practices as a result of a prolonged drought, then reacting adjustments will occur in many other elements. It follows that no cultural system is ever static. It is always changing in big and small ways, some of which can be studied in archaeological sites. A cultural system can be broken down into all manner of subsystems: religious and ritual subsystems, economic subsystems, and so on. Each of these is linked to the others. Changes in one system, such as a shift from cattle herding to wheat growing, will cause reactions in many others. Such relationships give the archaeologist a measure of the constant changes and variations in human culture that can accumulate over long periods, as cultural systems respond to external and internal stimuli. Many of the interacting components are highly perishable. So far, no one has been able to dig up a religious philosophy or an unwritten language. Archaeologists work with the *tangible* remains of human activity that still survive in the ground, such as clay potsherds and the foundations of dwellings. But these surviving remains of human activity are radically affected by the *intangible* aspects of human culture. For instance, the **Moche** people of the Peruvian coast buried their great lords with elaborate gold and copper ornaments, with fine textiles and elaborate ceremonial regalia. Thanks to Walter Alva's excavations in the great mounds at **Sipán,** we know of one lord who was buried in A.D. 400 with a golden rattle that showed a Moche warrior in full regalia beating a prisoner on the head with his war club (Chapter 14). The artistic masterpieces buried with the Lord of Sipán reflected a culture with an elaborate symbolism and complex religious beliefs that formed part of the intangible world of the Moche.

CULTURE HISTORY, TIME AND SPACE, AND THE "MYTH OF THE ETHNOGRAPHIC PRESENT"

The past extends back hundreds of thousands of years into remote prehistory, a featureless landscape that archaeologists people with cultures, each with their context in time and space. Culture history, the study of these many contexts, is a fundamental part of archaeology.

Culture history is the description of human cultures that extends back thousands of years into the past. Culture history is derived from the study of archaeological sites, and the **artifacts** and structures in them, within the context of time and space. By investigating groups of sites and the artifacts found there, it is possible to construct local and regional sequences of human cultures that extend over centuries, even millennia. The study of culture history depends on another important principle, that of context.

Context

Archaeological **context** is the position of an archaeological find in time and space, established by excavation, recording, and survey. The dimension of time combines in archaeological context with that of space—not the limitless space of the heavens, but a precisely defined location for every find made during an archaeological survey and excavation. Every archaeological find, be it a tiny pin or a large palace, has an exact location in latitude, longitude, and depth, which together identify any point in space and time absolutely and uniquely. When carrying out surface surveys or excavations, archaeologists use special methods to record the precise positions of sites, artifacts, dwellings, and other finds. They locate the position of each site on an accurate survey map so that they can use the grid coordinates on the map to define the location in precise terms. When investigating a site, they lay out recording grids made up from equal squares over the entire site, using the grids to record the exact position of every object on the surface or in the trenches, a context in time and space, determined by stratigraphic observation (Figure 1.6a), chronometric dating, and the law of association (Figure 1.6b).

Time

The time scale of the human past is hard to imagine. We are separated by 15,000 years from the end of the Ice Age, when great ice sheets covered much of Europe and North America. At least 150,000 years have passed since the first anatomically modern humans appeared in Africa. Fewer than a million archaic humans lived in Africa, Asia, and Europe, and the Ameri-

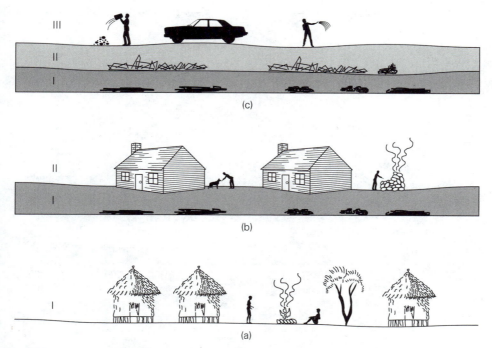

Figure 1.6a STRATIGRAPHY AND ASSOCIATION: TWO FUNDAMENTAL PRINCIPLES OF ARCHAEOLOGY   (a) Superposition and stratigraphy. A farming village built on virgin sub-soil. After a time, the village is abandoned and the huts fall into disrepair. Their ruins are covered by accumulating soil and vegetation. (b) After an interval, a second village is built on the same site, with different architectural styles. This in turn is abandoned; the houses collapse into piles of rubble and are covered by accumulating soil. (c) Twentieth-century people park their cars on top of both village sites and drop litter and coins, which when uncovered reveal to the archaeologists that the top layer is modern. An archaeologist digging this site would find that the modern layer is underlain by two prehistoric occupation levels; that square huts were in use in the upper of the two, which is the later under the law of superposition. Round huts are stratigraphically earlier than square ones here. Therefore village I is earlier than village II, but the exact date of either, or how many years separate village I from village II, cannot be known without further data.

cas were uninhabited 250,000 years ago. Two million years ago, the only humans on earth dwelt in tropical Africa. Some idea of the scale of prehistoric time can be gained by piling up 100 quarters. If the whole pile represents the entire time that humans and their culture have been on earth, the length of time covered by historical records would equal considerably less than the thickness of one quarter.

How, then, do archaeologists date the past? The chronology of world prehistory is based on stratigraphic observations, and on a variety of chronometric dating methods that take us far back into the past, long before the earliest historical records appear in western Asia about 5000 years ago (Table 1.2). Ninety-nine percent of all human existence lies in prehistoric times and can be measured only in millennia, and occasionally in centuries.

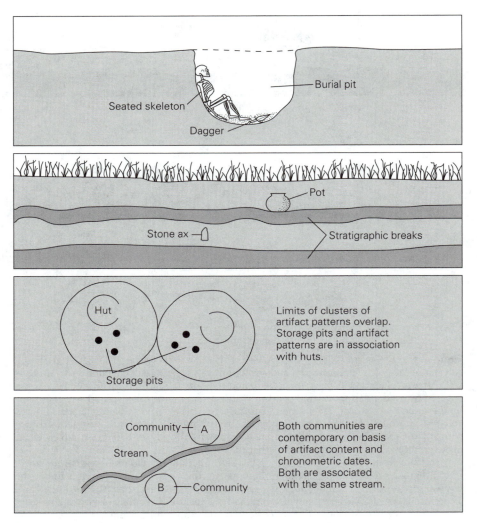

Figure 1.6b SOME ARCHAEOLOGICAL ASSOCIATIONS   (a) The burial pit, dug from the uppermost layer, contains not only a skeleton but also a dagger that lies close to its foot. The dagger is associated with the skeleton, and both finds are associated with the burial pit and the layer from which the grave pit was cut into the subsoil. (b) In contrast, a pot and a stone ax are found in two different layers, separated by a sterile zone, a zone with no finds. The two objects are not in association. (c) Two different household clusters with associated pits and scatters of artifacts. These are in association with one another. (d) An association of two contemporary communities.

Space

Spatial location is indispensable to archaeologists because it enables them to establish the distances between objects or dwellings, between entire settlements, or between settlements and key vegetational zones and landmarks.

Table 1.2 Major Chronological Methods

Date	Method	Major developments
Modern times (after A.D. 1)	Historical documents; dendrochronology; imported objects	Columbus in the New World; Roman Empire
2500 B.C.		
		Origins of cities Origins of culture Colonization of New World
40,000 B.C.	Radiocarbon dating (organic materials)	
75,000 B.C.	Uranium series dating	
100,000 B.C.	Potassium-argon dating (volcanic materials)	*Homo sapiens sapiens*
500,000 B.C.		Early humans
5,000,000 B.C.		

Such distances may amount to only a few inches, or they may extend for hundreds of miles as a team of fieldworkers traces the distribution of traded luxury goods in dozens of settlements. Thus, archaeologists think of space on two general scales: the distribution of artifacts within a settlement (Figure 1.7) and the **settlement pattern,** the placement of the settlements themselves over the landscape.

Context in space is closely tied to people's behavior. Archaeologists examine both an artifact itself and its association with other artifacts to gain insight into human behavior. For example, Belgian archaeologists investigated a 9000-year-old hunting camp in a sandy clearing at **Meer** in northern Belgium. By plotting all of the stone fragments on the ancient ground surface, they were able to identify not only a camping area but an outlying scatter of stone fragments where one or two people had sat down and fashioned several flint artifacts. The spatial relationships among the stone chips enabled them to reconstruct what had happened 9000 years ago in astounding detail. By fitting together the stone flakes, they were able to replicate the stoneworking technique and even to show that one of the workers had been left-handed!

Dating the Past

Four major chronological methods date the 2.5 million years of the human past (Table 1.2):

Historical Records (Present Day to 9500 B.C.)

Historical records can be used to date the past only as far back as the beginnings of writing and written records, which first appeared in western Asia in about 3000 B.C., much later in many other parts of the world.

Dendrochronology (Tree-ring Dating) (Present Day to 8000 B.C.)

The annual growth rings of long-lived trees such as sequoias, bristlecone pines, and European oaks, used for beams, posts, and other purposes by ancient people, can be used to date sites in some areas such as the American Southwest, the Mediterranean, and western Europe. Originally used on Southwestern pueblos, **dendrochronology** (tree-ring dating), using sequences of growth rings, is also used to calibrate radiocarbon dates (see "Tree-ring Dating" box in Chapter 7).

Radiocarbon Dating (c. A.D. 1500 to 40,000 Years Ago)

Radiocarbon dating is based on the measurement of the decay rates of ^{14}C atoms in organic samples like charcoal, shell, wood, hair, and other materials. When combined with accelerator mass spectrometry, it can produce dates from tiny samples, which are then calibrated, if possible, against tree ring dates to provide a date in calendar years. Radiocarbon chronologies date most of prehistory after about 40,000 years ago, well after modern humans appeared in Africa for the first time (see "Radiocarbon Dating" box in Chapter 4).

Potassium Argon Dating (250,000 Years Ago to the Origins of Life)

A chronological method used to date early prehistory, which measures the decay rate of ^{40}K atoms in volcanic rocks (see "Potassium Argon Dating" box in Chapter 2). **Potassium argon dating** is an excellent way of dating East African hominid fossils, many of which are found in volcanic levels.

Other dating methods include obsidian hydration, paleomagnetic dating, thermoluminescence, and uranium thorium dating, but none of them can be universally applied.

Analogy and the "Ethnographic Present"

The study of culture history depends heavily on **ethnographic analogy**—the comparisons of the artifacts and culture of living, modern-day societies with those of the past. Of course, there are numerous, and sometimes obvious, analogies that can be made between ancient and modern hunting weapons, or, for example between grindstones (metates) used by modern Maya Indians and

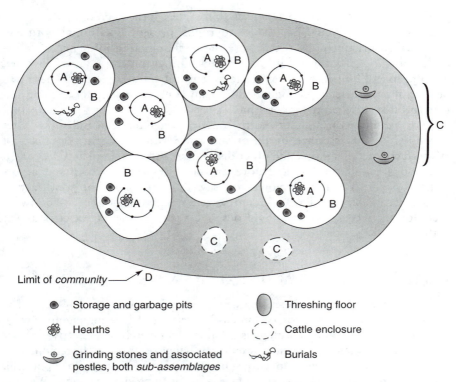

Limit of *community* ——→ D

⊚ Storage and garbage pits	▢ Threshing floor
✲ Hearths	⟨⟩ Cattle enclosure
⌣ Grinding stones and associated pestles, both *sub-assemblages*	✎ Burials

Figure 1.7 A Hypothetical Ancient Farming Village, Showing (a) Houses, (b) Household Areas, (c) Activity Areas, and (d) the Community

their remote ancestors. But to assume that prehistoric foragers thought the same way about the environment as modern San peoples from southern Africa do, or to consider late Ice Age hunters living in arctic environments as similar in many respects to living Eskimos, is nonsensical.

One approach is **ethnoarchaeology,** sometimes called "living archaeology," the study of living societies to aid in the understanding and interpretation of the archaeological record. For example, archaeologist John Yellen lived for many months among !Kung San foragers in the Kalahari Desert in southern Africa. He went back to their campsites, recorded the scatters of abandoned artifacts, the remains of brush shelters, even hearths and sleeping places. Yellen even excavated some of the sites, gathering a valuable body of information for studying ancient foragers. For instance, most artifact patternings at !Kung sites were the result of family activities, whereas communal events such as dancing and the first distribution of meat took place in open spaces and left no traces in the archaeological record.

Everywhere in the world, archaeologists work back from the known present into the remote past, from historic Pueblo settlements in the American Southwest, from modern African villages, and contemporary Australian

Aboriginal camps. These societies, be they Aztec, Inca, Pueblo, or Zulu, represent something often called the **ethnographic present,** traditional culture in its so-called pristine condition before the contaminating influence of Western civilization transformed it forever. The ethnographic present is, however, a myth, for all human societies are in a constant state of change. There was never a moment, let alone one at European contact, when any ancient culture stood still, when it was pristine.

For example, throughout North America, the American Indian societies encountered and described by Europeans had already suffered the effects of Western contact. Smallpox and other diseases spread far inland and decimated indigenous populations long before anyone physically encountered a foreigner. So even the first explorers of, say, the interior of the southeastern United States interacted with Indian societies that were often a shadow of their former selves. No one could describe their decimated societies as the "ethnographic present."

CULTURAL PROCESS AND PAST LIFEWAYS

Cultural process refers to the changes and interactions in cultural systems. The study of cultural process provokes intense theoretical debate among archaeologists, who assume that archaeology is far more than merely a descriptive activity and that it is possible to explain how cultural change occurred in the remote past.

Every cultural system is in a constant state of change. Its various political, social, and technological subsystems adjust to changing circumstances. We ourselves live in a time of rapid cultural change in which there are measurable differences between decades, let alone centuries. Consider the many small changes in automobile design that have occurred in the past few decades. In themselves, the changes often are not very significant, but the *cumulative* effect of several years of steady change toward safer cars is striking—air bags, energy-absorbing bumpers, padded steering wheels, and so on. The automobile of today is very different from that of the 1960s, and many of the changes are due to stricter government safety regulations, which in turn result from greater safety consciousness on the part of consumers. Here we see a major cumulative change in part of our enormous technological subsystem. By examining the relationships between these technological changes and the political and social subsystems, we can understand the processes through which culture has changed.

Most processes of culture change in human prehistory were cumulative, occurring slowly over a long time period. They were the result of adaptations to constantly changing external environments. Cultural systems were constantly adjusting and evolving in response to internal and external feedback, including changes in the natural environment. The study of past lifeways— that is, how people have made their living in the past—involves the examination of prehistoric cultures within their environmental context. Environmental data come from many sources, including ancient plant remains, fossil pollen grains, and animal bones. Ancient subsistence patterns, and even diet, can be reconstructed from food residues such as animal bones, carbonized seeds, and fish remains. This is also descriptive archaeology, but it relates archaeological cultures to the complex and continually changing patterns of settlement, subsistence, and environmental influences.

The fundamental questions about prehistory revolve around culture change. How did anatomically modern humans, *Homo sapiens sapiens,* evolve their more advanced cultures? What cultural processes came into play when people began to cultivate the soil, or when complex and elaborate urban societies developed in western Asia just over 5000 years ago? Clearly, no single element in a cultural system is the primary cause of cultural change, because a complex range of factors—rainfall, vegetation, technology, social restrictions, and population density, to mention only a few—interact with one another and react to a change in any element in the system.

THE MECHANISMS OF CULTURE CHANGE

Culture history is a sound way of describing the past, but it is of minimal use for studying variations in different prehistoric cultures, for answering fundamental questions about the nature of culture change in the past. But the archaeological record does not invariably reflect an orderly and smooth chronicle of culture change. A radically new artifact inventory may suddenly appear in contemporary occupation layers at several sites, while earlier tool kits suddenly vanish. A culture's economy may change rapidly within a century as the plow revolutionizes agricultural methods. How do such changes come about? What mechanisms of cultural change were at work to cause major and minor alterations in the archaeological record?

Archaeologists use four descriptive models to characterize culture change: inevitable variation, invention, diffusion, and migration.

- **Inevitable variation.** As people learn the behavior patterns of their society, inevitably some differences in learned behavior will appear from generation to generation. These, although minor in themselves, accumulate over a long period of time, especially in isolated populations. The snowball effect of such inevitable variation among isolated, thinly scattered populations can be considerable. For example, projectile point forms varied considerably between different, isolated big-game hunting groups on the North American Great Plains in 4000 B.C., even though they all pursued the same animals with much the same techniques.
- **Invention.** Humans are inquisitive, constantly innovating, having ideas. Invention is the creation or evolution of a new idea. The term *invention* refers to new ideas that originate in a human culture, either by accident or by design. All innovations in human society have their origin in such actions or chance occurrences, but only a very few inventions are truly unique and not introduced from outside by some other culture. It is one

thing to invent something, quite another to have it accepted by society as a whole. In general, technological innovations, like for example, the plow, are more readily accepted than social or religious innovations, for they are less likely to conflict with established value systems. The genius of humanity was that it recognized opportunities when they came along and adapted to new circumstances, often in similar ways in widely separated areas, resulting in independent invention of very similar ideas such as farming.

- **Diffusion.** The spread of ideas, over short or long distances, is termed diffusion. Neither the exchange of ideas nor of technological innovations necessarily involve actual movements of people. Diffusion can result from regular trade between neighboring communities. Commerce of any kind implies a two-sided relationship, in which both parties exchange goods, services, and, of course, ideas such as new religious beliefs. For instance, the highly distinctive Chavín religious beliefs and art style were diffused widely through highland and lowland Peru after about 900 B.C. (Figure 1.8) (Chapter 14).

- **Migration.** This involves movements of entire societies that deliberately decide to expand their spheres of influence. Spanish conquistadors occupied Mexico, the Polynesians deliberately voyaged from island to island across the Pacific. In each case, new land masses were found by purposeful exploration, then colonized. Smaller-scale migrations are more commonplace, such as when a group of merchants from lowland VeraCruz, Mexico, moved into the highland city of **Teotihuacán** and settled in their own barrio, identified from their distinctive artifacts. There are other types of migrations, too, unorganized movements of slaves and artisans, and of people fleeing religious persecution.

Figure 1.8 CHAVÍN ART Sculpted head from the outer wall of the temple at Chavín de Huantar, Peru, showing a shaman being transformed into a jaguar.

Invention, diffusion, and migration are far too general cultural mechanisms to explain the ever-changing relationships between human cultures and their environments. The identification of these mechanisms is largely a descriptive activity, based on artifacts and other material remains. The explanation of culture change requires more sophisticated research models that reflect the interaction of human societies with the natural environment.

CULTURE AS ADAPTATION

In the 1950s, American anthropologists Julian Steward and Leslie White developed what they called **cultural ecology,** the study of the total way in which human populations adapt to and transform their environments. Archaeologists who study cultural ecology are concerned with how prehistoric cultures as systems interacted with other systems: with other human cultures, the biotic community (other living things around them), and their physical environment. This is what is often called the **culture-as-adaptation** approach to human prehistory.

Culture as adaptation—this phrase is behind most contemporary interpretations of world prehistory. Leslie White called culture "man's extrasomatic [outside the body] means of adaptation." Culture is the result of human beings' unique ability to create and infuse events and objects with meaning that can be appreciated, decoded, and understood, with, among other things, ideology. Thus, human cultures differ greatly from place to place and from time to time, resulting in variations in prehistoric material culture—the data for studying prehistory.

Under the culture as adaptation rubric, human behavior is an adaptation not to a single site but to environmental regions. Thus, the archaeologist has to study not individual sites but entire regions. The archaeological record is not just a system of structured sites, but a continuous pattern of artifact distribution and density over the landscape. As individuals and groups hunt, forage, or farm their way across this landscape, they leave behind material remains of their presence, a record that reflects their continual behavior within the region.

Multilinear Cultural Evolution

The culture as adaptation approach attempts to interpret cultural variation and adaptation on a regional basis over long periods of time. This strategy means that the archaeologist must pay close attention to the relationships between ecological and social systems. Under this theory of **multilinear cultural evolution** (evolution along multiple tracks), each human society pursues its own evolutionary course, determined by the long-term success of an adaptation, via technology and social institutions, to its natural environment. Multilinear evolution is widely used as a general framework for interpreting world prehistory, which witnessed occasional dramatic incidents of cultural change.

Some societies achieve a broad measure of equilibrium with their environment, in which adaptive changes consist of little more than some refinements in technology and the fine-tuning of organizational structures. Others become involved in cycles of change that are triggered by external environmental change or from within society. If these changes involve either greater food supplies or population growth, there can be accelerated change resulting from the need to feed more people or the deployment of an enlarged food surplus. Such was probably the case in parts of southwestern Asia in 8000 B.C., when some communities living in favored regions began cultivating wild cereal grasses to expand their food supplies (Chapter 6). (See Figure 1.9.) Within generations of the first experiments with farming, many groups depended heavily on cereal crops. Major technological and social changes followed. People now settled in permanent villages under entirely different social conditions.

Every society has its growth limits imposed by the environment and available technology, and some environments, like, say, Egypt's Nile valley, have more potential for growth than others. Certain types of sociopolitical organization, such as centralized control of specialized labor, are more efficient than others. Adaptive changes triggered technological innovations that led to increased food supplies and higher population densities. Multilinear evolution assumes human societies have developed along many tracks.

Figure 1.9 EXPERIMENTAL HARVESTING OF WILD-TYPE EINKORN   A widely domesticated cereal crop, einkorn is shown here being harvested with a replica of an ancient Egyptian flint-bladed sickle.

The widespread use of multilinear evolution as an explanatory mechanism has led a number of archaeologists to talk of two broad stages of social development in prehistory: prestate and state-organized societies. These should not be thought of as universal stages through which all societies pass, as some Victorian anthropologists once argued, but as degrees of social development that are achieved by many groups quite independently in many environments.

Multilinear cultural evolution combines systems approaches to human culture and cultural ecology into a closely knit, highly flexible way of studying and explaining cultural process. The culture-as-adaptation approach requires that one look at cultural change in the context of the interrelationships among many variables. Thus, there is no one prime agent of cultural evolution that caused, say, farming in ancient Syria or Maya civilization in Mesoamerica (the area of Central America where prehistoric states flourished). Rather, a series of important variables, such as, for example, population growth, food shortages and a prolonged drought cycle, and intergroup competition, acted together to trigger cultural change.

When we seek to explain the major and minor events of prehistory, we have to consider the ways in which change takes place, the processes and mechanisms of change, and the social and economic stresses (population pressure, game scarcity, and so on) that trigger these mechanisms. Such multicausal models are a far cry from theories that speak of ancient Egyptian voyages or brilliant, solitary inventors. They require rigorous methodologies for identifying the many factors involved, using data that consist, for the most part, of material remains such as potsherds and stone implements.

Cultural Traditions and Cultural Change

The culture-as-adaptation approach to the past is concerned primarily with identifying variations in ancient human cultures and with explaining cultural change over long periods of time. Archaeologists espousing this approach have focused on explanations for culture change, and on relationships between people and their environments, to the point that many archaeologists have complained that this perspective is more concerned with the processes of culture change than with the people behind these changes. All human societies are made up of individuals—men and women, children and adults, families, entire communities, their neighbors near and far. They spend their lives interacting with one another, agreeing, disagreeing, negotiating, quarreling, and living in peace. From these interactions stem cultural traditions, which provide guidance for coping with the environment. The same traditions can be a powerful, conservative force, that inhibit change, or encourage innovation in times of stress.

Ecological and other external constraints can be culturally mediated, but they operate independently of human actions, which makes them susceptible to understanding in terms of evolutionary theory and other such generalizations. Cultural traditions are far more idiosyncratic and haphazard. This makes it difficult to impose evolutionary order on human history, for despite external constraints,

ANCIENT SOCIAL ORGANIZATION

Prestate societies are small-scale societies, based on the community, **band,** or village. They vary greatly in their degrees of political integration and are sometimes divided into three loosely defined categories (Figure 1.10):

1. *Bands* are associations of families that may not exceed 25 to 60 people. They are knit together by close social ties; they were the dominant form of social organization for most of prehistory, from the earliest times up to the origins of food production some 10,000 years ago.

2. *Tribes* are clusters of bands that are linked by *clans* (formal kin groups). A **clan** is not a **tribe,** which contains people from many kin groups, but a group of people linked by common ancestral ties that serve as connections between widely scattered communities. Clans are important because they are a form of social linkage that gives people a sense of common identity with a wider world than their own immediate family and relatives. Many early farming societies throughout the world can be classified as tribal societies.

3. *Chiefdoms* are a controversial category, for they display great differences in organization and social complexity, making them hard to define precisely. Fundamentally, they are societies headed by individuals with unusual ritual, political, or entrepreneurial skills and are often hard to distinguish from tribes. Society is still kin-based but more hierarchical, with power concentrated in the hands of kin leaders responsible for acquiring and then redistributing food and other resources throughout the group

    Chiefdoms tend to have higher population densities and vary greatly in their elaboration, and were politically very volatile, rising to power and collapsing with dramatic rapidity.

State–organized Societies (Preindustrial civilizations) operated on a large scale, with centralized political and social organization. Such societies were ruled by a tiny elite, who held monopolies over strategic resources, including food surpluses, and used force to impose authority. Their social organization can be likened to a pyramid, with a single ruler at the apex and stratified classes of nobles, priests, bureaucrats, merchants, artisans, and commoners below. Most were based in large cities, with populations that ranged upward from 5000 people.

The state-organized society was based on intensive agricultural production, which often relied heavily on irrigation or swamp farming—carefully watered lands that yielded several bountiful crops a year. These painstakingly administered and controlled agricultural works were the means by which society supported thou-

much cultural change is contingent on ever-changing circumstances and cultural traditions. By studying individual cultural traditions, archaeologists try to explain the distinctive features of cultures in ways that evolutionists and cultural ecologists can never hope to. Increasingly, we seek to explain the past in terms of both external (environmental) and internal (social) constraints.

	Prestate			
	Band	Tribe	Chiefdom	State-Organized Societies
Total Numbers	Less than 100	Up to few thousand	5000–20,000+	Generally 20,000+
Social Organization	Egalitarian Informal leadership	Segmentary society Pan-tribal associations Raids by small groups	Kinship-based ranking under hereditary leader High-ranking warriors	Class-based hierarchy under king or emperor Armies
Economic Organization	Mobile hunter-gathers	Settled farmers Pastoralist herders	Central accumulation and redistribution Some craft specialization	Centralized bureaucracy Tribute-based Taxation Laws
Settlement Pattern	Temporary camps	Permanent villages	Fortified centers Ritual centers	Urban: cities, towns Frontier defenses Roads
Religious Organization	Shamans	Religious elders Calendrical rituals	Hereditary Chief with religious duties	Priestly class Pantheistic or monotheistic religion
Architecture	Temporary shelters	Permanent huts Burial mounds Shrines	Large-scale monuments	Palaces, temples, and other public buildings
				Pyramids at Giza
	Paleolithic skin tents, Ukraine	Neolithic shrine Çatalhüyük, Turkey	Stonehenge England—final form	Castillo Chichén Itzá, Mexico
Archaeological Examples	All Paleolithic societies, including Paleo-indians	All early farmers (Neolithic/Archaic)	Many early metal-working and Formative societies Mississippian, USA Smaller African kingdoms	All ancient civilization, e.g., in Mesoamerica, Peru Near East, India and China, Greece and Rome
Modern Examples	Eskimos Kalahari San Australian Aborigines	Pueblos, Southwest USA New Guinea Highlanders Nuer and Dinka in East Africa	Northwest Coast Indians, USA 18th-century Polynesian chiefdoms in Tonga, Tahiti, Hawaii	All modern states

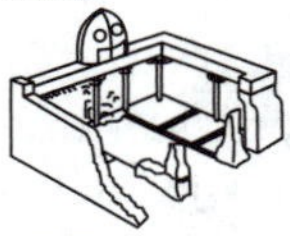

Figure 1.10 GENERAL CATEGORIES OF PREHISTORIC HUMAN SOCIETIES (Modified from Renfrew and Bahn, *Archaeology*, London: Thames and Hudson, 1995).

sands of nonfarmers, the artisans, officials, traders, and priests, also city dwellers. State economies were based on the centralized accumulation of capital and social status through tribute and taxation. Long-distance trade and the division of labor, also craft specialization, were often characteristic of early states, as were advances toward record keeping, science, and mathematics, and usually some form of written script.

Internal constraints include knowledge, beliefs, values, and other culturally conditioned habits, all of them different in every culture. Yet some of them are shared by cultures flourishing thousands of miles apart. For instance, two widely separated cultures may develop bronze metallurgy, which is based on a common body of technological know-how, but the cultural context of that knowledge is radically different, as it was, say, in the Shang civilization of China (Chapter 11) and the Moche culture in coastal Peru (Chapter 14). Some symbols, like the common practice of elevating chiefs or kings on a dais, or associations between rulers and the sun, have developed in many places. That does not mean, of course, that they are connected.

A new generation of archaeological research has moved beyond cultural process and ecology, to take a first, cautious look at what was going on inside the early human mind. Sometimes called **cognitive archaeology,** the study of the archaeology of mind, this new approach to the past is both controversial and stimulating, as it draws on lines of evidence from many disciplines, including evolutionary psychology.

INTANGIBLES: IDEOLOGY AND INTERACTION

Archaeologists study the remote human past from rare fossil human remains and the surviving consequences of human behavior—artifacts, food remains, and so on. The human mind, our speech, thought processes, beliefs, and interpersonal dealings are intangibles, which do not survive in the archaeological record. Nevertheless, this same record provides dramatic evidence for evolving human behavior and much enhanced intellectual capabilities over 2.5 million years. The appearance of toolmaking in East Africa 2.5 million years before present was one moment when major change occurred. Perhaps it was no coincidence that human brain size increased dramatically over the next million years. Another major moment came after the development of the fully modern brain, some 60,000 to 30,000 years ago, when *Homo sapiens sapiens* developed much more complex technology, the first art, and the earliest religious beliefs. Herein lie many fundamental questions about the past: what happened to the human mind during these great spurts in brain size? When did language and human consciousness first arise? What was the nature of human intelligence both before and after the development of the modern brain? Our increased understanding of cultural forces and constraints, and of cognitive issues, has caused archaeologists to focus more attention on people and groups rather than on the processes of culture change. Much new research has tried to look beyond the material aspects of the archaeological record to search for the complex, intangible ideas behind ancient societies. This approach, which has generated an extraordinary outpouring of (often verbose and irrelevant) theoretical argument, is sometimes called **post-processual archaeology.** The theoretical debate continues, but has had the effect of focusing attention on two important topics: ancient ideologies and beliefs, and the interactions between groups and individuals.

Ideology and Beliefs

The intangible ideologies and beliefs of ancient times are extremely difficult to reconstruct from material remains such as artifacts, art, and architecture. We can only guess at the beliefs and motivations behind late Ice Age cave art

(Chapter 4) or the celebrated plastered human portraits from the early farming settlement at **Jericho**, Jordan (Chapter 6). But the study of ancient ideology and beliefs offers great potential when written records such as Egyptian documents or Maya glyphs can be combined with excavations. One of the best examples of such research is Linda Schele and David Freidel's remarkable work on ancient Maya iconography in ancient Mesoamerica, based on a combination of deciphered glyphs and archaeological data (Chapter 12). Their work shows how ritual life, shrines, and temple structures helped shape past lives. "The Maya believed in a past which always returned . . . in endless cycles repeating patterns already set into the fabric of time and space," they write in their book *A Forest of Kings* (Schele and Freidel, 1990:18). "Our challenge . . . is to interpret this history, recorded in their words, images, and ruins, in a manner comprehensible to the modern mind, yet true to the Mayans' perception of themselves."

Interactions

In the final analysis, it is people who share culture, groups and individuals who make decisions about daily life. Men interact with women, children with adults; a kin group quarrels within itself, pitting small faction against small faction; ethnic groups compete for access to wealth or political power—such dealings between individuals, between individuals and groups, and between groups are the forces that constrain or encourage cultural change. By its very nature, the archaeological record tends to be impersonal, its artifacts and food remains chronicling the dealings of blurred groups rather than individuals, or even categories of people, like, say, women at a given moment in time.

Only rarely can the archaeologist go beyond artifacts and food remains to study the roles of groups or individuals, the work they undertook, the subtle ways in which they influenced the course of events. For example, at the early farming village of **Abu Hureyra** in Syria, dating to 7700 B.C., biological anthropologist Theya Molleson observed malformations of the toes, knees, and lower vertebrae in the skeletons of all the adult women, a condition due, almost certainly, to hours of grinding grain (Figure 1.11). Male skeletons did not display the same impairments. This is some of the earliest evidence for division of labor between men and women in human history.

Studying ancient beliefs, the intangibles of the past, can be likened to studying a series of pictures without the captions. Herein lies one of the great frustrations of archaeology. We can admire a giant bull from the 15,000-year-old frieze painted by Stone Age artists on the walls of **Lascaux** Cave in southwestern France (Chapter 4), or trace the intricate engraving on a freshwater shell from the **Mississippian culture** of the southeastern United States (Chapter 7). But while we can admire the artistry behind the image, we can only rarely discern the complex beliefs and motives behind these magnificent achievements. We cannot speak to the ancients, we can only seek to understand some of the brilliant, and often frustrating, complexity of their diverse societies.

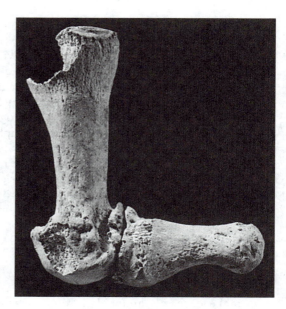

Figure 1.11 DEFORMED TOE BONES OF AN ABU HUREYRA WOMAN, SYRIA

British archaeologist Steven Mithen, an expert on the ancient human mind, has likened the long millennia of our past to an archaeological play with several acts, which reaches a climax with the appearance of farming a mere 10,000 years. In 10 short millennia, humanity moves away from a simple village existence into a world of automobiles, aircraft, vast industrial cities, and an emerging global, computerized society. *World Prehistory* performs most of this play, ending with the Spanish conquest of Mexico and Peru, with the climactic encounter between Westerners and the last of the preindustrial civilizations in the early 16th century A.D.

Our play begins 2.5 million years ago.

P A R T

2

THE WORLD OF THE
FIRST HUMANS

And God said, "Let us make man in our image, after our likeness; and let them have dominion over the fish of the sea, and over the birds of the air, and over the cattle, and over all the earth, and over every creeping thing that creepeth upon the earth."

GENESIS 1:26

CHAPTER 2

Human Origins

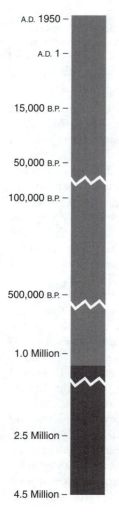

A.D. 1950 —

A.D. 1 —

15,000 B.P. —

50,000 B.P. —

100,000 B.P. —

500,000 B.P. —

1.0 Million —

2.5 Million —

4.5 Million —

Biologist Thomas Huxley called it "the question of questions," the nature of the exact relationship between humans and their closest living relatives such as the chimpanzee and the gorilla—the question of human origins. Ever since his day, scientists have been locked in controversy as they trace the complex evolutionary history of humanity back to its very beginnings. In this chapter, we examine some of the controversies that surround the biological and cultural evolution of humankind and describe what we know about the behavior and lifeways of our earliest ancestors.

THE GREAT ICE AGE
(1.6 million to 15,000 years ago)

The story of humanity begins deep in geological time, during the later part of the Cenozoic Era, the age of mammals. For most of geological time, the world's climate was warmer than it is today. During the Oligocene epoch, some 35 million years ago, the first signs of glacial cooling appeared with the formation of a belt of pack ice around Antarctica. This development was followed by a major drop in world temperatures between 14 and 11 million years ago. As temperatures fell, large ice sheets formed on high ground in high latitudes. About 3.2 million years ago, large ice sheets formed on the northern continents. Then, some 2.5 million years ago, just as humans first appeared on tropical Africa, glaciation intensified even more and the earth entered its present period of constantly fluctuating climate. These changes culminated during the **Quaternary** period or

---

D I S C O V E R Y

THE LEAKEYS AND *ZINJANTHROPUS*

It was a blazing hot day at Olduvai Gorge, East Africa, in 1959. Back in camp, Louis Leakey lay in his tent, suffering from a bout of influenza. Meanwhile, Mary Leakey, sheltered by a beach umbrella, was excavating the small scatter of broken bones and crude artifacts deep in the gorge. For hours she brushed and pried away dry soil. Suddenly, she unearthed part of an upper jaw with teeth so humanlike that she took a closer look. Moments later, she jumped into her Land Rover and sped up the track to camp. "Louis, Louis," she cried, as she burst into their tent, "I've found Dear Boy at last." Louis leapt out of bed, his flu forgotten. Together, they excavated the fragmentary remains of a magnificent, robust hominid skull. The Leakeys named it *Zinjanthropus boisei* ("African human of Boise"), a Mr. Boise being one of their benefactors. With this dramatic discovery, they changed the study of human evolution from a part-time science into an international detective story.

Pleistocene epoch, the most recent interval of earth history, which began at least 1.8 million years ago. This period is sometimes called the Age of Humanity, for it was during this epoch, the Great Ice Age, that humans first peopled most of the globe. The major climatic and environmental changes of the Ice Age form the backdrop for some of the most important stages of evolution.

The words *Ice Age* conjure up a vision of ice-bound landscapes and frigid, subzero temperatures that gripped the earth in a prolonged deep freeze. In fact, the Pleistocene witnessed constant fluctuations between warm and intensely cold global climates. Deep-sea cores lifted from the depths of the world's oceans have produced a complex picture of Ice Age climate (Table 2.1). These cores have shown that climatic fluctuations between warm and cold were relatively minor until about 800,000 years ago. Since then, periods of intense cold have recurred about every 90,000 years, with minor oscillations about 20,000 and 40,000 years apart. Many scientists believe that these changes are triggered by long-term astronomical cycles, especially in the earth's orbit around the sun, which affect the seasonal and north–south variations of solar radiation received by the earth.

There were at least nine glacial periods that mantled northern Europe and North America with great ice sheets, the last one retreating only some 15,000 years ago. Interglacial periods, with climates as warm or warmer than that of today, occurred infrequently, and the constant changes displaced plants and animals, including humans, from their original habitats. During colder cycles, plants and animals generally fared better at lower altitudes and in warmer latitudes. Populations of animals spread slowly toward more hospitable areas, mixing with populations that already lived there, and creating new communities with new combinations of organisms. For example, paleontologist Björn

Table 2.1 Major Events of the Ice Age

Temperature ←— Lower Higher —→	Dates (B.P.)	Periods	Epochs	Glacials	Human Evolution	Prehistory
	10,000	Holocene	Holocene	Holocene		Cities, agriculture
					Homo sapiens sapiens	Settlement of New World
	118,000	Quaternary	Brunhes	Würm (Wisconsin in North America)		
	128,000			Saale		
					Archaic Homo sapiens	Hunter-gatherers
		Pleistocene	Matuyama	Many cold episodes		
	730,000				Homo erectus	
			Olduvai Event			
		Pliocene				
	1,600,000	Tertiary			Early hominids	

Uncertain climatic detail before 130,000 years ago

Kurten has estimated that no fewer than 113 of the mammalian species living in Europe and adjacent Asia evolved during the past 3 million years. This repeated mixing surely affected human evolution in many ways.

The earliest chapter of human evolution unfolded during a period of relatively minor climatic change, indeed before the Pleistocene truly began. Between 4 and 2 million years ago, the world's climate was somewhat warmer and more stable than it was in later times. The African savanna, the probable cradle of humankind, contained many species of mammals large and small, including a great variety of the order of primates, of which we humans are a part.

EARLY PRIMATE EVOLUTION AND ADAPTATION

The Order Primates

All of us are members of the order primates, which includes most tree-loving placental mammals. There are two suborders: **anthropoids** (apes, humans, and monkeys) and **prosimians** (lemurs, tarsiers, and other so-called pre-monkeys). The many similarities in behavior and physical characteristics between the **hominids** (primates of the family Hominidae, which includes modern humans, earlier human subspecies, and their direct ancestors) and the **pongids** (our closest living nonhuman primate relatives) can be explained by identical characteristics that each group inherited millions of years ago from a common ancestor. In other words, humans and our closest nonhuman primate relatives evolved along parallel lines from a common ancestor (Table 2.2).

When did humankind separate from the nonhuman primates? Experts disagree violently about the answer. It was in Africa that humans and apes diverged from monkeys, but no one knows when this divergence took place. Several species of apes were flourishing in Africa at the beginning of the Miocene epoch, some 24 million years ago. The basic anatomical pattern of the large hominids appears in the Middle Miocene, 18 to 12 million years ago. A second radiation began in the Late Miocene, between 8 and 5 million years ago. This radiation eventually produced four lineages, at least one of which, human beings, is known to have been considerably modified. It is interesting to note that a similar evolutionary pattern occurs among herbivores such as elephants. In both cases, the patterns reflect changing climates and habitats—from warmer, less seasonal, more-forested regimens to colder, more-seasonal, and less-forested conditions. They also mirror changes in the configuration of continents, mountain systems, and antarctic ice.

For the hominids, the critical period was between 10 and 5 million years ago, when the segment of the African **hominoid** lineage radiated to produce gorillas, chimpanzees, and hominids. Unfortunately, this 5-million-year period is a black hole in our knowledge of early human evolution. We can only guess at the nature of the apelike animals that flourished in Africa during these millennia. Paleoanthropologist David Pilbeam theorizes that these animals were mostly tree-living, with long arms and legs and a broad chest.

Table 2.2   Evolution of the Primates

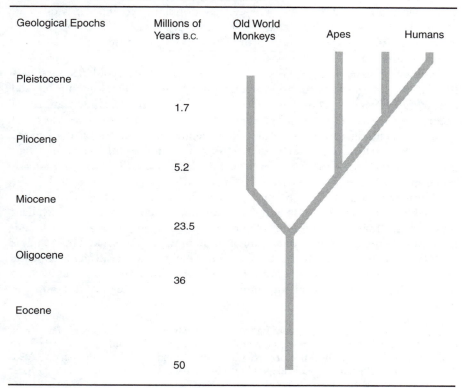

Geological Epochs	Millions of Years B.C.	Old World Monkeys	Apes	Humans
Pleistocene				
	1.7			
Pliocene				
	5.2			
Miocene				
	23.5			
Oligocene				
	36			
Eocene				
	50			

They would have used all four limbs in the trees, occasionally scrambling on the ground and even standing on their rear limbs at times. About 5 million years ago, Pilbeam believes, the hominoid lineage divided into western and eastern parts. The western segment, the proto-chimpanzee, remained dependent on fruit and other tree foods, scattered resources that required a flexible social organization.

Intense controversy surrounds the relationships between humans, chimpanzees, and gorillas, but many biologists agree that chimpanzees are humans' closest relatives. Using molecular time clocks, they calculate that these three primate forms last shared a common ancestor about 6 to 7 million years ago.

"Coming Down from the Trees"

A fall in world temperatures after 20 million years ago resulted in increasingly open environments in tropical latitudes. With this reduction in forested environments probably came a trend toward ground-adapted species. Many species of living and now-extinct primates, including hominids, adapted to this kind of existence some time after 10 million years ago. In other words, "they came down from the trees."

About 5 million years ago, the African savanna, with its patches of forest and extensive grassland plains, was densely populated by many mammalian species as well as specialized tree-dwellers and other primates. Some of these were flourishing in small bands, probably walking upright, and conceivably making tools out of stone and wood.

Coming down from the trees created three immediate problems. First was the difficulty of getting around in open country. Hominids adopted a **bipedal** posture as a way of doing so at least 4 million years ago. Our ancestors became bipedal (walking on two feet) over a long period of time, perhaps as a result of spending more and more time feeding on food resources on the ground. Bipedalism is a posture that is configured for endurance rather than power or speed. An upright posture and bipedal gait are the most characteristic hominid physical features.

Upright posture is vital because it frees the hands for other actions, like toolmaking. It contrasts with **knuckle walking,** which provides an excellent power thrust for jumping into a tree or a short sprint (think of a football lineman). It is a specialized way of moving around in which the backs of the fingers are placed on the ground and act as main weight-bearing surfaces. Knuckle walking was adaptive in the forest because long arms and hands as well as grasping feet were still vital for climbing (Figure 2.1). Human arms are too

Figure 2.1   KNUCKLE WALKING AND BIPEDALISM   (a) Human bipedal posture. The center of gravity of the body lies just behind the midpoint of the hip joint and in front of the knee joint, so that both hip and knee are extended when standing, conserving energy. Also, walking is more efficient. (b) Knuckle-walking chimpanzee, with the center of gravity lying in the middle of the area bounded by arms and legs. (c) The ape's quadruped stance. (Courtesy Adrienne Zihlman.)

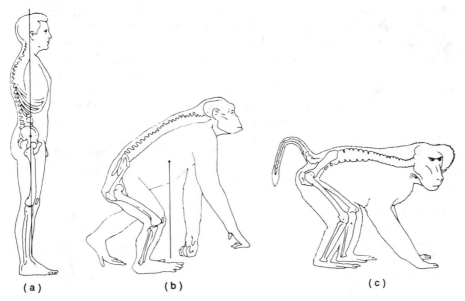

(a)   (b)   (c)

short for us to be comfortable with this posture. Bipedalism favors endurance and the covering of long distances, important considerations in open country. It was a critical antecedent of hunting, gathering, and toolmaking.

Second, the savanna abounded in predators, making it hard for primates to sleep safely. Large hominids made home bases, where they sheltered from the hot sun and slept in safety. What form these home bases took is a matter of great debate. Lastly, high-quality plant foods, abundant in the forests, were widely dispersed over the savanna. It is striking that later foragers subsisted off a broad range of game and plant foods. As part of human evolution, their hominid ancestors expanded their food range to include more meat, perhaps during long periods of plant scarcity. Among mammals, these characteristics are associated with a trend toward larger brain size. And, as brain size increased, so, gradually, the lifeways of evolving hominids became less ape-like, and closer to that of human foragers, a process that took hundreds of thousands of years to unfold.

Early hominids faced three major adaptive problems. They were large mammals, were terrestrial primates, and lived in an open, tropical savanna environment. Human beings are large and have additional food requirements due to higher metabolic rates. This means that each hominid has to range efficiently over a larger area to obtain food. Larger mammals are more mobile than their smaller relatives. They cover more ground, which enables them to subsist off resources that are unevenly distributed not only in space but also at different seasons. Mobility allows larger mammals like humans to incorporate unpredictable, often seasonal resources in their diets. They can tolerate extremes of heat and cold, a capacity that may have contributed to the spread of humans out of the tropics later in prehistory. Bipedal humans have sweat glands and are heavily dependent on water supplies. These glands are a direct adjunct to bipedalism, for they enhance endurance for long-distance foraging.

These and several other factors—such as increased longevity and brain enlargement—created adaptive problems for emerging humans. These problems resulted in a number of solutions, among them wider territorial ranges, the need to schedule food gathering, a broadening of diet, a high degree of mobility, and much greater behavioral flexibility. This flexibility included enhanced intelligence and learning capacity, parental care, and new levels of social interaction.

THE FOSSIL EVIDENCE FOR HUMAN EVOLUTION
(4 million to 1.5 million years ago)

What we know of early human evolution and lifeways comes almost entirely from archaeological and fossil finds in tropical Africa (Figure 2.2). Between 9 and 4 million years ago, the last common ancestral hominoid stock split into two main lineages, which evolved into apes and hominids. The details of this split are still a complete mystery, largely because fossil beds dating to this critical period are very rare in Africa. The fossil record increases after about 5 million years ago, but is still very fragmentary and controversial.

Figure 2.2   MAP OF ARCHAEOLOGICAL SITES DESCRIBED IN CHAPTER 2

Between 5 and 2 million years ago, the East African savanna was populated by a great variety of hominids. Paleoanthropologists divide them into two broad groups: the australopithecines and *Homo*.

Australopithecus

Australopithecus (Latin for "southern ape") was first identified by anatomist Raymond Dart at the Taung site in South Africa in 1925. He described a small, gracile primate that displayed both human and apelike features. Dart named his find *Australopithecus africanus*, a much lighter creature than another, more robust form of australopithecine that subsequently turned up at

POTASSIUM ARGON DATING

The world's first archaeological sites are so ancient that they lie far beyond the chronological range of radiocarbon dating (Chapter 1). Potassium argon dating allows the dating of volcanic rocks between 2 billion and 100,000 years old. Many of the earliest hominid sites occur in volcanically active areas. Human tools are found in direct association with cooled lava fragments or ash from contemporary eruptions, allowing the dating of the East Turkana locations, Olduvai Gorge, and other famous early sites.

Potassium (K), an abundant element in the earth's crust, is present in nearly every mineral. Potassium in its natural form contains only a small proportion of radioactive ^{40}K atoms. For every 100 ^{40}K atoms that decay, 11 percent become argon 40, an inert gas that can easily escape from its material by diffusion when lava and other igneous rocks are formed. As volcanic rock forms by crystallization, the argon 40 concentration drops to almost nothing, but the process of ^{40}K decay continues, and 11 percent of every 100 ^{40}K atoms will become argon 40. Thus, it is possible, using a spectrometer, to measure the concentration of argon 40 that has accumulated since the volcanic rock formed.

Recent advances in potassium argon dating involve computerized laser fusion, a variant of the method that uses a laser beam to analyze irradiated grains of volcanic ash that give off a gas that is purified and its constituent argon atoms measured in a spectrometer. The new method draws on crystals of volcanic materials from layers associated with hominid fossils to produce much more accurate dates, like recent readings of about 3.18 million years for Lucy, *Australopithecus afarensis.*

---

other South African sites and, later, in East Africa (Figures 2.3 and 2.4). The latter is known as *Australopithecus robustus*, a squat, massively built primate with a crested skull.

For years, paleoanthropologists thought that *Australopithecus africanus* was the direct ancestor of humankind, that human evolution had proceeded in a relatively linear way through time. More recent finds from East Africa have muddied the picture and revealed far earlier primates on the human line.

A Trio of Hominid Forms: Ardipithecus ramidus, Australopithecus anamensis, Australopithecus afarensis

Charles Darwin, the father of evolutionary theory, theorized that humans evolved from apes in tropical Africa, but, until very recently, no one had the fossil evidence to support his hypothesis. Now paleoanthropologist Tim White has unearthed the remains of at least 17 prehumans at *Aramis*, near the Awash River in Ethiopia, dating to almost 4.4 million years ago, that begin to document Darwin's theory. The Aramis fossils are a mosaic of apelike and more human characteristics, with the surviving jaws looking more like those of a chimpanzee, while other anatomical details are more suggestive of

Figure 2.3   *AUSTRALOPITHECUS AFRICANUS*

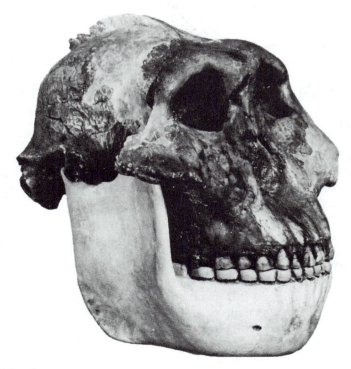

Figure 2.4   *AUSTRALOPITHECUS ROBUSTUS*

Figure 2.5 *ARDIPITHECUS RAMIDUS*

humans. Paleoanthropologist Tim White has classified the Aramis fossils as *Ardipithecus ramidus,* and believes they date from a time soon after hominids branched off from apes, perhaps as recently as 5 million years ago (Figure 2.5). The Aramis hominids are thought to have flourished not in a savanna, but in a wooded environment, as if they predate the movement of hominids into open country.[1]

About 3.9 million years ago, another form of upright-walking hominid flourished at Allia Bay and Kanapoi, the shores of Lake Turkana, northern Kenya. The fossil fragments, found by Meave Leakey and Alan Walker and named *Australopithecus anamensis* ("anam" is "lake" in Turkana), come from a hominid with large teeth and a mosaic of what appear to be apelike and more evolved features. The anatomical relationships between the Aramis fossils and this later find still remain highly uncertain.

---

[1]White originally named *Ardipithecus ramidus* as *Australopithecus ramidus.* His new terminology underlines the current difficulty in connecting these very early hominids with later Australopithecines.

Figure 2.6   "LUCY" *AUSTRALOPITHECUS AFARENSIS*

These recently discovered, and very old, hominids were the ancestors of a much better known, and somewhat later australopithecine, found at **Hadar**, about 45 miles (72 km) north of Aramis, also on the Middle Awash River. It was at Hadar in northern Ethiopia that Maurice Taieb and Donald Johanson discovered a remarkably complete skeleton of a small primate (the famous "Lucy"), together with fragments of at least 13 males, females, and children. Lucy, who dates to about 3.2 million years ago, stood just under 4.0 feet (1.2 m) tall and was 19 to 21 years old (Figure 2.6). She was a powerful, heavily muscled primate, fully bipedal, with arms slightly longer for their size than those of humans. Lucy and her contemporaries had humanlike hands and brains about the size of chimpanzees. Johanson and Tim White have classified Lucy as *Australopithecus afarensis,* implying that the Hadar hominids were direct ancestors of later australopithecines. Undoubtedly, they are correct.

A nearly intact *A. afarensis* skull and arm bones from several other males have come from another Awash location about a mile upstream and date to about 3 million years ago, some 200,000 years later than Lucy. This important find confirms that all the *A. afarensis* fragments found over the past 20 years are from a single australopithecine species. It also confirms that *A. afarensis* displays considerable size variation. Some individuals stood 5 feet (1.5 m) tall and probably weighed approximately 150 pounds (68 kg), a far cry from the small, slender Lucy. *Australopithecus afarensis* does not come only from Hadar.

These early australopithecines were powerful, heavily muscled individuals, thought to be as strong as chimpanzees. Like *Ardipithecus ramidus, A. afarensis* was an anatomical mosaic, bipedal from the waist down, **arboreal** in the upper part of the body. All were fully bipedal, with the robust, curved arms associated with tree climbers. The arms were slightly longer for their size than the arms of modern humans.

Even more remarkable evidence of bipedalism comes from fossil-bearing beds at **Laetoli** in Tanzania, where Mary Leakey uncovered not only hominid fossils like those at Hadar, but the actual 3.6-million-year-old footprints of big game and some fairly large bipedal primates. The footsteps are those of an adult male and female, the latter carrying a child (Figure 2.7). "The tracks indicate a rolling and probably slow-moving gait, with the hips swiveling at each step, as opposed to the freestanding gait of modern man," Mary Leakey wrote. Some scientists believe the Laetoli prints are from *Australopithecus afarensis,* flourishing 1000 miles (c. 1600 km) south of Hadar.

Originally, experts thought *Australopithecus afarensis* was confined to East Africa. French paleontologist Michel Brunet has discovered a 3- to 3.5-million-year-old fossilized *A. afarensis* jaw with seven teeth at **Koto Toro** in Chad, in the southern reaches of the Sahara Desert. The Chad hominid flourished in a savanna-woodland environment, much wetter than the arid landscape of today.

Figure 2.7   Hominid Footprints from Laetoli, Tanzania

Koto Toro is the first australopithecine find west of East Africa's Rift Valley and debunks a long-held theory that the great valley formed a barrier separating ape populations and causing those in more open country to move from the trees onto the ground. The evolutionary picture was much more complex than that.

Many scientists consider *A. afarensis* a primitive form of the australopithecines, which displayed considerable anatomical variation yet was hardy enough to adapt to harsh, changing savanna environments and survive for nearly a million years. Without question, there were several, as-yet largely unknown hominid forms in eastern Africa before 3 million years ago. And with this diversification, we emerge into a more complex chapter in human evolution marked by geographical and biological diversification.

Gracile and Robust Australopithecines

By 3 million years ago, tropical Africa supported a great variety of hominids, a primate form unique to Africa. They included the classic australopithecine forms and hominids on the direct evolutionary line to humans.

Raymond Dart identified both lightly built and more robust *Australopithecus* forms before World War II. *Australopithecus africanus*, the originally discovered australopithecine, has a small, almost delicate skull and prognathous (jutting out) face (see Figure 2.3). It is fairly similar to the earlier *Australopithecus afarensis*, but is confined in the main to southern Africa.

In contrast, *Australopithecus robustus* is heavily built, with large teeth and a small brain and was specialized for the chewing of coarse, fibrous plant foods (see Figure 2.4). Robust australopithecines abounded in East Africa. As a group, these squat, heavily built hominids were very diverse.

Neither *A. africanus* nor *A. robustus* was on the direct line to humans.

Homo habilis

Olduvai Gorge is a spectacular rift in the Serengeti Plains of northern Tanzania, made famous by the fossil discoveries of Louis and Mary Leakey. The gorge cuts through deep lake beds of a long-dried-up Pleistocene lake, frequented by early hominids. The Leakeys uncovered not only a robust *Australopithecus*, potassium-argon dated to 1.75 million years ago, but the bones of a more gracile hominid, found in the same levels as crude stone choppers and flakes that were more primitive than any previously discovered in the world. Louis Leakey called this hominid *Homo habilis* ("handy person"), on the grounds that it was quite different from *Australopithecus*, even if it lived in the same general area.

At first, experts thought *Homo habilis* was perhaps a form of australopithecine. But far north of Olduvai Gorge, in the East Turkana region of Kenya, Richard Leakey, son of Louis and Mary, and an international team of scientists, have recovered not only robust and gracile australopithecines, but more *Homo habilis* specimens (Figure 2.8), placing the very first humans on a firmer scientific footing.

Figure 2.8   OLDUVAI GORGE, TANZANIA

These very early humans were hominids with unmistakably larger brains. Their brain capacities were between 650 and 800 cubic centimeters (cc), but otherwise they were about the same size as *Australopithecus*, weighing about 88 pounds (44 kg) and standing just over 4 feet, 3 inches (1.3 m) tall. Both were bipedal and predominantly fruit eaters, but *Homo habilis* would have looked less apelike around the face and skull (Figure 2.9). Their heads were higher and rounder, the face less protruding. Their hand bones were more curved and robust than those of modern humans. This was a powerful grasping hand, more like that of chimpanzees and gorillas than humans, a hand ideal for climbing trees. But an opposable thumb allowed both powerful gripping and precise manipulation of fine objects. This feature would have enabled *Homo habilis* to make tools.

A recent *Homo habilis* find at Olduvai reinforces the impression that the earliest hominids were closer to apes than to human beings. This individual has upper arm bones that are almost as long as its thigh bone, a characteristic of chimpanzees and other apes, not of humans, whose arms are only about 70 percent of the length of the leg bones. Most likely, *Homo habilis* spent a great deal of time climbing trees, an adaptation that would make them much less human in their behavior, and presumably in their social structure.

Homo habilis is a somewhat generic term, which probably covers a wide variety of closely related toolmaking hominids, still unknown to us. But most experts agree that *Homo habilis* is the probable ancestor of the later human species *Homo erectus* and *Homo sapiens*. Much more controversial are the evolutionary relationships between *Australopithecus afarensis* and later australopithecines on the one hand, and between *Homo habilis* and the australopithecines on the other. The simple linear evolutionary schemes that passed

Figure 2.9   SKULL 1470 FROM EAST TURKANA, KENYA, A SPECIMEN OF EARLY *HOMO*, SOMETIMES CALLED *HOMO HABILIS*

from *Australopithecus* to *Homo* and then on to more modern forms have been replaced by branching models that stem from a realization that hominid evolution involved a far higher level of species diversity than was previously thought. Human evolution is more like a bush than the ladder that has been used for an analogy for so long (Figure 2.10).

The current view of early human evolution accepts that the process began with the australopithecines, followed by the emergence of *Homo habilis,* then later, by more modern forms. But there was considerable diversity at each stage, so much so that one cannot think of human evolution as merely a trend toward more modern forms. Between 5 and 1 million years ago, there was considerable **adaptive radiation** of australopithecines leading to great hominid diversity. The earliest members of the genus *Homo* were probably part of the radiation, *Australopithecus*-like forms with larger brains relative to body size. They are classified as *Homo habilis,* but it is certain that there was considerable variability. A more modern form, *Homo erectus* (Chapter 3), appeared about 1.9 million years ago and may also have been part of this adaptive radiation.

This same pattern of adaptive radiation may have continued much later in prehistory, during the long millennia when *Homo erectus* flourished in Africa, Asia, and Europe, with only a small part of this evolutionary process resulting in modern humans, *Homo sapiens,* probably in Africa.

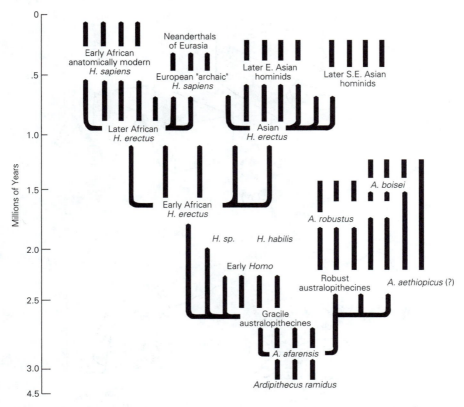

Figure 2.10   Diagram Showing the Process of Human Evolution as a Series of Adaptive Radiations   The basis for each radiation was a mixture of adaptations to local conditions and geographic isolation. The result was the evolution of diverse behavioral and ecological strategies and different species and subspecies of hominids.

TOOLMAKING AND EARLY HUMAN BEHAVIOR

"Humans the toolmakers . . ."—this phrase has served to distinguish the earliest toolmaking humans from all other primates of the day—their ability to manufacture tools, a clear sign of that uniquely human attribute, culture (see Chapter 1). Other animals like chimpanzees make tools to dig for grubs or other specific purposes, but only people manufacture artifacts regularly and habitually as well as in a much more complex fashion. We have gone much further in the toolmaking direction than other primates. One reason is that our brains allow us to plan our actions much more in advance.

The earliest human tools may well have been made of perishable wood, perhaps rudimentary clubs, digging sticks, or spears, but they have not survived. Simple stone tools, made by knocking one rock against another, appeared in East Africa about 2.6 million years ago, the conventionally agreed upon date for the origin of human culture. These stone artifacts have been found in large numbers throughout East and southern Africa, and associated

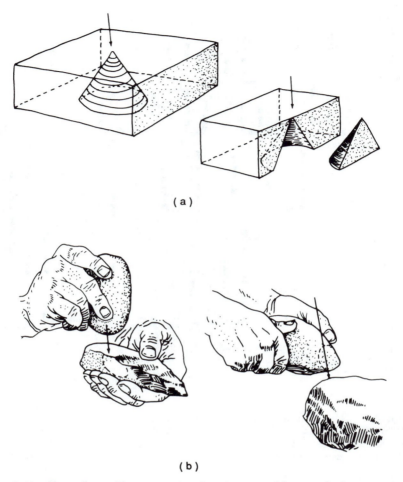

(a)

(b)

Figure 2.11   EARLY STONE TECHNOLOGY   Certain types of flinty rocks fracture in a distinctive way, as illustrated in (a). When a blow is struck on such rock, shock waves form a cone of percussion by rippling through the stone (*left*). A flake is formed (*right*) when the block (or core) is hit at the edge, and the stone fractures along the edge of the ripple. (b) The earliest stoneworkers used a heavy hammer to remove edge flakes or struck lumps of rock against boulders to produce the same effect. Oldowan technology was simple, often consisting of little more than a few flakes removed from lava cobbles.

with broken animal bones in the East Turkana region and at Olduvai Gorge. They were made from convenient pebbles, some perhaps converted into simple choppers by removing one or two flakes (Figure 2.11).

Stone tool expert Nicholas Toth has shown that the most important artifacts were not pebbles or even crude choppers, but the sharp-edged flakes removed from them. Angular flakes and lumps of lava made weapons, scrapers, and cutting tools, used to cut meat, butcher animals, and perhaps to shape wood. There are few formal tools, but Toth's controlled experiments show that the first toolmakers had a clear understanding of the potential of stone as the basis for a simple, highly effective technology that grew more complex over time. Eventually, the simple choppers evolved into crude axe-like tools, flaked on both surfaces—the hand axe used widely over a million years ago. The earliest human technology is called the **Oldowan,** after Olduvai Gorge, where it was first described in detail (see Figure 2.11b).

Nicholas Toth has replicated thousands of Oldowan artifacts and shown by experiment that sharp-edged flakes are highly effective for slitting skin and butchering game animals. By studying the working edges of the tools under microscopes, he has detected wear from three possible uses: butchery and meat cutting, sawing and scraping wood, and cutting soft plant matter. Toth believes our earliest ancestors had a good sense of the mechanics of stone tool manufacture. They were able to find the correct acute angle for removing flakes by percussion. Not even modern beginners have this capacity; it takes hours of intensive practice to acquire the skill.

Unlike chimpanzees, who rarely tote the sticks and stones they use more than a few yards, *Homo habilis* carried flakes and pebbles over considerable distances, up to 9 miles (14 km). This behavior represents a simple form of **curation,** retaining tools for future use rather than just utilizing convenient stones, as chimpanzees do.

Toth hypothesizes that the hominids tested materials in stream beds and other locations; transported the best pieces to activity areas; and sometimes dropped them there, carrying the rest off with them. He also points out that they must have relied heavily on other raw materials, like wood and bone, and that stone artifacts do not necessarily give an accurate picture of early hominid cognitive abilities.

What does the Oldowan mean? Did the early toolmakers possess a form of "protohuman culture," with its simple stone artifacts a first step on the long evolutionary trail to modern humanity? Or were the Oldowan hominids at an apelike grade of behavior? After all, the conceptual abilities and perceptions needed to manufacture Oldowan tools also appear in ape-manufactured tools like termite-fishing tools and sleeping platforms. Furthermore, not only Oldowan hominids but also chimpanzees scavenged and hunted for game—chasing down small animals, carrying meat over considerable distances, and using convenient objects to break open animal bones and nuts.

Chimpanzees, like early hominids, use the same places again and again, pounding nuts at the same locations and carrying food to their favorite eating sites. Even if the specifics vary in some instances and the natural environments are different, the behavioral pattern of Oldowan hominids is generally similar to that of apes. There are, however, two behavioral differences between apes and early hominids. First, hominids were at an advantage in that they were bipedal, a posture that is far more efficient for carrying objects than is walking on four limbs. Second, the Oldowan humans were adapted to savanna living, where they had to organize and cover far larger territories in open country than their primate relatives in the forest. In the long term, this may have resulted in new concepts of space and spatial organization, concepts that were definitely reflected in more complex stone tool forms after a million years ago.

Early hominids with their larger brains probably would not have behaved the same way as modern apes. We can be certain that there were significant differences between nonhuman primates and hominids 2 million years ago, but these changes may not be reflected in stone artifacts. Without question, our ancestors became more and more dependent on technology. The opportunistic nature of primeval stone technology is in sharp contrast to the better designed, much more standardized stone artifacts of later humans.

THE ARCHAEOLOGY OF EARLY HUMAN BEHAVIOR

Two sources of information on very early human behavior survive in East Africa—the first is manufactured artifacts, the second scatters of tools and food remains found at a few locations like **Koobi Fora** in East Turkana and Olduvai Gorge.

Concentrations of broken animal bones and stone tools in these two regions and a few others have been excavated and studied with meticulous care. The concentrations are usually only some 20 to 30 feet (c. 6 to 9 m) across, places that were visited and used by hominids either once or on several occasions. Later prehistoric foragers made habitual use of central places, places where they returned to sleep, cook food, and engage in a wide variety of social activities. Are we, then, to assume that the Koobi Fora and Olduvai concentrations are evidence that our earliest ancestors also used central places like their successors did? Did they hunt and kill big-game animals, or did they merely scavenge flesh from abandoned predator kills?

At Koobi Fora in northern Kenya, a group of hominids found the carcass of a hippopotamus in a stream bed about 1.8 million years ago. They gathered around and removed bones and meat from the dead animal with small stone flakes. The sandy deposits in which the artifacts lay are so fine that we can be certain that every stone cobble was carried in to make tools at the carcass, some of them from as far as 9 miles (14 km) away. The site contains abundant evidence of butchering and of tool manufacture, but we do not know if the hominids actually killed the animal.

Site FxJj50, also at Koobi Fora, is also in an ancient watercourse, a place where the hominids could find shade from the blazing sun, located close to water and abundant toolmaking stone. The site is a cluster of stone artifacts and fragments, including sharp flakes, choppers, and scraping tools. More than 2000 bones from at least 17 mammalian species, mostly antelope, are associated with the tools, some of which have been chewed by hyenas and other carnivores. There are clear signs the bones were smashed and cut by hominids, for reconstructed fragments show traces of hammer blows and fine linear grooves that may have resulted only from cutting bone with stone flakes. Many of the FxJj50 bones have their articular ends chewed off by carnivores, a characteristic of bone accumulations resulting from carnivore kills. Perhaps the hominids simply chased away lions and other predators, then moved in on a fresh kill; we cannot be sure.

At Olduvai Gorge, Mary Leakey plotted artifact and bone scatters in the lowest levels of the ancient lake bed. Many artifacts and bones were concentrated in areas about 15 feet (4.6 m) across. At one site, a pile of shattered bones and rocks lay a short distance away, the bones perhaps piled in heaps as the marrow was extracted from them. Recent microscopic studies of the Olduvai scatters have shown that many of the bones were heavily weathered. They had lain on the surface for considerable periods of time, some for perhaps as long as a decade. The bones of many different animals come from the scatters, parts of carcasses from a very ecologically diverse set of animals. Limb bones predominate, as if these body parts were repeatedly carried to the sites.

At both Koobi Fora and Olduvai, meat- and marrow-rich bones occur concentrated in small areas with stone tools. The percentage of carnivore bones is somewhat higher than in the natural environment, as if there was intense competition between hominids and other carnivores. Perhaps the presence of such predators restricted the activities of hominids at Olduvai. They may have grabbed meat from fresh carnivore kills and then taken their booty to a place where they had a collection of stone tools near water or other predictable food supplies. There they would hastily cut off meat and extract the marrow before abandoning the fresh bones to the carnivores hovering nearby. Without fire or domesticated animals, scientists believe that *Homo habilis* probably had to rely on opportunistic foraging for game meat, it being unsafe for them to camp in open watercourses or on lake shores. It is worth noting that one hominid bone found at Olduvai Gorge had been gnawed by carnivores.

Most of the bones from the Olduvai accumulations are of smaller animals that could be run down and thrown to the ground with ease. This is more of an apelike form of behavior, although apes have been observed scavenging meat. Microscopic studies of the Olduvai bones show that the hominids rarely butchered and disarticulated large animals and carried their bones back to base. They seem to have obtained meat without cutting up too many carcasses, as if they scavenged it from already dismembered predator kills. In some cases, human cutting marks overlay predator tooth marks, as if the hominids had scavenged bones from carcasses that had already been killed by other animals. In others, predators have chewed bones abandoned by *Homo*.

Archaeologist Robert Blumenschine has spent several field seasons studying animal predators on the game-rich Serengeti Plains of northern Tanzania. Semiarid grassland crossed by occasional streams lined with trees, this was the kind of environment that early hominids shared with other predators like lions and hyenas. Blumenschine observed dozens of predator kills, studying the abandoned, shattered bones and comparing them to the archaeological finds at Olduvai Gorge. As a result of these observations, he believes the hominids could take unique advantage of two scavenging opportunities. The first was near streams, because lions kill close to water in the dry season. Sometimes more than a day would elapse before hyenas moved in, ample time, Blumenschine believes, for hominids to seize their share. It is here, too, that leopards hide small antelope kills in trees, high above the ground, but not out of reach of humans. Scavenging would have been most common in the dry months, when game (and its predators) stayed near to permanent water supplies and plant foods were in short supply. During the rains, both antelope and predators would range far over the plains, where it was easy for hyenas to find lion kills. But these were the months when hominids relied on plant foods and fruit in more wooded environments. Blumenschine argues that scavenging and plant gathering went hand-in-hand, each complementing the other at different times of year. Opportunism has always been an important quality of humankind, from the earliest times. Undoubtedly, however, plants and all kinds of vegetable foods were an important, if not the most important, part of very early human diet.

THE MIND OF THE EARLIEST HUMANS

By 2 million years ago, there were probably several species of early *Homo*, but, for convenience sake, we can group them under a single toolmaking species, *Homo habilis*. What, then, were the specialized mental processes found in these earliest humans as opposed to much earlier, non-toolmaking hominids?

Some clues lie in stone tool manufacture. Chimpanzees shape termite twigs with their teeth from convenient wood fragments, removing leaves so they could poke the "artifact" down a small hole. The making of stone tools requires good hand-eye coordination, the ability to recognize acute angles in stone, and the mental processes necessary to shape one tool by using another. But the Oldowan stoneworkers were carrying out simple tasks: shaping stones so they could hold them in one hand to crack bones and striking off sharp-edged flakes. Their artifacts defy precise classification in the way that one can subdivide later stone tools into forms such as choppers, scrapers, and knives, for example. Their lumps and flakes display continuous variability, an understanding of basic fracture mechanics, not the ability to impose standardized forms, or to choose easily worked raw materials. Could chimpanzees have made such tools, as has been suggested? When Nicholas Toth tried to train a pygmy chimpanzee named Kanzi to make Oldowan tools, he found that Kanzi could make sharp flakes, but he never mastered the art of recognizing acute angles in stone, or other flaking. Archaeologist Steven Mithen argues for two possibilities: either a more general intelligence had evolved, or some mental processes for basic stone working had appeared—intuitive physics in the mind of *Homo habilis*.

Oldowan stone tools were mainly used to process animal carcasses, for skinning, cutting joints and meat, and breaking open bones. But how did *Homo habilis* interact with the natural world?

One obvious and significant difference between *Homo habilis* and chimpanzees appears in the archaeological record of 2 million years ago: a dramatic rise in meat consumption. In practice, *Homo habilis* was probably a behaviorally flexible, nonspecialized forager, whose lifeway was marked by diversity, by shifts between hunting and scavenging, and between food sharing and feeding on the move. The larger brain of *Homo habilis* would have required the consumption of more energy and a higher quality of diet. The stable basal metabolic rate was maintained by a reduction in the size of the gut, which could only become reduced as a result of a higher-meat diet, as a high-fiber diet requires more intestinal action.

Steven Mithen believes that this need for more meat required another cognitive ability as opposed to that for toolmaking—that of being able to use one's knowledge of the environment to develop ideas about where to find predator kills and high densities of animals. He argues that the presence of toolmaking stone up to 6 miles (10 km) from its source is a sign that *Homo habilis* was moving not only stone but meat to different, sometimes third, ever-changing locations. Such ability suggests a relatively sophisticated interaction with the environment when compared with chimpanzees who only transport "tools" to fixed locations.

Homo habilis was so far confined to tropical Africa, and to a relatively narrow range of savanna and grassland environments, in contrast with later humans who adapted to every kind of climate imaginable. Many groups lived close to permanent water, tethered, as it were, to places like the shallow lake at Olduvai, where sites are "stacked" one above another over considerable periods of time. Many animal species appear in the Olduvai caches, as if our ancestors ranged widely over the surrounding landscape, but they may have transported much of their food to well-defined locations.

Homo habilis shared the ability of its earlier ancestors to "map" resources over wide areas. But it may also have possessed additional cognitive abilities: to develop ideas about where food might be found, and to use tell-tale signs such as animal droppings to find it—within a relatively narrow environmental setting. At the same time, its general intelligence was supplemented by some specialized abilities in artifact manufacture, which were to be an important foundation for environmental intelligence in later millennia.

Social intelligence may have evolved significantly. Anthropologist Robin Dunbar has studied living primates and discovered evidence for larger brain size in individuals living in larger groups, developing an equation for relating brain to group size. He then estimated the brain size of *Homo habilis,* and applied his figures to the chimpanzee equation. Chimpanzees lived in predicted group sizes of about 60 individuals. In contrast, he predicted that australopithecines lived in groups with a mean size of about 67 individuals, whereas *Homo habilis* flourished in larger groups of about 81. Group living was an essential for *Homo habilis,* which lived in an environment teeming with carnivores, often competing with them for meat with only the simplest of weaponry for protection. Large group living has dramatic advantages for hominids living in environments where resources come in large "parcels" that are irregularly distributed across the landscape. Members of a group can search for food individually or in pairs, then share it with others, allowing the group as a whole to cover a much larger area. Mithen believes the larger brain of the first humans allowed for greater social intelligence, for coping with the complexities of living in closer juxtaposition to others, where assuming that others know things is of vital importance.

THE DEVELOPMENT OF LANGUAGE

Cooperation, the ability to get together to solve problems of both subsistence and potential conflict, is a vital quality in human beings. We are unique in having a spoken, symbolic language that enables us to communicate our most intimate feelings to one another. One fundamental question about early prehistory surrounds this development: At what point did hominids acquire the ability to speak?

Our closest living relatives, the chimpanzees, communicate with gestures and many voice sounds in the wild, whereas other apes use sounds only to convey territorial information. However, chimpanzees cannot talk to us because they do not have the vocal apparatus to do so. Articulate speech was an important threshold in human evolution because it opened up whole new vistas of cooperative behavior and unlimited potential for the enrichment of life. When did hominids abandon grunts for speech? We cannot infer language from the simple artifacts made by *Homo habilis*, but there are two potential lines of research open.

Both comparative anatomy and actual fossils can be used to study differences between apes and humans. Biological anthropologist Jeffrey Laitman and others studied the position of the larynx in a wide variety of mammals, including humans. They found that all mammals except adult humans have a larynx high in the neck, a position that enables the larynx to lock into the air space at the back of the nasal cavity. Although this position allows animals like monkeys and cats to breathe and swallow at the same time, it limits the sounds they can produce. The pharynx—the air cavity part of the food pathway—can produce sounds, but animals use their mouths to modify sounds since they are anatomically incapable of producing the range of sounds needed for articulate speech.

Until they are about 18 months to 2 years old, human children's larynxes are also situated high in the neck. Then the larynx begins to descend, ending up between the fourth and seventh neck vertebrae. How and why are still a mystery, but the change completely alters the way the infant breathes, speaks, and swallows. Adult humans cannot separate breathing and swallowing, so they can suffocate when food lodges in an airway. However, an enlarged pharyngeal chamber above the vocal cords enables them to modify the sounds they emit in an infinite variety of ways, which is the key to human speech.

Using sophisticated statistical analyses, Laitman and his colleagues ran tests on as many complete fossil skulls as possible. They found that the australopithecines of 4.0 to 1.0 million years ago had flat skull bases and high larynxes, whereas those of *Homo erectus*, dating to about 1.9 million years and later, show somewhat more curvature, suggesting that the larynx was beginning to descend to its modern position. It was only about 300,000 years ago that the skull base finally assumed a modern curvature, which would allow for fully articulate speech to evolve. *Homo habilis* probably had very limited speaking abilities.

The real value of language, apart from the stimulation it gives brain development, is that with it we can convey feelings and nuances far beyond the power of gestures or grunts to communicate. We may assume that the first humans had more to communicate with than the gestures and grunts of non-human primates, but it appears that articulate speech was a more recent development.

SOCIAL ORGANIZATION

The few early sites that have been excavated show that the first phase of human evolution involved shifts in the basic patterns of subsistence and loco-motion as well as new ingredients—food sharing and toolmaking. These led to enhanced communication, information exchange, and economic and social insight, as well as cunning and restraint. Human anatomy was augmented with tools. Culture became an inseparable part of humanity, and social life acquired a new, and as yet little understood, complexity.

What sort of social organization did *Homo habilis* enjoy? However much we look at contemporary nonhuman primates, we cannot be sure. Most primates are intensely social and live in groups in which the mother–infant relationship forms a central bond. The period of infants' dependency on mothers found in, say, chimpanzees was probably lengthened considerably with *H. habilis*. The larger brain size would mean that infants were born with much smaller heads than adults, at an earlier stage of mental maturity. This biological reality would have had a major impact on social organization and daily habits.

Chimpanzees have flexible, matriarchal social groups. They occupy a rel-atively small territory, one with sufficient vegetable resources to support a considerable population density; this pattern contrasts sharply with the aver-age hunter-gatherer band, typically a closely knit group of about 25 people of several families. The kind of systematic hunting such people engage in requires much larger territories and permits much lower densities per square mile. The few sites that have been excavated suggest that *Homo habilis* tended to live in bands that were somewhat more akin to those of modern hunter-gatherers. But in all probability their social organization resembled more closely that of chimpanzees and baboons, which is very different from those of humans.

The world of *Homo habilis* was much less predictable and more demand-ing than that of even *Australopithecus*. What was it that was more complex? Why do we have to be so intelligent? Not for hunting animals or gathering food but for our interactions with other people. The increased complexity of our social interactions is likely to have been a powerful force in the evolution of the human brain. For *H. habilis,* the adoption of a wider-based diet with a food-sharing social group would have placed much more acute demands on the ability to cope with the complex and unpredictable. And the brilliant techno-logical, artistic, and expressive skills of humankind may well be a consequence of the fact that our early ancestors had to be more and more socially adept.

CHAPTER 3

African Exodus

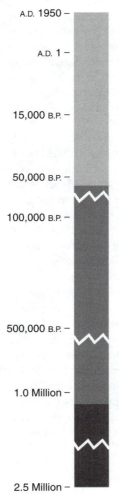

A.D. 1950 —

A.D. 1 —

15,000 B.P. —

50,000 B.P. —

100,000 B.P. —

500,000 B.P. —

1.0 Million —

2.5 Million —

About 1.9 million years ago, *Homo habilis* gave way to more advanced humans capable of far more complex and varied lifeways. These new human ancestors were the first to tame fire and the first to settle outside the tropical savannas of Africa. They did so at the beginning of the last geological epoch, the Pleistocene, sometimes called the Ice Age.

ICE AGE BACKGROUND

The Pleistocene began about 1.8 million years ago, after an intensification of glaciation worldwide about 2.5 million years ago. By this time great mountain chains had formed in the Alps, Himalayas, and elsewhere. Land masses had been uplifted; connection between these latitudes and southern areas was reduced, lessening their heat exchange and causing greater temperature differences between them. Northern latitudes became progressively cooler after 3 million years ago, but climatic fluctuations between warmer and colder climatic regimens were still relatively minor during the first million years of the Ice Age. This was a critically important time when a new human form, *Homo erectus*, evolved in Africa and moved out of the tropics into Asia and Europe.

About 730,000 years ago, the earth's magnetic field changed abruptly from a reversed state it had adopted about 2.5 million years ago to a normal one (see Table 2.1). This Matuyama/Brunhes boundary, named after the geologists who first discovered it, marks the beginning of constant climatic change for

Chronological Table A

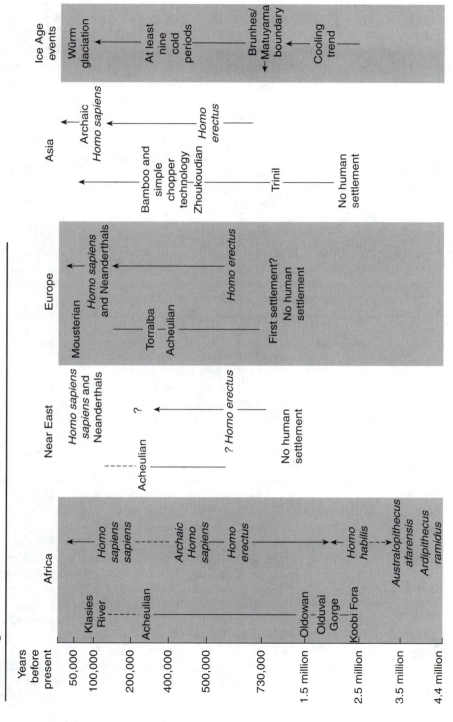

D I S C O V E R Y

Eugene Dubois and *Homo erectus*

Eugene Dubois was a Dutchman obsessed with the "Missing Link," the mythical human that was the evolutionary connection between apes and modern people. A surgeon by profession, young Dubois even wangled a posting as an army physician to distant Sumatra in southeast Asia in 1887, where, he was convinced, the Missing Link would be found. Incredible though it may seem, Dubois actually found what he claimed was such an ancestor on nearby Java in 1891. Digging into fossil-rich ash and river sediments at Trinil on the Solo River in northeastern Java, he found not only the bones of extinct animals but a human tooth, a thick-walled skull, and a human thigh bone.

Dubois was ecstatic and named his fossil *Pithecanthropus erectus,* "ape-human which stood upright." This, he claimed, was the missing link between apes and humans, a very primitive human being. On his return to Europe in 1895, he was greeted with skepticism, then scorn. Dubois's reaction was to withdraw from the scientific arena. He is said to have kept his fossils under his bed. Modern science has vindicated Eugene Dubois, for he was the first to discover what is now known as *Homo erectus,* a direct ancestor of modern humanity.

the remainder of the Ice Age. Deep sea cores give us a record of changing sea temperatures. They tell us that ice sheets formed gradually, but deglaciation and global warming trends took place with great rapidity. These corresponded with major sea level rises that flooded low-lying coastal areas. During glacial maxima, ice sheets covered a full third of the earth's surface, mantling Scandinavia and the Alps in Europe, as well as much of northern North America (see Figure 4.2). Sea levels fell dramatically as a result, hundreds of feet below modern levels. The glaciers were about as extensive as they are today during warmer periods, the so-called interglacials, when sea levels were close to present shorelines. Much less is known about changes in tropical regions, although it is thought that the southern fringes of Africa's Sahara Desert expanded dramatically during cold periods.

Both *Homo erectus* and its successor, *Homo sapiens,* evolved during a long period of constant climatic transition between warmer and colder regimens in northern latitudes. Experts believe that the world's climate has been in transition from one extreme to the other for over 75 percent of the past 730,000 years, with a predominance of colder climate over the period (see Table 2.1). There were at least nine glacial episodes, a major one about 525,000 years ago, when there was ice as far south as Seattle, St. Louis, and New York in North America, and sea levels were as much as 650 feet (197 m) below modern levels. In contrast, there were periods of more temperate conditions between 515,000 and 315,000 years ago. This was the period when human settlement outside Africa expanded, as small bands of foragers exploited the rich animal and plant resources of European and Asian river valleys and forests.

Another intensely cold cycle lasted from about 180,000 to 128,000 years ago, a cycle that coincided in general terms with the period when *Homo sapiens,* modern humans, were evolving in Africa. Between 100,000 and 15,000 years ago, the last Ice Age glaciation saw the spread of *Homo sapiens* throughout the Old World and into the Americas. These constant climatic changes played an important role in the spread of early human beings throughout temperate and tropical latitudes.

HOMO ERECTUS (c. 1.9 million to after 200,000 years ago)

All paleoanthropologists agree that the new human form, known generically as *Homo erectus* evolved in tropical Africa. They point to the continuous record of human evolution in that continent, from *Australopithecus afarensis* to the australopithecines, then *Homo habilis* and *H. erectus*. However bushlike the evolutionary tree, and it was much more complex than we know today, the best and longest fossil record comes from Africa. As we shall see later in this chapter, the same continent may have been the cradle of modern humans, *Homo sapiens sapiens,* also.

Current estimates place the emergence of *Homo erectus* (the earliest African form is sometimes called *Homo ergaster*), probably in Africa, at about 1.9 million years ago. That the new human evolved from a *Homo habilis*–like hominid seems unquestionable, but we still await the discovery of largerbrained transitional forms.

The Earliest African Examples

The early East African *Homo erectus* specimens come from northern Kenya. Skull KNM-ER 3733 from East Turkana dates to between 1.6 and 1.5 million years ago (Figure 3.1).[1] This fossil, with its massive brow ridges, enlarged brain size, and high forehead, is morphologically very close to examples of later *H. erectus* specimens dating to a million years ago. Another fossil find, this time of a 12-year-old boy from the western shore of Lake Turkana, dates to about the same time period (Figure 3.2). From the neck down, the boy's bones are remarkably modern looking. The skull and jawbone are more primitive, with brow ridges and a brain capacity perhaps as high as 700 to 800 cc, about half the modern size. The boy stood about 5

---

[1] For clarity, *Homo erectus* is used here as a generic classification. Numerous new terms, *Homo ergaster* among them, have proliferated in recent years but are irrelevant at this level of discussion.

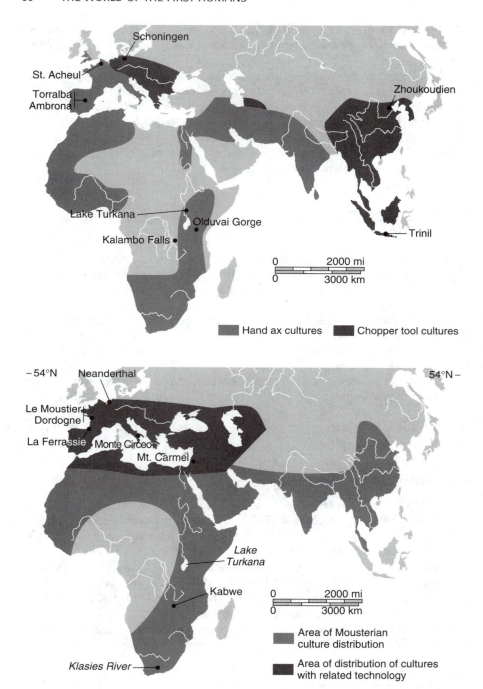

Figure 3.1   Maps of Sites Mentioned in Chapter 3

Figure 3.2 Lake Turkana, East Africa   A reconstruction of a young *Homo erectus* boy, who died in a small lagoon on the western shores of Lake Turkana about 1.5 million years ago. Drawing by Ian Everard.

feet 6 inches (1.8 m) tall, taller than most modern 12-year-olds. The Turkana boy seems to confirm the theory that different parts of the human body evolved at different rates, the body achieving fully modern form long before the head.

Unlike its predecessors, *Homo erectus* spread far out of Africa and adapted to a wide range of temperate, tropical, and cold environments throughout Europe and Asia. However, these archaic humans never crossed into the Americas. We know that the earliest hominids could adapt to a variety of climates and habitats. Both *Australopithecus* and *Homo habilis* adjusted to plunging global temperatures during a glacial episode between about 2.7 and 2.5 million years ago. The colder conditions turned much of Africa's moist woodlands into much drier, open savanna. The hominids thrived in these conditions, as tree-dwelling primates yielded to bipedal forms better able to survive in the open. This adaptability let hominids move into new environments, where their mixed diet of meat and plant foods caused them to move over large home territories. *Homo erectus* was just as adaptable and mobile, but was the first human to use fire, fashion more elaborate tools, and leave Africa.

Homo erectus Radiates Out of Africa

If new potassium argon dates for *Homo erectus* fossils in Indonesia are to be believed, then these new humans radiated out of Africa with remarkable speed, appearing on the savanna by 1.9 million years ago, and in the southeast Asian rainforest by 1.8 million years ago. But would a radiation of *H. erectus* populations from Africa into Asia occur within a such a short time frame as 100,000 years? Such a rapid spread is theoretically possible. With *Homo erectus* covering large, open territories where food resources were scattered unevenly over the landscape, even an expansion of 20 to 30 miles (c. 30 to 50 km) a year soon translates to hundreds, then thousands of miles, within a few generations. Unfortunately, the archaeological and fossil evidence for this extraordinary radiation is still tantalizingly incomplete.

Why did this sudden movement occur? Around 2 million years ago, hominids were adjusting to cyclical alterations among savanna, forest, and desert, as the Ice Age began. They did so by migrating with changing vegetational zones, as many mammals did, or by adapting to new environments, changing their dietary emphasis from meat to plant foods. Finally, they could move out of tropical latitudes altogether, into habits that human beings had never occupied before.

Very likely *Homo erectus* adapted to changed circumstances in all these ways, radiating out of Africa by way of the Sahara, when the desert was capable of supporting human life. Geologist Neil Roberts has likened the Sahara to a pump, sucking in population during wetter savanna phases and forcing foragers out northward to the margins of the desert during drier cycles. In radiating out of Africa, *H. erectus* behaved just like other mammals in its ecological community.

H. erectus was a carnivore and a plant eater, and thus linked ecologically with other predators. There was widespread interchange of mammals between Africa and more temperate latitudes during the Pliocene and Lower Pleistocene. For example, a major change in the mammalian populations of Europe took place about 700,000 years ago. Hippopotamuses, forest elephants, and other herbivores and carnivores like the lion, leopard, and spotted hyena seem to have migrated northward from Africa at this time. Migrations by the lion, leopard, and hyena—the animals with which hominids shared many ecological characteristics—were in the same direction as that taken earlier by *Homo erectus*. That the first successful human settlement of tropical Asia, then, apparently later, of temperate Europe, coincided with radiations of mammalian communities out of Africa seems plausible. It may also have coincided with the taming of fire.

Homo erectus may have domesticated fire as early as 1.6 million years ago. Early humans would have been familiar with the great grass and brush fires that swept across the savanna during the dry months. Fire offered protection against predators and an easy way of hunting game, even insects and rodents fleeing from a line of flames. Perhaps *Homo erectus* developed the habit of conserving fire, taking advantage of long-smoldering tree stumps ignited by lightning strikes and other natural causes to kindle flames to light dry brush or simply to scare off predators.

It may be no coincidence that the radiation of *Homo erectus* out of tropical Africa into temperate environments in Asia and Europe occurred after the taming of fire and during a period of accelerated climatic change. Archaic humans were well established in northern Spain by 800,000 years ago, and far north in China by 500,000 years ago, probably earlier.

Homo erectus in Asia

The classic *Homo erectus* fossils come from Asia, from the **Trinil** area of Java, where they date to between 1.8 million and 600,000 years ago, and from northern China, dating to between 500,000 and 350,000 years ago (Figure 3.3). These well-preserved specimens show that these archaic humans had a brain capacity between 775 and 1300 cc, showing much variation. It is probable that their vision was excellent and that they were capable of extensive reasoning. The *H. erectus* skull is more rounded than that of earlier hominids. It also has conspicuous brow ridges and a sloping forehead. *Homo erectus* had limbs and hips fully adapted to an upright posture. Males stood over 5 feet 6 inches (1.8 m) tall and had hands fully capable of precision gripping and many kinds of toolmaking.

During *Homo erectus*'s long history, humanity adapted to a far wider range of environments, ranging from tropical savannas in East Africa to forested Javanese valleys, temperate climates in North Africa and Europe, and the harsh winters of northern China and central Europe. *Homo erectus* was certainly capable of a far more complex and varied lifeway than previous hominids. With such a wide distribution, it is hardly surprising that

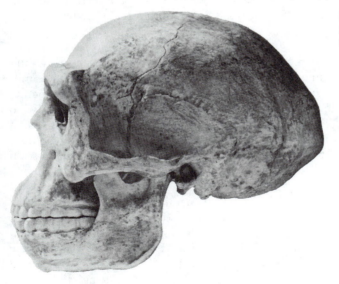

Figure 3.3 *HOMO ERECTUS* FROM ZHOUKOUDIAN, CHINA

some variations in population occur. For example, Chinese scholars claim that the *Homo erectus* fossils from the famous **Zhoukoudian** cave near Beijing display a gradual increase in brain capacity from about 900 cc 600,000 years ago to about 1100 cc in 200,000-year-old individuals. In any case, *Homo erectus* was far more human than *Homo habilis,* a habitual biped, who had probably lost the thick hair covering that is characteristic of non-human primates.

THE LIFEWAY OF HOMO ERECTUS

We still know little of the world of *Homo erectus,* beyond a certainty that, between 1.8 million and half a million years ago, humans had radiated far beyond their tropical African homeland (see Figure 3.1). Nowhere were human beings abundant, and the global population of archaic humans was undoubtedly minuscule. As far as is known *Homo erectus* did not settle in extreme arctic latitudes, in what is now Eurasia and Siberia, nor did these archaic humans cross into the Americas. Nor did they develop the watercraft needed to cross from the islands of Southeast Asia to New Guinea and Australia, landmasses that remained isolated by the ocean until the late Ice Age.

Throughout this enormous area of the Old World, *Homo erectus* populations developed a great variety of lifeways and local tool kits that reflected different needs. The hominids were part of a vast animal community and their long-term success resulted from their ability to adapt to the cyclical changes in the Ice Age environment, from temperate to much colder, then to full glacial conditions and then, more rapidly, to warmer again. Many of these early human populations flourished in regions where dense, abundant, and predictable resources were to be found, isolated from other regions where similar conditions existed.

The climatic conditions of the Ice Age sometimes brought these isolated populations together, then separated them again, ensuring gene flow and genetic drift and continued biological and cultural evolution over the millennia. As it had been for *Homo habilis,* the key to adapting to temperate environments was mobility. Human bands could respond quickly to changes in resource distribution by moving into new areas. Theirs was a primarily opportunistic adaptation based on knowledge of where resources were to be found, rather than on deliberate planning, as was the case in much later times.

Separated as we are from *Homo erectus* by hundreds of thousands of years, it is difficult for us to obtain even a general impression of their simple but opportunistic lifeway. Almost invariably, the only signs of their existence are scatters of stone artifacts, most frequently discovered near lakes and in river valleys, where the most plentiful food resources were to be found. These many finds have enabled us to divide the world of *Homo erectus* into two broad and still ill-defined provinces: Africa, Europe, and some parts of Asia—

more open country where hunting was important and multipurpose stone axes were commonly used; and a vast area of forested and wooded country in Asia where wood artifacts were all-important and stone technology far more conservative. This is almost certainly a gross simplification of a very complex picture, but it provides us with a general portrait of an archaic lifeway far removed from that of more modern humans.

The Issue of Big-Game Hunting

The simple Oldowan technology of *Homo habilis* remained in use for more than a million years before evolving slowly into a more diverse, stone technology that itself remained in use for a further half-million years. Neither *Homo habilis* nor *Homo erectus* relied exclusively on stone, for we can say with confidence that our remote ancestors also made use of wood, one of the most versatile raw materials known to humanity. The earliest known wooden artifacts are three throwing spears and a possible thrusting spear dated to 400,000 years ago, found with broken animal bones and stone tools in an open coal mine at **Schoningen**, Germany. The spears are between 2 feet 9 inches and 7 feet 6 inches (0.78–2.30 m) long, with tapering tails, to give them better direction when thrown. However, most insights into the technology of *H. erectus* come from stone tools and the byproducts associated with them, because wood and other organic materials are rarely preserved.

In Africa, Europe, and some parts of Asia, *Homo erectus* is associated with a distinctive tool kit that includes not only a variety of flake tools and sometimes choppers, but also one of the most common exhibits in the world's museums—the hand axe (Figure 3.4). Unlike the crude flakes and choppers of the Oldowan, the **Acheulian** hand axe (named after the northern French town Saint Acheul) was an artifact with converging edges that met at a point. The maker had to envision the shape of the artifact, which was to be produced from a mere lump of stone, then fashion it not with opportunistic blows but with carefully directed hammer strokes.

Acheulian hand axes come in every size, from elegant oval types a few inches long to heavy axes more than a foot (0.3 m) long and weighing 5 pounds (2.3 kg) or more. They were multipurpose tools, used for woodworking, scraping skins, and especially skinning and butchering of animals. The hand axe and its near relative the cleaver (see Figure 3.4) were ideal for butchery because the artifact could be sharpened again and again. When it became a useless lump of stone, it could be recycled into flake tools. But one can achieve effective butchery with simple flakes as well. A number of researchers have wondered whether the hand axe was not used for other purposes such as throwing at game or digging for roots.

Hand axes and related artifacts occur over an enormous area of the Old World and underwent considerable refinement during the million years or so they were in use. But what do we know of the behavior of their makers? Without question, *Homo erectus* hunted and foraged for food, probably in

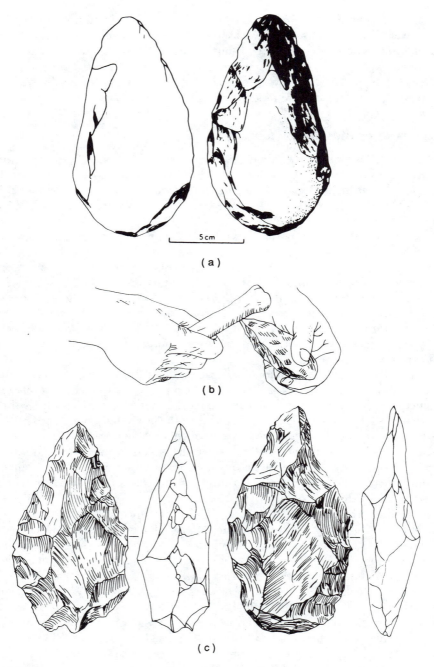

Figure 3.4 ACHEULIAN TECHNOLOGY   (a) Hand axes were multipurpose artifacts shaped symmetrically around a long axis. (b) A stoneworker thins the edge of a hand ax with a bone hammer. (c) Acheulian hand ax from Swanscombe, England and cleaver from **Kalambo Falls**, Zambia.

far more effective ways than *Homo habilis*. Time and time again, hand axes and other butchering artifacts have been found in association with the bones of large game animals. But did the hunters actually kill such formidable herbivores as the elephant and the rhinoceros? To do so would require social mechanisms to foster cooperation and communication abilities far beyond those of their predecessors.

Evidence for butchery and perhaps big-game hunting comes from two remarkable Acheulian sites at **Ambrona** and **Torralba** in central Spain. The Acheulians probably lived in this deep, swampy valley either 200,000 or 400,000 years ago (the date is controversial). Torralba has yielded most of the left side of an elephant, which had been cut into pieces, while Ambrona contained the remains of 30 to 35 dismembered elephants. Concentrations of broken bones lay all over the site and the skulls of the elephants had been broken open to get at the brains. In one place, elephant bones had been laid out in a line, perhaps to form stepping stones in the swamp where the animals had been killed. Both sites were littered with crude hand axes, cleavers, scrapers, and cutting tools.

The original scenario for the sites had hunters watching the valley floors, which may have lain astride an important game trail (Figure 3.5). At a strategic moment several bands would gather quietly, set brush fires, and drive the

Figure 3.5 Torralba, Spain A remarkable linear arrangement of elephant tusks and leg bones that were probably laid out by those who butchered the animals.

unsuspecting beasts into the swamps, where they would be killed and butchered at leisure. Other archaeologists challenge this scenario. They believe the hunters were actually scavenging meat from animals that had perished when they became mired in the swamps.

Bamboo and Choppers

The eastern portions of the archaic human world lay in Asia, in an enormous region of woodland and forest with great environmental diversity. The tropical forests of east Asia are rich in animal and plant foods, but these food resources are widely dispersed over the landscape. Thus, *Homo erectus* bands were constantly on the move, carrying tools with them. Under these circumstances, it was logical for them to make use of bamboo, wood, and other fibrous materials—the most convenient materials at hand. There was no need for the specialized, often complicated artifacts used in the open country of the West either for spear points or for the butchering tools used on large animals. As archaeologist Geoffrey Pope has pointed out, the distribution of the simple choppers and flakes used by eastern populations coincides very closely with the natural distribution of bamboo, one of the most versatile materials known to humankind. Bamboo was efficient, durable, and ⌐ ʳtable. It could be used to manufacture containers, sharp knives, spears, weapon tips, ropes, and dwellings. To this day, it is widely used in Asia as scaffolding for building skyscrapers. It is an ideal material for people subsisting not off large game but off smaller forest animals such as monkeys, rats, squirrels, lizards, and snakes, as well as plant foods. Simple stone flakes and jagged-edged choppers, the only artifacts to survive the millennia, would be ideal for working bamboo and may, indeed, have been used for this purpose for hundreds of thousands of years, long after *Homo erectus* had been superseded by more advanced human forms.

Everything points to *Homo erectus* having been eclectic and flexible hunter-gatherers, who relied on hunting, scavenging, and plant foods. They may have understood the telltale signs of the passage of seasons, the meanings of cloud formations, the timing of game and bird migrations, and the geography of their territories. But they never exploited small game, birds, fish, or sea mammals on any significant scale, as modern humans did almost at once.

Homo erectus probably lived in relatively large groups at times, both to reduce the danger from carnivores and to improve the chance of finding food, especially from larger animals. At other times, band size may have been much smaller, especially when plant foods were more abundant and easily obtained by individuals. All of this argues for considerable social flexibility and intelligence on the part of *Homo erectus* reflected in their larger brain size. However, they may have been unable to integrate their social intelligence—their ability to share food and cooperate in the hunt—with other aspects of human intelligence.

Language

Homo erectus had a large brain with a well-developed Broca's area, the zone associated with speaking ability. Its vocal tracts were more modern, suggesting considerable potential for articulate speech. Anthropologists Leslie Aiello and Robin Dunbar have argued that the basis for language ability appeared in humans by at least 250,000 years ago. They believe it first evolved as a way to handle increasingly complex social information. As group sizes increased, so did a capacity for language, used primarily to talk about social relations. It was only later that humans developed the kind of general-purpose language we use today, which allows us to communicate freely, whatever the behavioral domain. So like us in many ways, *Homo erectus* lacked the cognitive flexibility characteristic of modern humans, yet it was from this archaic human that ultimately *Homo sapiens sapiens* evolved.

ARCHAIC HOMO SAPIENS
(c. 400,000 to 130,000 years ago)

Homo erectus has long been considered the single human form to have lived on earth between about 1.8 million and 400,000 years ago. However, this all-embracing classification dates from the days when scholars thought of human evolution in more linear terms. They linked anatomically primitive features such as heavy brow ridges and bun-shaped skull-caps, which are indeed common to the various *Homo erectus* fossils from Africa, Asia, and Europe.[2] Specialized features, such as the massive faces found on Asian individuals, may in fact be evidence for geographically defined forms, only one of which evolved into *Homo sapiens,* anatomically modern humans. This branching view sees *Homo erectus* as an adaptive radiation of hominids after 1.9 million years ago, with only a small part of this evolution resulting in the emergence of *Homo sapiens.*

Between about 400,000 and 130,000 years ago, *Homo erectus* was evolving toward more modern forms of human throughout the Old World. Fossil fragments from Africa, Asia, and Europe display both *erectus*-like and *sapiens*-like traits, sufficient for them to be classified under the general label archaic *Homo sapiens*. These anatomical advances take several forms. Brain capacities are larger, the sides of the skull are wider, and the rear of the cranium is now more rounded. Human skeletons become less robust and molar teeth are smaller.

These general trends occur in African fossils, such as the well-known, massive Broken Hill skull from **Kabwe**, Zambia, in central Africa. They are

---

[2]Again, in the interests of clarity the generic term *Homo erectus* is used to describe many newly classified local forms, such as Europe's *Homo heidelbergensis*. For information on the new classifications, please consult a physical anthropology text.

found in China, too, where both archaic and *sapiens* traits appear, traits that Chinese anthropologists also claim appear in modern populations there. In Europe, too, fossil remains dating to this long period display a mosaic of *erectus* and *sapiens* features. But the fossils from each continent differ considerably. European fossils, for example, often appear somewhat more robust than those from Asia. Everywhere, however, brain sizes increase gradually and skull shapes become rounder. In Asia and Africa, the changes seem to have a trend toward modern sapiens, whereas the European fossils are evolving toward a Neanderthal form (see below). This evolutionary trend toward more modern anatomy appears everywhere, but it was only on one continent, Africa, that *Homo erectus* gave rise to modern *Homo sapiens*. In other words, the pattern of human evolution based on the adaptive radiation seen with the australopithecines hundreds of thousands of years earlier persisted into much later prehistory.

THE NEANDERTHALS (c. 150,000 to 32,000 years ago)

Much of what we know about archaic *Homo sapiens,* the descendant of *Homo erectus,* comes from the Neanderthals, long-term inhabitants of Europe and Eurasia, whose anatomical features appear in archaic European populations such as those from **Atapuerca**, Spain, at least 300,000 years ago (Figure 3.6). The Neanderthals are still the subject of great controversy among physical anthropologists. Some people use the word *Neanderthal* to describe dim-witted, ugly people who are like apes, an insult aimed at those they consider dumb. This stereotype and that of the shambling cave people so beloved by cartoonists come from mistaken studies of

Figure 3.6 Archaic *Homo sapiens* Skull from the Pit of Bones, Atapuerca, Spain

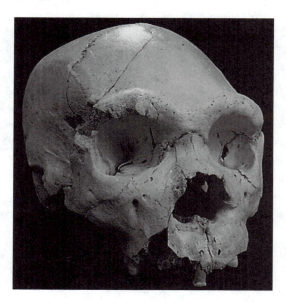

Neanderthal skeletons in the early years of this century. In fact, the Neanderthals were strong, robustly built humans with some archaic features. Their skulls display retreating foreheads, projecting faces, and sometimes eyebrow ridges, when compared with modern people. There is every reason to believe they were expert hunters and beings capable of considerable intellectual reasoning.

There are, of course, striking anatomical differences between Neanderthals and modern humans, both in the robust postcranial skeleton of the Neanderthal and in its more bun-shaped skull, sometimes with heavy brow ridges and a forward projecting face (Figure 3.7). These features are the reason this extinct hominid form is classified as *Homo sapiens neanderthalensis,* a subspecies of *Homo sapiens,* and not as *Homo sapiens sapiens,* a fully modern human.

Researchers at the University of Munich, Germany, and at Pennsylvania State University were able to extract deoxyribonucleic acid (DNA) from the first Neanderthal arm bone ever discovered in the Neander Valley near Dusseldorf, Germany, in 1856. The scientists pulverized a small amount of the bone and were able to extract several small fragments of **mitochondrial DNA** (see below). By overlapping the small fragments of Neanderthal DNA and using a technique known as polymerase chain reaction to make many copies of the molecules, the scientists were able to identify a sequence of 378 base pairs (chemicals that form the fundamental units of the genetic code) in a specific region of the Neanderthal DNA. This area, known as hypervariable region 1, is known to show changes over many generations. In general, the greater the dissimilarity in this region between two species, the more remote the relation is thought to be.

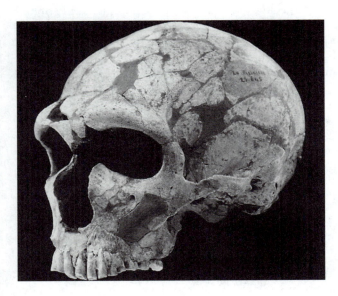

Figure 3.7 CLASSIC NEANDERTHAL SKULL FROM LA FERRASSIE, FRANCE

The researchers compared the Neanderthal DNA sequence to sequences in the same region of DNA for 994 modern human lineages, which included Africans, Asians, Australians, Europeans, Native Americans, and Pacific Islanders. The Neanderthal DNA sequence differed from all the modern human DNA by either 27 or 28 base pairs. In contrast, modern human sequences in this region of DNA differ from each other on average by 8 base pairs. The difference between modern human DNA and chimpanzee DNA in this region is much greater, at about 55 base pairs.

As a result, the geneticists concluded that Neanderthals and modern humans are distant relations and did not interbreed or evolve from one another. If chimpanzees and humans diverged about 4 million to 5 million years ago, then we can estimate Neanderthals may have split from early modern humans between 550,000 and 690,000 years ago.

The Neanderthals flourished in Europe, Eurasia, and part of southwestern Asia from about 150,000 years ago until around 32,000 years ago. Their anatomical pattern stabilized for 50 millennia before changing rapidly to essentially modern human anatomy within a brief period of 5000 years approximately 40,000 years ago. Neanderthal populations displayed great variation, but everywhere had the same posture and manual abilities as modern people. They differed from us in having massive limb bones, often somewhat bowed in the thigh and forearm, features that reflect their greater muscular power (Figure 3.8). For their height, the Neanderthals were bulky and heavily muscled, and their brain capacity was slightly larger than that of modern humans. Their antecedents are in earlier archaic *Homo sapiens* Europeans, from which they inherited their heavy build and their ability to withstand extreme cold, an adaptation so successful that it lasted for more than 100,000 years.

Neanderthal culture and technology was far more complex and sophisticated than that of their Acheulian predecessors. Many of their artifacts were not multipurpose tools, but were made for specific purposes, as stone spear points mounted on wooden spears, or curved scrapers for treating pegged-out hides (Figure 3.9). Like their predecessors, they occupied large territories, which they probably exploited on a seasonal round, returning to the same locations year after year when game migrated or plant foods came into season.

The Neanderthals were skilled hunters, especially when one realizes that they had to attack game at close quarters with spears and clubs rather than with the bow and arrow (Figure 3.10, *top*). They were not afraid to tackle such formidable animals as mammoth, bison, or wild horses. Many western European bands lived in caves and rock shelters during much of the year as a protection against arctic cold. During the brief summer months they may have fanned out over the open plains, living in temporary tented encampments, also exploiting plant foods (Figure 3.10, *bottom*). There can be little doubt the Neanderthals knew their local environments intimately and that they planned their lives around migration seasons and such factors as herd size and the predictability of animal movements. By this time, too, humans had learned how

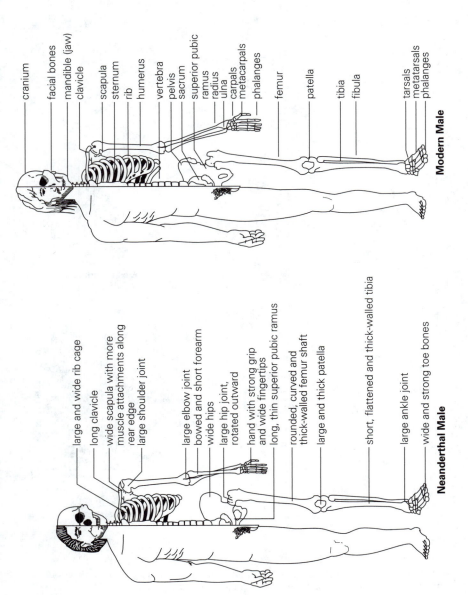

Figure 3.8   The Skeleton of a Male Neanderthal (*Left*) Compared With That of a Modern Male   The Neanderthal is more robust and stocky than his modern counterpart. (After Stringer and Gamble, *In Search of the Neanderthals* 1992).

Labels (Modern Male):
cranium
facial bones
mandible (jaw)
clavicle
scapula
sternum
rib
humerus
vertebra
pelvis
sacrum
superior pubic ramus
radius
ulna
carpals
metacarpals
phalanges
femur
patella
tibia
fibula
tarsals
metatarsals
phalanges

Modern Male

Labels (Neanderthal Male):
large and wide rib cage
long clavicle
wide scapula with more muscle attachments along rear edge
large shoulder joint
large elbow joint
bowed and short forearm
wide hips
large hip joint, rotated outward
hand with strong grip and wide fingertips
long, thin superior pubic ramus
rounded, curved and thick-walled femur shaft
large and thick patella
short, flattened and thick-walled tibia
large ankle joint
wide and strong toe bones

Neanderthal Male

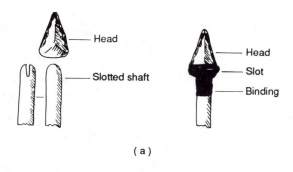

(a)

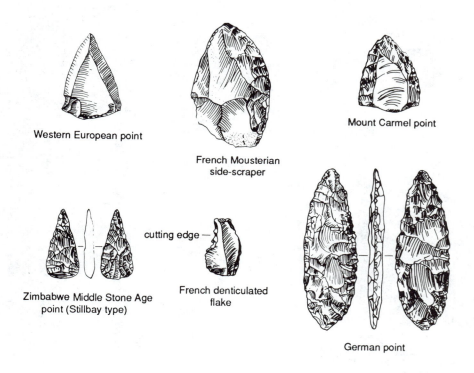

(b)

Figure 3.9 COMPOSITE SPEAR POINTS   Stone artifacts fabricated by archaic *Homo sapiens* included (a) composite tools that mounted stone points to the ends of wooden shafts and (b) a variety of spear points, also cutting and scraping tools.

to store food for the lean months, maximizing the meat taken from seasonally migrating herds of reindeer and other animals.

The resulting cultural variability is reflected in the diverse **Mousterian** tool kits of Neanderthal groups (named after the site of Le Moustier in

Figure 3.10 RECONSTRUCTION OF NEANDERTHAL LIFEWAYS   (*top*) Hunters during the early Würm glaciation. (*bottom*) Neanderthal woman gathering fruit in early summer.

southwestern France). Unlike the hand-ax makers, the Neanderthals made most of their artifacts of flakes, the most common being scraping tools and spear points. Some of their weapons were **composite tools,** artifacts made of more than one component—for example, a point, a shaft, and the binding that secured the head to the shaft, making a spear. Their technology was simple, highly variable, and a logical development of earlier technologies developed over hundreds of thousands of years (see Figure 3.9). Neanderthal sites in France have yielded a great diversity of tool kits. Some levels include hand axes; others notched flakes, perhaps used for stripping meat for drying or pressing fibrous plants. Such wide variation in Mousterian tool kits is found not only in France but at other Neanderthal sites throughout Europe and Southwestern Asia and in North Africa, where other archaic *Homo sapiens* made similar tools. No one knows exactly what all these variations in tool kits mean, but they reflect the ability of the Neanderthals and other archaic *Homo sapiens* to develop tools for different, highly specific activities, perhaps at a time of rising human populations and slightly enhanced social complexity.

The Neanderthals and their archaic contemporaries elsewhere were foragers and the world's population was still small, but life was gradually becoming more complex. We find the first signs of religious ideology, of a preoccupation with the life hereafter. Many Neanderthals were buried by their companions. Neanderthal burials have been recovered from caves and rock shelters, and from open campsites. One rock shelter, **La Ferrassie** near Les Eyzies in France, yielded the remains of two adult Neanderthals and four children buried close together in a campsite. Group sepulchers occur at other sites, too, signs that the Neanderthals, like most later foragers, believed in life after death.

We find in the Neanderthals and their increasingly sophisticated culture the first roots of our own complicated beliefs, societies, and religious sense. But the Neanderthals, like other archaic *Homo sapiens* forms, gave way to fully modern humans, after 40,000 years ago, people whose awesome intellectual and physical powers created a late Ice Age world unimaginably different from that of earlier prehistory.

THE ORIGINS OF MODERN HUMANS
(?c. 180,000 to 150,000 years ago)

Homo sapiens sapiens means the "wise person." We are the clever people, capable of subtlety, of manipulation, of self-understanding. What is it that separates us from earlier humans, scientists wonder? First and foremost must be our ability to speak fluently and articulately. We communicate, we tell stories, we pass on knowledge and ideas, all through the medium of language. Consciousness, cognition, self-awareness, foresight, and the ability to express oneself and one's emotions—these are direct consequences of fluent speech. They can be linked with another attribute of the fully fledged human psyche: the capacity for symbolic and spiritual thought, concerned not only with subsistence and technology but also with the boundaries of existence and the relationships among the individual, the group, and the universe.

Fluent speech, the full flowering of human creativity expressed in art and religion, expert toolmaking—these are some of the hallmarks of *Homo sapiens sapiens*. With these abilities humankind eventually colonized not just temperate and tropical environments but the entire globe. With the appearance of modern humans we begin the study of people anatomically identical to ourselves, people with the same intellectual potential as our own.

For hundreds of thousands of years, both *Homo erectus* and early *Homo sapiens* survived and evolved with the aid of multiple intelligences, separated by walls analogous to those dividing the chapels of a Medieval cathedral. As archaeologist Steven Mithen says, the thoughts in one chapel could barely be heard in another. Archaic humans lacked one vital component of the modern mind: cognitive flexibility, the ability to bridge the walls between their many intelligences. Such flexibility appears to have been the prerogative of modern humans, *Homo sapiens sapiens*.

The controversies surrounding the origins of modern humanity, of ourselves, rank among the most vigorous in archaeology.

Continuity or Replacement?

Over generations of debate, two major, and diametrically opposed, hypotheses have developed to explain the origins of modern humans (Figure 3.11):

- *The so-called candelabra (or multiregional) model* hypothesizes that *Homo erectus* populations throughout the Old World evolved independently, first to archaic *H. sapiens,* then to fully modern humans. This continuity model argues for multiple origins of *H. sapiens* and no migrations later than those of *Homo erectus*. Thus, modern geographic populations have been separated from one another for a long time, perhaps for nearly 2 million years. Under this scenario, continuous gene flow within the group meant that highly adaptive, novel anatomical features spread rapidly, thereby keeping all human populations on the same fundamental evolutionary path toward anatomically modern people, even if some evolved into fully modern humans before others.

- *The Noah's ark (or out-of-Africa) model* takes the diametrically opposite view. According to it, *Homo sapiens* evolved in one place, then spread to all other parts of the Old World. This model, which assumes population movement from a single point of origin, implies that modern geographic populations have shallow roots and were derived from a single source in relatively recent times.

These two models represent extremes, which pit advocates of anatomical continuity against those who favor rapid replacement of archaic populations.

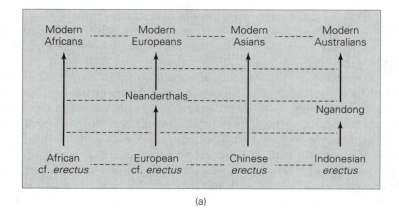

(a)

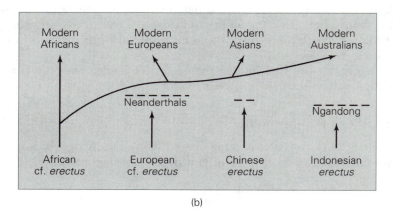

(b)

Figure 3.11   THEORIES OF THE ORIGINS OF MODERN HUMANS, EACH OF WHICH INTER-
PRETS THE FOSSIL EVIDENCE IN VERY DIFFERENT WAYS   (a) The Candelabra or multiregional model, which argues for the evolution of *Homo sapiens sapiens* in many
regions of the Old World. The dotted lines between different columns represent gene
flow between regions. (b) The Noah's Ark (Out-of-Africa) model, which has modern
humanity evolving in Africa, then spreading to other parts of the world (After Stringer
and Gamble, 1992).

Until recently, most anthropologists favored the multiregional model, as both
human artifacts and fossil finds from Europe and southwestern Asia appeared
to document slow biological and cultural change over long periods of time.
Today, however, a torrent of new discoveries have shown that archaic human
populations displayed great variation and were morphologically more different from anatomically modern humans than once suspected. Advocates of the
multiregional model rely heavily on anatomical traits from surviving fossils to
argue their case, whereas out-of-Africa supporters make use not only of fossils
but of genetics, an approach their opponents regard as highly controversial.
The debate continues, despite a lack of new fossils, and is likely to continue
for generations as both new discoveries and more refined genetic researches

radically alter our knowledge of archaic *Homo sapiens* and its contemporaries and successors.

Molecular Biology and Homo sapiens

Molecular biology has played a significant role in dating earlier human evolution and is now yielding important clues to the origins of *Homo sapiens*.

Researchers have zeroed in on mitochondrial DNA (mtDNA), a useful tool for calibrating mutation rates because it accumulates mutations much faster than nuclear DNA. Mitochondrial DNA is inherited only through the maternal line; it does not mix and become diluted with paternal DNA. Thus, it provides a potentially reliable link with ancestral populations. When genetic researchers analyzed the mtDNA of 147 women from Africa, Asia, Europe, Australia, and New Guinea, they found that the differences among them were very small. Therefore, they argued, the five populations were all of comparatively recent origin. There were some differences, sufficient to separate two groups within the sample—a set of African individuals and another comprising individuals from all groups. The biologists concluded that all modern humans derive from a 200,000-year-old African population, from which populations migrated to the rest of the Old World with little or no interbreeding with existing, more archaic human groups.

A storm of criticism has descended on this hypothesis, most of it directed against the calculations of the rate of genetic mutation. The methodology is very new and evolving rapidly. Nevertheless, with mitochondrial data from some 5000 modern individuals, there is evidence that Africans display more diverse types of mitochondrial DNA than other present-day populations elsewhere in the world, which suggests they had more time to develop such mutations. An even larger database of normal (nuclear) DNA, also of its products (blood groups and enzymes), displays a hierarchy of clusters. There was a primary split between Africans and non-Africans, then a later one between Eurasians and southeast Asians. This also implies that modern humans originated in Africa then dispersed from there to split again in Asia. It is thought that the ancestral population lived in Africa before 100,000 years ago. This also means that, assuming a constant rate of genetic diversification, all human variation could have arisen in the past 150,000 years.

Fortunately, there is some archaeological and fossil evidence that tends to confirm an early appearance of anatomically modern humans in sub-Saharan Africa. According to German physical anthropologist Günter Bräuer, there were at least three forms of *Homo sapiens* in sub-Saharan Africa. An archaic *Homo sapiens* form was distributed from southern to northeast Africa some 200,000 years ago. These archaic populations had evolved from earlier *Homo erectus* populations and had higher cranial vaults and other anatomical features akin to those of anatomically modern humans. Between about 150,000 and 100,000 years ago, Bräuer believes, late archaic *Homo sapiens* populations flourished throughout Africa—people displaying mosaics of both archaic and modern features. Bräuer believes that very early anatomically modern humans were widely distributed in eastern and southern Africa as early as 115,000 years ago, and perhaps earlier. He also believes that the biological developments that led to the appearance of modern humans had run their course as early as between 100,000 and 70,000 years ago, earlier than anywhere else in the world, including Europe, where archaic human forms such as the Neanderthals still flourished.

We can now be certain *Homo sapiens sapiens* lived in southern Africa. Recently, archaeologists have found well-preserved footprints of an anatomically modern human preserved in a fossilized sand dune at **Langebaan Lagoon** near Cape Town, South Africa, dating to at least 117,000 years ago.

Ecology and Homo sapiens

Ecological anthropologist Robert Foley points out that the savanna woodland of Africa 100,000 years ago was an ideal environment for promoting the speciation of modern humans. He has studied monkey evolution in Africa and found that the widely dispersed populations had diverged; they did not continue on a single evolutionary course. Africa experienced considerable habitat fragmentation and reformation during the constant cold and warm cycles of the Ice Age, fluctuations that enhanced the prospects of speciation among the continent's animals and plants. For example, says Foley, one monkey genus alone radiated into 16 species at about the same time as modern humans may have evolved in Africa. Foley's monkey studies have convinced him that modern humans evolved in just such a fragmented mosaic of tropical environments, developing distinctive characteristics that separated them from their archaic predecessors. There were areas where food resources were predictable and of high quality. In response to such regions, some human populations may have developed wide-ranging behavior, lived in larger social groups with considerable kin-based substructure, and been highly selective in their diet.

As part of these responses, some groups may have developed exceptional hunting skills, using a technology so effective that they could prey on animals from a distance with projectiles. With more efficient weapons, more advance planning, and better organization of foraging, our ancestors could have reduced the unpredictability of the environment in dramatic ways. Few archaeologists would be so bold as to associate ancient technologies with specific fossil forms, but we do know that tens of thousands of years later, *Homo sapiens sapiens* relied on much more sophisticated tool technology than their predecessors. The new tool kits were based on antler, bone, wood, and parallel-sided, stone-blade manufacture. This technology was far more advanced than anything made by their predecessors and took many millennia to develop. There is no question but that it would have conferred a major advantage on its users, both in terms of hunting efficiency and energy expended in the chase.

Interestingly enough, there are signs of technological change throughout eastern and southern Africa between 200,000 and 130,000 years ago, as age-old hand ax technology gave way to lighter tool kits that combined sharp stone flakes with wooden spear shafts, and to other more specialized artifacts used for woodworking and butchery. Such simple artifacts, made on medium-sized flakes, could have been the archaic prototypes of far more efficient tools and weapons developed by anatomically modern humans after 100,000 years ago (Figure 3.12). But again, one must emphasize that the existence of such artifacts in Africa at the time when modern humans apparently first appeared there is not necessarily proof they were developed by *Homo sapiens sapiens*.

To summarize the controversy over modern human origins—the weight of such evidence as there is, and it is not much, tends to favor an African origin for modern humans.

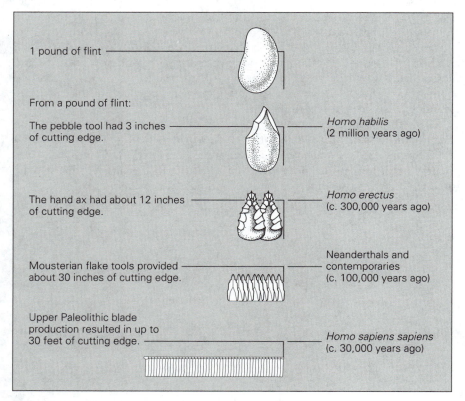

1 pound of flint

From a pound of flint:

The pebble tool had 3 inches of cutting edge.   *Homo habilis* (2 million years ago)

The hand ax had about 12 inches of cutting edge.   *Homo erectus* (c. 300,000 years ago)

Mousterian flake tools provided about 30 inches of cutting edge.   Neanderthals and contemporaries (c. 100,000 years ago)

Upper Paleolithic blade production resulted in up to 30 feet of cutting edge.   *Homo sapiens sapiens* (c. 30,000 years ago)

Figure 3.12   THE GROWING EFFICIENCY OF STONE AGE TECHNOLOGY, SHOWN BY THE ABILITY OF ANCIENT STONEWORKERS TO PRODUCE EVER-LARGER NUMBERS OF CUTTING EDGES FROM A POUND OF STONE OR OTHER FINE-GRAINED ROCK   The Neanderthals were far more efficient stone artisans than their predecessors. By the same token, *Homo sapiens sapiens* used blade and other technologies that produced up 30 feet (9.1 m) per pound of rock (see Figure 4.6).

OUT OF TROPICAL AFRICA

If tropical Africa was the cradle of modern humans, how and why did *Homo sapiens* spread into Europe and Asia? The critical period was between 100,000 and 45,000 years ago, the date by which anatomically modern people were certainly living in southwest Asia. The only major barrier to population movement between tropical Africa and the Mediterranean Basin is the Sahara desert, today some of the driest territory on earth. Bitterly cold glacial conditions in the north brought a cooler and wetter climate to the desert from before 100,000 until about 40,000 years ago. For long periods, the country between East Africa and the Mediterranean was passable, supporting scattered game herds and open grassland. The Nile Valley was always habitable, even during periods of great aridity in the desert. Thus, small groups of modern people could have hunted and foraged across the Sahara into the Nile Valley and southwest Asia as early as 100,000 years ago. From there, their successors may have moved into south and southeast Asia at a still unknown date, but perhaps between 70,000 and 50,000 years ago. As southwest Asia became increasingly dry and less productive after 50,000 years ago, small numbers of modern people may have responded to population pressure and food shortages by moving across the wide land bridge that joined Turkey to southeastern Europe at the time, spreading into the homeland of the European Neanderthals within a few millennia.

With these still little known population movements, the initial radiation of modern humans throughout the Old World ended, perhaps by about 40,000 years ago. As we shall see in Chapter 5, the next 30,000 years saw the greatest of all human diaspora take our ancestors into island southeast Asia, to New Guinea, Australia, Siberia, and, ultimately, the Americas.

PART

3

THE BIRTH OF
THE MODERN WORLD

Three thousand, four thousand years maybe, have passed and gone since human feet last trod the floor on which you stand, and yet, as you note the signs of recent life around you—the half-filled bowl of mortar for the door, the blackened lamp, the finger-mark on the freshly painted surface, the farewell garland dropped on the threshold—you feel it might have been but yesterday. . . . Time is annihilated by little intimate details such as these, and you feel an intruder.

EGYPTOLOGIST HOWARD CARTER,
notebook entry on Tutankhamun's tomb, November 26, 1922

CHAPTER 4

Diaspora

A.D. 1950 —

A.D. 1 —

15,000 B.P. —

50,000 B.P. —

100,000 B.P. —

500,000 B.P. —

1.0 Million —

2.5 Million —

Something dramatic happened to humanity about 50,000 to 60,000 years ago. Suddenly, the pace of human life, of cultural evolution, accelerated rapidly. Some scientists have called these changes a "cultural explosion," but a better term is probably a series of "sparks," where there was rapid cultural change in one area, but not in others. One such spark was the development of new stone technologies in southwest Asia by 50,000 years ago, another the first appearance of art in Europe about 40,000 years ago, a third the first settlement of Australia by 35,000 years before present. Only after about 30,000 years ago, during the late Ice Age, did rapid cultural change take hold in all parts of the world. This chapter describes the rapidly late Ice Age world of about 50,000 to 15,000 years ago. We show how humans first adapted to extreme arctic climates and developed highly specialized forager cultures that subsisted off cold-loving animals such as the mammoth and steppe bison. We discuss, also, the radiation of *Homo sapiens* throughout the Old World, and then turn to one of the most controversial subjects in modern archaeology—the first settlement of the Americas (Figure 4.1).

Archaeologist Steven Mithen believes that the new types of behavior associated with the cultural explosion resulted from the development of full cognitive fluidity. Some 50,000 years ago, human beings developed new connections between previously isolated mental domains— environmental, technical, and social intelligence, knocking down the walls between the chapels of the metaphorical medieval cathedral referred to in Chapter 2. One consequence was much more sophisticated social relations,

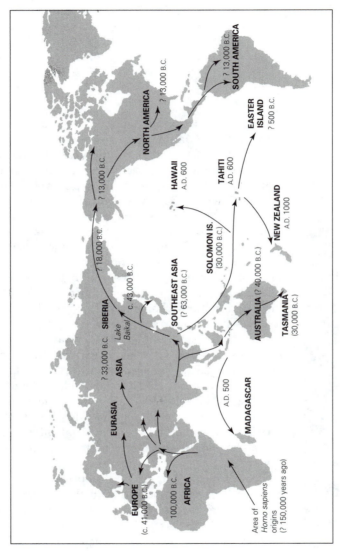

Figure 4.1   MAP SHOWING THE SETTLEMENT OF THE WORLD BY MODERN HUMANS

D I S C O V E R Y

ALTAMIRA CAVE PAINTINGS

Spanish landowner Marcellino de Sautuola had a casual interest in archaeology. He had visited an exhibit of some of the fine stone tools from French caves in Paris. In 1875, he decided to dig for some artifacts of his own in the caverns of Altamira on his estate in northern Spain. Sautuola's five-year-old daughter Maria begged for the chance to dig with him, so he good-naturedly agreed. Maria soon tired of the muddy work and wandered off with a flickering lantern into a low side chamber of the cave. Suddenly, he heard cries of ¡Toros! ¡Toros! ("Bulls! Bulls!"). Maria pointed excitedly at brightly painted figures of bison and a charging boar on the low ceiling. Daughter and father marveled at the fresh paintings arranged so cleverly around bulges in the rock that they seemed to move in the flickering light.

Sautuola was convinced the paintings were executed by the same people who had dropped stone tools in the cave. But the experts laughed at him and accused the Marquis of smuggling an artist into Altamira to forge the bison. It was not until 1904 that the long-dead Spaniard was vindicated, when some paintings with strong stylistic links to Altamira came to light in a French cave that had been sealed since the prehistoric artists had worked there.

another visual symbolism, the development of art as a means of expression and communication. As the great cave paintings of western France show (described below), humankind now had the ability to bring the natural and social worlds together in a seamless synthesis that is characteristic of many human societies, whether hunter-gatherers or farmers, to this day.

The evolution of cognitive fluidity gave *Homo sapiens sapiens*, spreading throughout the world after 45,000 years ago, perhaps earlier, a competitive edge over resident earlier human populations. With their superior intellectual capabilities, they pushed earlier populations into extinction, perhaps occasionally interbreeding with them. Once the move toward cognitive fluidity began, there was no stopping the process. By 30,000 years ago, the final step on the path to full modernity had been taken everywhere.

THE LATE ICE AGE WORLD
(50,000 to 15,000 years ago)

For most of the past 45,000 years, the world was very different from that of today. At the height of the last Ice Age glaciation, some 18,000 years ago, vast ice sheets mantled Scandinavia and the Alps, leaving a chilly corridor of open tundra between them. Sea levels were more than 300 feet (90 m) lower than today. Britain was joined to the European continent, the North Sea was under ice, and the Baltic Sea did not exist. One could walk from Turkey to Bulgaria

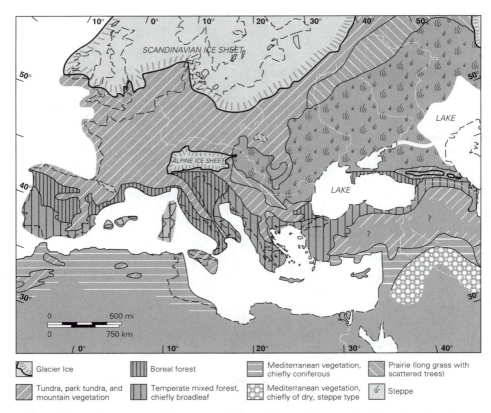

Figure 4.2   Generalized Vegetation Map of Europe During the Late Ice Age

dry-shod (Figure 4.2). Vast, treeless plains stretched north and east from central Europe to the frontiers of Siberia and beyond, a landscape of rolling scrub country dissected by occasional broad river valleys. The only signs of life were occasional herds of large big-game animals like the mammoth, bison, and reindeer, and they were often confined to river valleys. For humans to survive in these exposed landscapes required not only effective hunting methods and weaponry, but well-insulated winter dwellings and layered, tailored clothing that could keep people warm in subzero temperatures.

In more temperate and tropical latitudes, the effects of the last glaciation are harder to detect in geological strata. Tropical regions were often drier, many rain forests shrank, and there were more open grasslands and woodlands. In Africa, the Sahara Desert was as dry, if not drier, than today, as cold polar air flowed south of the Mediterranean. Much lower sea levels exposed enormous areas of continental shelf in Southeast Asia. Many offshore islands became part of the Asian mainland. Great rivers meandered over what were then exposed coastal plains, across another sunken Ice Age continent known to scholars as **Sunda.** Offshore lay two large land masses—**Wallacea,** made up of the present islands of Sulawesi and Timor, and **Sahul,** a combination of New Guinea, Australia, and the low-lying and now flooded shelf between them.

Let us now look at how late Ice Age humans peopled this diverse, often harsh, world.

THE PEOPLING OF SOUTHEAST ASIA AND AUSTRALIA (45,000 to 15,000 years ago)

Homo sapiens had appeared in Southeast Asia, including Indonesia and the Philippines, by at least 50,000 years ago. At the time, sea levels were much lower than today, so human settlement on Sunda, the exposed continental shelf, may have been concentrated in river valleys, along lake shores and on the coasts. If there were technological changes associated with *Homo sapiens,* they probably involved more efficient ways of exploiting the rich and highly varied environments of the mainland and offshore islands. The coastlines that faced offshore were relatively benign waters that probably offered a bounty of fish and shellfish to supplement game and wild plant foods. Perhaps coastal peoples constructed simple rafts for fishing in shallows or used rudimentary dugout canoes for bottom fishing. At some point, some of these people crossed open water to Wallacea and Sahul.

Sahul was a landscape of dramatic contrasts, of rugged mountain chains and highland valleys in the north, and rolling semiarid lowlands over much of what is now Australia. Colonizing Sahul meant an open-water downwind passage of at least 62 miles (98 km), an entirely feasible proposition in simple watercraft in warm tropical waters and smooth seas.

The earliest documented human settlement of New Guinea comes from the **Huon Peninsula** in the southeastern corner of the island, where some 40,000-year-old **ground stone** axes came to light. The Huon Peninsula faces New Britain Island, 30 miles (48 km) offshore. Fishermen were living in caves on the island by at least 32,000 years ago. Some 4000 years later, people had sailed between 81 and 112 miles (130 to 180 km) to settle on Buka Island in the northern Solomons to the south (Figure 4.3). From Buka it would have been an easy matter to colonize the remainder of the Solomon chain, for the islands are separated by but short distances. All these data point to a rapid spread of late Ice Age foragers through Sahul by at least 40,000 years ago, using some form of quite effective watercraft.

Human occupation in what is now Australia is well documented by 35,000 years ago, but may extend back 10,000 to 15,000 years earlier—the evidence is highly controversial. The **Willandra Lakes** region has yielded shell middens and campsites dating from perhaps as early as 37,000 to about 26,000 years ago. They include the skulls and limb bones of robustly built, anatomically modern people, the earliest human remains found in Australia. By 33,000 years ago, human beings had crossed the low-lying strait that joined the island of

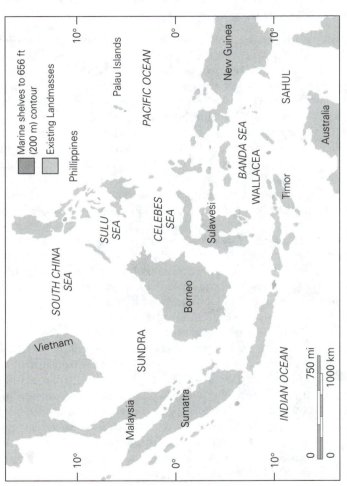

Figure 4.3   Sunda and Sahul During the Late Ice Age

RADIOCARBON DATING

Radiocarbon dating is the primary dating method used between about 40,000 years ago and the past 2000 years. The method is based on the knowledge that living organisms build up their own organic matter by photosynthesis and by using atmospheric carbon dioxide. The percentage of radiocarbon in the organism is equal to that in the atmosphere. When the organism dies, the carbon 14 (^{14}C) atoms disintegrate at a known rate, with a half-life of 5730 years. It is possible then to calculate the date of an organic object by measuring the amount of ^{14}C left in the sample. The initial quantity in the sample is low, therefore the limit of detectibility is soon reached, so the oldest reliable radiocarbon dates are about 40,000 years old.

Radiocarbon dates can be obtained from many types of organic material, including charcoal, shell, wood, and hair. The beta particle decay rate is conventionally measured with a proportional counter, but the use of accelerator mass spectrometry has refined the procedure dramatically. Every radiocarbon date arrives with a statistical error, a standard deviation. For example, a date of 2200 ±200 years, means that the date has a probable range of 200 years, with a two-out-of-three chance that the date lies between the span of one standard deviation (2400 and 200 years).

Unfortunately, the concentration of radiocarbon in the atmosphere has varied considerably over time, as a result of alterations in solar activity and changes in the strength of the earth's magnetic field. It is possible to correct dates by calibrating them against accurate dates from tree rings, by radiocarbon dating rings and developing a master correction curve. Dates as far back as nearly 9000 B.C. can be calibrated with tree rings.

Tasmania to the Australian mainland in the far south, to colonize the most southerly region of the earth settled by Ice Age people. At the height of the glacial maximum, people lived in the rugged landscape of the Tasmanian interior, hunting red wallabies and ranging over a wide area for many centuries.

The ancient Australians adapted to a remarkable variety of late Ice Age environments, as did people living in northern China, Japan, and on coastlines bordering chilly Ice Age seas. We do not have the space to cover all the diverse societies of the late Ice Age world, but, on the other side of the globe from Australia, the hunter-gatherer societies of Europe and Eurasia offer insights into the remarkable adaptive and opportunistic skills of the inhabitants of this long vanished world.

LATE ICE AGE EUROPE: THE CRO-MAGNONS (40,000 to 15,000 years ago)

The first fully modern Europeans are known to biological anthropologists as the **Cro-Magnons,** named after a rock shelter near the village of Les Eyzies in southwestern France. Anatomically, the Cro-Magnons are indistinguishable from ourselves (Figure 4.4), strongly built, large-headed people, whose appearance contrasts dramatically with that of their Neanderthal predecessors. The Cro-Magnons had settled in southeast and central Europe by at least 40,000 years ago, apparently near Neanderthal groups. Some of them had penetrated into the sheltered, deep river valleys of southwestern France by 35,000 to 40,000 years ago. By 30,000 years ago, the Neanderthals had vanished and the density of Cro-Magnon settlement intensified considerably.

Subsistence

The Cro-Magnons entered Europe during a brief period of more temperate climate. Even then, climatic conditions and seasonal contrasts may have been such as to require new artifacts and much more sophisticated hunting and foraging skills. These adaptations developed rapidly, indeed spectacularly, after 30,000 years ago. It was during these millennia that *Homo sapiens* finally mastered winter, for it was in northern latitudes that human ingenuity and endurance were tested to the fullest. The Cro-Magnons of western and central Europe developed elaborate and sophisticated hunting cultures during this period. Their cultures were marked not only by many technological innovations, but by a flowering of religious and social life, reflected in one of the earliest art traditions in the world.

The center of these activities was away from the open plains, in the river valleys of southwestern France and northern Spain, and in parts of central Europe like the Danube Basin. Here, deep valleys supported lush summer meadows and a mix of open steppe and forest where cold-tolerant animals ranging in size from the mammoth and bison to the wild horse and boar flourished. High cliffs often provided caves and rock shelters warmed by the winter sun. The area lay astride reindeer migration routes in spring and fall, while salmon ran up the fast-running rivers. The Cro-Magnons may have migrated to open country during the short summer months, concentrating in more sheltered river valleys from fall through spring. They hunted not only big game, but smaller animals such as arctic fox, beaver, rabbits, wolves, and many birds; they also gathered plant foods. After about 16,000 years ago, they also fished for salmon, trout, perch, and eels from rivers and streams.

The Cro-Magnons survived in a harsh and unpredictable environment not only because they were expert hunters and foragers, but because they had effective ways of keeping warm outside in the depth of winter and the ability to store large amounts of meat and other foods to tide them over lean periods. Above all, anyone living in late Ice Age Europe had to be adaptable, capable of cooperating with others, and ready to grab opportunities to obtain food when they arose. Survival depended on diversification, on never concentrating on one or two animals to the exclusion of others.

For most of the year, the Cro-Magnons lived in small groups, subsisting off a wide range of game and stored foods. The times when they came together in larger groups may have been in spring, summer, and early fall, when reindeer, and in later times, salmon, were abundant. This period of coming together was an important annual occasion, when social life was at its most intense. It was then that people arranged marriages, conducted initiation rites, and bartered raw materials, artifacts, and other commodities with one another. Then, as winter closed in, the groups would disperse through the sheltered river valleys, returning to their stored foods and the small herds of game animals that also took refuge from the bitter winds.

Reindeer were vital to survival. At the **Abri Pataud** rock shelter near Les Eyzies in France's Dordogne, reindeer provided up to 30 percent of all prey for more than 10,000 years (Figure 4.4). The hunters located their camps close to shallow river crossings where they knew migrating reindeer were likely to pass. This complex rhythm of reindeer hunting was but a part of a constant pattern of group movements that persisted over many thousands of years. It survived for thousands of years from at least 32,000 years ago right up to the end of the Ice Age, when the glaciers finally melted and dense forest spread over the open plains and deep valleys of central and western Europe. Not that life stayed exactly the same through these many millennia, for climatic conditions changed constantly. The Cro-Magnons had an efficient and highly versatile tool kit and a wide range of food resources to choose from, so they could readily adjust to changing circumstances.

Figure 4.4   EXCAVATIONS AT THE ABRI PATAUD ROCK SHELTER, LES EYZIES, FRANCE

Cro-Magnon Technology

Cro-Magnon technology was versatile, yet fundamentally very simple. It depended on four interrelated foundations:

1. Careful selection of fine-grained rock such as chert, flint, or obsidian for blade cores;
2. The production of relatively standardized, parallel-sided artifact blanks from these cores that could be used to make more specialized cutting, piercing, and scraping tools;
3. The refinement of the burin (engraving tool), which enabled people to work antler and bone efficiently;
4. The use of the so-called **groove-and-splinter** technique for working antler and bone.

These technological innovations had a profound impact on the future course of human prehistory, for they were the material means by which humans adapted to the climatic extremes of Eurasia and Siberia.

Late Ice Age stoneworkers everywhere were highly selective in their use of flint and other fine-grained rock. The Cro-Magnons' primary objective was to produce **blades,** long, parallel-sided artifact blanks that could then be turned into a wide spectrum of specialized artifacts for hunting, for butchery and processing skins, for woodworking and clothing manufacture, and for the production of the raw materials needed to create specialized antler and bone tools in treeless environments. So great was Cro-Magnon concern for good toolmaking stone that they bartered it with neighbors over considerable distances. Once procured, the precious raw materials were turned into carefully prepared blade cores that were carried around from one camp to the next. The cores were a kind of savings bank, an account of toolmaking stone used to produce tool blanks whenever they were needed. Thus, Cro-Magnon people were able to respond at a moment's notice to an opportunity to butcher an animal or to cut long slivers from fresh reindeer antlers.

The closest analogies in our own technology are the Leatherman and Swiss army knife (or "snap-on" mechanics' tools) (Figure 4.5). Both are multipurpose artifacts built on a strong chassis with a special spring system that enables the user to call on a wide variety of different tools, everything from a pair of scissors to pliers. The late Ice Age equivalents were the cores and the blades that came from them.

One important Cro-Magnon artifact was the **burin,** a delicate chisel for carving fine lines. The burin was used for woodworking, for cutting grooves in animal hides, for engraving designs on antler, bone, and cave walls, and, above all, for cutting the long antler blanks for making artifacts of antler, bone, and ivory (see Figure 4.6). Many of these were specialized tools like barbed points, mounted with foreshafts which snapped off when the spear entered its quarry (see Figure 4.6). Some were important innovations, especially the eyed needle, essential for making tailored winter clothes, and the

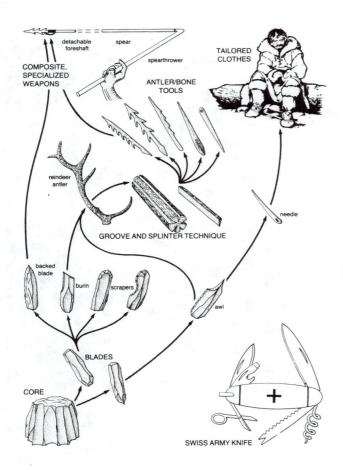

Figure 4.5 BLADE CORE TECHNOLOGY ACTS LIKE A SWISS ARMY KNIFE, PRODUCING BLANKS FOR MAKING MANY SPECIALIZED ARTIFACTS FOR WORKING ANTLER AND BONE

spearthrower, a hooked and sometimes weighted device that extended the range and accuracy of hunting weapons (see Figure 4.6). The same technology of fine-barbed antler head spears and stone-barbed weapons could be used for hunting big game, as well as for taking salmon in shallow water, for dispatching rabbits, even for developing bows and arrows, which appeared some time during the late Ice Age.

The archaeological record reflects many refinements in Cro-Magnon technology over more than 15,000 years. In the early years of this century, French archaeologist Henri Breuil classified the late Ice Age cultures of southwestern France into four basic cultural traditions that culminated in the celebrated **Magdalenian** culture of about 18,000 to 12,000 years ago. The Magdalenian, named after the **La Madeleine** rock shelter on the Vezère River, was not only a technologically sophisticated culture, but one with a new concern for artistic expression and body ornamentation.

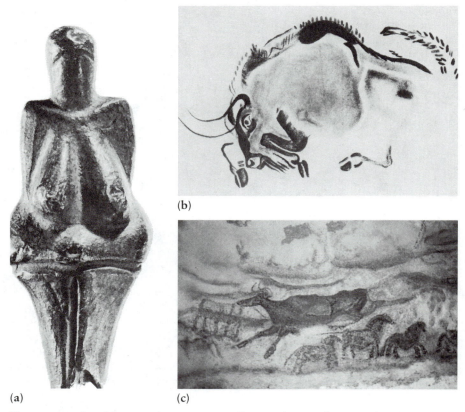

(a)   (c)

Figure 4.6   Cro-Magnon Art   (a) Venus figurine from Dolni Vestonice, Moravia, central Europe. (b) Wild bull from Lascaux, France. (c) Bison painted on a natural bulge of a chamber in Altamira cave, northern Spain. All three works date to the period 25,000 to 12,000 B.C.

Cro-Magnon Art

The symbolic and ceremonial life of the Cro-Magnons was probably no more elaborate than that of their contemporaries known to have been painting in southern Africa and Australia at much the same time. However, it is the best known and most thoroughly explored. Fortunately, much has survived, for Cro-Magnon artists used cave walls as their canvas, durable antler and ivory, not wood and skins, as palettes.

The first appearance of cave art coincides with a new concern with body ornamentation, especially perforated carnivore teeth and sea shells. This explosion in body ornamentation probably coincided with realizations that such adornments could define and communicate social roles— gender, group affiliation, and so on. Late Ice Age people mastered the ability to think in specific visual images, using them as well as chants, recitations, and songs to share and communicate images and ideas. This resulted in complex and diverse art traditions that lasted for more than 20,000 years.

The surviving Cro-Magnon art of Europe and Eurasia is but a minor proportion of their artistic output, for the artists almost certainly used many perishable materials—clay, wood, fiber, bark, hides, and bird feathers. Without question, too, they used red ocher and other pigments as body paint, for decoration. The surviving art occurs over a vast area from North Africa to Siberia, with major concentrations in northern Spain, southwestern France, also central and Eastern Europe. On cave walls, the artists engraved and painted animals and occasional humans, also schematic patterns: lines, elaborate panels, and complex shapes. The same artists engraved antler, bone, and ivory with consummate skill. They created animals in the round, engraved bison with delicate strokes that etched in every detail of eyes, manes, and hair. There are figurines of animals and humans in ivory, soft stone, and baked clay, such as the celebrated Venus figurines that depict women of all ages.

Cro-Magnon art is full of compelling images, many of them concentrated at major sites such as Lascaux and **Trois Frères** in southwestern France, and **Altamira** in northern Spain (Figure 4.6; see also Figure 1.1). These may have been places of unusual religious and symbolic importance. They were ritual shrines, not only for local groups, but for people from far wider areas, too. Other locations were sacred places used occasionally for major ceremonies. These are illustrated dramatically by **Le Tuc d'Audoubert** Cave in Ariège, France, where two carefully modeled clay bison lie in a remote, low-ceilinged chamber far from the entrance, placed against a rock (Figure 4.7). The bison are about one-sixth the full size, shaped with a skilled artist's fingers and a spatula, the eyes, nostrils, and other features marked with a pointed object. Ancient human heel marks can be seen around the figures in this remote and dark chamber. In many other caves, paintings and engravings are far from daylight. There are several instances in which the footprints of both adults and children are preserved in damp clay, perhaps left by small parties of initiates who attended ceremonies in remote subterranean chambers. Some caves may also have been chosen for their echoes and other resonant effects.

Upper Paleolithic art defies easy interpretation, for the symbolic messages it communicates come from a world that is remote from our own. Yet the paintings and engravings still seem to come alive and appear larger than life when seen by modern candlelight flickering in the intense darkness. Did the artists paint art for art's sake, as some art historians and archaeologists allege? Or were they symbolically killing their prey before setting out on the chase? Such explanations are too simplistic, for we can be sure that the motivations for the art extended far beyond mere environmental and subsistence concerns.

Today, we know a great deal more about symbolic behavior and the art that goes with it, and much more about how forager societies function. In such societies, visual forms are manipulated to structure and give meaning to

Figure 4.7   Two Clay Bison from Tuc d'Audoubert, Ariège, France

existence. For Cro-Magnon artists, there were clearly continuities between animal and human life and with their social world. Thus, their art was a symbolic depiction of these continuities.

Shamans, priests or spirit mediums, (the word comes from the Siberian Tungus word *saman,* meaning priest) are important members of forager and subsistence farming societies all over the world. They are individuals perceived as having unusual spiritual powers, the ability to cross over into the world of the gods and ancestors. Through trance and chant, they would intercede with the ancestors and define the order of the world and the creation—the relationship between the living and the forces of the environment. Perhaps, argue some experts, much of the cave art was involved with shamanistic rituals, the animal figures being images of spirit creatures or the life force for the shamans.

Some of the art may also have been associated with initiation rites, the journey through dark passages adding to the disorienting ordeal of initiation. Almost certainly, the art was a way of transmitting environmental and other knowledge from one generation to the next. Australian Aborigines, for example, commit to memory vast quantities of information about their territory that is closely tied to the mythical and symbolic world of their ancestors. Much of this data is vital to survival, constantly imparted to the young in ceremonies and rituals.

HUNTER–GATHERERS IN EURASIA
(35,000 to 15,000 years ago)

The open steppe-tundra plains that stretched from the Atlantic to Siberia were a far harsher environment than the sheltered valleys of southwestern Europe. To live there permanently, late Ice Age people had to find sheltered winter base camps, have the technology to make tailored, layered clothing with needle and thongs, and the ability to build substantial dwellings in a treeless environment. Only a handful of big-game hunting groups lived in the shallow valleys that dissected these plains before the glacial maximum 18,000 years ago. Thereafter, the human population rose comparatively rapidly, each group centered on a river valley where game was most plentiful, and where plant foods and fish could be found during the short summers. It was here that the most elaborate winter base camps lay. One such base camp lay at **Mezhirich** on the Dneipr River, a complex of well-built, dome-shaped houses fashioned of intricate patterns of mammoth bones. The outer retaining walls were made of patterned mammoth skulls, jaws, and limb bones. The completed oval-shaped dwellings were about 16 feet (4.8 m) across, roofed with hides and sod, entered through subterranean tunnels. The use of mammoth bone for houses was a logical strategy in a largely treeless environment. American archaeologist Olga Soffer has calculated that it would have taken some 15 workers about 10 days to build a Mezhirich dwelling, much more effort than would have gone into a simpler base camp or hunting settlement.

Soffer believes that these base camps were occupied by groups of about 30 to 60 people for about six months of the year. Mezhirich was but one of several important base camp locations in the Ukraine, sites that contain the bones of a greater variety of game animals than smaller, more specialized settlements (Figure 4.8). The mammoth bone dwellings also yielded many bones from fur-bearing animals like the beaver, and exotic materials and ornaments such as shiny amber from near Kiev and shells from the Black Sea, far to the south. The items from afar exchanged between neighboring communities were predominantly nonutilitarian, luxury goods that had social and political significance. Much of the trade may have been ceremonial, a means of validating important ideologies, of ensuring exchange of information and cooperation in daily life, just as it was elsewhere in the late Ice Age world at the time.

Late Ice Age groups settled much of the steppe-tundra as far east as Lake Baikal in Siberia, not through a deliberate process of migration, but as a result of the natural dynamics of forager life. The tundra hunters lived in small, highly flexible bands. As the generations passed, one band would coalesce into another, sons and their families would move away into a neighboring, and empty, valley. And, in time, a sparse human population would occupy thousands of square miles of steppe-tundra, concentrated for the most part in river valleys, at times venturing out onto the broad plains, and always on the move. It was through these natural dynamics of constant movement, of extreme

Figure 4.8 Artist's Reconstruction of Late Ice Age Life on the Central European Plains

social flexibility and opportunism, that people first settled the outer reaches of Siberia and crossed into the Americas.

North and east of Lake Baikal, the steppe-tundra extends all the way to the Pacific, the home of more late Ice Age hunting groups that are known from a handful of settlements along lake shores and in river valleys. They are part of a widespread late Ice Age cultural tradition that reflects a varied adaptation by *Homo sapiens* to an enormous area of central Asia and southern Siberia from well west of Lake Baikal to the Pacific coast by 30,000 to 20,000 years ago. But where did these Siberian hunters come from? Did they originate in the west, or were their cultural roots in China to the south? These questions have a direct bearing on one of the most debated questions of world prehistory—the date of the first Americans.

EAST ASIA (35,000 to 15,000 years ago)

We know enough about prehistoric Asia to realize that this was not a backward, peripheral region of the late Ice Age world. We cannot just argue that big-game hunters from the Ukraine and the western steppe-tundra migrated steadily northeastward into Siberia and then into the Americas. Rather, the spread of modern humans into central Asia, northern China, and the extreme northeast was a complex process that began at least 35,000 years ago.

Many biological anthropologists assume that *Homo erectus,* originally a tropical and subtropical animal, settled in the warmer southern parts of China first, then radiated northward into more temperate environments. But how far north? It is not until just before 35,000 years ago that a few signs of human settlement appear along the banks of the Huang-Ho River in the arid grasslands of Mongolia. Open landscapes such as this and the neighboring steppe-tundra could support only the sparsest of forager populations, people who placed a high premium on mobility and portable tool kits. They were some of the first late Ice Age people to develop diminutive microliths.

The **microlith** (a term derived from the Greek *micros:* small and *lithos:* stone) is a highly distinctive artifact, manufactured from carefully prepared wedge-shaped, conical, or cylindrical cores (Figure 4.9). By their very size, microliths were designed to be mounted in antler, bone, or wooden hafts to serve as spear barbs, arrow points, or small knives and scraper blades. Such diminutive artifacts came into use almost everywhere in the post–Ice Age

Figure 4.9 Microlith Technology (a) Siberian microblade artifacts were made by striking small blades of a wedge-shaped core, which produced fine, sharp artifacts that could be mounted on spears or in bone heads. (b) Later microliths used after the Ice Age were made by notching and snapping blades.

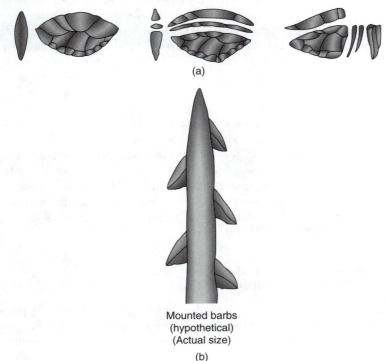

(a)

Mounted barbs
(hypothetical)
(Actual size)

(b)

world, for they were highly adaptive when used with slender wooden arrow shafts or with stout wooden handles. They first appear in a crude form in northern China at least 30,000 years ago, were in widespread use by 25,000 to 20,000 years ago, and soon became popular in the arid open country of the steppe-tundra, an area where high mobility and portable tool kits were at a premium. A somewhat similar microblade technology developed in Siberia late in the Ice Age. We do not know, however, whether the first human inhabitants of northeast Asia were people with such diminutive tool kits, or whether they used a heavier weaponry that included stone-tipped spears with sharp projectile points.

Unfortunately, the archaeology of northern China, northeastern Siberia, and Alaska is little known because harsh environmental conditions make fieldwork possible for a mere two months or so a year in many places. We can only guess at a possible scenario for first settlement of this vast area, and of the Americas.

Sinodonty and Sundadonty

That the first Americans came from Siberia is unquestionable, but their ultimate ancestry is a matter of much debate. Christy Turner of Arizona State University has long studied the dental characteristics of native American populations and compared them to other groups in the Old World. He has shown that the crowns and roots of human teeth give clues to the degree of relationship between prehistoric populations. These tooth features are more stable than most evolutionary traits, with a high resistance to the effects of environmental differences, sexual distinctions, and age variations. In particular, he has focused on a pattern of specialized tooth features he calls **Sinodonty.**

Sinodont hallmarks include incisor shoveling (the scooped-out shape on the inside of the tooth), double-shoveling (scooping out on both sides), single-rooted upper first premolars, and three-rooted lower first molars. Sinodonty is characteristic of all native Americans. They share this feature with northern Asians, including northern Chinese. The morphological difference between Sinodonts and the other Mongoloid populations, whom Turner labels Sundadonts, is so great that he believes Siberia and the Americas were settled by Sinodont populations from northern Asia. It was in China, he believes, that Sinodonty evolved, at least 40,000 years ago. The problem is to find the archaeological sites to confirm his theory.

Early Human Settlement of Siberia (?before 20,000 to 15,000 years ago)

If the ancestry of the first Americans lies in Siberia, what, then, is the earliest evidence for human settlement in extreme Northeast Asia? At present, there is no reliable evidence for late Ice Age occupation any earlier than about 20,000 years ago, although it is fair to say that field investigations have hardly begun.

Some of the earliest evidence of human settlement comes from the **D'uktai Cave** in the Middle Aldan Valley. There, Russian archaeologist Yuri Mochanov found 14,000- to 12,000-year-old mammoth and musk ox bones associated with flaked-stone spear points, burins, microblades, and other Upper Paleolithic tools. The earliest securely dated D'uktai-like site is **Verkhene-Trotiskaya,** also on the Aldan River, which has been radiocarbon dated to about 18,000 years ago. Subsequently, microblades and characteristic wedge-shaped cores have been found over a wide area of northeast Asia, across the Bering Strait in Alaska, and as far south as British Columbia.

With its microblades and wedge-shaped cores, the D'uktai culture has plausible links with widespread microblade cultures to the south, in China. A case can be made, then, for linking D'uktai cultural traditions with northern China, where Sinodonts have been found, as well as with microblade finds in Alaska and British Columbia. Were the D'uktai people thus the first Americans? Almost certainly not, for recent discoveries in Alaska have shown that foragers without microlithic tool kits flourished in the far north of North America just after the end of the Ice Age. D'uktai-style microliths appear late, by about 9000 B.C

When D'uktai people or even earlier settlers first crossed the windy, steppe–tundra-covered land bridge that joined Alaska to Siberia remains a mystery. We do not even know how they subsisted, except for a likelihood that they preyed on all kinds of arctic game. They may also have hunted sea mammals and taken ocean fish. Unfortunately, their settlements are deep beneath the waters of the Bering Strait.

THE FIRST AMERICANS
(?before 15,000 years ago to 9000 B.C.)

During all of the last glaciation, the Bering Land Bridge joined extreme northeast Siberia and Alaska. During warmer intervals, it was little more than a narrow isthmus, during the glacial maximum a broad plain. Thus, it was theoretically possible for humans without canoes to cross into North America from the Old World dry shod for all of the past 100,000 years. Therein lies one of the great questions of world prehistory. When and how did the first human beings settle the New World?

The controversies that surround the first Americans are still unresolved. Most authorities agree that the first Americans were anatomically modern humans. This is a strong argument in favor of first settlement during the past 45,000 years, especially since recent mitochondrial DNA research suggests there were four mtDNA lineages for the Americas, with a considerable, as yet undefined, time depth. The chronology of first settlement divides archaeologists into two camps. Some scientists argue passionately for a late Ice Age occupation before 30,000 years ago, perhaps as much as 15,000 years earlier. Their theories pit them against most American archaeologists, who believe humans first crossed into Alaska at the very end of the Ice Age, perhaps as the land bridge flooded, after 15,000 years ago. We must examine these two viewpoints more closely.

Settlement before 30,000 Years Ago?

The case for early settlement rests on a handful of sites, most of them in South America, none of them yielding much more than a scatter of alleged stone artifacts and sometimes animal bones. Therein lies the controversy, for what one archaeologist claims as a stone tool is rejected out of hand by another. Unfortunately, most of the claims for early settlement are based not on fine-grained, scientific examination of the artifacts and their context in the surrounding deposits, but on an individual archaeologist's subjective belief that a handful of chipped stones are humanly manufactured rather than of natural origin. For example, if one finds 35,000-year-old "stone artifacts" deep in a hypothetical Peruvian cave, it is not sufficient to state they are manufactured by humans. One must prove beyond all measure of reasonable scientific doubt that they were made by prehistoric people, and not formed, for example, by stones falling from a cliff face or by pebbles being knocked together in a stream that once ran through the cave. Such research is extremely time-consuming and very difficult and has not yet been carried out at most of the sites where early settlement has been claimed. Let us briefly examine some of the early sites.

In South America, French archaeologist Niède Guidon has reported evidence of hearths and stone artifacts dating back to as early as 47,000 years ago in the bottom layers of a rock shelter named **Boqueirão da Pedra Furada** in northeastern Brazil. Many experts have expressed doubt about how these early levels and the artifacts in them were formed. They are concerned that a stream once ran through the rock shelter and about the possibility that rockfalls from the surrounding cliffs manufactured tools. Almost certainly, human occupation did not begin here until after 10,000 years ago.

Further south, in northern Chile, Tom Dillehay has uncovered a remarkable settlement on the edge of a stream. **Monte Verde** was occupied by foragers living in simple wooden dwellings between 10,850 and 10,350 B.C. A 31,000-year-old lower level is said to contain split pebble and wood fragments, but, to date, excavations in these levels have been relatively limited, insufficient to document the proven presence of human occupation at such an early date.

There is no theoretical reason why *Homo sapiens* could not have moved south from Beringia well before 25,000 years ago, but we still lack credible proof of such early human settlement in Siberia, let alone the Americas. Whether this is because the Americas were still uninhabited, or because the human population was so mobile and tiny that little or no material survived, continues to be hotly debated. As an outside observer, African archaeologist Nicholas Toth has made the important observation that it is pointless to place too much reliance on isolated finds. Rather, we should be searching for patterns of very early human settlement, characteristic distributions of artifacts and human activity that occur over wide areas, that indeed reflect widespread early occupation. Such patterns document the very earliest human occupation on earth. There is no theoretical reason why similar patterns should not turn up to chronicle the first Americans. So far, consistent distributions of human settlement in the New World date to after the Ice Age, to after 15,000 years ago. But we stress again that there is no reason why earlier settlement might not be found one day. So far, however, the evidence is unconvincing.

Another scenario places first settlement during a brief warmer spell of the last glaciation, between 30,000 and 20,000 years ago. This would be shortly before the late Ice Age maximum cut off movement south of Alaska until after about 13,000 years ago.

Settlement after 15,000 Years Ago?

Most American archaeologists consider first settlement a much later phenomenon. Under the late scenario, a few families may have moved into Alaska during the very late Ice Age, perhaps before 15,000 years ago. At that time, vast ice sheets mantled much of northern North America, effectively blocking access to the midcontinent. After 14,000 years ago, these ice sheets retreated rapidly, allowing a trickle of human settlers to move onto the plains and into a new continent.

This hypothesis is based on the earliest indisputable archaeological evidence for human settlement, which dates to between 14,000 and 12,000 years ago. In North America, a handful of sites, among them **Meadowcroft Rock Shelter** in Pennsylvania, and **Fort Rock Cave,** Oregon, may belong in this time frame. So do scattered sites from Central and South America, among them **Valsequillo** in Mexico, **Taima Taima** in Venezuela, and Monte Verde in northern Chile. All these sites have yielded small scatters of stone artifacts, occasionally a projectile point. After about 9200 B.C. the trickle of archaeological sites turns into a flood. There are now traces of **Paleo-Indian** (Greek *paleos:* old) settlement between the southern margins of the ice sheets in the north and the Straits of Magellan in the far south. (The term *Paleo-Indian* is conventionally used to refer to the prehistoric inhabitants of the Americas from earliest settlement up to the beginning of the **Archaic** period in about 6000 B.C.)

How, then, did Paleo-Indians travel southward from the arctic to the heart of North America? Were they big-game hunters who followed small herds of animals southward through a widening corridor between the two great North American ice sheets to the east of the Rockies as the ice sheets melted? Or were the first Americans expert sea-mammal hunters and fish-erfolk, who crossed from Siberia along low-lying coasts in canoes while fishing and sea-mammal hunting? Did their successors then travel south-ward along the Pacific coast into more temperate waters? Again, fierce con-troversy surrounds what is virtually nonexistent archaeological evidence. Perhaps both coastal settlement and terrestrial occupation took hold in the rapidly changing world of the late Ice Age. We simply do not know, partly because the coastal sites of the day are buried hundreds of feet below mod-ern sea levels.

At present, the consensus of archaeological opinion favors a relatively late human occupation of the Americas at the very end of the Ice Age, but it is entirely possible that this scenario will change dramatically as a result of future research. But why did first settlement take place? In all probabil-ity, the first Americans were probably behaving in the same way as other animal predators. They spent their days tracking the game herds, and per-haps sea mammals, that formed an important part of their subsistence, and when Siberian game herds moved onto the Bering Land Bridge during the coldest millennia of the last glaciation, their human predators followed. The higher ground to the east—Alaska—formed part of the same hunting grounds.

THE CLOVIS PEOPLE (c. 9200 to 8900 B.C.)

The earliest well-documented Paleo-Indian settlement is associated with the distinctive Clovis **fluted** point (Figure 4.10). The **Clovis tradition,** named after a town in New Mexico, once flourished in various forms over much of North and Central America from about 9200 to 8900 B.C. Clovis may be an indige-nous North American cultural tradition, but its roots lie in northern forager cultures such as flourished in Alaska at such locations as the **Hidden Mam-moth** and **Mesa** sites as early as 9800 B.C., where foragers used simple bifacial spear points in the chase. These locations, little more than tiny scatters of bones, hearths, and stone artifacts, are the earliest evidence for human settle-ment in Alaska and have no direct equivalents in earlier traditions such as D'uktai in Siberia.

Clovis is best, and misleadingly, known from occasional mammoth and bison kills on the Northern American plains. These plains expanded at the end of the Ice Age, their short grasses providing ample feed for all kinds of big game, including bison, mammoth, and other ruminants. Clovis bands on the plains preyed on these and many other game species, large and small. They were constantly on the move, often camping along rivers and streams and close to permanent waterholes. Here they killed their prey, camping near where the carcass lay.

It would be a mistake, however, to think of the Clovis people as purely big-game hunters. They settled not only on open grasslands, but in wood-

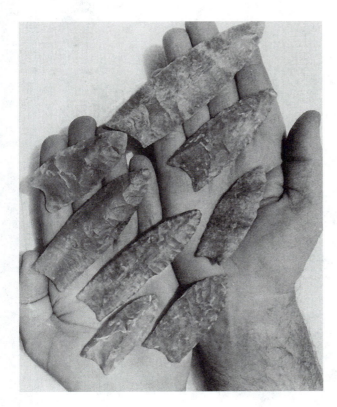

Figure 4.10 Clovis
Points Found with a
Mammoth Skeleton at
Naco, Arizona

lands, tundra, deserts, and along sea coasts. In some areas, wild plant foods
were probably as important as, if not more important than, game. Fish and
sea-mammal hunting may also have assumed great local importance, especially along rising coastlines. But wherever Clovis people and their contemporaries settled, large game was of great importance, simply because it was a relatively abundant meat source.

Nowhere were Clovis populations large. Their tool kit was highly
portable, based on an expert stone-flaking technology that produced fine,
fluted-based points. The hunters mounted these on long wooden shafts, sometimes attaching the head to a detachable foreshaft that acted as a hinge. When
the spear penetrated an animal, the foreshaft would snap off, ensuring that the
lethally sharp point stayed in the wound. Like other later Paleo-Indian groups,
and like Ice Age hunters in the Old World, the Clovis people hunted their prey
on foot, relying on their stalking skill and the accuracy of their throwing sticks
(**atlatls**) to dispatch their quarry.

The origins of the Clovis people remain a complete mystery. However,
most experts believe their ultimate origins were among late Ice Age forager
populations in Alaska and Northeast Asia. If the first Americans crossed into
the New World about 15,000 years ago, then the peopling of the uninhabited

continent took place remarkably quickly. By 9000 B.C., Stone Age foragers occupied every corner of the Americas. The overall human population probably numbered no more than a few tens of thousands, but they had adapted to every form of local environment imaginable.

By this time, the last glaciation was long over and the great ice sheets of the north were in rapid retreat. Climatic conditions were warming up rapidly and many species of Ice Age big game vanished. The descendants of the first Americans adapted to these new circumstances in very diverse ways, along trajectories of cultural change that led, ultimately, to the brilliant array of Native American societies encountered by Europeans in the late fifteenth century A.D.

With the first settlement of the Americas, the great radiation of *Homo sapiens sapiens,* the wise person, was nearly complete. This was the second great radiation of humanity, the climactic development of world prehistory. From it stemmed not only the great biological and cultural diversity of modern humankind, but food production, village life, urban civilization, and the settlement of the Pacific Islands—the very roots of our own diverse and complex world.

CHAPTER 5

The Origins of Food Production

A.D. 1950 —

A.D. 1 —

15,000 B.P. —

50,000 B.P. —

100,000 B.P. —

500,000 B.P. —

1.0 Million —

2.5 Million —

Agriculture and animal domestication ("food production") were a major turning point in human history, the foundation for all early civilizations and, ultimately for our own modern industrial world. Before describing the development and spread of farming, we must examine some of the major theories that explain this development and review some of its consequences. Also, we must describe the intensification of hunter-gatherer societies that came immediately after the Ice Age (Figure 5.1).

Serious discussion of the origins of food production began in the 1930s. Australian-born archaeologist Vere Gordon Childe was an eccentric genius, who regarded artifacts and archaeological sites as the equivalent of historical documents and actual characters on the ancient world stage. Childe's main claims to fame were an encyclopedic knowledge of the clay and metal tools of Europe and southwestern Asia, and a priceless ability to write popular accounts of the prehistoric past. To Childe, southwestern Asia, from Turkey to the Nile Valley and Mesopotamia, was the cradle of both farming and early civilization. In his famous syntheses of the origins of civilization, he wrote of two great revolutions in the early human past. An Agricultural (or Neolithic [New Stone Age]) Revolution resulted from the development of village farming, followed a few thousand years later by an **Urban Revolution** and the beginnings of cities, writing, metallurgy, and literate civilization.

The notion of an Agricultural and Urban Revolution appealed to historians like George Trevelyan and Will and Ariel Durant, who adopted Gordon Childe's revolutions for the early chapters of their widely read world histories. The revolutions were convenient labels,

115

CHRONOLOGICAL TABLE B

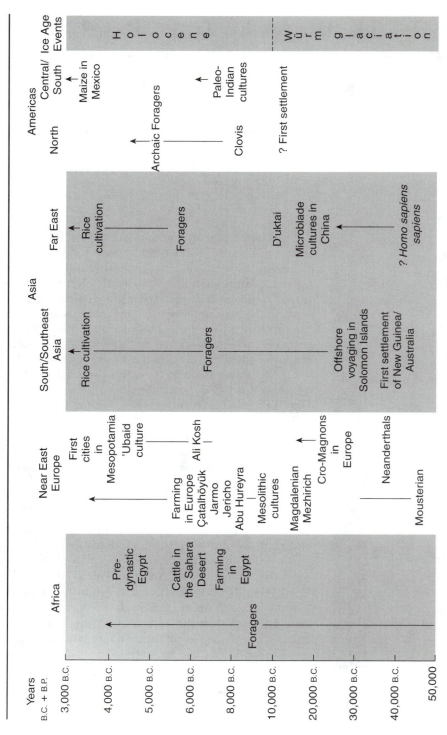

just like the Industrial and Information Revolutions we talk about today. To archaeologists, the Agricultural Revolution is a simplistic label, long outdated by a flood of new field data unavailable in Childe's day. However, the term does have merit in the sense that it draws attention to a catalytic development in the human past and, above all, to its consequences. Animal and plant domestication had awesome consequences for all of humankind—new economies and great interdependence, permanent settlement, and more complex social organization, accelerating population growth, and increasing social inequality—to mention only a few.

THE HOLOCENE (after 10,000 B.C.)

Some 15,000 years ago, the great ice sheets began to retreat, at times very rapidly, ushering in postglacial times, often called the **Holocene** (Greek *Holos:* recent). At the same time, world sea levels rose dramatically, if irregularly, from their previous lows up to 300 feet (90 m) below modern levels, leading to major changes in world geography. The chilly waters of the Bering Sea flooded central Beringia and separated Siberia and Alaska by 11,000 B.C. Sunda in Southeast Asia became an enormous archipelago. Britain became an island and the North Sea and Baltic assumed their modern configurations. The most striking climatic and vegetational transformations took place in northern latitudes, in areas like western and central Europe and in regions of North America contiguous to the great ice sheets. Only 7000 years after the Scandinavian ice sheet began retreating, forests covered much of Europe. There were major vegetational changes in warmer latitudes, too. Rainfall patterns changed at the end of the Ice Age, bringing large, shallow lakes and short grasslands to the Sahara. As late as 6000 B.C., forager populations flourished in the desert, in areas that are now arid wilderness.

In southwestern Asia, warmer conditions saw the immigration of new plant species into highland areas such as the Zagros mountains in Iran, among them wild cereal grasses. Their distribution now expanded dramatically, to the point that wild wheat and barley became important staples for forager groups in the highlands and fertile river valleys like the Euphrates. Far away, in Mexico, rising temperatures brought a rich forest of cacti and legume trees to mountain valleys of the central highlands. This thorn-scrub-cactus forest included many wild ancestors of domesticated plants, among them the maguey, squash, bean, and teosinte, the wild grass that was probably the ancestor of wild maize, the crop that was to become one of the staples of native American life.

CHANGES IN FORAGER SOCIETIES

The above and other Holocene climatic changes had profound effects on forager societies throughout the world, especially on the intensity of the food quest and the complexity of their societies. So did natural population growth. By 15,000 years ago, the world's forager population was probably approaching about 10

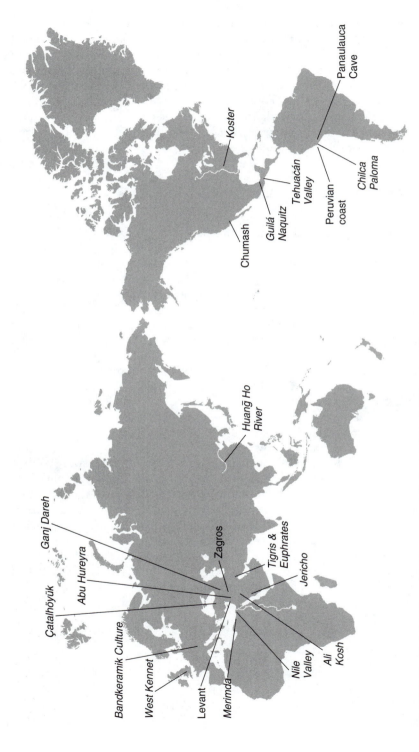

Figure 5.1 Map Showing Archaeological Sites and Major Centers of Food Production Mentioned in Chapter 5

million people. Except in the most favored areas, like southwestern France or the Nile valley, late Ice Age environments were incapable of supporting anything but the sparsest of human population densities—well under one person per square mile. As a result, in early Holocene times, after 10,000 B.C., still-rising human populations began to match the ability of the world's environment to support them as foragers. It was no longer possible to solve a subsistence problem simply by moving elsewhere. People began to exploit a wider range of food resources with greater efficiency, both to avert starvation and to protect themselves from food shortages caused by short-term droughts and other unpredictable changes. In time, forager societies underwent profound changes and in some areas acquired greater complexity.

Nowhere can these changes be seen more clearly than in the Americas, settled by a handful of forager bands by 15,000 years ago. By 9000 B.C., the big game that formed a staple part of their diet was extinct. The Paleo-Indians responded to changed circumstances by developing ever more intensive and specialized ways of exploiting local environments. The change is especially marked in areas of exceptional resource diversity like parts of the West Coast, the Peruvian coast, and the fertile river valleys of the southern Midwest and southeastern United States. In all these areas, forager populations became more sedentary, developed specialized technologies for hunting, foraging, and fishing, and in the process, developed some form of social ranking.

The famous **Koster** site in the Illinois River valley provides a chronicle of this process of intensification taking place over many thousands of years, from about 7500 B.C. until A.D. 1200 (Figure 5.2). The first visitors were Paleo-Indian hunters who camped on the edge of the valley. About 6500 B.C., some

Figure 5.2   EXCAVATIONS AT KOSTER, ILLINOIS

later inhabitants founded a base camp that covered about 0.75 acre (0.1 ha). An extended family group of about 25 people returned repeatedly to the same location, perhaps to exploit the rich fall hickory nut harvests in the area. Between 5600 and 5000 B.C., there were substantial settlements of permanent mud and brush houses that were occupied for most of the year, if not all of it. During spring and summer the inhabitants took thousands of fish, gathering mussels and hickory nuts in fall and migratory birds in spring. Even when hunting deer on the nearby uplands, the people could find most of their food resources within 3 miles (4.8 km).

After 2500 B.C., Koster's population had risen to the point at which the people were exploiting a much wider range of food resources, including acorns, which require much more preparation than hickory nuts. Eventually, they experimented with the deliberate planting of wild native grasses like goosefoot, simply to increase supplies of wild plant foods.

The Koster excavations document several long-term trends in many Holocene forager societies, trends toward more sedentary settlement, intensive exploitation of locally abundant and predictable food resources such as salmon or nuts, and carefully organized mass processing and storage of staple foods.

Such intensive exploitation, processing, and storage was adaptive in environments where seasonal phenomena such as salmon runs, caribou migrations, or hickory nut harvests required not only efficient harvesting of quantities of food in a short time, but also their processing and storage for later use. By using storage, and by careful seasonal exploitation of game, plant, and aquatic resources like fish and waterfowl, Holocene foragers compensated for periodic food shortages caused by short-term climatic change and seasonal fluctuations. For example, Native American societies developed a remarkable expertise with wild plant foods. They also evolved an array of simple pestles, grinders, and other tools to process seeds and other wild plant foods. Later, it was an easy matter to adapt these tool kits to new, specialized tasks such as farming.

More restricted territories, less mobility, rising population densities, unpredictable environmental variations, and seasonal flood fluctuations were problems common to Holocene foragers throughout the world. A few of these societies, especially those in areas with rich and diverse food resources that included fish and sea mammals, achieved a greater complexity than any Ice Age society, with some signs of social ranking.

Social Complexity among Foragers

Complex forager societies did not appear everywhere, but they developed in a remarkable variety of environments, from fertile river valleys to coastal deserts. Everywhere, however, certain general conditions were necessary. First, population movements had to be limited by either geography or the presence of neighbors. Second, resources had to be abundant and predictable in their seasonal appearance. Such resources included fish, shellfish, nuts, and seeds, species that are abundant and seldom exhausted. Third, population growth might reach a point at which food shortages occur and there is an imbalance between people and their food supply. Again, a solution was to intensify the food quest, an intensification that might result in a more complex society, or, as we shall see, in food production.

Social complexity was most common in areas where freshwater or marine fish, shellfish, or sea mammals were abundant. The full potential of marine and freshwater resources was realized only in a relatively few areas like northern Europe, Peru, and western North America. Here, higher than normal population densities were concentrated in restricted territories circumscribed by geography or neighbors. These populations acquired a more varied diet by using more specialized tool kits and sophisticated food storage systems and preservation techniques. These groups often lived in sedentary, large base camps ruled by important kin leaders who monopolized trade with neighboring groups. For example, the Chumash Indians of the southern California coast were skilled navigators, fishers, and sea-mammal hunters. Some Chumash communities numbered as many as 1000 people, living under hereditary chiefs (*wots*). There was a small elite of ceremonial officeholders, shamans, and such experts as canoe builders. Chumash culture was a maritime adaptation made possible by a specialized fishing technology that included planked canoes about 25 feet (7.6 m) long (Figure 5.3). Each community maintained exchange contacts with other coastal communities and with people living far in the interior.

Chumash culture achieved a degree of social elaboration that represents about the limit of such complexity possible without adopting agriculture. Why did such social complexity develop? Some scholars see the ocean as a kind of Garden of Eden, an environment sometimes so productive that foragers could maintain permanent, sedentary settlements and maintain high population densities. Perhaps people turned to fish, shellfish, and sea mammals in a period of rapid environmental change, like that at the end of the Ice Age. Unfortunately, however, we do not know how decisive marine or riverine resources were in allowing dense populations and sedentary living, both essential prerequisites for social complexity.

Away from coasts, rivers, and lake shores, and especially among groups living at the edges of several ecological zones, people living in more or less permanent settlements in rich inland environments turned to another strategy. They experimented with the planting of wild plant staples to supplement food resources in short supply. The cultural changes forced upon them by Holocene climate change made it easier for their descendants to adopt radically new economic strategies such as deliberate cultivation of the soil and animal domestication—food production.

THEORIES OF FARMING ORIGINS

Victorian scientists believed agriculture was a brilliant invention, fostered by a rare genius. One day, went the scenario, a solitary forager was carrying home a bundle of edible grasses when she stumbled, spilling some of her load on

Figure 5.3 Recon-struction of a Chumash Indian *Tomol* (canoe), Used on the Waters of the Santa Barbara Channel, California The Chumash were among the most sophisticated forager societies on earth.

damp ground. A few days later, she passed the same way and noticed small green shoots sprouting from the soil. With startling insight, the woman realized the potential of her new invention, planted more seeds near her hut, and fed her family off the bountiful harvest. Other families soon copied her example and agriculture was born.

Such captivating scenarios offer simple explanations, but have no foundation in scientific fact. Firstly, no one ever "invented" agriculture, because all hunter-gatherers knew that grasses germinated each year. Root crops like the African yam can be propagated simply by cutting off the top and placing it in the soil. Foragers living on the fringes of the African rainforest as early as 40,000 years ago may have planted yams in that way, but such practices are a far cry from the cultivation of cereal grasses, which began in Old World and New after the Ice Age. Reality was more complex than mere invention, and is still little understood.

Nor did a single society "invent" agriculture, for farming appeared at widely different times in many parts of the world. Farmers in southwestern Asia's Euphrates and Jordan River Valleys cultivated wheat and barley by about 8000 B.C. Central American cultivators grew domesticated squashes by about the same date. Chinese villagers harvested rice by 6000 B.C., perhaps earlier. Most scientists believe that a set of complex cultural and environmental factors combined with population growth to cause societies in widely separated parts of the world to shift from foraging to food production, usually within a relatively short time, sometimes a few generations.

At the end of the Ice Age, foragers in drought-prone subtropical zones such as southwestern Asia and highland Mesoamerica were exploiting potentially domesticable wild grasses and root plants with greater intensity. Dependence on such foods probably came earlier in these regions, where there were only a few forageable plant foods. Such dependence was essential to long-term survival and led almost inevitably to experimentation with deliberate planting of wild cereals and ultimately to cultivation. In contrast, populations in more humid, plant-rich tropical regions, like the African and Amazonian rainforests, probably did little more than plant a few wild species to minimize risk of starvation in lean years long after farming appeared in more temperate regions. Cereal agriculture came to tropical Africa only within the past 3000 years, and it spread widely after the introduction of iron technology some centuries later.

During the 1920s, University of Chicago Egyptologist Henry Breasted popularized the term **Fertile Crescent** to describe the cradle of agriculture and civilization in southwestern Asia. The Crescent has its arms in Mesopotamia and the Nile Valley, joined by a great arch across the Jordan Valley and Zagros Mountains of Iran. The label has fallen into disuse in recent years, but is apt in the sense that it spans the vast arc of contrasting terrain where agriculture, and urban civilization, first began. Most speculation about agricultural origins has surrounded the Fertile Crescent.

Early Theories: Oases and Hilly Flanks

Gordon Childe's Agricultural Revolution offers a good starting point, for it was the first modern attempt to explain agricultural origins. Drought conditions formed the core of his revolution thesis. He speculated that after the Ice Age the southwestern Asian climate became increasingly dry, forcing both animals and humans to concentrate in areas like the Jordan Valley, where permanent water supplies were available and plant foods perennially abundant. The arid conditions brought animals, humans, and plants into a close symbiosis (Greek: "life together"), creating favorable conditions for foragers to experiment with cereal grasses and with herding wild goats and sheep. These experiments revolutionized human existence and spread rapidly throughout southwestern Asia and further afield.

Childe proposed the Agricultural Revolution long before pollen analysis, deep sea cores, and other highly sophisticated tools for climatic reconstruction were applied to Asian sites. The theory was simple, but unproven. During the 1950s, University of Chicago archaeologist Robert Braidwood took a multidisciplinary team of botanists, geologists, and zoologists on a major field expedition to the Zagros Mountains, what he called the "hilly flanks" of southwestern Asia. He recovered the first climatic data for Holocene times and found evidence of increased forest cover and high rainfall after the Ice Age. He also excavated early farming settlements high above the fertile low-lands, which, at the time, were considered exceptionally early, as they radio-carbon dated to about 6000 B.C.

Braidwood rejected Childe's oasis theory and argued that agriculture and animal domestication began in the mountainous terrain at the periphery of fertile lands. Higher rainfall meant more wild food supplies and denser game populations in the lowlands. Highland peoples were not so fortunate and adopted agriculture to increase food supplies in the face of rising populations. In other words, agriculture began on the flanks, not in the center.

THE RECOVERY REVOLUTION

Braidwood and Childe theorized at a time when multidisciplinary research was still in its infancy. Since the 1950s, archaeology has gone through what one may call a "recovery revolution," a dramatic refinement of field and lab-oratory methods that has produced infinitely more fine-grained data. The recovery revolution has taken place alongside other important developments:

- Multidisciplinary studies of Holocene climatic change, which combine pollen samples from lakes and marshes with deep sea and tree-ring data to produce a chronicle of large- and small-scale climatic change since 10,000 B.C. These data allow archaeologists to place early farming sites within much more precise environmental contexts.
- A mass of new botanical data acquired through systematic use of flota-tion methods (see "Flotation" box) which allow the recovery of large samples of wild and domesticated seeds from occupation levels.
- Major advances in zooarchaeology, the study of animal bones, have provided a wealth of new information on the domestication of cattle, goats, pigs, sheep, and other animals.
- Accelerator mass spectrometry (AMS) radiocarbon dating (see "AMS Dating" box) permits the dating of individual seeds, root fragments, or maize cobs. For the first time, we can date early farming with high pre-cision, as opposed to merely dating layers in which tiny seeds are found (and into which they may have fallen from higher levels).

The past 20 years have seen the development of more sophisticated ecological interpretations of the origins of food production, which result in large part from much larger data bases of archaeological and environmental data.

MULTICAUSAL THEORIES

The recovery revolution has spawned complex, *multivariate models,* which take into account the emerging realization that many early Holocene hunter-gatherer societies were more complex and well preadapted to food production

FLOTATION AND BOTANICAL REMAINS

Until the 1960s, archaeologists knew little of early domesticated plants. They lacked a recovery technology to excavate more than a few handfuls of carbonized seeds preserved in storage pits or hearths. **Flotation** methods, first developed in the North American Midwest, revolutionized our knowledge of ancient farming. By passing soil samples through water or chemicals, today's excavators can recover thousands of seeds, as they float to the surface while the heavier soil matrix sinks to the bottom of the screen. Elaborate flotation machines can process dozens of samples an hour. The sample is poured into a screened container and agitated by water pouring into the screen. The light plant materials float on the water and are carried out of the container by a sluiceway that leads to fine mesh screens, where the seeds are trapped and wrapped in fine cloth for further study. Flotation is rewriting the early history of both foraging and farming. Botanist Gordon Hillman has reconstructed the foraging habits of 16,000-year-old hunter-gatherers living alongside the Nile River during the late Ice Age. His studies of the environment at Abu Hureyra, Syria, described in Chapter 6, document how tree cover receded from the site as drought became endemic. The inhabitants responded by gathering wild grasses, then cultivating them to amplify their food supply. Flotation has also been used extensively in eastern North America, the Southwest and the Andean area, with similarly dramatic results.

---

before anyone started planting wild cereal grasses or penning animals. For example, as recently as the 18th century A.D., the Kumeyaay Indians of southern California reduced the risk of starvation by "domesticating" their landscape. They lived in semiarid valleys, encouraging the growth of wild grasses by burning of harvested stands, then broadcasting some of the seed over the burnt ground. They created groves of oaks and pines by planting edible nuts at high elevations and planted agave and other desert plants in suitable habitats. In this way they flourished by means of a complex mosaic of manipulated wild plants.

Population and Resources Theories

All of us take risks in our lives and try to protect ourselves against the dangers of a sudden catastrophe. This is why wise investors diversify their holdings, and why parents carry life insurance policies. This is known as risk management. In the case of prehistoric people, it meant minimizing anything that would threaten long-term survival. All environments, however favorable, involve some form of risk for foraging societies—drought cycles, long, cold winters, and unpredictable floods, to mention only a few. Often people respond to these risks by moving away or by developing new storage and food preservation technologies.

ACCELERATOR MASS SPECTROMETRY (AMS) RADIOCARBON DATING

Until the 1980s, archaeologists collected handfuls of charcoal and other organic materials for radiocarbon dating. Most samples came from hearths, hut posts, and other larger features, or just charcoal concentrations. This meant that the samples dated entire levels, not individual artifacts within them, so that dates for, say, early maize cobs, were at best general approximations. In many cases, small cobs or seeds may have been trodden into earlier levels, resulting in inaccurate dates. **Accelerator mass spectrometry (AMS)** radiocarbon dating needs such small samples that the archaeologist can date a single seed, maize cob, or speck of wood preserved in the socket of a bronze axe. For the first time, we can date actual botanical specimens planted and harvested by early farmers.

AMS radiocarbon dates result from using an accelerator mass spectrometer to date the age of sample material by counting the number of ^{14}C atoms present as opposed to counting decay events (beta counts). By doing this researchers can date samples 1000 times smaller than the handful of charcoal used a generation ago. Ionized carbon 14 atoms from the sample are pulled in beam form toward the accelerator, then counted by a detector as a magnetic lens focuses the beam, allowing calculation of the age of the sample. AMS has dated maize in Mesoamerica to earlier than 2600 B.C. and cereal grains in Syria to earlier than 8500 B.C.

One logical and straightforward solution to rising populations, resulting food shortages, or risk factors may be to go one step further, to cultivate familiar plants and domesticate common prey so that people can draw on familiar stored food during scarce periods. In other words, food production arose as a result of risk management, as a way of increasing food supplies.

Ecological Theories

Proponents of ecological models talk of so-called opportunities for the introduction of food production, of people turning to superior local resources when the moment arrived. In this kind of scenario, some resources, say wild wheat or barley or wild oats, are seen as attractive. People use them more and more, to the extent that they eventually become domesticated.

Ecological theories are founded on the assumption that human societies are cultural systems operating within much larger environmental systems. The classic exposition of this point of view is that of University of Michigan archaeologist Kent Flannery, who works in Mexico's southern highlands. He discovered that between 8000 and 4000 B.C. the local people relied on five basic food sources—deer, rabbits, maguey, legumes, and prickly pears—for their sustenance. By careful prediction of the seasons of each food, they could schedule their hunting and gathering at periods of abundance and before animals gained access to the ripe plants. Flannery assumed that the southern highlands and their inhabitants were part of a large, open environmental system consisting of many subsystems—economic, botanical, social, and so on—that interacted with one another. Then something happened to jolt the food procurement system toward the deliberate growing of wild grasses.

Flannery's excavations at dry caves dating to between 5000 and 2000 B.C. showed maize cobs slowly increasing in size as well as other signs of genetic change. Thus, he suggested that the people began to experiment with the deliberate planting of maize and other crops, intentionally expanding the areas where they would grow. After a long period, these intentional deviations in the food procurement system caused the importance of wild grass collecting to increase at the expense of other collecting activities until it became the dominant one. Eventually, the people created a self-perpetuating food procurement system, with its own vital scheduling demands of planting and harvesting that competed with earlier systems and won out because it was more durable. By 2000 B.C., the highly nutritious bean and corn diet of the highland people was well established.

The crux of all these theoretical approaches is to identify the processes that caused people to shift to deliberate cultivation and domestication. For example, were there new cost-benefit realities that favored farming? What about such factors as the nutritive value and seasonal availability of different foods? Did genetic changes in plants and animals play a role? Unfortunately, it is difficult to link complex theoretical models with actual field data, largely because the factors involved in such profound cultural change (the reasons why people make the changeover) do not lend themselves to easy documentation.

THE CONSEQUENCES OF FOOD PRODUCTION

Once successful, food production spread rapidly, partly because population growth after the fact prevented people from reverting to hunting and gathering. Food production spread to all corners of the world except where an environment with extreme aridity or heat or cold rendered agriculture or herding impossible or where people chose to remain hunters and gatherers. In some places, food production was the economic base for urbanization and literate civilization; but most human societies did not go further than subsistence-level food production until the industrial power of 19th- and 20th-century Europe led them into the machine age.

Food production resulted, ultimately, in much higher population densities in many locations, for the domestication of plants and animals can lead to an economic strategy that increases and stabilizes available food supplies, although more energy is used to produce them (Figure 5.4). Farmers use concentrated tracts of territory for agriculture and for grazing cattle and small stock if they practice mixed farming. Their territory is much smaller than that of hunter-gatherers (although pastoralists need huge areas of grazing land for seasonal pasture). Within a smaller area of farming land, property lines are

Figure 5.4   Bemba Women from Central Africa Hoeing a Freshly Cleared Field

carefully delineated as individual ownership and problems of inheritance arise. Shortages of land can lead to disputes and to the founding of new village settlements on previously uncultivated soil.

More enduring settlements brought other changes. The portable and lightweight material possessions of many hunter-gatherers were replaced by heavier tool kits and more lasting houses (Figure 5.5). Grindstones and ground-edged axes were even more essential to farming culture than they were to gathering societies. Hoes and other implements of tillage were vital for the planting and harvesting of crops. New social units came into being as more lasting home bases were developed; these social links reflected ownership and inheritance of land and led to much larger settlements that brought hitherto scattered populations into closer and more regular contact.

Food production led to changed attitudes toward the environment. Cereal crops were such that people could store their food for winter (see Figure 5.6). The hunter-gatherers exploited game, fish, and vegetable foods, but the farmers did more; they *altered* the environment by the very nature of their exploitation. Expansion of agriculture meant felling trees and burning vegetation to clear the ground for planting. The same fields were then abandoned after a few years to lie fallow, and more woodland was cleared. The original

Figure 5.5 A Mud-and-Pole Hut Typical of the Middle Zambezi Valley, Central Africa (*LEFT*) Such dwellings, often occupied 15 years or longer, are more lasting than the wind break or tent of the hunter-gatherer or cattle herder. At right is a grain bin from an African village, used for cereal crops. Storing food is a critical activity of many foragers and farmers.

vegetation began to regenerate, but it might have been cleared again before reaching its original state. This shifting pattern of farming is called slash-and-burn, or swidden, agriculture. Voracious domesticated animals stripped pastures of their grass cover; then heavy rainfalls denuded the hills of valuable soil, and the pastures were never the same again. However elementary the agricultural technology, the farmer changed the environment, if only with fires lit to clear scrub from gardens and to fertilize the soil with wood ash. In a sense, shifting slash-and-burn agriculture is merely an extension of the age-old use of fire to encourage regeneration of vegetation.

Food production resulted in high population densities, but population growth was controlled by disease, available food supplies, water supplies, and particularly famine. Also, early agricultural methods depended heavily on careful selection of the soil. The technology of the first farmers was hardly effective enough for extensive clearing of the dense woodland under which many good soils lay, so potentially cultivable land could only be that which was accessible. Gardens probably were scattered over a much wider territory than is necessary today. One authority estimates that even with advanced shifting agriculture, only 40 percent of moderately fertile soil in Africa is available for such cultivation. This figure must have been lower in the early days of agriculture, with the simpler stone tools and fewer crops.

In regions of seasonal rainfall, such as southwestern Asia, sub-Saharan Africa, and parts of Asia, periods of prolonged drought are common. Famine was a real possibility as population densities rose. Many early agriculturalists must have worriedly watched the sky and had frequent crop failures in times of drought. Their small stores of grain from the previous season would not have carried them through another year, especially if they had been careless with their surplus. Farmers were forced to shift their economic strategy in such times.

We know that the earliest farmers availed themselves of game and vegetable foods to supplement their agriculture, just as today some farmers are obliged to rely heavily on wild vegetable foods and hunting to survive in bad years. Many hunter-gatherer bands collect intensively just a few species of edible plants in their large territories. Aware of many other edible vegetables, they fall back on these only in times of stress; the less-favored foods can carry a comparatively small population through to the next rains. A larger agricultural population is not so flexible and quickly exhausts wild vegetables and game in the much smaller territory used for farming and grazing. If the drought lasts for years, famine, death, and reduced population can follow.

NUTRITION AND EARLY FOOD PRODUCTION

Was food production a real improvement in human lifeways? For generations archaeologists have argued that human health improved dramatically as a result of agriculture, because people worked less and lived on more reliable food supplies. But the economist Ester Boserup and others have argued that in fact agriculture brought diminishing returns in relation to labor expended in the new systems that were adopted to feed many more people. Richard Lee's studies of the !Kung San of the Kalahari Desert tend to support her views. They show that these hunter-gatherers, and presumably others, had abundant leisure and worked less than farmers. Some nutritionists point out that foragers may have had better-balanced diets than many farmers, who relied heavily on root or cereal crops. Further, farmers, with their sedentary settlements and higher population densities, were much more vulnerable to famine than their hunter-gatherer predecessors. They would also have been more vulnerable to gastrointestinal infections and epidemics because of crowded village populations.

Nutrition studies based on the skeletons of early farmers suggest some incidence of anemia and slow growth resulting from malnutrition. Regional studies of prehistoric populations have suggested a *decline* in mean age life expectancy in agricultural populations, which contradicts the commonly held perception. Taken as a whole, paleopathological studies suggest a general decline in the quality, and perhaps the length, of human life with the advent of food production. However, there are many unknowns involved, among them changes in fertility and population growth rates, which caused the world's population to rise even if general health standards and life expectancy fell.

What impact these studies will have on population-pressure theories about the origins of agriculture is still uncertain. Certainly, any shift to food production caused by increasing population pressure could be reflected in a decline in the overall health and nutrition displayed by prehistoric skeletons.

In the final analysis, some people probably turned to food production only when other alternatives were no longer practicable. The classic example is the Aborigines of extreme northern Australia, who were well aware that their neighbors in New Guinea were engaged in intensive agriculture. They, too, knew how to plant the top of the wild yam so that it regerminated, but they never adopted food production simply because they had no need to become dependent on a lifeway that would reduce their leisure time and produce more food than they required. We should never forget that humans have always been opportunistic, and the planting of food crops and the first taming of animals may have been the simple result.

CHAPTER 6

The Earliest Farmers

A.D. 1950 —

A.D. 1 —

15,000 B.P. —

50,000 B.P. —

100,000 B.P. —

500,000 B.P. —

1.0 Million —

2.5 Million —

Whatever the complex factors that led to agriculture and animal domestication, the new food-producing economies proved dramatically successful. In 8000 B.C., virtually everybody in the world lived by hunting and gathering. By A.D. 1, most people were farmers or herders, and only a minority were still hunter-gatherers, most of them living in environments where extreme cold or aridity prevented the growth of domesticated crops. The spread of food production throughout the world took only about 8000 years. This chapter examines the archaeological evidence for the origins and initial spread of farming in the Old and New Worlds, a process that was the foundation for subsequent, more complex human societies and the early civilizations.

As we saw in Chapter 5, hunter-gatherers everywhere had a profound knowledge of the food resources in their local environments. Nevertheless, many fewer animals and wild vegetable foods were domesticated than foraged over the millennia. In the Old World, early farmers tamed wheat, barley, and other cereals that grow wild over much of Asia and Europe. In the New World, Native Americans developed a remarkable expertise with plants of all kinds—indigenous cereal grasses, root species, and nuts of all kinds. From this proficiency came the staples of American farming: Indian corn (*Zea mays*), the only important wild grass to be domesticated, beans, squashes, and many minor crops. Root plants such as manioc and sweet potatoes, chili peppers, tobacco, and many forms of potato were vital parts of Indian life.

Potentially tamable animal species like the wild ox, goat, pig, and sheep were widely distributed in the Old

World during the late Ice Age. Native American farmers domesticated only such animals as the llama, the guinea pig, and the turkey, and then only under special conditions and within narrow geographic limits.

OLD WORLD: DOMESTICATION OF ANIMALS

Having one's own herds of domesticated mammals ensured a regular meat supply. The advantages to having a major source of meat under one's control are obvious. Later, domesticated animals provided byproducts such as milk, cheese, and butter, as well as skins for clothes and tent coverings and materials for leather shields and armor. In later millennia, people learned how to breed animals for specialized tasks such as plowing, transportation, and traction.

Domestication implies a genetic selection emphasizing special features of continuing use to the domesticator. Wild sheep have no wool, wild cows produce milk only for their offspring, and undomesticated chickens do not lay surplus eggs. Changes in wool bearing, lactation, or egg production could be achieved by isolating wild populations for selective breeding under human care. Isolating species from a larger gene pool produced domestic sheep with thick, woolly coats and domestic goats providing regular supplies of milk, which formed a staple in the diet of many human populations.

No one knows exactly how domestication of animals began. Three elements are vital to domestication: constraining the movement of the target populations, regulating their breeding, and controlling their feeding to shape future generations. At the end of the Ice Age, hunters in southwestern Asia were concentrating on gazelles and other steppe animals. Wild sheep and goats were intensively hunted on the southern shores of the Caspian Sea. Gregarious, highly social animals like goats and sheep are the most easily domesticated beasts; they follow the lead of a dominant herd member or all move together. They also tolerate feeding and breeding in a confined environment.

Hunters often fed off the same herd for a long time, sometimes deliberately sparing young females and immature beasts to keep the source of food alive. Young animals captured alive in the chase might be taken back to the camp to grow dependent on those who caged them, thus becoming partially tamed. A hunter could grasp the possibility of gaining control of the movements of a few key members of a herd, who would be followed by the others. Once the experience of keeping pets or of restricting game movements had suggested a new way of life, people might experiment with different species. As part of domestication, animals and humans increased their mutual interdependence.

The process of animal domestication undoubtedly was prolonged, developing in several areas of southwestern Asia at approximately the same time. Although animal bones are scarce and often unsatisfactory as evidence of early domestication, most authorities now agree that the first species to be domesticated in southwestern Asia were goats and sheep, about 8500 B.C. Goats and sheep are small animals who live in herds, whose carcasses yield much meat for their size. They can readily be penned and isolated to develop a symbiotic relationship with people.

Cattle are much more formidable to domesticate, for their prototype was *Bos primigenius,* the wild ox much hunted by Stone Age people (Figure 6.1). South African archaeologist Andrew Smith, an expert on herding, believes that the first domesticated animals came from better disciplined wild herds in arid environments, where it was easier to control the movements of animals. Such conditions may have persisted over much of southwestern Asia and the Sahara Desert as the climate became drier after 7000 B.C.

Some animals, such as sea mammals, resist domestication because much of their lives is spent out of range of human influence. Most early successes with domestication took place with gregarious animals. They can be thought of as a food reserve, as "grain on the hoof."

OLD WORLD: DOMESTICATING WHEAT AND BARLEY

The qualities of wild wheat, barley, and similar crops are quite different from those of their domestic equivalents. In the wild, these grains occur in dense stands. They can be harvested by tapping the stem with the hands and gathering the seeds in a basket as they fall off or by uprooting the plant. The tapping technique is effective because the wild grain is attached to the stem by a brittle joint, or **rachis.** When the grass is tapped, the weak rachis breaks and the seed falls into the basket.

The first cultivated wheat and barley crops were of the wild, brittle-rachised type, and the resulting crops would probably have been large enough to generate domestic-type mutants in the first two to five years. Selection for the semi-tough rachised forms was an unconscious process during the earliest stages of domestication, perhaps accelerated by the use of sickles or uprooting of individual plants to harvest ripe seeds rather than merely tapping them into waiting baskets (Figure 6.2). Computer simulations have shown that domestic, semi-tough rachised forms may have been rare at first, but they would have been fully domesticated within 20 to 30 generations—for these cereals, between 20 and 30 years. Even with less-intense selective pressures than those assumed in the experiment, domestication could have been achieved within one or two centuries. Archaeobotanist Gordon Hillman of London University believes that the farmers would have started conscious selection as soon as the domesticates became sufficiently common to be recognized, perhaps 1 to 5 percent of the crop. From then on, domestication would have been completed in three or four years.

Although the broad outlines of the process of domestication can be reconstructed through controlled experimentation and computer simulation, it is most unlikely that anyone will ever find "transitional" grains in Southwestern Asian sites that will document the actual process underway. The changeover from wild to domesticated strains was so rapid that we are more likely to find wild seeds in one level and domesticated ones in the next. This is precisely what has been found at Southwestern Asian sites such as Abu Hureyra in Syria, where farming appears abruptly about 8500 B.C. (see below).

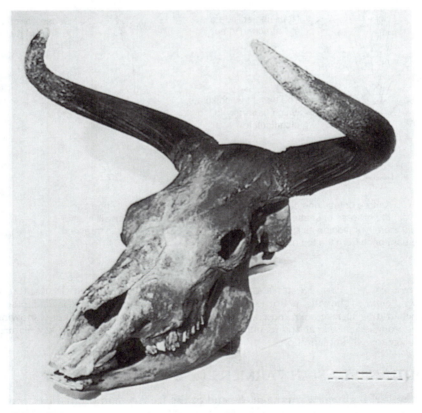

Figure 6.1   THE AUROCHS, *BOS PRIMIGENIUS*, THE WILD PROTOTYPE FOR DOMESTIC CATTLE   (*top*) The aurochs as depicted by S. Von Herbenstain in 1549.   (*bottom*) A *Bos primigenius* skull from Cambridgeshire, England.

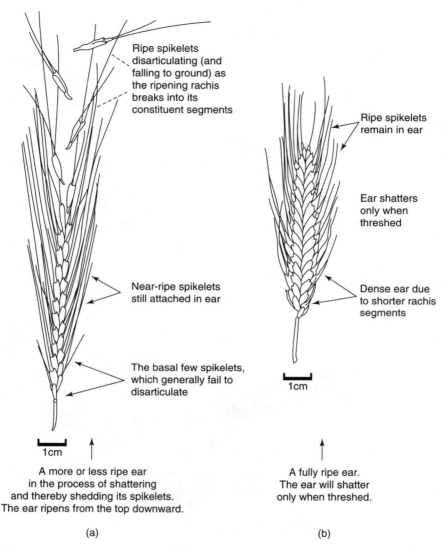

Ripe spikelets disarticulating (and falling to ground) as the ripening rachis breaks into its constituent segments

Ripe spikelets remain in ear

Ear shatters only when threshed

Near-ripe spikelets still attached in ear

Dense ear due to shorter rachis segments

The basal few spikelets, which generally fail to disarticulate

1cm

1cm

A more or less ripe ear in the process of shattering and thereby shedding its spikelets. The ear ripens from the top downward.

A fully ripe ear. The ear will shatter only when threshed.

(a)

(b)

Figure 6.2   Wild and Domesticated Einkorn, Showing Brittle and Tough Rachis (a) Wild einkorn showing its brittle-rachised ear and arrow-shaped spikelets adapted for penetrating surface litter and cracks on the ground. (b) Domestic einkorn, showing its semitough rachised ear and its plumper spikelets, which have lost some key features necessary for self-implantation.

SOUTHWEST ASIAN FARMERS (c. 8000 to 5000 B.C.)

The universal global warming at the end of the Ice Age had dramatic effects on temperate regions of Asia, Europe, and North America. Ice sheets retreated, sea levels rose. The climatic changes in southwestern Asia were more subtle, in that they involved shifts in mountain snow lines, rainfall patterns, and vegetational cover. However, these same cycles of change had momentous impacts on the sparse human populations of the region. At the end of the Ice Age, no more than a few thousand foragers lived along the eastern Mediterranean coast, in the Jordan and Euphrates Valleys. Within 2000 years, the human population of the region numbered in the tens of thousands, all as a result of village life and farming. Thanks to new environmental and archaeological discoveries, we now know something about this remarkable change in local life.

Pollen samples from freshwater lakes in Syria and elsewhere tell us forest cover expanded rapidly at the end of the Ice Age, for the southwestern Asian climate was still cooler and considerably wetter than today. Many areas were richer in animal and plant species than they are now, making them highly favorable for human occupation. About 9000 B.C., most human settlements lay in the Levant (the area along the Mediterranean coast) and in the Zagros mountains of Iran and their foothills (see Figure 5.1). Some local areas, like the Jordan River valley, the Middle Euphrates valley, and some Zagros valleys, were more densely populated than elsewhere. Here more sedentary and more complex societies flourished. These people exploited the landscape intensively, foraging on hill slopes for wild cereal grasses and nuts, while hunting gazelle (a small desert antelope) and other game on grassy lowlands and in river valleys. Their settlements contain exotic objects such as sea shells, stone bowls, and artifacts made of obsidian (volcanic glass), all traded from afar. This considerable volume of intercommunity exchange brought a degree of social complexity in its wake.

Thanks to extremely fine-grained excavation and extensive use of flotation methods, we know a great deal about the foraging practices of the inhabitants of **Abu Hureyra** in Syria's Euphrates Valley (Figure 6.3). Abu Hureyra was founded about 9500 B.C., a small village settlement of cramped pit dwellings (houses dug partially in the soil) with reed roofs supported by wooden uprights. For the next 1500 years, its inhabitants enjoyed a somewhat warmer and damper climate than today, living in a well-wooded steppe area where wild cereal grasses were abundant. They subsisted off spring migrations of Persian gazelles from the south. With such a favorable location, about 300 to 400 people lived in a sizable, permanent settlement. They were no longer a series of small bands, but lived in a large community with more elaborate social organization, probably grouped into clans of people of common descent. The flotation samples from the excavations allowed botanist Gordon Hillman to study changing plant-collecting habits, as if he were looking through a telescope at a changing landscape. Hundreds of tiny plant remains show how they exploited nut harvests in nearby pistachio and oak forests. However, as the climate dried up, the forests retreated from the vicinity of the settlement. The inhabitants turned to wild cereal grasses instead, collecting them by the thousands, while percentages of nuts fell. By 8200 B.C., drought conditions were so severe that the people abandoned their long-established settlement, perhaps dispersing into smaller camps.

Five centuries later, about 7700 B.C., a new village rose on the mound. At first, the inhabitants still hunted gazelle intensively. Then, about 7000 B.C., within the space of a few generations, they switched abruptly to herding domesticated goats and sheep and to growing einkorn, pulses, and other cereal grasses.

Figure 6.3 ABU HUREYRA, SYRIA   Excavations in the earlier settlement, showing interconnecting pits that were roofed with poles, branches, and reeds to form small huts. Part of a later rectangular house can be seen at a higher level (*top right*).

Abu Hureyra grew rapidly until it covered nearly 30 acres (12 ha). It was a close-knit community of rectangular, one-story mud-brick houses, joined by narrow lanes and courtyards, finally abandoned about 5000 B.C.

Many complex factors led to the adoption of the new economies, not only at Abu Hureyra, but at many other locations such as **'Ain Ghazal,** also in Syria, where goat toe bones showing the telltale marks of abrasion caused by foot tethering (hobbling) testify to early herding of domestic stock. Most settlements lay on low ground, near well-watered, easily cultivable land. Their inhabitants usually lived in small, densely clustered villages of circular or oval one-room houses. The most famous of these many settlements is at the base of the Biblical city of **Jericho,** famous for the siege in which Joshua collapsed the city walls with the blast of trumpets.

A small camp flourished at the bubbling Jericho spring by at least 8500 B.C., but a more permanent farming settlement quickly followed. Soon the

---

DISCOVERY

PLASTERED SKULLS AT JERICHO

It was the final day of the 1953 excavation season at Jericho. For weeks, the top of a human skull had projected from the side of the trench dug deep into one of the earliest farming communities in the world. Excavator Kathleen Kenyon had given strict instructions that it was not to be disturbed until the stratigraphic layers in the trench wall had been drawn and photographed. Then the excavators recovered a complete cranium, with facial features carefully modeled in clay, the eyes inset with shells (see Figure 7.1). Kenyon looked closely at the small hole in the wall. She could see two more plastered skulls within. They were removed. Three more now appeared behind them, then a final seventh head. It took five days to extract the nest of skulls from the wall, for the crushed bones were packed tightly with stones and hard earth. They formed the earliest portrait gallery in the world, each head modeled with individual features—nose, mouth, ears, and eyebrows molded with delicacy. Kenyon believed she had found the heads of revered ancestors, who were critical intermediaries between the living and the spiritual world, linking people closely to the land that brought forth their crops.

---

inhabitants built massive stone walls complete with towers and a rock-cut ditch more than 9 feet (2.7 m) deep and 10 feet (3 m) wide around their settlement. Their beehive-shape huts clustered inside the walls. The communal labor of wall and ditch building required both political and economic resources on a scale unheard of a few thousand years earlier. Why the walls were needed remains a mystery, but they may have been flood works or for defense, resulting from competition from neighboring groups for scarce food resources. Jericho also yielded compelling evidence of ancestor worship in the form of human skulls with plastered faces, a clear sign that people enjoyed a close link with the supernatural and the land, guarded traditionally by the dead.

The population of the Levant increased considerably between 7600 and 6000 B.C., scattered in permanent villages as far east as the more arid Syrian plateau. Emmer wheat, barley, lentils, and peas were grown in small fields, crops were rotated with pulses to sustain soil fertility. Some communities like Jericho became important trading centers. The farmers were using obsidian from Turkey, turquoise from Sinai, and sea shell ornaments from the Mediterranean and the Red Sea. The volume of trade was such that many villages used small clay spheres, cones, and disks to keep track of commodities traded. These tokens are thought to represent a simple recording system that later evolved into written script (Chapter 8).

In the Zagros highlands of Iran, the herding of goats and sheep probably began somewhat earlier than in the lowlands. Here, open steppe was ideal country both for intensive hunting of wild goats and sheep, and after about 8000 B.C. for herding them as well. At the village of **Ganj Dareh** near Kermanshah in Iran, foragers occupied a seasonal hunting camp in about 8500 B.C. About 1500 years later, a small farming village of rectangular mud-brick houses stood on the same spot, a settlement based on goat and sheep herding and cereal horticulture. One of the best-known prehistoric farming villages in the Zagros is **Jarmo**, little more than a cluster of 25 mud houses, forming an irregular huddle separated by small alleyways and courtyards. Jarmo was in its heyday in about 5000 B.C., by which time more than 80 percent of the villagers' food came from their fields or herds.

Below, on the lowlands, farming began along the eastern edge of the flat Mesopotamian plain as early as it did in the Levant. The village of **Ali Kosh** on the plains of Khuzistan, north of where the Tigris and Euphrates become one river, started off life as a small settlement of rectangular mud-brick houses as early as 8000 B.C. As time went on, the houses became larger, separated one from another by lanes or courtyards. The people drove their herds of goats and sheep to the highlands during the hot summer months, bringing them back to lush lowland pastures in fall. These same seasonal herding practices continue to this day. Ali Kosh documents more than 2000 years of farming and herding on the lowlands, a period that saw the development of improved cereal strains and the development of irrigation as a means of intensifying agricultural production.

Only 5000 years after food production first appeared, people in the Levant and Mesopotamia were living in cities with thousands of inhabitants.

EARLY EGYPTIAN AND AFRICAN FARMERS (earlier than 6000 B.C. to 1000 B.C.)

The same dynamics of growing populations crowded into restricted territories developed in the Nile valley as a result of Holocene climatic change. During the late Ice Age, the valley was a rich, diverse habitat, abounding in game, fish, and wild plant foods. Wild cereal grasses were important in human diet from at least 15,000 years ago.

The Nile valley is unusual in that its water supplies depend not on local rains but on floods from rainfall gathered far upstream in Ethiopia. The fluctuations in these yearly inundations had a profound effect on the pattern of human settlement downstream. The irregular cycles of higher and lower rainfall may have caused people to manage wild food resources very carefully. Like their southwest Asian counterparts, they turned to the deliberate cultivation of wild barley and wheat.

By 6000 B.C., dozens of farming villages flourished in the Nile valley, settlements that are now buried beneath deep layers of sand and gravel laid down by thousands of years of river floods. Only 1500 years later, the inhabitants of the valley were subsisting almost entirely off agriculture, living in small villages like **Merimda Beni Salama** near the Nile valley. Merimda was a cluster of oval houses and shelters, built half underground and roofed with mud and sticks. The farmers planted barley and wheat as the annual floods receded, while their animals grazed in flat river grasslands. Population densities were still low, so the average Nile flood allowed early Egyptian farmers

Figure 6.4 AN ANCIENT EGYPTIAN TOMB PAINTING SHOWS A NOBLE'S ESTATE WORKERS CULTIVATING THE SOIL   The roots of ancient Egyptian agriculture date back to at least 6000 B.C.

to harvest grain over perhaps two-thirds of the river floodplain (Figure 6.4). Thus, there was no need for irrigation works, which first appear in about 3000 B.C., when Egypt became a unified state (Chapter 10).

After 6000 B.C., cattle herders ranged widely over the semiarid grasslands of what is now the Sahara Desert. These nomads left superb wall paintings of their beasts in the caves and rock shelters of the Saharan highlands, grazing their herds along the shores of shallow lakes like a much larger Lake Chad on the southern edge of the desert. The Sahara dried up rapidly after 6000 B.C., forcing its cattle-herding population into permanent oases or to the fringes of the desert. But it was not until much later, around 1000 B.C., that herders moved into sub-Saharan Africa, and that West Africans domesticated such tropical cereals as sorghum and millet.

EUROPEAN FARMERS (c. 6500 to 3000 B.C.)

The new economies were so successful that they spread rapidly from southwestern Asia into contiguous areas, especially as forager populations rose and natural food supplies were no longer sufficient to support increasingly sedentary forager groups. Many of them turned to food production to supplement their age-old game, plant, and fish diet. By using a mosaic of key sites and radiocarbon dates, we can trace the spread of farming over wide areas of Europe and southern Asia.

Agriculture and animal domestication spread rapidly north into Turkey after 8000 B.C., and from there into Greece, the Balkans, and temperate Europe. Between 7500 and 5000 B.C., long-distance exchange, especially of obsidian for ornaments and toolmaking, became a major factor in daily life. From Turkey's Lake Van it traveled to the Levant and as far afield as the Persian Gulf. A few settlements like **Çatalhöyük** prospered by controlling the trade. Between 6000 and 5000 B.C., Çatalhöyük covered 32 acres (12.9 ha), a settlement of numerous small mud-brick houses backed onto one another, the outside walls serving as a convenient defense wall. But the large village never became a full-fledged city. There were no powerful leaders who monopolized trade and production. It was a community of individual households and families that lacked the elaborate, centralized organization of a city (Figure 6.5).

Figure 6.5   SCHEMATIC RECONSTRUCTION OF A CLUSTER OF FLAT-ROOFED, MUD-BRICK HOUSES FROM LEVEL VI AT ÇATALHÖYÜK, TURKEY   The inhabitants entered through the roof, the outside walls forming natural protection against intruders.

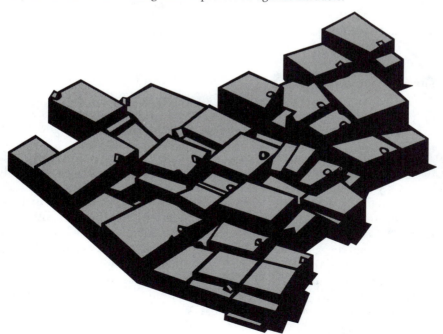

At the time Çatalhöyük was a bustling village, farming was already well established on the Aegean Islands, in Greece, and in parts of southeastern Europe. Since the end of the Ice Age, Europe had been the home of numerous, scattered forager groups who lived off forest game, plant foods, and sea and freshwater fish and mollusks. As in Asia, these populations were preadapted to cultivation and animal domestication, especially in areas where short-term population shifts and local environmental change may have required new subsistence strategies. Domesticated animals and grains were probably introduced into southeast Europe from Asia by local bartering. The plants were cereals like emmer and bread wheat, which were demanding crops that extracted large quantities of nutrients from the soil. The farmers had to husband their land carefully, rotating cereals with nitrogen-fixing legumes and revitalizing their fields with animal manure. Thus was born the European farming system that carefully integrated cultivation and animal rearing into a close-knit subsistence strategy based on individual households supplying their own food needs. Temperate Europe has year-round rainfall and marked contrasts between summer and winter seasons. With plentiful wood and cooler temperatures, timber and thatch therefore replaced the mud-brick architecture of southwestern Asia.

The expansion of farming society into central and western Europe coincided with a cycle of higher rainfall and warmer winters around 5500 B.C. Within a thousand years, farming based on cattle herding combined with spring-sown crops developed over an enormous area of continental Europe. As farming groups spread across lighter soils, clearing forest for fields and grazing their animals in once-forested lands, many indigenous forager bands adopted the new economies.The best-known early European farming culture is named the **Bandkeramik complex** after its distinctive, line-decorated pottery. It first appeared in the Middle Danube valley in about 5300 B.C., then spread rapidly along sheltered river valleys far west to southern Holland and east into parts of the Ukraine. Bandkeramik communities were well spaced, each with territories of some 500 acres (202 ha). The people lived in long, rectangular timber-and-thatch houses, from 18 to 46 feet (5.4 to 14.0 m) long, presumably sheltering families, their grain, and their animals (Figure 6.6). Between 40 and 60 people lived in Bandkeramik villages.

As the centuries passed, the population rose rapidly and the gaps between individual settlements filled in. In time, village territories became more circumscribed, their settlements protected by earthen enclosures. This was a time when communal tombs came into fashion, among them the celebrated **megaliths** (Greek *mega-lithos:* big stone) of western Europe. These were sepulchers fashioned from large boulders and buried under earthen mounds (Figure 6.7). Such corporate burial places may have been locations where revered kin leaders were buried; people with genealogical ties with the ancestors were of paramount importance to a group of farming communities with strong attachments to their fertile lands. Judging from modern analogies, the ancestors were seen as the guardians of the land, the links between the living and the forces of the spiritual world that control human destiny.

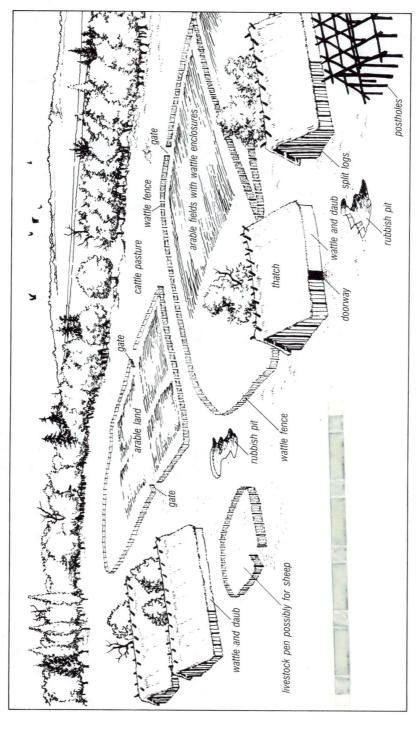

Figure 6.6 Reconstruction of a Bandkeramik Farming Settlement

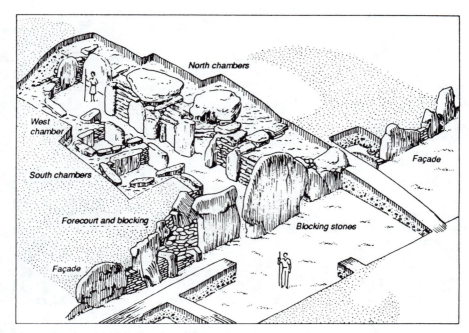

Figure 6.7 WEST KENNET LONG BARROW, WILTSHIRE, ENGLAND   A megalithic tomb buried under an earthen mound, the side chambers filled with burials.

Somewhat later, between about 2800 and 2300 B.C., individual graves as well as communal sepulchers appeared (Figure 6.8). These may have been the burial sites of individual leaders, prominent men who were laid to rest with their elaborate regalia of rank. They may have been the sole male ancestor of the group, the source of authority over land ownership. Chieftainship, inheritance of land and wealth, was now legitimized, as the character of European agriculture changed rapidly, partly as a result of the introduction of the plow by about 2800 B.C.

EARLY AGRICULTURE IN ASIA (before 6000 B.C.)

Rice was the staple of ancient agriculture over an enormous area of southern and southeastern Asia, and southern China. Today, rice accounts for half the food eaten by 1.7 billion people and 21 percent of the total calories consumed by humankind. Unfortunately, we still know almost nothing about the origins of this most important of domesticated crops.

Rice was one of the earliest plants to be domesticated in the northern parts of Southeast Asia and southern China. Botanists believe that the rices and Asian millets ancestral to the present domesticated species radiated from perennial ancestors around the eastern borders of the Himalaya Mountains at the end of the Ice Age. The initial cultivation of wild rice is thought to have

Figure 6.8 STONEHENGE, WILTSHIRE, ENGLAND A celebrated Stone Age and Bronze Age shrine that developed over many generations after 3000 B.C. and was used for more than 1500 years.

taken place in an alluvial swamp area, where there was plenty of water to stimulate cereal growth. The first form to be domesticated may have flourished in shallow water, where seasonal flooding dispersed the seed on the border zone between permanently dry and permanently inundated lands. Perhaps this cultivation occurred under conditions in which seasonal flooding made field preparation a far from burdensome task. Such conditions could have been found on the Ganges Plain in India and along the rich coastal habitats of Southeast Asia and southern China with their dense mangrove swamps.

Perhaps the first efforts to cultivate rice resulted from deliberate efforts to expand seasonally inundated habitats by constructing encircling dams to trap runoff. The dams could then be breached, flooding dry land that could be used for rice planting, thereby creating additional stands of wild rice. From there, it was a short step to deliberate sowing and harvesting in wet fields (paddies). Most likely, a sedentary lifeway based on the gathering of wild rice developed in low-lying, seasonally flooded areas at the beginning of the Holocene. Systematic cultivation resulted from a response to population growth, climatic change, or some other stress.

During the early Holocene, warmer conditions may have allowed wild rice to colonize the lakes and marshes of the middle and lower Yangtze Valley of southern China, when hunter-gatherer societies throughout China were exploiting a broad spectrum of animal and plant resources. At the time of this writing, the earliest known rice farming sites come from the Yangtze River region of southern China. Although the Yangtze Valley now lies outside the modern range of wild rice, warmer, more humid conditions before 5000 B.C. may have supported extensive wetlands where the cereal once flourished. Many Chinese scholars believe the middle and lower Yangtze was the most likely heartland of all rice domestication by 6000 B.C., perhaps considerably earlier.

By 3000 B.C., much more sophisticated agricultural societies were flourishing on the Yangtze River and farther afield. The archaeology of these traditions is known primarily from cemetery excavations that show slow changes in grave goods. The earliest graves indicate few social differentiations, but later sepulchers show not only a much wider variety of artifacts—pottery, bone and stone tools, jade objects, and other ornaments—but also an increase in the number of elaborately adorned burials. China specialist Richard Pearson, who has analyzed several cemeteries, argues that they demonstrate an increase in the concentration of wealth, a trend toward ranked societies, and a shift in the relative importance of males at the expense of females; the last trend may be associated with the development of more intensive agriculture, an activity in which males are valued for their major roles in cultivation.

A second great center of early Chinese agriculture lies nearly 400 miles (650 km) north of the Yangtze, where the Huang Ho River flows out of mountainous terrain into the low-lying plains of northern China. Northern Chinese agriculture was based on millet, whereas the southern staple was rice. The first northern agricultural communities were sited in the central regions of the Huang Ho River Valley. The area is a small basin, forming a border between the wooded western highlands and the swampy lowlands to the east. As in the south, the early Holocene saw a warming trend, followed by a cooler interval, then a more prolonged period of climatic amelioration. It was during the colder period, dating to after 6500 B.C., that the first sedentary farming villages appear in the Huang Ho Valley.

The fine, soft-textured earth of the valley was both homogeneous and porous and could be tilled by simple digging sticks. Because of the concentrated summer rainfall, cereal crops, the key to agriculture in this region, could be grown successfully. The indigenous plants available for domestication included the wild ancestors of foxtail millet, broom-corn millet, sorghum, hemp, and the mulberry. Many villages lay near small streams on lower river terraces, along foothills and plains. Ancient Chinese farmers developed their own cultivation techniques, which persisted for thousands of years.

The earliest farming villages in central and northern China date to as early as 5500 to 5200 B.C. Many settlements consisted of semisubterranean houses with large storage pits. By far the best known of China's early farming cultures is the **Yangshao,** which flourished over much of the Huang Ho River Basin, an area as large as the early centers of agriculture in Egypt or Mesopotamia, from before 4800 B.C. to about 3200 B.C.

Each Yangshao village was a self-contained community, usually built on a terrace overlooking fertile river valleys, situated to avoid flooding or to allow maximal use of floodplain soils (Figure 6.9). Using hoes and digging sticks, the farmers cultivated foxtail millet as a staple, mainly in riverside gardens that were flooded every spring. By 3000 B.C., Yangshao was a characteristic, and thoroughly Chinese, culture, with its own naturalistic art style, and expert potters who made cooking pots for steaming food, the technique that forms

Figure 6.9 Reconstruction of Yangshao Houses, Northern China

the basis of much Chinese cuisine to this day. The Chinese language may have its roots in Yangshao as well.

Many regional variations of peasant farming culture developed throughout China. Agriculture developed over wide areas at about the same time, with people adapting their crops and farming techniques to local conditions. In time, the success of the new economies led to local population increases, more complex cultures, and the concentration of wealth in privileged hands.

EARLY AMERICAN AGRICULTURE (8000 B.C. onward)

Food production developed independently, also, in the Americas. For thousands of years after first settlement, the native Americans subsisted off hunting and gathering, developing an increasing expertise with wild plant foods of all kinds. In some regions, they exploited such resources intensively, especially in the Midwest and Southeast, where some groups were able to occupy more or less permanent settlements for many generations. In time, however, they also started planting wild grasses as a means of supplementing wild plant resources. In time, too, this led to agriculture, especially in areas where wild grasses were plentiful.

By the time of Columbus, the ancient Americans had developed a truly remarkable expertise with all kinds of native plants, using them not only for food but for medicinal and many other purposes. The most important staple crop was maize, the only significant wild grass in the New World to be fully domesticated. It remains the most important food crop in the Americas, used in more than 150 varieties as both food and cattle fodder. Root crops formed another substantial food source, especially in South America, and included manioc, sweet potatoes, and many varieties of the potato. Chili peppers were grown as hot seasoning. Amaranth, sunflowers, cacao, peanuts, and several types of beans were also significant crops. In contrast to Old World farmers, the Indians had few domesticated animals. Among them were the llama of the Andes and alpacas, which provided wool. The dog, the guinea pig, the raucous turkey, and the muscovy duck were also tamed.

Most archaeologists now agree there were at least three major centers of native plant domestication in the Americas: Mesoamerica for maize, beans, squash, and sweet potatoes; the highlands of the central Andes for root crops like potatoes and manioc; and the southeastern United States for pepo squash, sunflowers, and other local plants. There were also four areas of later cultivation activity: tropical (northern) South America, the Andean area, Mesoamerica, and southwestern and eastern North America.

Mesoamerica: Guilá Naquitz and Early Cultivation

The process of plant domestication is still little understood. Archaeologist Kent Flannery bases his arguments on ecological considerations (Chapter 5). He believes plant cultivation began as a result of strategies designed to cope with continuous short-term climatic fluctuations and constant population shifts. Flannery bases his arguments on his own excavations at the **Guilá Naquitz** rock shelter in the Valley of Oaxaca (see Figure 1.3). Guilá Naquitz was occupied about six times over a 2000-year period between 8750 and 6670 B.C. The tiny forager groups who visited the cave faced unpredictable climatic fluctuations due to periodic droughts in an area that could support very few people per square mile.

The Guilá Naquitz people foraged 11 different edible plant species over the year. In wet years, they experimented with deliberate planting of beans. Bean cultivation near the cave allowed people to collect more food and travel less. At first the experiments were confined to wet years, but as time went on and they gained more confidence, plant yields rose and they relied more heavily on their own cultivation as opposed to foraging. In time, the Guilá Naquitz people simply added squashes, beans, and a simple form of maize to a much earlier foraging adaptation. Recent AMS radiocarbon dates date squash cultivation at the cave to about 8000 B.C., as early as cereal agriculture in southwestern Asia. Flannery believes that this kind of changeover occurred in many areas of Mesoamerica.

Maize

The wild ancestor of maize was a perennial grass named teosinte, which still grows in Central America today. The process of domestication may have started as an unintentional byproduct of gathering wild teosinte. What may have happened was that the foragers favored the most harvestable of teosinte grasses, those whose seeds scattered less easily when ripe. In time, this favored type of teosinte would become established near campsites and in abandoned rubbish dumps. In time, too, people would remove weeds from these teosinte stands, then start deliberately planting the more useful types. Eventually, the grass became dependent on human intervention. A genetic revolution followed, which led to maize.

The hypothetical scenario for maize domestication goes as follows (Figure 6.10). The process may have started as an unintentional byproduct of gathering

Figure 6.10   THE VARIOUS STAGES IN THE TRANSITION FROM TEOSINTE TO MAIZE
The earliest teosinte is (a), the stabilized maize phenotype (e). The harvesting process
increased condensation of teosinte branches and led to the husks becoming the enclosures for corn ears.

wild teosinte, for gathering would lead to selective pressure for harvestable types
of the grass, then to deliberate planting. At first the planted teosinte was no more
productive than wild forms, but it was easier to harvest, a critical stage in the
process of domestication. When people began selective harvesting and planting
of transitional forms of teosinte, the grass became dependent on human intervention. A genetic revolution followed, in which attributes that made harvesting
easier and favored teosinte's use as a human food had a selective advantage.

The best archaeological evidence for early maize cultivation comes from
the dry caves and open sites of the dry, highland **Tehuacán Valley** in southern
Mexico (Figure 6.11). Archaeologist Richard MacNeish found that the earliest Tehuacán people lived mainly by hunting deer and other mammals and
also by collecting wild vegetable foods. MacNeish estimates that in 10,000

Figure 6.11 EXCAVATIONS AT COXCATLÁN CAVE, TEHUACÁN VALLEY, MEXICO

B.C. 50 to 60 percent of the people's food came from game. After 8000 B.C., the game population declined, and the people turned more and more to wild plant foods. By at least 4500 B.C., about 90 percent of the Tehuacano diet consisted of tropical grasses, and such plants as cacti and maguey. So much grain was necessary that some form of cultivation or domestication of native plants may have been essential by this time. AMS radiocarbon dates on early maize cobs from **San Marcos Cave** date this staple to at least 3600 B.C.

More than 24,000 maize specimens have come from the caves of the Tehuacán Valley. They document a long sequence of maize evolution, beginning with 71 small cobs from the lowest levels of San Marcos Cave and from deep in the **Coxcatlán Cave** (see Figure 6.12). The cobs are less than 2 inches (20 mm) long, and lack the ability to disperse their kernels naturally, a clear sign of full domestication. We do not know how many centuries earlier teosinte was transformed into maize, but archaeologist Bruce Smith believes the process took place more than 155 miles (250 km) west of Tehuacán, in river valleys that flow from the highlands into the Pacific—areas where the wild teosinte that is most biochemically similar to maize still grows today.

Maize was domesticated in Mesoamerica at about the time the Pyramids of Giza were built along the Nile River (Chapter 10).

The primitive form of domesticated eight-rowed maize (*Maiz de ocho*) represented at Tehuacán was the common ancestral corn that spread thousands of miles from its original homeland. Subsequent derivatives of this basic maize developed elsewhere throughout the Americas.

If Kent Flannery's hypothesis is correct, plant domestication in Mesoamerica was not so much an invention in one small area as a shift in ecological adaptation deliberately chosen by peoples living where economic strategies necessitated intensive exploitation of plant foods. It appears that the evidence from both Tehuacán and Guilá Naquitz bears out this hypothesis.

Andean Farmers

The story of plant domestication in Mexico shows how it was a deliberate shift in ecological adaptation. The same shift occurred in two areas of the Andean region: in the mountain highlands and along the low-lying, arid Pacific coast.

The great 18th-century German naturalist Alexander von Humboldt was the first European scientist to explore the high Andes. He marveled at the great variety of wild plants and animals that thrived in the harsh and varied landscape of high peaks and mountain valleys. Only a handful of these many species had been tamed by the farmers living in the foothills of the great mountains. Five important Andean species were of vital importance to highland economies: the llama, alpaca, and guinea pig, also the potato and a grain crop, quinoa. Llamas were perhaps domesticated alongside quinoa, perhaps as early as 2500 B.C. (Figure 6.12). Llama herding was widespread throughout the highlands and along the north coast of Peru by 900 B.C. Guinea pigs, an important wild food for many thousands of years, may have been domesticated in high mountain valleys at about the same time.

At the time of European contact in the 15th century A.D., Andean farmers used literally hundreds of potato varieties. Four major strains were domesticated in the highlands, of which one, *Solanum tuberosum,* is now grown all over the world. Wild potatoes were an important food for highland Andean foragers from the time of earliest settlement. Well-documented potato tubers come from midden sites dating to about 2000 B.C. at the mouth of the Casma Valley on the Peruvian coast, but earlier specimens will undoubtedly come to light in the south-central highlands, where other animal and plant species, including lima beans, were domesticated, between 3000 and 2000 B.C.

The Peruvian coast forms a narrow shelf at the foot of the Andes, an arid desert strip dissected by river valleys with deep, rich soils and plentiful water for some of the year. For thousands of years, coastal communities lived off the incredible bounty of the Pacific and gathered wild plants in summer. Fishing may have assumed greater importance after 5000 B.C., when the climate was warmer and drier than today. By this time the people were also cultivating some plant species like squash, peppers, and tuberous begonias.

At large, more or less permanent, coastal settlements like **Chilca** and **Paloma,** fish and mollusks were staples, but the inhabitants also ground up

Figure 6.12 Panaulauca Cave near Lake Jumin, Peru   Excavations here have
yielded evidence of early quinoa cultivation and llama domestication by 2500 B.C.

wild grass seeds into flour and grew squashes. By 3800 B.C., the Chilca people
were growing several types of beans, including the ubiquitous lima, and
squashes. They lived in circular matting and reed huts erected on frameworks
of canes or occasionally whale bones. The succeeding millennia saw many
permanent settlements established near the Pacific, the people combining agriculture with fishing and mollusk gathering. But fish and sea mammals were so
abundant that agriculture remained a secondary activity much later than it did
in Mesoamerica.

Within a remarkably short time, more-complex farming societies developed out of the simple village communities of earlier centuries. In some
regions, these developments led rapidly to the emergence of state-organized
societies, the world's first civilizations. In others, egalitarian farming cultures
became elaborate chiefdoms, in remarkably effective adaptations to challeng-
ing environments. Chapter 7 examines some of these remarkable societies and
the issue of greater cultural complexity in farming societies.

C H A P T E R 7

Chiefs and Chiefdoms

A.D. 1950 —

A.D. 1 —

15,000 B.P. —

50,000 B.P. —

100,000 B.P. —

500,000 B.P. —

1.0 Million —

2.5 Million —

Food production was the foundation of the world's earliest civilizations, but agriculture did not lead, invariably, to state-organized societies or cities. As we saw in Chapter 1, the archaeologists of a century ago often thought in linear, evolutionary terms, of an inevitable ladder of human progress from simple hunting and gathering to civilization. This linear approach, with its overtones of cultural superiority and racism, was intellectually bankrupt by 1910. Multilinear evolution, developed a half century later and a common model for studying the past, likens human cultural evolution to a complex tree with many branches leading cultures in many different environments in bewilderingly diverse ways. The branching model argues that no single society, however simple or complex, is superior to another. In other words, civilization, for all its variety, also social and technological complexity, is only one way of adapting to the world's many environments.

A generation ago, the anthropologist Elman Service made a fundamental distinction between prestate and state-organized societies, dividing the former into bands, tribes, and chiefdoms (see "Ancient Social Organization" box in Chapter 1, page 30). Ferocious academic debates about the nature of tribes and chiefdoms have erupted in recent years, many of them revolving around the relative complexity of chiefdoms both in the ancient and modern worlds. At issue here is not so much stages of social complexity, but the whole issue of complexity itself. This chapter describes several examples of emerging social complexity in the ancient world, which did not result in literate civilizations. The chiefdoms surveyed here, from the Pacific Islands and the American

D I S C O V E R Y

Frank Cushing and the Zuni

In 1879, a young anthropologist from the Smithsonian Institution named Frank Cushing arrived at Zuñi pueblo on a mule. A pall of wood smoke covered the town as the sun set behind the settlement. The mudbrick walls melted into the landscape. He wrote: "It seemed still a little island of mesas, one upon the other, reared from a sea of sand, in mock rivalry of the surrounding grander mesas of Nature's rearing." A pioneer of the anthropological method known as participant observation, Cushing lived among the Zuñi for four-and-a-half years, learning their language and recording their traditional life in great detail.

After three years, the Zuñi initiated him into the secret Priesthood of the Bow. Cushing now dressed in Indian clothing. He spent many hours sitting in kivas watching: "the blazes of the splinter-lit fire on the stone altar, sometimes licking the very ladder-poles in their flight upward toward the skyhole, which served at once as door-way, chimney, and window." He listened to: "the shrill calls of the rapidly coming and departing dancers, their wild songs, and the din of the great drum, which fairly jarred the ancient, smoke-blackened rafters" (quotations from Frank Cushing, *Zuni* [Lincoln, NE: University of Nebraska Press, 1979], pp. 48 and 112).

Frank Cushing enjoyed the confidence of the Zuñi, but unfortunately died before he could set down his account of their culture. Cushing's observations have been of priceless value to archaeologists, as they work back from the present into the remote Southwestern past.

Southwest and Southeast, represent a wide range of complexity, which resulted from diverse environmental and cultural circumstances.

Inevitably, multilinear cultural evolution has acquired somewhat of a step-like association. Some scholars choose to consider "evolution" a racist and pejorative creation of Western science, ignoring in the process the branch-like model, which allows for many forms of equally successful human society without recourse to ethnocentric or racist assumptions.

RECIPROCITY AND "BIG MEN"

As we saw in Chapter 2, precise definitions of chiefdoms, or of cultural complexity, are virtually impossible to formulate. There is no question, however, that all more-complex human societies depend heavily on ties of kin and reciprocity for their long-term viability. And all the world's more-intricate ancient societies, whether foragers or farmers, were based on permanent, or at least semipermanent, settlements.

While a considerable degree of cultural complexity arose in some hunter-gatherer societies, like, for example, those of the Chumash of southern California or the Pacific Northwest, the most profound changes in human society arose after the advent of farming. Perhaps the most profound changes in the new farming societies were social and political rather than economic. They stemmed in large part from the necessity for farmers to live in compact, permanent settlements, to adopt sedentary lifeways and maintain very close ties to their lands.

Early agricultural villages like Abu Hureyra or Merimda in western Asia, or permanent farming settlements in Mexico's Tehuacán valley, brought households into much closer juxtaposition than ever before. The members of a small forager band could always move away when factional disputes threatened to disrupt the band. Farmers, anchored to their land, did not have such a luxury. As a result, kinship ties, not only of immediate family, but of more distant kin, assumed much greater importance in daily life. Subsistence farming households produce their own food needs, but their survival depends both on cultivating a diversity of soil types and on reciprocal obligations with fellow kin. Reciprocity was vital to survival, for it created networks of obligation between near and more distant kin. These allowed people to ask for help when their crops failed, knowing that one day their kin would need help in turn, assistance given without question.

The ties of kinship, of membership in hereditary clans and lineages, with all their reciprocal obligations, provided not only institutions that allowed for the settlement of domestic disputes, but also mechanisms for the ownership and inheritance of farming and grazing land. The ownership of land was vested not in individual hands, but in a clan or lineage founded by a powerful ancestor. Thus, the relationship between people and their land was closely related to their links to their ancestors, who were the guardians of the soil. It is probably for this reason that early farmers in the Levant and Turkey maintained figurines or the plastered skulls of their forebears (Figure 7.1).

Trade and exchange played an important role in the development of more-complex societies. Everywhere the new farming economies developed, farmers relied increasingly on their neighbors. While late Ice Age hunter-gatherers traded fine-grained rock and exotic objects over long distances, the more sedentary agriculturalist was forced to obtain many more commodities from elsewhere. These include foodstuffs, game meat and hides, hut poles, obsidian, and other vital materials, to say nothing of ornaments and other rare objects from afar. Complicated exchange networks linked village with village, household with household, narrow trails that carried visitors from one community to the next, brought objects bartered from hand to hand over enormous distances. It was such networks that brought Gulf Coast seashells deep into the North American Midwest and obsidian from Turkey to the distant Jordan Valley. The individuals who controlled such exchange networks, or the supplies of key commodities and exotic luxuries, became natural leaders of newly complex village societies.

Everything points to the earliest farming villages having been egalitarian communities, for signs of social ranking do not appear in burials until long after food production took hold. In time, however, this egalitarian form of village life often gave way to new, more complex agricultural societies

Figure 7.1 Plastered Skull from Jericho A cache of such heads hints strongly at a family ancestor cult.

headed by powerful kin leaders. These were individuals, often shamans or people with extraordinary supernatural powers, linked to their followers by close kin ties and by their ability to reward loyalty with gifts of food and exotic commodities and goods obtained from afar. Anthropologist Marshall Sahlins, who has studied modern-day Pacific Island societies, calls such people Big Men. They are clever entrepreneurs, whose power is based strictly on their above-average abilities and the loyalty they command from their followers. This loyalty is but transitory, for it does not pass from one generation to the next. This makes for volatile, ever-changing political, economic, and social orders. In time, some Big Men acquired such power that they were able to create hereditary dynasties, which passed chiefly authority from one generation to the next.

Prestate societies of this greater complexity developed in almost every part of the prehistoric world, in late prehistoric Europe, in sub-Saharan Africa, Polynesia, and parts of North America. Everywhere chieftainships of this type evolved, they were exceptionally volatile, as the reins of political and economic power passed from one chiefly family to another, from one center to the next. None of these elaborate prestate societies was able to maintain tight political, economic, and social control over little more than a local area. It was state-organized societies that achieved such larger-scale integration, which often transcended local ecological zones. Some complex prestate societies, notably those in western Europe, eventually came under the sway of expanding civilizations like that of Rome. Others, like those of Africa, Polynesia, and North America, survived into historic times, until the arrival of European explorers during the Age of Discovery, which began in the 15th century A.D.

We cannot hope to describe all the more complex prestate farming societies that developed throughout the world, so we shall confine our discussion to the first settlement of the Pacific and to the emergence of chiefdoms in North America.

NAVIGATORS AND CHIEFS IN THE PACIFIC (2000 B.C. to modern times)

By the closing of the millennia of the Ice Age some 15,000 years ago, *Homo sapiens* had settled in most areas of the Old and New Worlds. Only two areas remained uncolonized by human beings. One was Antarctica, not even visited until the 18th century A.D., the other the remote islands of Melanesia and Polynesia in the Pacific (Figure 7.2). In Chapter 4, we saw how late Ice Age foragers voyaged across open straits to colonize Sahul and the Solomon Islands. Small groups of them had settled on the islands close to New Guinea, in the Bismarck Archipelago of the southwestern Pacific, by at least 32,000 years ago. Here colonization paused for many thousands of years. The successful settlement of islands even further offshore depended on the development of large offshore sailing craft and the ability to navigate far out of sight of land. It also hinged on the successful cultivation of root crops like taro and yam, also on small, portable animals like chickens and pigs that could be penned and transported in canoes. These conditions were met by 2000 B.C.

The first settlement of offshore Melanesia and Polynesia was closely connected to the cultivation of yams and taro, which enabled people to live on islands far from the mainland, land masses too isolated for animals or plants to migrate to. The maritime expansion to the more distant Melanesian islands took place after 2000 B.C. and covered 3100 miles (5000 km) of island chains and open ocean during a period of six centuries. The voyages took place in ocean-going double-hulled canoes capable of carrying heavy loads (Figure 7.3). They are associated with the so-called **Lapita culture,** named after a site on New Caledonia Island in the southwestern Pacific. The Lapita people originated in the Bismarck Archipelago region of western Melanesia some millennia earlier. Their canoes carried obsidian, foodstuffs, and other commodities from island to island over long distances. Lapita trade networks were part of a chain of such contacts that extended from Malaysia in the east to coastal New Guinea and offshore.

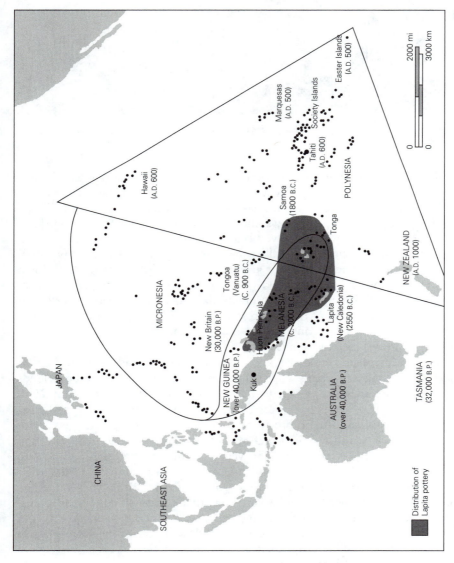

Figure 7.2 Human Settlement of the Pacific Islands

Figure 7.3 Double-Hulled Canoes Pass in Review off Tahiti, as Depicted by the 18th-Century Artist Sydney Parkinson

The rapid expansion to more remote islands occurred among people who lived in an island environment where short interisland passages were an integral part of daily life. But the journeys to off-lying islands like Fiji and Tonga involved much longer passages, some as many as 600 miles (c. 1000 km). Here, one-way journeys may have been rare and trade was at best sporadic. Navigation out of sight of land required expert skills. Canoe navigators became a respected and close-knit group, who passed their knowledge down from generation to generation by word of mouth. Young apprentices acquired their skills over many years of sailing under expert supervision. They learned the angles of rising and setting stars, the trends of ocean swells, the telltale and often inconspicuous phenomena that indicate the general direction and distance of islands.

From Melanesia, canoes voyaged from island to island through western Polynesia, taking the plants and domesticated animals of their homelands with them. Melanesians voyaged to Micronesia and Polynesia about 2000 years ago. After a lengthy period of adaptation in western Polynesia, small groups began to settle the more remote islands. The Marquesas were colonized by 200 B.C. and the Society Islands and Tahiti by A.D. 600. The first canoes arrived in Hawaii some 1350 years ago and on Easter Island by A.D. 500. New Zealand, the largest and among the most remote of all Pacific islands, has a temperate climate, not the tropical warmth of Polynesia. Despite this ecological difference, New Zealand was first settled by Polynesian ancestors of the **Maori** people, who voyaged southward, perhaps as early as A.D. 1000. New Zealand's temperate North Island made the cultivation of yams and other tropical island crops difficult, so the early settlers relied heavily on hunting, fishing, and foraging.

Technologically, Micronesia and Polynesia were still in the Stone Age. They relied heavily on stone axes and an elaborate array of bone and shellfish hooks. The crops people planted varied from island to island, but breadfruit, taro, coconut, yams, and bananas were the staples. By combining fish with simple agriculture, the islanders were able to accumulate significant food surpluses that were the basis of powerful chiefdoms. In Polynesia, as elsewhere in the world, agricultural surpluses generated on the larger islands were used as a form of wealth. This wealth, in turn, concentrated political power in the hands of a relatively few people. When European explorers visited Tahiti in the mid-18th century, they chanced on a center of a vigorous eastern Polynesian society (Figure 7.4). The islands were ruled by a powerful hierarchy of warlike chiefs and nobles, descendants of the canoe crews who had first settled the archipelago. The chiefs acquired prestige by controlling and redistributing wealth and food supplies just as they did in Europe, North America, and elsewhere in the prehistoric world. Their formidable religious and social powers led, inevitably, to intense competition, to warfare, and to ever more ambitious agricultural projects.

Tahitian society was riddled with factionalism and vicious infighting, as were the chiefdoms that developed far to the north, in the Hawaiian Islands, at about the same time. Polynesian chiefdoms were highly volatile and politically unstable. This volatility is well documented in New Zealand, where the introduction of the sweet potato in about A.D. 1400 made a dramatic difference to

Figure 7.4   A Tahitian *Marae*, Temple, as Drawn by 18th-Century Artist William Watson

local life. The population of North Island grew rapidly as agricultural surpluses created new wealth and greater social complexity. Soon, overcrowding on the best sweet potato lands led to intense competition between neighboring chieftains. When Europeans arrived in 1769, they found the Maori people living in fortified villages and engaged in constant warfare (Figure 7.5). Their military campaigns on land and sea were short and violent, often launched from elaborately carved war canoes up to 80 feet (24.3 km) in length. By this time, warfare was a key element in Maori society, to the extent that it was institutionalized and an important factor in maintaining cohesion and leadership.

The chiefdoms of Polynesia were fully as elaborate and hierarchical as those elsewhere in the ancient world. But they were still based on kin ties and on communal ownership of land. These were societies in which leadership, even when inherited, depended heavily on the personal qualities of leaders and on their ability to retain the loyalty of their followers. Their chieftains were not despotic monarchs, exercising supreme political, religious, and economic authority, but people who ruled because of their inborn abilities and because of their close ties to their people. As we shall see in the case of North America, some of these prestate societies achieved remarkable levels of elaboration, but they were very different from the tightly controlled, socially stratified states of Western Asia, China, or the Americas, described later in this book.

Figure 7.5   Maori *Pa*, a Fortified Village, as Drawn by 19th-Century Artist Augustus Earle

The transformation in Maori society that resulted from the introduction of the sweet potato can be mirrored by the history of maize in North America. Both in the Southwest and in the South and Southeast, the arrival of corn led to major changes in indigenous society; but these changes varied greatly from one region to the next. In each area, highly variable ecological factors and social realities led to the development of complex farming societies.

THE AMERICAN SOUTHWEST
(300 B.C. to modern times)

Chapter 6 describes how maize was domesticated from an indigenous grass called teosinte in southern Mexico before 3500 B.C. and was in common use a millennium later. Maize originated in Mexico and was widely grown by 2500 B.C. The new staple did not, however, spread northward across the Rio Grande into the North American Southwest until some centuries later.

Human occupation of the Southwest dates back to before 9000 B.C. For thousands of years, the descendants of these early southwesterners gathered many plant foods, including yucca seeds, cacti, and sunflower seeds, adapting skillfully to the harsh realities of desert living. They developed a remarkable expertise with all kinds of plant foods, which preadapted them for maize agriculture. Maize, beans, and squash agriculture came to the Southwest from northern Mexico, after generations of sporadic contacts between desert foragers and settled farmers. Knowledge of domesticated plants, even gifts of seeds or seedlings, passed from south to north.

Climatic data from tree rings tells us that between about 2500 and 100 B.C. the Southwestern climate was relatively stable, perhaps somewhat wetter than today (see "Dendrochronology" box). However, it was a semiarid environment where hunting and gathering were high-risk occupations, mainly because rainfall was always unpredictable. Domesticated plants like maize and beans might have low yields in these dry environments, but they had one major advantage: they were predictable food sources. Cultivators of the new crops could control their location and their availability at different seasons by storing them carefully. The people living in the southern deserts of the Southwest may have adopted maize and beans as supplementary foods not because they wanted to become farmers, but so they could become more effective foragers and maximize the potential of their environment.

Maize first entered the Southwest during a period of higher rainfall between 2000 and 1500 B.C. The new crop spread rapidly through the region, especially when combined with beans after 500 B.C. Beans helped return vital nitrogen to the soil, maintaining fertility for longer periods of time. Maize farming in the dry Southwest was never easy, for the farmers were working close to the limits of corn's range. They selected moisture-retaining soils very carefully, used north- and east-facing slopes that received little direct sun,

DENDROCHRONOLOGY (TREE-RING DATING)

Dendrochronology was the brainchild of University of Arizona astronomer A.E. Douglass in about 1913. He developed a tree-ring chronology for Southwestern pueblos, using roof beams, also ancient and modern trees like long-growing sequoias and bristle-cone pines. Everyone is familiar with tree rings, the concentric circles visible in the cross-section of a felled tree trunk. Each represents annual growth, and are especially marked in environments where there are seasonal weather changes, or alternating wet and dry seasons. The rings are formed of cambium, the growth layer formed by cells between the bark and the wood. Weather variations within a region tend to run in cycles of wet and dry years. These cycles are reflected in patterns of thicker and thinner rings, repeated from tree to tree within a limited area.

Tree-ring samples are taken with special core borers or by V-cutting large logs. Once in the laboratory, the sample is carefully leveled to a precise plane, then computer-matched with the master tree-ring chronology for the region.

Extremely accurate tree-ring chronologies for Southwestern pueblos allow not only the dating of entire sites, but even of individual rooms. Dendrochronology has also been applied to European oaks, with a sequence going back more than 10,000 years, and also to Aegean sites. Tree-ring chronologies are so accurate that they can be used to calibrate the radiocarbon ages from ^{14}C samples. The telltale cycles of tree rings are often valuable indicators of drought and wet periods, such as the drought that affected Anasazi settlement in the Southwest in about A.D. 1100.

planted near canyon mouths and diverted water from streams and springs. They did everything they could to minimize risk, dispersing their gardens to reduce the danger of local drought or flood.

The appearance of maize did not trigger a dramatic revolution in Southwestern life. The earlier corns were not very productive, but more bountiful local forms soon became a vital staple to many Southwestern groups who were now living in permanent hamlets and much smaller territories. They also led to more complex Southwestern societies that adjusted to changing climatic conditions with remarkable flexibility.

Hohokam, Mogollon, and Anasazi

By 300 B.C., many centuries of experimentation had produced much more productive domestic crops and a greater dependence on farming. The cultural changes of these centuries culminated in the great southwestern cultural traditions: Hohokam, Mogollon, and Anasazi.

Hohokam people occupied much of what is now lower Arizona. They were desert farmers, who grew not only maize and beans, but cotton, which flourishes in hot environments. Where they could, they practiced irrigation from flowing streams; otherwise they cultivated floodplains and caught runoff from local storms with dams, terraces, and other devices. For centuries, much Hohokam life and trading activity centered around **Snaketown,** a large settlement and ceremonial center near the Gila River (Figure 7.6). The inhabitants maintained trading relationships not only with other parts of the Southwest and with the Pacific coast to the west, but also with Mexico. The Hohokam obtained tropical bird feathers, copper artifacts, and other exotic objects from the South, but scholars are sharply divided on the amount of Mexican influence on Hohokam culture and religious beliefs. The Hohokam vanished after A.D. 1500, its cultural heirs the Papago and Pima Indians of today.

Mogollon was a more highland cultural tradition, which flourished mainly in what is now New Mexico from about 300 B.C. to between A.D. 850 and 1150. Mogollon farmers relied on direct rainfall and used little irrigation, living in small villages of pit dwellings with timber frames and mat or brush roofs. In only a few areas did more elaborate settlements develop, but by this time Mogollon was becoming part of the western pueblo Anasazi tradition.

Figure 7.6 THE HOHOKAM SETTLEMENT AT SNAKETOWN, ARIZONA, DURING 1965 EXCAVATIONS, SHOWING KIVAS AND DWELLINGS

Anasazi developed out of indigenous forager roots and was centered on the Four Corners area, where Utah, Arizona, Colorado, and New Mexico meet. Anasazi people made heavy use of wild plant foods, even after they took up serious maize farming after A.D. 400. Most of their farming depended on seasonal rainfall, although they used irrigation where practicable.

At first the Anasazi lived in small pithouse villages, but after A.D. 900 much of the population congregated in above-ground settlements of adjoining rooms. These became the famous pueblos, often clustered in small arcs to make them equidistant from the subterranean ceremonial rooms, the **kivas,** in the middle of the settlement. The largest and most spectacular pueblos were located in densely populated areas like Chaco Canyon in New Mexico and Mesa Verde in Arizona. It was in areas like these that Pueblo society sometimes achieved a higher degree of complexity, with larger, densely populated towns that controlled large exchange networks.

Chaco Canyon, with its dramatic cliffs was the center of a remarkable flowering of Anasazi culture that lasted for two centuries after A.D. 900. During this time, the **Chaco phenomenon,** as it is called, expanded from its canyon homeland to encompass an area of 25,000 square miles of the San Juan Basin and adjacent uplands. The people constructed large, well-planned towns, extensive road and water control systems, and outlying sites linked to the canyon by ceremonial roadways and visual communication systems. The "great houses," large pueblos of Chaco Canyon contained many luxury items, including turquoise from near Santa Fe, seashells, copper bells, even the skeletons of macaws, colorful birds from the lowland rainforests of Mesoamerica much prized for their bright feathers (Figure 7.7).

When Chaco was in its heyday between A.D. 1075 and 1115, the canyon was not only a focus for turquoise ornament manufacture, but an important ceremonial center for dozens of outlying settlements. Chaco flourished during a period of uncertain rainfall, and the local farming land could never have supported more than about 2000 people, although population estimates for the pueblos rise as high as 5600. Thus, archaeologists argue, Chaco may have had a relatively small permanent population and been a place where much food was stored and where large crowds of Anasazi congregated for major ceremonial observances.

What, then, was Chaco? Was it a highly centralized chieftainship, controlled by a small, but powerful elite of chiefs and nobles, who had a monopoly over trade and important spiritual powers? Or was it what archaeologist Gwinn Vivian calls an egalitarian enterprise, a cooperative mechanism developed by dozens of communities living in a harsh and unpredictable environment? We do not know, but elaborately decorated burials were discovered in Chaco by early archaeologists. The Anasazi lived in a society where kin ties were all important, where everyone had complex obligations to fulfill both to his own community and to the clan. Without such obligations, it would have been impossible to carry large quantities of

Figure 7.7   Pueblo Bonito, a Chaco Canyon "Great House," Dated to Between A.D. 850 and 1130   The round structures are kivas.

food to Chaco's storerooms, or to transport the more than 200,000 wooden beams needed to build its large pueblos and kivas. Perhaps the Chaco phenomenon was an adaptive mechanism whereby local kin leaders regulated and maintained long-distance exchange networks and ceremonial life as a means of supporting far more people than the environment would normally carry. They used economic, social, and ritual ties among a scattered rural population to encourage cooperation between isolated communities in times of need.

The Chaco phenomenon reached its peak between A.D. 1100 and 1130, when a prolonged drought and environmental degradation caused the system to collapse. The Anasazi moved away into more dispersed settlements, maintained alliances with one another, or flourished in scattered, independent pueblos. Perhaps the most famous of all Anasazi cultural developments is that centered on the **Mesa Verde** canyon system in the northern San Juan Basin. By 1100, as many as 30,000 people lived in the nearby Montezuma valley, mainly concentrated in villages of 1000 people or more. Only about 2500 of them lived in Mesa Verde. Between A.D. 1200 and 1300, people moved from open locations into crowded pueblos. **Cliff Palace,** which was the largest settlement, had 220 rooms and 23 kivas.

Both in Mesa Verde itself and in the surrounding countryside, large villages, almost towns, were homes for between 1000 and 2500 people, living in room clusters associated with kivas and other ceremonial buildings. Everywhere in Mesa Verde, the emphasis was on individual communities. Judging from the numerous kivas, there was considerable cooperative and ritual activity, and there were numerous occasions when inhabitants of different communities organized large labor parties to carry out sophisticated water control works and other communal projects. This Anasazi tradition was quite similar to Chaco Canyon, with its intricate mechanisms for integrating dispersed communities, or the chiefdoms of the South and Southeast with their large centers and satellite villages.

The 12th and 13th centuries saw the culmination of four centuries of rapid social and political development in the Mesa Verde region. About 1300, however, the entire San Juan drainage, including Mesa Verde, was abandoned by Pueblan peoples. They moved in scattered groups south and southeastward into the lands of the historic Hopi, Zuñi, and Rio Grande pueblos, where their ultimate descendants live to this day. Following the abandonment of large areas of the Southwest in the late 13th and early 14th centuries, large settlements formed in previously sparsely inhabited areas. Some of these pueblos are recognized as those of direct ancestors of modern communities.

Southwestern pueblo society never achieved the cultural complexity found in eastern North America or among the Hawaiians or Tahitians, but it achieved the limits of regional integration possible for a region where rainfall was irregular and the climate harsh. Perhaps the best way to describe much Southwestern organization is as a theocracy, a government that regulated religious and secular affairs through both individuals, like chiefs, and kin groups or associations (societies) that cut across kin lines. The basic social and economic unit was the extended family, but for hundreds of years Southwestern peoples fostered a sense of community and undertook communal labors like irrigation works using wider social institutions that worked for the common good.

MOUNDBUILDERS IN EASTERN NORTH AMERICA (2000 B.C. to A.D. 1650)

No one knows exactly when maize spread across the southern Plains into the eastern Woodlands of North America, but at least sporadic corn cultivation may have diffused to the Mississippi River and beyond in the early first millennium A.D. Like all ancient native Americans, eastern groups had developed a great expertise with native plants of every kind soon after first settlement before 9500 B.C. The densest populations gathered by lakes and estuaries, and in the fertile river valleys of the Midwest and Southeast. By 2000 B.C., local river valley populations in some areas had increased to the point that group mobility was restricted, and there were periodic food shortages. Under these circumstances, it was almost inevitable that some groups turned to the deliberate cultivation of native food plants like goosefoot and marsh elder to sup-

plement wild cereal grass yields. At the same time, the first signs of social
ranking appear in local burials. We find, also, an increasing preoccupation
with burial and life after death. For the first time, individual communities and
groups maintained cemeteries on the edges of their territories, which may
have served to validate territorial boundaries. As the centuries passed, the
funeral rites associated with death and the passage from the world of the living to that of the ancestors became ever more elaborate and important. This
elaboration was associated not only with increasing social complexity and an
explosion in long-distance exchange, but with the building of ceremonial
earthworks as well.

Adena and Hopewell

Thousands of years of long-distance exchange between neighboring communities had given certain raw materials and exotic artifacts high prestige value
in eastern North American society. Such imports were scarce and hard to
come by, important gifts exchanged between kin leaders and chiefs. They
assumed great social value and significance in societies that placed a high premium on prestige. Hammered copper artifacts, conch shells from the Atlantic
and Gulf coasts, certain types of stone axes—these became status symbols,
buried with their powerful owners at death. By 500 B.C., the individuals who
controlled these exchange networks were influential not only in life, but in
death, for they were buried under large burial mounds.

The **Adena culture,** which flourished in the Ohio Valley between 500 B.C.
and about A.D. 400, was one of the first to build extensive earthworks. Adena
earthworks follow the contours of flat-topped hills and form circles, squares,
and other shapes, enclosing areas as much as 350 feet (107 m) across. These
were ceremonial enclosures rather than defensive works, sometimes built to
surround burial mounds, other times standing alone. Adena burial mounds
were usually communal rather than individual graves. The most important
people were buried in log-lined tombs, their corpses smeared with red ocher
or graphite. Nearby lie soapstone pipes and tablets engraved with curving
designs or birds of prey. Some prestigious kin leaders were buried inside
enclosures or death huts that were burned down as part of the funeral ceremony. Occasionally the burial chamber was left open so that other bodies
could be added later.

The building of these mounds was invariably a communal effort, probably
involving fellow kin from several settlements who piled up basketfuls of earth.
The earthworks grew slowly as generations of new bodies were added. Apparently, only the most important people were interred in the mounds. Most
Adena folk were cremated and their ashes placed in the communal burial
place.

Between 200 B.C. AND A.D. 400, the **Hopewell tradition,** an elaboration of
Adena with a distinctive religious ideology, appeared in Ohio. Hopewell cults
were such a success that they spread rapidly from their heartland as far afield

as upper Wisconsin and Louisiana and deep into Illinois and New York State. The Midwest experienced a dramatic flowering of artistic traditions and of long-distance trade that brought copper from the Great Lakes region, obsidian from Yellowstone, and mica from southern Appalachia. The Hopewell people themselves dwelt in relatively small settlements and used only the simplest of artifacts in daily life. They wore leather and woven clothes of pliable fabrics. All the wealth and creative skill of society was lavished on a relatively few individuals and their life after death.

At first glance, Hopewell exotic artifacts and ritual traditions seem completely alien to the simple indigenous culture of the area, but they are deeply rooted in local life. The cult objects buried with the dead tell us something of the rank and social roles of their owners. Some of the exotic grave goods, such as pipe bowls or ceremonial axes, were buried as gifts from living clan members to a dead leader. Others were personal possessions, cherished weapons, or sometimes symbols of status or wealth. Hopewell graves contain soapstone pipe bowls in the form of beavers, frogs, birds, bears, and even humans. Skilled artisans fashioned thin copper and mica sheets into head and breast ornaments that bear elaborate animal and human motifs (Figure 7.8). There were copper axes and arrowheads, trinkets and beads fashioned from native copper nuggets, not smelted.

Most of these artifacts were manufactured by a few specialists, perhaps produced in workshops within large earthwork complexes, themselves close to major sources of raw materials. Ceremonial objects of all kinds were traded from hand to hand throughout Hopewell territory along the same trade routes that carried foodstuffs and everyday objects from hamlet to hamlet. However, the prized manufactures may have passed from one person to another in a vast network of gift-giving transactions that linked different kin leaders with lasting, important obligations to one another. The closest, but very far-fetched, modern analogy to such an arrangement is the famous *kula* ring exchange system of the Trobriand Islands of the southwestern

Figure 7.8   Hopewell Sheet-Mica Ornament in the Form of a Claw of a Bird of Prey

Figure 7.9 CIRCULAR HOPEWELL MOUNDS AT MOUND CITY NATIONAL MONUMENT, OHIO Each covers a charnel house where cremated dead were deposited.

Pacific. There, distinctive types of shell ornaments pass in perennial circles among individuals, linking them in lasting ritual and trading partnerships, in ties of reciprocal obligation. This kind of environment encourages individual initiative and competition, as kin leaders and their followers vie with one another for prestige and social status that is as transitory as life itself. Perhaps somewhat similar practices were commonplace in Hopewell times. Once dead and buried with their prized possessions, the deceased were no longer political players, for their mantles did not necessarily pass to their children or relatives.

Hopewell burial mounds are much more elaborate than their Adena forebears (Figure 7.9). Some Hopewell mounds rise 40 feet (12 m) high and are more than 100 feet (30.5 m) across. Often, the builders would deposit a large number of bodies on an earthen platform, burying them over a period of years before erecting a large mound over the dead. Hopewell burial complexes reached imposing sizes. The 24 burial mounds at Mound City, Ohio, lie inside an earthen enclosure covering 13 acres (5.26 ha).

The Mississippian Tradition

The center of religious and political power shifted southward after A.D. 400, as the Hopewell tradition declined. It was then that the people of the densely populated and lush Mississippi flood plain may have realized the great potential of maize as a high-yielding food staple. Much of the local diet always came from game, fish, nuts, and wild or cultivated native plants, but maize added a new, and valuable, supplement to the diet; it was demanding to grow, but eventually maize became a vital staple, especially when combined with beans in the late first millennium A.D. Beans had the advantage of a high protein value but also the asset of compensating for the nutritional deficiencies of corn. The new crops assumed greater importance as rising populations, and, perhaps, the insatiable demands of a small but powerful elite, were causing considerable economic and social stress.

Maize and beans may have been planted initially as supplementary foods, but they differ from native plants such as goosefoot in that they demand more start-up labor to clear land. Within a short time, the river valley landscape was transformed in such a way that hunting and fishing provided less food for energy expended than farming. Major social and political changes and an entirely new economic pattern followed, changing eastern North American society beyond recognition. Thus was born the **Mississippian tradition,** the most elaborate prehistoric cultural tradition to flourish in North America.

Regional Mississippian societies developed in river valleys over much of the Midwest and Southeast and interacted with one another for centuries. Many Mississippian populations lived in fertile river valleys with lakes and swamps. They lived by hunting, fishing, and exploiting migrating waterfowl. Every family harvested nuts and grew maize, beans, squashes, and other crops. The cultivation of native plants like goosefoot and marsh elder, as well as sunflowers—to mention only a few species—was of vital importance. Theirs was a complex adaptation to highly varied local environments. Some groups flourished in small, dispersed homesteads, while others lived in compact villages, some so large they might be called small towns; thousands of people lived near locations like **Cahokia,** on the banks of the Mississippi opposite the modern city of St. Louis.

Cahokia flourished on the so-called American Bottom, an extremely bountiful flood plain area with a great diversity of food resources and fertile soils. The greatest of all Mississippian centers, Cahokia presided over a population of several thousand people in its heyday after A.D. 1000. The great mounds and plazas of its ceremonial precincts dominated the countryside for miles. Monk's Mound at the center of Cahokia rises 102 feet (31 m) above the Mississippi floodplain and covers 16 acres (6.5 ha) (Figure 7.10). On the summit stood a thatched temple at the east end of an enormous plaza. Around the plaza rose other mounds, temples, warehouses, administrative buildings, and the homes of the elite. The entire ceremonial complex of mounds and plazas covered more than 200 acres (c. 80 ha) and depicted the ancient cosmos of the eastern Woodlands, divided into four opposing segments and oriented toward the cardinal points.

Why did Cahokia achieve such political and religious importance? The great center lay at a strategic point close to the Mississippi River and near its

Figure 7.10 A Reconstruction of the Central Precincts of Cahokia in its Heyday, c. a.d. 1100

confluence with the Missouri, in a region where northern and southern trade routes met. The ruling families of Cahokia achieved enormous political and spiritual power within a few generations, perhaps by virtue of their supernatural abilities as mediators between the spiritual and living worlds, between those on earth and the ancestors. At the same time, they must have been adept traders, with economic and political connections over a wide area. Their political power was sufficient to command the loyalty and labor of satellite settlements and religious centers throughout the American Bottom, to the point that elite families may have lived in subordinate centers, where they presided over critical rituals such as the annual Green Corn festival, which celebrated the new harvest. Sacred figurines and distinctive clay vessels bear motifs that are familiar in later native American religious belief and have deep roots in more ancient cultures.

Cahokia was the most elaborate of all Mississippian chiefdoms, its core territory minuscule by, say, ancient Egyptian standards. Politically volatile, based on ancient religious beliefs, its power and prosperity depended heavily on the authority, charisma, and ability of a handful of rulers. The great center was destined, inevitably, for collapse, which came in about a.d. 1250, when other polities to the south and east rose to a prominence that never rivaled that of the Mississippian's greatest chiefdom.

Cahokia was in the north of Mississippian lands. A major center now developed to the south, at **Moundville** in Alabama. Dozens of small centers and towns sprang up between the two. More than just sacred places for annual planting and harvest ceremonies, all Mississippian centers were markets and focal points of powerful chiefdoms. For example, Cahokia owed some of its importance to the manufacture and trading of local salt, and chert, a fine-grained rock used to make hoes and other tools.

We know little about how Mississippian society functioned, but each major population center was probably ruled as a series of powerful chiefdoms by an elite group of priests and rulers who lived somewhat separated from the rest of the population. Unlike their recent predecessors, these individuals may have inherited political and economic power, also social position, as the offices of the elite were passed from one generation to the next. The chieftains controlled long-distance trade and were the intermediaries between the living, the ancestors, and the gods.

As in the Hopewell culture, high-ranking individuals went to the next world in richly decorated graves, with clusters of ritual objects of different styles that symbolized various clans and tribes. Excavations at burial mound 72 revealed at least 6 different burial events that involved 261 people, including 4 mutilated men and 118 women, who were probably retainers sacrificed to accompany a chief in the afterlife. One such chief lay on a layer of thousands of shell beads, accompanied by grave offerings from as far afield as Wisconsin and Tennessee. Cahokia and most other larger Mississippian communities had more or less standardized layouts. The inhabitants built platformlike mounds and capped them with temples and the houses of important individuals. These mounds were grouped around an open plaza, while most people lived in thatched dwellings clustered nearby. As we shall see in Chapter 11, somewhat similar architectural groupings are typical of Mesoamerican ceremonial centers and cities, tempting many earlier scholars to claim that Mississippian chiefs were under strong cultural influence from Mexico, claims now discounted.

Mississippian graves and mound centers contain finely made pottery and other artifacts that bear elaborate designs and distinctive artistic motifs. These artifacts include stone axes with handle and head carved from a single piece of stone, copper pendants adorned with circles and weeping eyes, shell disks carved with woodpeckers and rattlesnakes, elaborately decorated clay pots, and engraved shell cups adorned with male figures in ceremonial dress (Figure 7.11). The themes and motifs on these objects have many common features throughout the South and Southeast and as far afield as the borders of the Ohio valley. At first, experts thought that these ceremonial artifacts represented a **Southern Cult,** that its ideology and motifs like a weeping eye had arrived in North America in the hands of Mexican artisans and priests. But a closer look at indigenous art traditions show that such motifs were commonly used by many North American groups. Many Mississippian ceremonial artifacts served as badges of rank and status, and as clan symbols. They were traded from hand to hand over long distances as symbolic gifts between widely separated chieftains who shared many common religious beliefs.

The Mississippian was an entirely indigenous cultural tradition, the climax of millennia of steady cultural evolution in eastern North America with some significant Mesoamerican influences. Cahokia, Moundville, and other great Mississippian centers were past the height of their powers by the time European explorers reached the Mississippi valley in the 16th century. But numerous chiefdoms still flourished in the mid-South and Southeast right up

Figure 7.11   A MISSISSIPPIAN SHAMAN CAVORTS ON A SHELL GORGET   He carries a death's head in one hand and a ceremonial mace in the other. Diameter: 4 inches (10 cm).

to the time of European contact and beyond. It is interesting to speculate what trajectory the successors of Mississippian society would have taken if Europeans had not arrived. Would they have evolved into a full-fledged, state-organized society, to rival that of the Maya and Aztec to the south? Experts believe they would not have, simply because the growing seasons for maize and beans in North America are too short and the climate too harsh to support either speculated agriculture or high urban population densities under preindustrial conditions. It would have been difficult for any chieftain to accumulate the food surpluses necessary to maintain authority over more than a relatively limited area. In sum, the most important cultural consequences of food production were a long-term trend toward greater political elaboration, a degree of social ranking, and greater interdependency in a wide range of village farming societies.

The trends toward complexity that developed in eastern North America and the Pacific also unfolded in temperate Europe and in sub-Saharan Africa (Chapter 10). In Europe, the most able of village kin leaders eventually became warrior chieftains and even hereditary leaders ruling from small towns. One catalyst for such development was an explosion in long-distance exchange that coincided with the widespread use of bronze, and later iron—metallurgy that linked even isolated communities together in larger economic, and later political, units. Roman general Julius Caesar's legions found the Iron Age people of western Europe a tough enemy to conquer. Centuries later, the descendants of these people were to shatter Rome's reputation as an invincible power. However, the most momentous consequences of food production were those that led to the emergence of the state-organized society, the urban civilizations that developed in many parts of the world after 3000 B.C., described in Part 4.

P A R T

4

EARLY CIVILIZATIONS

When Enlil, lord of all the lands, had given the kingship of the Land to Lugalzagezi, had directed to him the eyes [of all the people] of the Land from east to west, had prostrated [all the people] for him . . . from the lower sea, along the Tigris [and] Euphrates to the upper sea . . . from east to west, Enlil gave him no rival . . . the Land rejoiced under his rule; all chieftains of Sumer [and lords] of foreign lands bowed down before him. . . .

SUMERIAN VASE COMMEMORATING KING LUGALZAGEZI OF MESOPOTAMIA'S RULE OVER THE ANCIENT WORLD. SAMUEL KRAMER, *THE SUMERIANS* (CHICAGO: UNIVERSITY OF CHICAGO PRESS, 1963, P. 323).

CHAPTER 8

State-Organized Societies

About 3100 B.C., the first state-organized societies appeared in Egypt and Mesopotamia, ushering in a new chapter in human history (Figure 8.1). The development of the world's first states was a complex process that took many centuries. This chapter defines a state-organized society and discusses some of the factors that contributed to the development of early civilization. We also examine some of the theories surrounding their origins.

WHAT IS A STATE-ORGANIZED SOCIETY?

Everyone who has studied the prehistory of human society agrees that the emergence of civilization in different parts of the world was a major event in human adaptation. The word civilization has a ready, everyday meaning. It implies "civility," a measure of decency in the behavior of the individual in a civilization. Such definitions inevitably reflect ethnocentrism or value judgments because what is "civilized" behavior in one civilization might be antisocial or baffling in another. These simplistic understandings are of no use to students of early civilizations seeking basic definitions and cultural processes.

Today, archaeologists use the term *civilization* as a shorthand for urbanized, state-level societies. Those described in these pages are sometimes called "preindustrial civilizations," because they relied on manual labor rather than on fossil fuels such as coal. There are many variations between the preindustrial civilizations, but the following features are characteristic of all of them:

- Societies based on cities, with large, very complex social organizations. The preindustrial civilization was invariably based on a larger territory, such as the Nile Valley, as opposed to smaller areas owned by individual kin groups.
- Economies based on the centralized accumulation of capital and social status through tribute and taxation. For instance, Sumerian kings in Mesopotamia monopolized trading activity in the name of the state. This type of economy allows the support of hundreds, often thousands,

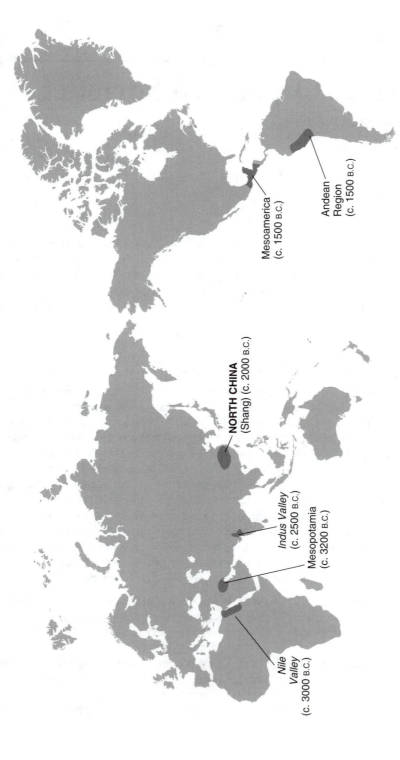

Figure 8.1 AREAS OF EARLY STATE FORMATION

Mesoamerica (c. 1500 B.C.)

Andean Region (c. 1500 B.C.)

NORTH CHINA (Shang) (c. 2000 B.C.)

Indus Valley (c. 2500 B.C.)

Mesopotamia (c. 3200 B.C.)

Nile Valley (c. 3000 B.C.)

of nonfood producers such as smiths and priests. Long-distance trade and the division of labor, as well as craft specialization, are often characteristic of early civilizations.

- Advances toward formal record keeping, science, and mathematics, and some form of written script. This took many forms, from Egyptian hieroglyphs to the knotted strings used by the Inca of the Andes.
- Impressive public buildings and monumental architecture, like Egyptian temples and Maya ceremonial centers.
- Some form of all-embracing, state religion, in which the ruler plays a leading role. For example, the Egyptian pharaoh was considered a living god on earth.

CITIES

Archaeological research into early civilization concentrates on the origin and development of the city. Today the city is the primary human settlement type throughout the world, and it has become so since the industrial revolution altered the economic face of the globe. The earliest cities assumed many forms, from the compact, walled settlement of Mesopotamia to the **Mesoamerican** ceremonial center, with a core population in its precincts and a scattered rural population in villages arranged over the surrounding landscape. The palaces of the Minoans and Mycenaeans of Crete and mainland Greece functioned as secular economic and trading centers for scattered village populations nearby.

A city can be defined by its population, which is generally larger and denser than that of a town or village. A generally used rule of thumb is a lower limit of 5000 people for a city. However, numbers are not a sufficient definition. Economic and organizational complexity as well as population size and density distinguish the city from other settlement types:

- A city is a large and relatively dense settlement, with a population numbered in at least the thousands. Small cities of the ancient world had 2000 or 3000 inhabitants; the largest, such as Rome or Changan in China, may have had over a million.
- Cities are also characterized by specialization and interdependence, between the city and its rural hinterland, and between specialist craftspeople and other groups within the city. The city is a central place in its region, providing services for the villages of the surrounding area, at the same time depending on those villages for food. Most cities, for example, had a marketplace where agricultural produce could be exchanged.
- Cities also have a degree of organizational complexity well beyond that of small farming communities. There are centralized institutions to regulate internal affairs and ensure security. These usually find expression in monumental architecture such as temples or palaces, or sometimes a city wall. Here we must recognize an overlap between the concept of the

CHRONOLOGICAL TABLE C

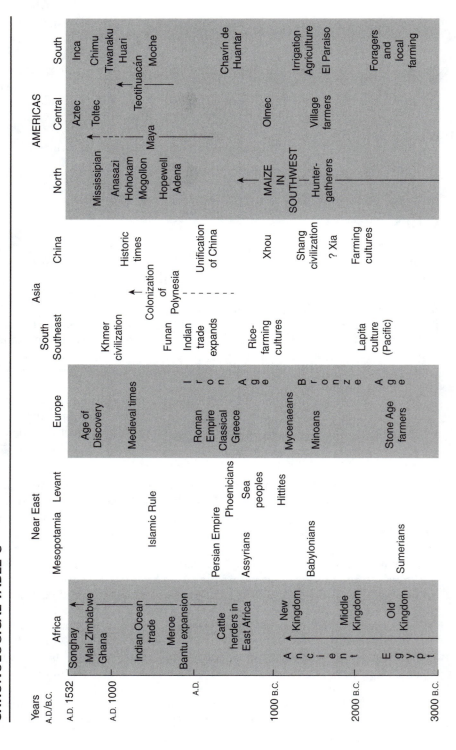

city and the concept of the state. States, too, are characterized by centralized institutions. It may be possible to have states without cities; but it is hard to envisage a city that was not embedded within a state.

An ancient city site will usually be obvious to archaeologists, from both its size and the scale of its remains. The state is more difficult to define. It is a political unit governed by a central authority whose power cross-cuts bonds of kinship. Kin groups do not disappear, of course, but their power is reduced, and a new axis of control emerges based on allegiance to a ruling elite.

THEORIES OF THE ORIGINS OF STATES

Few developments in world prehistory have generated as much theoretical debate as the origins of states. Modern hypotheses build on theories developed as early as the 1930s.

The "Urban Revolution"

The Victorians, like the Greeks and Romans before them, assumed that civilization had originated along the Nile, in the "Land of the Pharaohs." Eventually, early theorizing used a broader canvas, embracing all of the Fertile Crescent.

The first relatively sophisticated theories about the origins of civilization were formulated by Vere Gordon Childe of "Neolithic Revolution" fame. He wrote of a later "Urban Revolution," which saw the development of metallurgy and the appearance of a new social class of full time artisans and specialists, who lived in much larger settlements: cities. However, the artisans' products had to be distributed, and raw materials obtained, often from long distances away. Both needs reduced the self-sufficiency of peasant communities, Childe argued. Agricultural techniques became more sophisticated as a higher yield of food per capita was needed to support a growing nonagricultural population. Irrigation increased productivity, leading to centralization of food supplies, production, and distribution. Taxation and tribute led to the accumulation of capital. Ultimately, said Childe, a new class-stratified society came into being, based on economic classes rather than traditional ties of kin. Writing was essential for keeping records and for developing exact and predictive sciences. Transportation by land and water was part of the new order. A unifying religious force dominated urban life as priest kings and despots rose to power. Monumental architecture testified to their activities.

Gordon Childe considered technology and the development of craft specialization in the hands of full-time artisans a cornerstone of the Urban Revolution.

Early Ecological Models

With much more data to work with, modern scholars now agree that three elements of Gordon Childe's "Urban Revolution" were of great importance in the development of all the world's early civilizations: large food surpluses, diversified farming economies, and irrigation agriculture.

The Fertile Crescent model assumed that the exceptional fertility of the Mesopotamian flood plain and the Nile Valley was the primary cause for the appearance of cities and states in these regions. Larger grain surpluses resulted from increased agricultural efficiency, as well as social and cultural changes. Some scholars, among them the economist Esther Boserup, took the opposite tack. They believed that population growth, not food surplus, was the incentive for intensified agriculture and eventually more-complex societies. But, though important, dense populations did not characterize all state-organized societies, as the Mycenaean or Inca civilizations show.

The same theorists pointed out how the ecological diversity of local environments varied greatly from one area to another. Diversified agricultural economies tended to focus on fewer, more productive crops, but the ultimate subsistence base remained wide. For instance, the Egyptians farmed wheat and barley on a large scale, but also raised large herds of cattle and goats. The highland Andean states relied heavily on their lowland neighbors for fish meal, cotton, and other resources. The resulting diversity of food resources protected the people against famine and stimulated trade and exchange for food and other products as well as the growth of distributive organizations that encouraged centralized authority.

The adoption of irrigation agriculture was also considered a major factor in the rise of civilization, as it supported far higher population densities. Early ecological theories were closely tied to the apparent widespread use of irrigation agriculture by early states to enhance agricultural output. Anthropologist Julian Steward and historian Karl Wittfogel argued during the 1950s that irrigation lay behind the development of socially stratified societies in Egypt, Mesopotamia, and elsewhere, which Wittfogel famously called "hydraulic civilizations." In areas where irrigation was practiced, both scholars argued, the relationship between the environment, food production, and social institutions was identical. Wittfogel was a China specialist, who argued that early Asian civilizations became "mighty hydraulic bureaucracies," which owed their despotic control over densely populated areas like China, Egypt, and India to the technological and environmental demands required by large-scale water control projects in areas of scant rainfall. Thus, the social requirements of irrigation led to the development of states and urban societies in several parts of the Old World. And the same requirements led to remarkable similarities in their economic and social structure.

A mass of new data, including large-scale landscape surveys, has sharpened our perceptions of early irrigation. For example, archaeologist Robert Adams carried out major field surveys of ancient irrigation works in Mesopotamia in the 1960s. Adams found that early Mesopotamian irrigation consisted of cleaning natural river channels and building just a few smaller feeder canals. Most settlements lay near major rivers and made the most of the natural hydrology of the waterways. Each community controlled its own small-scale irrigation works. Only centuries later did a highly centralized state government organize irrigation schemes on a massive scale. The same was true of Egypt, where the greatest irrigation works were undertaken during the New Kingdom, using thousands of laborers fulfilling tax obligations to the state. In contrast, early Egyptian agriculture relied on natural basins to hold back Nile water: a village-level, small-scale operation requiring no official supervision.

While some form of irrigation was a necessary precondition for the settlement of the southern Mesopotamian plains, where the world's first cities arose, large-scale irrigation does not everywhere appear to have been a factor in the rise of early civilization. By the same token, modern researchers have shown that ecology was only one component in a mosaic of many changes that led to state-organized societies.

Technology and Trade

The origins and evolution of complex societies have long been linked to technological innovation and to growing trade in raw materials like obsidian, copper, and luxuries of all kinds. Gordon Childe considered metallurgy an important component in the Urban Revolution, but, in fact, copper and other exotic materials were at first used in southwest Asia for small-scale production of cult objects and jewelry. In many cases the technological innovations that did appear, like the wheel in Mesopotamia and the sailing ship in Egypt, were of more benefit in transportation than production. Not until several centuries after civilization started were copper and bronze more abundant, as demands for transportation and military needs burgeoned. Technology did evolve, but only in response to developing markets, new demands, and the expanded needs of a tiny segment of the population—the elite.

Any form of trade involves two elements, both the goods and commodities being exchanged and the people doing the exchanging. People make trade connections when they need to acquire goods and services that are not available to them within their local area. This trade (more conventionally called "exchange") can be gift-giving, the exchange of gifts that reinforce a social relationship between both individuals and groups as a whole. The gifts serve as gestures that place obligations on both parties and are often a preliminary to bartering for all manner of commodities. This kind of preliminary gift exchange is commonplace in New Guinea and the Pacific and was widespread in Africa during the past 2000 years. Bartering, the exchange of commodities or goods, was another basic trading mechanism for many thousands of years, often sporadic, and usually based on notions of reciprocity, the mutual exchange of commodities or objects between individuals or groups. Redistribution of these goods through society lay in the hands of chiefs, religious leaders, or kin groups. As we have seen, such redistribution was a basic element in chiefdoms. The change from redistribution to impersonal market economy trade, often based on regulated commerce, involving, perhaps, fixed prices, even currency, was a change closely tied to growing political and social complexity, and hence, to the development of the state.

In the 1970s, a number of archaeologists gave trade a primary role in the rise of states. In the Aegean area, British archaeologist Colin Renfrew attributed the dramatic flowering of Minoan civilization on Crete and through the Aegean to intensified trading contacts and to the impact of olive and vine cultivation on local communities. As agricultural economies became more diversified and local food supplies could be purchased both locally and over longer distances, a far-reaching economic interdependence resulted. Eventually, this led to redistribution systems for luxuries and basic commodities, systems that were organized and controlled by Minoan palaces and elsewhere in the Aegean where there were major centers of olive production.

Now that we know much more about ancient exchange and commerce, we know that trade can never be looked upon as a unifying factor or as a primary cause of ancient civilization, simply because no one aspect of it was an overriding cause of cultural change or evolution in trading practices. Extensive long-distance trade, like large-scale irrigation, was a consequence rather than a cause of civilization.

Warfare

In the 1970s, anthropologist Robert Carneiro used the archaeology of coastal valleys in Peru to argue that warfare played a key role in state formation. His "coercive theory" of state origins argued that the amount of agricultural land in these valleys was limited and surrounded by desert. So a series of predictable events led to the development of states. At first, autonomous farming villages flourished in the valley landscape. But as the population grew and more land was taken up, the communities started fighting over land and raided each others' fields as they competed for limited acreage. Some of the village leaders emerged as successful warlords, became chieftains, and presided over large tribal polities. The valley population continued to grow, and warfare intensified until the entire region fell under the sway of a single, successful warrior, who presided over a single state centered on the valley. Then this ambitious ruler and his successors start raiding neighboring valleys. Eventually a multivalley state developed, creating a much larger civilization.

Carneiro's theory is hard to test in the field, but an attempt to do so in Peru's Santa Valley showed no sign of autonomous villages. Rather, it depicted a much more complex, evolving settlement pattern over many centuries. Archaeologist David Wilson points out that the only "coercive" processes came about in about A.D. 400, when the Moche people carved out a multivalley state by military conquest of neighboring valleys (Chapter 14). The conquest took place long after complex irrigation-based societies flourished in the

Santa Valley. As with irrigation hypotheses, reality is more complex than the straightforward Carneiro scenario.

Warfare can be rejected as a primary cause of civilization on other grounds, also. In earlier times, the diffuse social organization of village communities had not yet led to the institutional warfare that resulted from the concentration of wealth and power in a few hands. Only when absolute and despotic monarchs came into power did warfare become endemic, with standing armies to control important resources, solve political questions, and ensure social inequality. This type of warfare presupposes authority and is a consequence of civilization.

Cultural Systems and Civilization

Most archaeologists agree that urban life and preindustrial civilization came into existence gradually, during a period of major social and economic change. Everyone agrees, also, that linear explanations invoking irrigation, trade, or warfare are inadequate. Recent theories of the rise of states invoke multiple, and often intricate, causes and are frequently based on systems models.

In the 1960s, Robert Adams, an expert on ancient Mesopotamia, introduced a new generation of complex theories when he argued that irrigation agriculture, increased warfare, and "local resource variability" were three factors vital in newly appearing urban civilizations. Each affected society and the other factors with positive feedback, helping to reinforce each other. The creation of food surpluses and the emergence of a stratified society were critical developments. Irrigation agriculture could feed a bigger population. Larger populations, an increase in permanent settlement, and trade with regular centers for redistributing goods were all pressures for greater production and increased surpluses, actively fostered by dominant groups in society. The greatly enlarged surpluses enabled those who controlled them to employ larger numbers of artisans and other specialists who did not themselves grow crops.

Adams argued that some societies were better able to transform themselves into states because of the favorable variety of resources on which they could draw. Higher populations led to monopolies over strategic resources. These communities eventually were more powerful than their neighbors, expanding their territories by military campaigns and efficiently exploiting their advantages over other peoples. Such cities became early centers of major religious activities, of technological and artistic innovations, and of writing. Literacy, a skill confined to a few people, became an important source of power.

Archaeologists like Kent Flannery, who works in Mesoamerica, now saw the state as a very complicated "living" system, the complexity of which could be measured by the internal differentiation and intricacy of its subsystems, such as those for agriculture, technology, or religious beliefs. The way these subsystems were linked, and the controls that society imposed on the system, were vital. This model seemed to work well with Mesoamerican states, where pervasive religious beliefs formed close links between public architecture, the economy, and other subsystems of civilization.

The management of a state is a far more elaborate and central undertaking than that of a small chiefdom. Indeed, the most striking difference between states and less-complicated societies is the degree of complexity in civilizations' ways of reaching decisions and in their hierarchic organization, not necessarily in their subsistence activities. Systems models of early states are bound to be complex, for they have to distinguish between mechanisms and processes of cultural change, and the socioenvironmental pressures by which we have sought to explain the origins of civilization. Religion and control of information now appear to be key elements in the regulation of environmental and economic variables in early civilizations, and, indeed in any human society.

Environmental Change

Ecologically based theories, which also rely heavily on systems approaches, have enjoyed a relatively long life compared with many other hypotheses. For example, in a classic study of the Valley of Mexico, William Sanders and a group of archaeologists showed how the Aztec state created and organized huge agricultural systems that spread over the shallow waters of the lakes that once filled the Valley. The variability of the local environment meant that the Aztecs had to exploit every environmental opportunity afforded them. Thus, Sanders argues, the state organized large-scale agriculture to support a population of up to 250,000 in and close to the Aztec capital, Tenochtitlán. Environmental factors were decisive in each area where civilization began, he believes. Another important factor was centralized leadership.

The ecological approach has serious problems. How, for example, does one tell which environments would foster state formation? Fertile flood plains like those in Mesopotamia and Egypt? Coastal river valleys like those in Peru? Highland plateaus like those of Mesoamerica? Or areas where land is in short supply (also coastal Peru)? States have arisen in regions where there are few geographical constraints, like the Maya lowlands of Mesoamerica. Further, preindustrial civilizations have developed without any sign of rapid population growth, in Iran and other parts of Southwest Asia. But there can be no doubt that environmental factors were major players in a very complex process of cultural change and response.

SOCIAL APPROACHES: POWER IN THREE DOMAINS

In recent years, archaeology has shifted away from systems-ecological approaches toward a greater concern with individuals and groups. The former theories have often been somewhat impersonal, treating states as rather impersonal, mechanical, entities that operated according to complex processes of cultural change. A new generation of researchers is carrying social approaches and the study of power in new directions, arguing that all human societies consist, ultimately, of individuals and groups interacting with one another, and each pursuing their own agendas.

Archaeologically, one can look at power in three domains: economic power, social and ideological power, and political power. The *combination* of economic productivity, control over sources and distribution of food and wealth, the development and maintenance of the stratified social system and its ideology, and the ability to maintain control by force was the vital ingredient of early states. Each of these domains was closely linked to the others, but they can be studied separately in the archaeological record.

Economic power depends on the ability to organize more-specialized production and the diverse tasks of food storage and food distribution. In time, stored wealth in food and goods develops into relationships of dependency between those who produce or acquire the wealth and those who control and distribute it. A state comprises elites (the noble class), officials (the managers), and dependents (the commoners). The land-owning class and the estate—whether owned by a temple, the ruler, or a private individual—provided security for the estate's dependents. All early states developed from foundations where agricultural production became more intensified and diverse. At the same time, early states moved away from purely kin-based organization into centralized structures that cross-cut or overrode kinship ties.

Economic power also rested in trade and long-distance exchange networks, which provided access to commodities that were not available locally. Sumer obtained its metal from Anatolia, Iran, and the Persian Gulf. Egypt acquired gold and ivory from Nubia. Highland Andean civilizations imported fish meal from the Pacific coast. The acquisition of exotic commodities or goods on any scale required organization, record keeping, and supervision. The archaeological record shows that the extent of state supervision of trade and traders varied considerably from civilization to civilization.

Social power means ideological power, and comes from the creation or modification of certain symbols of cultural and political commonality. Such common ideology, expressed in public and private ceremonies, in art and architecture, and in literature, served to link individuals and communities with common ties that transcend those of kin. Those who create and perpetuate these ideologies are held in high honor and enjoy considerable prestige, for they are often perceived as interceding with the spiritual world and the deities, and sometimes even seen as flesh and blood divines themselves. The guardians of ideology are privileged individuals, for their spiritual powers give them special social status and allow them to perpetuate social inequality.

So important was ideology that one can speak of the Mesopotamian or Maya areas not in a political sense, for they were made up of patchworks of city-states, but in an ideological one. Many great cities of the past, like Teotihuacán in the Valley of Mexico, were a combination of the spiritual and the

Figure 8.2   THE CENTRAL PRECINCTS OF TIKAL, GUATEMALA, ONCE A SYMBOLIC DEPICTION OF THE MAYA SPIRITUAL WORLD

secular. They all boasted powerful priesthoods and religious institutions, which owed their wealth to their ability to manage the spiritual affairs of the state and to legitimize rulers as upholders of the cosmic order. The temples and public buildings they erected formed imposing settings for elaborate public ceremonies that ensured the continuity of human life and the universe (Figure 8.2).

Political power rested in the ruler's ability to impose authority throughout society by both administrative and military means. Those who held positions of authority within either the bureaucracy or the army did not come from within the kin system, but were recruited outside it. This political power lay in foreign relations and in defense and making war. It also operated at a statewide level, dealing with the resolution of major disputes between different factions. But a great deal of power lay outside the political estate, in the hands of community and kin leaders who handled many legal matters revolving around such issues as land ownership and family law.

Archaeologist Norman Yoffee believes that the interplay between these three sources of power led to the development of new, societywide institutions—to supreme rulers and the state. There was, he says, no one moment when civilization came into being, for social evolution did not end with the rise of the state. Preindustrial states functioned in an atmosphere of continual change and constant disputation. Some collapsed, others survived for many centuries.

This approach to the origin of states argues not for neoevolutionary ladders, but for many trajectories for the development of social complexity. Many societies operated under significant constraints; they may have lacked, say, dependable crops or domesticated animals or the ability to store large amounts of food. Constraints like these took human societies along very different evolutionary paths than those of the state. That some societies did not become civilizations does not mean that they were stuck in a backward "stage," but simply that constraints on growth prevented the interplay of the major factors that led to state formation elsewhere. Thus, the chiefdom is an alternative trajectory to the state. In the chiefdom, social inequality came from within the kin system; in the state, inequality was based on access to resources and the power this control provided.

Factionalism and Ideology

Every early civilization had a pervasive set of religious beliefs and philosophies that reached out to every corner of society. Such ideologies shaped society and ensured the conformity of its members, but to study such intangibles is a formidable task. Ideologies come down to us in distinctive art styles, like those of the Egyptians, or the Moche art style of the Andes (Figure 8.3). Such styles are visual reminders of a state's ideology, reinforcing the power of supreme rulers and their special relationships to the gods and the spiritual world. In societies where only a minority, those with power, are literate (or have scribes in their employ), art and public architecture have powerful roles to play in shaping society and reinforcing ideology.

The Maya lived in cities like Copán and Tikal, which were depictions in stone, wood, and stucco of a symbolic landscape of sacred hills, caves, and forests. Here, great lords appeared before the people atop high pyramids in elaborate public ceremonies (see Figure 8.3). Through ritual bloodletting and shamanistic trance, they entered the realm of the Otherworld, the world of the deities and ancestors. These sacred rituals validated the world of the Maya, and linked noble and commoner, ruler and humble village farmer in a complex social contract. The leaders were the intermediaries, the people who interceded with the gods to guarantee plentiful crops and ensure the continued existence of human life. The ceremonial centers, with their pyramids, plazas, and temples, were reassuring settings where the drama of life and death, of planting and harvest were played out against a backdrop of ever-changing seasons. These ceremonies justified social inequality, the great distinctions between the ruler and the ruled.

Ancient ideologies were as complex as our own, and they defy ready archaeological analysis by their very complexity and nonmaterial nature. The recent decipherment of Maya script has shown just how important and pervasive ideologies were in ancient civilizations. Until decipherment, most authorities assumed Maya rulers were peaceful priest-kings, who used their power as astronomers to preside over small city states. But Maya glyphs reveal an intricate and complex pantheon of deities, and religious beliefs that

Figure 8.3 Arti-
facts as Ideological
Statements   A
Moche ceramic vessel
from coastal Peru,
c. A.D. 400, depicts a
man, probably a
shaman, dressed as a
deer carrying a cere-
monial mace.

often defy modern analysis. Each day in the Maya calendar possessed a combination of qualities, every compass direction colors and characteristics, each
deity many roles and moods. Nothing in Maya society occurred without
acquiring symbolic and often ideological meaning. In Egypt, too, the ancient
precedents of the pharaohs' rule and the teachings of the gods permeated all
society and governed even the collection of taxes and the distribution of
rations.

With ideology comes factionalism. As we have seen, ancient societies were
as diverse as modern ones, especially when their rulers traded with neighbors
near and far. The state functioned for the benefit of a minority—privileged
rulers and nobles to whom all wealth and power flowed. A ruler governed his

domains by deputing governance to relatives and loyal followers who became provincial governors. But, inevitably, some individuals were more ambitious than others, rebelling against authority, plotting to gain supreme power. Competing factions within local groups and in different regions triggered further social inequality and changing patterns of leadership, increased specialization, and the development of states. And once civilizations came into being, they would challenge royal successions, even trigger civil war when a ruler was perceived as weak or indecisive. Competition and emerging factionalism were powerful catalysts in the development of many early states.

In an era when archaeological research has become increasingly specialized, it is probably futile to search for a theory of state formation that can be applied to all civilizations. There are some common questions, however, that revolve around the implications of ecological variables in societies about to become states: How is ecological opportunity or necessity translated into political change? What were the goals of the political actors who were pursuing their individual goals while states were coming into being? Which ecological variables were obstacles? Which were opportunities? The answers to these questions will come from sophisticated researches that combine systems-ecological approaches with careful research into what British archaeologist Colin Renfrew has called "the archaeology of mind," the elusive intangibles behind the material record of the past.

THE COLLAPSE OF CIVILIZATIONS

Many historians have written about cycles of history, the rise of civilizations, their brilliant apogees, and their sudden declines. Eventually one civilization falls and another rises to take its place, which in turn goes through the same cycle of rise and fall. The record of early civilizations could easily be written in cyclical terms, for states have risen and then collapsed with bewildering rapidity in all parts of the world within the past 5000 years. In the Mexican highlands, for example, the great city of Teotihuacán flourished between about 200 B.C. and A.D. 700. In A.D. 600, it had a population of more than 125,000 people. For 600 years, more than 85 percent of the population of the Valley of Mexico lived in or close to Teotihuacán (see Figure 8.4). Then the city collapsed in the eighth century A.D. Within half a century, the population shrank to a quarter of its former size.

When a complex society collapses, it suddenly becomes smaller, simpler, and much more egalitarian. Population densities fall; trade and economic activity dries up; information flow declines; and the known world shrinks for the survivors. Joseph Tainter, one of the few archaeologists to have made a comparative study of collapse, points out that an initial investment by a society in growing complexity is a rational way of trying to solve the needs of the moment. At first the strategy works. Agricultural production increases through more intensive farming methods; an emerging bureaucracy works well; expanding trade

Figure 8.4   The Pyramid of the Sun at Teotihuacán, Mexico, a Vast Edifice Erected as a Sacred Mountain to Mirror the Peak Behind it, Which Was Still a Sacred place 800 Years After the City Collapsed, c. a.d. 750

networks bring wealth to a new elite, who use their authority and economic clout to undertake great public works such as pyramids and temples, that validate their spiritual authority and divine associations.

As the most costly solutions to society's needs are exhausted, so does it become imperative that new organizational and economic answers be found, which may have much lower yields and cost a great deal more. As these stresses develop, argues Tainter, a complex society such as that of the Maya is increasingly vulnerable to collapse. There are few reserves to carry society through droughts, famines, floods, or other natural disasters. Eventually, collapse ensues, especially when important segments of society perceive that centralization and social complexity simply do not work any more and that they are better off on their own. The trend toward decentralization, toward collapse, becomes compelling. Collapse was not a catastrophe but a rational process that occurs when increasing stress requires some organizational change. The population decline and other catastrophic effects that just preceded, accompanied, or followed collapse may have been traumatic at the time, but they can be looked at as part of what one might call an economizing process.

There is, of course, more to collapse than merely an economizing process. Complete collapse can occur only under circumstances in which there is a power vacuum. In many cases, there may be a powerful neighbor waiting in the wings. In early times, numerous city-states traded and competed with one another within a small area. Sumerian cities, Minoan and Mycenaean palace-kingdoms in Greece and the Aegean, the Maya in Mesoamerica—all lived in close interdependence within their culture areas, in a state of constant "peer-polity interaction." They traded, fought, and engaged in constant diplomacy. Under these circumstances, to collapse is an invitation to be dominated by one's competitors. There is only loss of complexity when every polity in the interacting cluster collapses at the same time.

The collapse of early civilizations may, then, be closely connected to declining returns from social complexity, and to the normal political processes of factionalism, social unrest, succession disputes, even civil war.

CHAPTER 9

Mesopotamia and the East Mediterranean World

A.D. 1950 –

A.D. 1 –

15,000 B.P. –

50,000 B.P. –

100,000 B.P. –

500,000 B.P. –

1.0 Million –

2.5 Million –

The Victorians thought of Mesopotamia (Greek for "land between the rivers") as the location of the biblical Garden of Eden. Today, it is a far from paradisal place, for the delta regions and flood plain between the Tigris and Euphrates rivers form a hot, low-lying environment, much of it inhospitable sand, swamp, and dry mud flats. Yet this now-inhospitable region was the cradle of the world's earliest urban civilization.

From north to south, Mesopotamia is approximately 600 miles (965 km) long and 250 miles (402 km) wide, extending from the uplands of Iran to the east to the Arabian and Syrian deserts in the west. The plains are subject to long, intensely hot summers and harsh, cold winters and would be desert but for the Euphrates and Tigris Rivers. There are few permanent water supplies away from these great rivers and their tributaries. Rainfall is slight and not dependable and is insufficient for growing crops. However, with irrigation, the alluvial soils of the lower plain can be farmed and their natural fertility unlocked. Farmers can achieve high crop yields from relatively limited areas of land, sufficient to feed relatively dense populations. By 5000 B.C. and perhaps earlier, village farmers were diverting the waters of the rivers. Within 2000 years the urban civilization of the Sumerians was flourishing in Mesopotamia.

This chapter describes this, the earliest of the world's civilizations, and the complex western Asian societies that developed out of the first Mesopotamian states (Figure 9.1).

D I S C O V E R Y

THE FLOOD TABLETS

In 1872, an earnest banknote engraver turned clay tablet expert named George Smith was sorting through the dusty fragments of Assyrian King Assurbanipal's royal library in the British Museum. Suddenly, he came across a tablet bearing a reference to a large ship grounded on a mountain. Immediately, he realized he had found an account of a flood that bore a remarkable resemblance to the biblical story of the Flood in Genesis. A prophet named Hasisadra is warned of the gods' intention to destroy all of sinful humankind. He builds a large ship, loads her with his family, "the beast of the field, the animal of the field . . . ." The flood destroys "all [other] life from the face of the earth." The ship goes aground on a mountain. Hasisadra sends out a dove, which returns. Eventually a raven is dispatched and never returns. Hasisadra releases the animals, becomes a god, and lives happily ever after.

George Smith's discovery caused a public sensation at a time when people believed in the literal historical truth of the Scriptures. Seventeen lines of the story were missing, so the London *Daily Telegraph* paid for him to go to Nineveh to find the missing fragments. Incredible though it may seem, Smith found them within five days. The tablets can be seen on display in the British Museum, duly labeled "DT"—"Daily Telegraph."

ORIGINS (5500 to 3000 B.C.)

Controversy surrounds the first settlement of the land between the rivers. Intensely hot in summer, bitterly cold in winter, the plains were far from a hospitable environment for village farmers. We know that by 5500 B.C. hundreds of small farming villages dotted the rolling plains of northern Mesopotamia upstream, settlements connected by long-distance trade routes that carried obsidian, finely painted pottery, and other goods over hundreds of miles, from Turkey as far as southern Iraq. By this time, much of the trade, especially in pottery, was concentrated in the hands of a small elite, living in key centers along water routes. However, we do not know whether the uninhabited plains were settled by village farmers from the north around 6000 B.C., as many scholars believe, or whether much earlier indigenous foragers adopted farming along the shores of the Persian Gulf at this time, or even earlier.

No one knows when foragers first settled on the shores of the Persian Gulf, which, during the late Ice Age, was a large river estuary. One school of thought believes that, as sea levels rose after 15,000 years ago, the Gulf spread far up into what is now southern Iraq, perhaps creating rich coastal and riverside marshlands rich in fish and plant foods. The ancient coastlines of the early and middle Holocene now lie below many feet of river alluvium and sand, as does the archaeological record of potential early occupation. As the

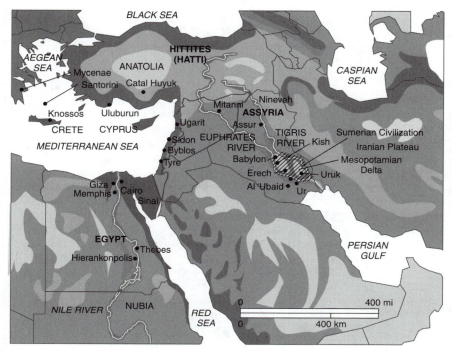

Figure 9.1   MAP SHOWING ARCHAEOLOGICAL SITES IN CHAPTERS 9 AND 10 (NUBIA OMITTED)

climate dried up during the Holocene, goes this argument, forager populations tended to concentrate in more resource-rich areas. As elsewhere in Western Asia, it may have been in such locations that people first experimented with growing cereal grains. Within a few thousand years, farming villages clustered along river banks and better-watered areas of the desert.

Whatever their origins, the earliest farmers developed methods of cultivation using canals and natural waterways, which allowed higher crop yields. The first known farming communities date to around 5800 B.C., small communities located in clusters along the Euphrates river channels. As early as 5000 B.C., a few farming communities were diverting flood waters from the Euphrates and Tigris onto their fields, then draining them away to prevent salt buildup in the soil. The largest of these clusters consisted of small rural communities located around a larger town that covered about 28 acres (11.3 ha) and housed between 2500 and 4000 people. Some of their small irrigation canals extended out about 3 miles (4.8 km) from the river. From the very beginning some of these 'Ubaid culture settlements (named after a village near ancient Ur) boasted of substantial buildings, alleyways, and courtyards. Others consisted of little more than humble mud-brick and reed huts. Each cluster was a group of villages linked by kin ties, with a clan leader living in one larger settlement overseeing village affairs and, probably, the irrigation schemes that connected them.

We do not know anything about how the first inhabitants of the Mesopotamian flood plain acquired or developed the skills needed to survive in their harsh environment. Interdependence among members of the community was essential because raw materials suitable for building houses had to be improvised from the plentiful sand, clay, palm trees, and reeds between the rivers. Digging even the smallest canal required at least a little political and social leadership. The annual backbreaking task of clearing silt from clogged river courses and canals could only have been achieved by communal efforts. Distinctive social changes came from the more-efficient systems for producing food that were essential in the delta. As food surpluses grew and the specialized agricultural economies of these 'Ubaid villages became successful, the trend toward sedentary settlement and higher population densities increased. Expanded trade networks and the redistribution of surpluses and trade goods also affected society, with dominant groups of 'Ubaid people becoming more active in producing surpluses, which eventually supported more and more people who were not farmers.

As Mesopotamian society grew rapidly in complexity in the centuries that followed, so did the need for social, political, and religious institutions that would provide some form of centralized authority. In time, the small village ceremonial centers grew. Eridu, a rapidly growing town, consisted of a mud-brick temple with fairly substantial mud-brick houses around it, often with a rectangular floor plan. The craftsworkers lived a short distance from the elite clustered around the temple, and still farther away were the dwellings of the farmers who grew the crops that supported everyone. By 4500 B.C., the Eridu temple had grown large, containing altars and offering places and a central room bounded by rows of smaller compartments. The population of Eridu was as high as 5000 at this time, but exact computations are impossible. Places like Eridu assumed great importance after 4500 B.C., among them Uruk, the world's first city.

The First Cities: Uruk

Uruk began life as a small town and soon became a growing city, quickly absorbing the populations of nearby villages. During the fourth millennium B.C., Uruk grew to cover an estimated 617 acres (250 ha). Satellite villages extended out at least 6 miles (c. 10 km), each with their own irrigation systems. All provided grain, fish, or meat for the growing urban population. The city itself was a densely packed agglomeration of houses, narrow alleyways, and courtyards, probably divided into distinct quarters where different kin groups or artisans such as potters, sculptors, and painters lived. Everything was overshadowed by the stepped temple pyramid, the ziggurat, that towered over the lowlands for miles around. The ziggurat complex and its satellite temples were the center of Uruk life, not only were they places of worship, but storehouses, workshops, and centers of government (Figure 9.2).

The ruler of Uruk and the keeper of the temple was both a secular and spiritual ruler. His wishes were carried out by his priests and by a complex hierarchy of minor officials, wealthy landowners, and merchants. Tradespeo-

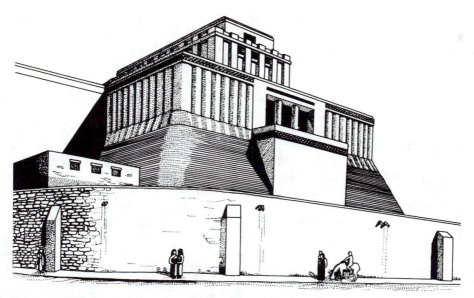

Figure 9.2   ARTIST'S RECONSTRUCTION OF A ZIGGURAT AT ERIDU, IRAQ, ONE OF THE
EARLIEST TEMPLES IN THE REGION

ple and artisans were a more lowly segment of society. Under them were thousands of fisherfolk, farmers, sailors, and slaves that formed the bulk of Uruk, and other cities' burgeoning populations. By 3500 B.C., the Mesopotamian city had developed an elaborate system of management. This system organized and regulated society, meted out reward and punishment, and made policy decisions for the thousands of people who lived under it.

Writing and Metallurgy

Two innovations appeared as Uruk and other cities grew rapidly. The first was writing, the second metallurgy. The origins of written records go back thousands of years before the Sumerians, to a time soon after the adoption of food production when the volume of intervillage trade demanded some means of tracking shipments. As early as 8000 B.C., villagers were using carefully shaped clay tokens, which they carried around on strings. By 5000 B.C., commercial transactions of all kinds were so complex that there were endless possibilities for thievery and accounting errors. Some clever officials made small clay tablets and scratched them with incised signs that depicted familiar objects such as pots or animals. From there it was a short step to simplified, more conventionalized, **cuneiform** signs (Figure 9.3).

At first, specially trained scribes dealt almost entirely with administrative matters, compiling lists and inventories. Eventually, the more creative among them explored the limitless opportunities afforded by the ability to express themselves in writing. Kings used tablets to trumpet their victories.

Figure 9.3 CUNEIFORM TABLET OF C. 2500 B.C. This tablet records transactions between different temple herds. The vertical line divides into two columns; each horizontal line then begins with marks that indicate a number (e.g., six in the third line of the right-hand column) or with the name of a god (e.g., the third line on the left, with the name of the god Shuruppak).

Fathers chided their errant sons, lawyers recorded complicated transactions. Sumerian literature includes great epics, love stories, hymns to the gods, and tragic laments.

The Sumerians' homeland had no metals, so they imported copper, gold, and other ores from the Iranian highlands and elsewhere as early as 3500 B.C. At first these shiny metals had high prestige value, but the advent of lead and tin alloying after 2000 B.C. led to widespread use of bronze artifacts for farming tools and weapons of war. The adoption of bronze-edged weapons had momentous consequences for Sumerian life, for their appearance in local armies can be linked directly to a rising penchant for using war as a means of attaining political ends. Cities like Eridu and Uruk were not isolated from other centers. Indeed they were only too aware of their neighbors. For example, the city-states of Lagash and Umma were uneasy neighbors and engaged in a tendentious border dispute that dragged on for three or four centuries. Cities soon had walls, a sure sign that they needed protection against marauders. Sumerian seals bear scenes with prisoners of war.

By this time, too, there were southern Mesopotamian "colonies" in what is now northern Iraq, at Susa across the Tigris, in the Zagros, and elsewhere on the northern and northeastern peripheries of the lowlands. Some of these colonies were entire transplanted communities; others are represented by characteristic Uruk-style artifacts far from their homelands. Artifacts and artistic styles characteristic of Uruk have come from the Nile Valley during centuries when long-distance caravan trade was expanding rapidly in Egypt and across the Sinai.

THE SUMERIAN CIVILIZATION (c. 3100 to 2334 B.C.)

With the emergence of the Sumerian civilization in about 3100 B.C., a new era in human experience begins, one in which the economic, political, and social mechanisms created by humans begin to affect the lives of cities, towns, and villages located hundreds, if not thousands, of miles apart. No human society has ever flourished in complete isolation, but the real launching point in long-distance exchange and organized trade took place during the fourth millennium B.C., the first millennium when the history of an individual society can be understood only against a background of much broader regional developments. In a real sense, a rapidly evolving "world system" linked hundreds of Southwest Asian societies all the way from eastern Iran and the Indus Valley in Pakistan to Mesopotamia, the eastern Mediterranean, Anatolia, and the Nile Valley with ever-changing cultural tentacles. By the third millennium B.C. this system not only embraced Southwest Asia but also extended to Cyprus, the Aegean, and mainland Greece.

This nascent world system developed as a result of insatiable demands for nonlocal raw materials in different ecological regions where societies were developing along very similar general evolutionary tracks toward greater complexity. The broad, and apparently linear, cultural sequence in southern Mesopotamia just described can be matched by equivalent developments in northern Mesopotamia and east of the Tigris. In each area, these developments and many technological innovations were triggered not only by basic economic needs but also by the competitive instincts of newly urbanized elites, who used lavish display and exotic luxuries to reaffirm their social prestige and authority. Sumerian civilization is a mirror of this developing regional interdependence.

Writing and metallurgy were symbols of a rapidly changing western Asian world. By 3250 B.C., expanding trade networks linked dozens of cities and towns from the Mediterranean to the Persian Gulf and from Turkey to the Nile valley. By this time, states small and large flourished not only in Egypt and Mesopotamia, but in the coastal Levant and in highland Iran. Each of them depended on the others for critical raw materials such as metal ore or soapstone vessels, for timber or even grain. In northern Mesopotamia, east of the Tigris, and in the Levant, expanding trade and a host of important technological innovations resulted, also, not only from basic economic needs, but from the competitive instincts of a new elite. All, however bitter their enmity, depended on their neighbors and more distant trading partners.

Sumerian civilization came into being as a result of a combination of environmental and social factors. The Sumerians lived in a treeless, lowland environment with fertile soils, but no metal, little timber, and no semiprecious stones. They obtained these commodities by trading with areas where such items were in abundance. Sumerian rulers controlled not only large grain surpluses that could be moved in river craft but also a flourishing industry in textiles and other luxuries. The trade moved up and down the great rivers, especially the placid Euphrates. Ancient overland trade routes linked the Tigris and Euphrates with the distant Levant cities and ports. Even as early as Sumerian times, caravans of pack animals joined Anatolia to the Euphrates, the Levant to Mesopotamia, and Mesopotamia to isolated towns on the distant Iranian highlands to the east.

Bronze technology produced tougher-edged, more durable artifacts that could be used for more arduous, day-to-day tasks. One resulting innovation was the metal- and wood-tipped plow, an implement dragged by oxen that was capable of digging a far deeper furrow than the simple hoes and digging sticks of earlier times. The plow, which incidentally was never developed in the Americas, was developed as irrigation agriculture assumed greater importance in Sumer, and the combined innovations increased agricultural yields dramatically. These yields not only supported larger urban and rural populations but also provided a means for the rulers of city-states both in Sumer and farther afield to exercise more control over food surpluses and over the wealth obtained by long-distance exchange. Eventually, Sumerian rulers became more despotic, controlling their subjects by military strength, religious acumen, and economic incentive.

An intricate and ever-changing system of political alliances and individual obligations of friendship linked community with community and city-state with city-state. In time, financial and logistical checks and balances were maintained by an administrative system based in the temples to bring order to what had begun as informal bartering. Specialized merchants began to handle such commodities as copper and lapis lazuli. There was wholesaling and contracting, loans were floated, and individual profit was a prime motivation. Increasingly, every city-state, and indeed entire civilizations, came to depend on what we have called a nascent world system, not so much for political stability but for survival. Reliable, long-term interdependency became a vital factor in the history of Southwest Asian states by 3000 B.C.

By 2800 B.C., Mesopotamia was home to several important city-states, states that were in contact with the Levant and the Iranian Plateau, even, sporadically, with the pharaohs of Egypt. As the Mesopotamian delta became an environment increasingly controlled by human activities and the volume of long-distance trade increased dramatically, so competition over resources intensified. Both clay tablets and archaeological finds tell of warfare and constant bickering between neighbors. Each state raised an army to defend its

Figure 9.4 The Reconstructed Sumerian Ziggurat at Ur, Iraq, Originally Built in about 2300 B.C.

water rights, trade routes, and city walls. The onerous tasks of defense and military organization passed to despotic kings supposedly appointed by the gods. Such city-states as **Erech, Kish,** and **Ur** had periods of political strength and prosperity when they dominated their neighbors (Figure 9.4). Then, just as swiftly, the tide of their fortunes would change and they would sink into obscurity. There was a constant threat from nomadic peoples of the surrounding mountains and deserts, who encroached on settled Sumerian lands. At times, they disrupted city life so completely that any form of travel became an impossibility. In a real sense, city-states were the settings for economic and social strife in early Mesopotamia.

Some Sumerian cities nurtured powerful and wealthy leaders. When British archaeologist Sir Leonard Woolley excavated a royal cemetery at Ur, he found the remains of a series of kings and queens who had been buried in huge graves with their entire retinue of courtiers. One tomb contained the remains of 59 people. Each wore his or her official dress and regalia and had laid down to die in the correct order of precedence, after taking a fatal dose of poison (Figure 9.5).

Inevitably, the ambitions of some of these proud Sumerian leaders led them to entertain bolder visions than merely the control of a few city-states in the lowlands. They were well aware that the control of lucrative sources of raw materials and trade routes was the secret of vast political power. In about 2400 B.C., a monarch named Lugalzagesi boasted of overseeing the entire area from the Persian Gulf to the Mediterranean. This boast was probably false. It is likely that Sumerian cities dominated the overland routes that linked Mesopotamia, Turkey, and the Levant, but their influence was never permanent, their control probably illusory. Lugalzagesi and others were characteristic of a tradition of Mesopotamian civilization: the combination of trade, conquest, ruthless administration, and tribute to create large, poorly integrated, and highly volatile empires. Each sought to control an enormous territory between the Mediterranean and the Persian Gulf.

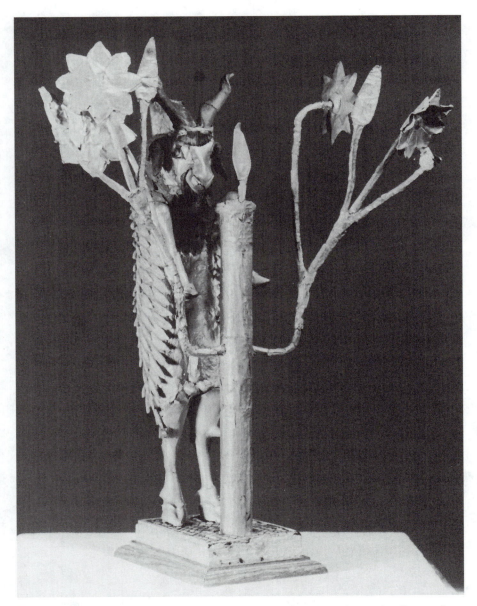

Figure 9.5 AN OFFERING FROM THE ROYAL CEMETERY AT UR   A wooden figure of a ram covered with gold leaf and lapis lazuli. The body is in silver leaf, the fleece in shell.

The tenuous and sometimes more regular contacts maintained by Mesopotamia with dozens of city-states in Anatolia and along the eastern Mediterranean coast foreshadow the constant political and economic rivalry that was to dominate Southwest Asian history during the second millennium B.C.—rivalry over control of Mediterranean coastal ports. Here two oceans and three continents meet. The eastern Mediterranean coast had no natural harbors, so the control of its overland routes was the key to dominating a vast area of the known world, resource-rich Anatolia and grain-rich Egypt. The history of this region was bound inextricably to the fortunes of the larger powers that surrounded it.

AKKADIANS AND BABYLONIANS (2334 to 1650 B.C.)

While Sumerian civilization prospered, urban centers waxed and waned in neighboring areas. In these regions, too, lived rulers with wider ambitions, who had a vision of a larger role. By 2500 B.C., Akkadian cities to the north of Sumer were competing with lowland cities for trade and prestige. In approximately 2334 B.C., a Semitic-speaking leader, Sargon, founded a ruling dynasty at the town of Agade, south of **Babylon.** By skillful commercial ventures and judicious military campaigns, his northern dynasty soon established its rule over a much larger kingdom that included both Sumer and northern Mesopotamia. After a short period of economic prosperity, northern Mesopotamia went through a catastrophic drought that lasted some 300 years. Starving farmers thronged to the rich southern cities. Violent clashes followed and the Akkadian kingdom collapsed.

Fifty years of political instability ensued before King Ur-Nammu of Ur took control of Sumer and Akkad in 2112 B.C. and created an empire that extended far to the north. Sargon had forged an empire by military conquest but had never followed up his victories with proper administrative governance. Tablets from royal archives tell us that Ur-Nammu and his successors of Ur's Third Dynasty were a new breed of ruler, who placed great emphasis on consolidating their new empire into a powerful and well-organized bureaucracy.

Ur in turn gave way to Babylon and its Semitic rulers by 1990 B.C. Babylon's early greatness culminated in the reign of the great king Hammurabi in 1792 B.C., famous for his law code. He integrated the smaller kingdoms of Mesopotamia for a short period, but his empire declined after his death as Babylonian trade to the Persian Gulf collapsed and trade ties to Assur in the north and for Mediterranean copper in the west were strengthened.

HITTITES AND SEA TRADERS (1650 to 1200 B.C.)

All these developments came from ever-closer economic ties between different regions of southwest Asia. These ties were a sign of an economic interdependency that persisted regardless of political change or war. The desert caravans of black asses and the ships that plied Mediterranean waters resulted from a more durable world system that transcended the boundaries of local societies and even entire civilizations. At the center of this world system lay the strategic eastern Mediterranean coast.

During the second millennium B.C. the eastern Mediterranean coastlands were divided among a network of small and prosperous states. They lived in the shadow of the great kingdoms that lay inland: Egypt to the south (see Chapter 10), **Mitanni** to the east of the Euphrates, and Hatti (the kingdom of the Hittites) in Anatolia. Each of these three kingdoms controlled a large area of territory surrounded by a hinterland that lay more or less under their influence (see Figure 9.1). The three states competed directly in the coastal zone, and they had complex dealings on all frontiers. Mitanni, for example, tried to prevent the city-state of Assur in northern Mesopotamia from going its own way, and the famous Amarna tablets, an archive of Egyptian diplomatic correspondence, tell of shifting allegiances among the city-states of the coast. By this time, the eastern Mediterranean shore was a land of many cities, a regular military and diplomatic battlefield for its powerful neighbors.

The Hittites

The Hittites were the newest, and perhaps the most able, diplomatic players. Originally the rulers of **Kanesh,** they expanded their domains and seized control of the rest of Anatolia just before 1650 B.C. Hittite kings exercised enormous political influence in southwest Asia from their capital at Boghazkoy, with its 4 miles (6.4 km) of city walls. In the 15th century B.C., Syria had been a province of the Egyptian empire. The Hittites pressed hard on the Egyptians on both diplomatic and military fronts, until the Great King of Hatti, Suppiluliumas I (1375–1335 B.C.), could claim Lebanon as his frontier. Diplomatic archives in Akkadian cuneiform contain records of a peace treaty of about 1269 between the Hittite and Egyptian kings, which confined Egyptian interests to southern Palestine. The grandiloquent public architecture of the period commonly depicted Egyptians and Hittites locked in battle with state-of-the-art weaponry. This included light, two-wheeled chariots manned by archers and new siege machinery for use against the many walled cities in the disputed areas.

By 1200 B.C., Hatti was in trouble. The Hittites had prospered by virtue of their well-organized, professional army, long a stabilizing influence in the eastern Mediterranean. They were expert diplomats, who controlled what is now northern Syria through their rule over two great cities—Carchemish on the Euphrates and Alalakh of Mukish in the west. There were also treaty relationships with other powerful neighbors, including **Ugarit** (Ras Shamra) on the northern Levant coast. Ugarit was a cosmopolitan city ruled by a monarch who was almost like a merchant-prince. He controlled vast supplies of gold and a fleet of more than 150 ships, some of considerable size. These ventured as far afield as Cyprus and the Nile, the former being a center of exchange with the Aegean. Ugarit was vital to the Hittites, who had never become a maritime power, for they depended on its ships.

Both the lack of maritime power and a rigid feudal system contributed to Hatti's undoing. About 1200 B.C., repeated migrations of foreigners flowed into Anatolia from the northwest. The central Hittite government collapsed, partly because of attacks from outside but also because powerful vassals threw off their allegiance to the king. Anatolia dissolved into the homeland of dozens of small city-states, each striving to maintain its independence.

Uluburun and Maritime Trade

All this diplomatic and military activity on the part of the great kingdoms was aimed at control of the lucrative gold, copper, and pottery trade of the eastern Mediterranean. This trade, in the hands of eastern Mediterranean and Mycenaean traders, is vividly illustrated by investigations of Bronze Age shipwrecks off the southern Turkish coast.

The advantage of shipwrecks from the archaeological point of view is that they provide sealed capsules of maritime trade frozen at a moment in time. The famous **Uluburun** ship, excavated by Çemal Pulak from the waters near Kas off southern Turkey, was shipwrecked in about 1310 B.C. The ship carried over 350 copper ingots, each weighing about 60 pounds (27 kg), a load of 10 tons, enough to equip a small army with weapons and armor (Figure 9.6). A ton of resin traveled in two-handled jars made by people living in the Syria region; it was used, so Egyptian records tell us, as incense for Egyptian rituals. There were dozens of blue glass disks, ingots being sent to Egypt from Tyre.

Figure 9.6   EXCAVATIONS ON THE BRONZE AGE SHIP AT ULUBURUN, TURKEY

The cargo also included hardwood, Baltic amber, tortoise shells, elephant tusks and hippopotamus teeth, ostrich eggs, jars of olives, and even large jars holding stacked Canaanite and Mycenaean pottery.

The Uluburun ship's cargo contains items from Africa, Egypt, the eastern Mediterranean coast, the Greek mainland and the Aegean, Cyprus, and even copper from Sardinia. It is a dramatic reflection of the truly international nature of eastern Mediterranean trade in the second millennium B.C., when the Hittites were at the height of their power. It is hardly surprising that the great powers of the day competed savagely for control of the eastern Mediterranean shore, for it lay at the very center of an interlocking maze of trade routes that spanned the entire civilized world.

Iron Technology

Maritime trade played a major role in the diffusion of iron tools and weapons over the eastern Mediterranean. Iron is thought to have been first smelted in the middle of the second millennium B.C., perhaps in the highlands immediately south of the Black Sea. The new metal had many advantages, for its tough, sharp edges were invaluable for military tasks and for farming and carpentry. Iron was plentiful, unlike the tin used to alloy bronze. Iron tools soon became commonplace over a wide area of Europe and southwest Asia, although it was some time before domestic artifacts such as axes and hoes were invariably made with the new technology.

MINOANS AND MYCENAEANS (1900 to 1200 B.C.)

Eastern Mediterranean trade extended far west of Greece, to Sardinia, North Africa, and Spain. But the main western frontier lay in the Aegean Islands and on the Greek islands, where the Minoan and Mycenaean civilizations flourished during the second millennium B.C.

The Aegean abounds in sheltered bays and many straits, allowing even primitive, heavily laden seagoing vessels to take shelter and sail from island to island. The interisland trade expanded rapidly, not only in metal objects but in olive oil and wine carried in fine pots, also in marble vessels and figurines. A constant flow of new products and ideas flowed across the region. By 2500 B.C., numerous small towns housed farmers, traders, and skilled artisans on the mainland and the islands. The beginnings of town life fostered considerable cultural diversity in the Aegean, a diversity fostered by constant trading connections and increasingly complex political and social organization.

Minoan Civilization (1900 to 1400 B.C.)

Minoan civilization developed out of earlier indigenous farming cultures by 1900 B.C. It is best documented at the famous Palace of Minos at **Knossos** near Heraklion on the north coast, a site first settled as early as 6000 B.C., at about the same time that Çatalhöyük flourished in Anatolia. Parts of the Greek mainland and Aegean Islands were settled by farming peoples as early as 6500 B.C., but it was not until considerably later that village communities sprang up throughout the region. This development coincided with the cultivation not only of cereals, but of olives and vines. By 3500 B.C., the inhabitants of the Aegean and Greece were exploiting local ores to make fine metal tools and precious ornaments. The Knossos farmers lived in sun-dried mud and brick huts of a rectangular ground plan that provided for storage bins and sleeping platforms. By 3730 B.C., signs of long-distance trading increased in the form of exotic imports such as stone bowls. The first palace at Knossos was built by about 1930 B.C.; it was a large building with many rooms grouped around a rectangular central court.

In about 1700 B.C., the first royal residence on the site was destroyed by an earthquake, just as Minoan civilization reached the height of its powers. The palace that rose in its place was an imposing structure that rambled around a central courtyard (Figure 9.7). Some buildings had two stories; the plastered walls and floors were painted with brightly colored geometric designs, with landscapes, dolphins, and other sea creatures (Figure 9.8). The most remarkable art depicted dances and religious ceremonies, including acrobats leaping vigorously along the backs of prancing bulls. Part shrine, part royal residence, part storehouse, and part workshop, the Palace of Minos at Knossos was the hub of predominantly rural civilization centered on large country houses and chieftains' residences.

Figure 9.7   General View of the Palace of Knossos, Crete

Figure 9.8 THE THRONE ROOM AT KNOSSOS, WITH STONE THRONE AND FRIEZE DEPICTING MYTHICAL BIRDS   This chamber was used for formal appearances of priests or priestesses costumed as deities.

The dramatic flowering of Minoan civilization resulted from intensified trading contacts throughout the Aegean and as far afield as Egypt and the Levant. The Minoans were expert seafarers and middlemen in international trade. Their ships handled all manner of cargos. But this time, olive and vine cultivation had added welcome diversity to local village farming economies, as well as providing valuable export commodities. This led to the development of distribution systems organized and controlled by important leaders, who controlled ships, shipping lanes, and marketplaces, and lived in palaces large and small. Minoan society developed from entirely local roots, which was an adaptation to a mountainous environment where population densities were never high and much wealth came from the export trade.

A massive volcanic explosion devastated the island of **Santorini,** a Minoan outpost 70 miles (113 km) north of Crete, in about 1450 B.C. This cataclysmic eruption caused massive tidal waves and ash falls that mantled many Minoan fields, but Knossos continued to flourish long afterward. Nevertheless, the Santorini disaster may have accelerated the decline of Minoan civilization. Some time later, many Minoan sites were destroyed and abandoned. Warrior farmers, probably from mainland Greece, established sway over Minoan domains and decorated the walls of Knossos with military scenes. In about 1400 B.C., the great palace was destroyed by fire. By this time, the center of the Aegean world had shifted west to the Greek mainland, where Mycenae reached the height of its power.

Mycenaean Civilization (1600 to 1200 B.C.)

Mycenaean civilization, centered on the fertile plain of Argos in southern Greece, developed in about 1600 B.C. The chieftains who ruled over the walled fortress of **Mycenae** gained their wealth and economic power not only from their warrior skills, but from far-flung trading contacts in the Aegean and further afield (Figure 9.9). Mycenaean kings were expert charioteers and horsemen, whose material culture and lifeways are immortalized in Homer's epic poems, the *Iliad* and the *Odyssey*. These epics were written many centuries after the Mycenaeans themselves had become folk memories. However, they give a splendid impression of the wealth and glitter of Bronze Age Greek life. So do Mycenaean graves. Mycenae's rulers and their relatives took their wealth with them to the next world. They were buried in spectacular shaft graves wearing fine gold face masks modeled in the likeness of their owners, and weapons adorned with copper, gold, and silver (Figure 9.10).

Mycenaean commerce took over where Minoan trade left off. Much of the rulers' prestige was based on their contacts in the metal trade. Minerals, especially tin for alloying bronze, were in constant demand in eastern Mediterranean markets. Both copper and tin were abundant in Turkey and central Cyprus, so Mycenaean traders became middlemen, developing the necessary contacts in both areas and in the Aegean to obtain regular supplies. So complex did their trading relationships become that the Mycenaeans found it necessary to establish their own writing system. They refined a simple picto-

Figure 9.9   AERIAL VIEW OF MYCENAE, GREECE

Figure 9.10
GOLDEN FUNERARY
MASK OF A MYCE-
NAEAN RULER FROM A
SHAFT GRAVE AT
MYCENAE

graphic script known to archaeologists as Linear A, which had been used by the Minoans, and wrote it in the Greek language, creating what scholars call Linear B. Large numbers of clay tablets from a Mycenaean palace at **Pylos** in western Greece show that the script was used for inventories and records of commercial transactions, ration issues, and so on, for the daily affairs of estate administration.

Like Minoan civilization, Mycenaean society was based on small towns and palaces where the elite lived, and where trade, centralized food storage, and major religious ceremonies took place. Mycenae itself was a formidable citadel ringed with a defense wall of large boulders. The main entrance passed under a portico carved with two seated lions and led up the hill to the stone-built palace with its magnificent views of the Plain of Argos. Everything was set up for storage and defense. There was a water cistern within the defense walls and rows of clay storage jars held large quantities of olive oil, with storerooms for many foodstuffs and the wealth of the palace. The rulers and their immediate relatives were buried in a circular enclosure to the west of the gate, but the Mycenaeans also used beehivelike communal burial chambers outside the citadel for many of their dead.

Mycenae continued to dominate seaborne eastern Mediterranean trade routes until about 1200 B.C., when its power was destroyed, probably as a result of warrior incursions from the north. In the same century, other northern barbarian raids overthrew the Hittite kingdom in Turkey. These incursions were the result of unsettled political conditions and overpopulation in Europe, and threw the eastern Mediterranean world into confusion.

SEA PEOPLES AND PHOENICIANS (1200 to 800 B.C.)

The Hittite civilization collapsed during a period of political upheaval, but the trade routes that joined states large and small continued to link every corner of the Mediterranean world. The imperial powers and petty kingships that had made up much of the economic world of 1200 B.C. were governed by highly centralized palace bureaucracies. These bureaucracies controlled specialized activities such as trade in glass ingots and ivory ornaments, which allowed significant economies of operation and dense population concentrations.

When the Hittite and Mycenaean civilizations came apart in an almost dominolike effect and Egypt declined at the same time, centralized bureaucracies lost their power over economic activities. The infrastructure for controlled, specialized trade came apart and the power of urban elites declined. For 300 years, there was a political vacuum, a period of widespread suffering and piracy, much of it at the hands of warlike bands known to archaeologists as the **Sea Peoples.** In the Levant, many rural groups moved to the highlands, loosening their dependence on trading cities like Ugarit and became herders and farmers. Some of them formed loose federations of towns, villages, and nomadic bands to preserve their sovereignty in the face of new and aggressive outside powers like the Assyrians of northern Mesopotamia. One such federation became the state of Israel, which acquired its own monarchy after 1000 B.C. and protected itself with a network of walled cities. By this time, eastern Mediterranean trade was recovering and the hillside federation expanded into the lowlands, hemmed in by the sea and the desert and by still-powerful Egyptian and Mesopotamian civilizations on either side.

A slow economic recovery during the first millennium B.C. came at the hands of the **Phoenicians.** At first, they acted as middlemen in the Cyprus and Aegean trade. Their ships were soon carrying Lebanese cedarwood to Cyprus and the Nile, copper and iron to the Aegean. Powerful cities like Byblos, Sidon, and Tyre extended their trading as far as the copper and tin mines of

Spain. Phoenician merchants made enormous profits from purple dye extracted from seashells and much used for expensive fabrics. By 800 B.C., Phoenician merchants were everywhere in the Mediterranean, as Assyria became the dominant power in the Levant. Their need for a highly accurate record-keeping system played a significant part in the development of the Western alphabet.

ASSYRIANS AND BABYLONIANS (900 to 539 B.C.)

The city of **Assur** on the Tigris River in northern Mesopotamia had been a major force in the eastern Mediterranean world since Sumerian times. The merchants of Assur controlled strategic desert and river trade routes and commerce downstream to Babylon and beyond. The Assyrian empire expanded dramatically in the ninth century B.C., when a series of despotic, grandiose kings expanded their domains with relentless annual campaigns. These were absolute monarchs, who boasted of their conquests on their palace walls, living in magnificent splendor. They were well aware of the value of conspicuous display. When King Assurnasirpal completed his palace at Nimrud on the Tigris he threw a party for the 16,000 inhabitants of the city, 1500 royal officials, "47,074 men and women from the length of my country," and 5000 foreign envoys. The king fed this throng of more than 69,000 people for 10 days, during which time his guests ate 14,000 sheep and consumed more than 10,000 skins of wine.

The last of the great Assyrian kings was Assurbanipal, who died in approximately 630 B.C. (see Figure 1.13). Eventually, the Assyrian capital, **Nineveh,** fell to Persian and Babylonian warriors. For 43 years, the mighty King Nebuchadnezzar of Babylon ruled over Mesopotamia and turned his capital into one of the showplaces of the ancient world. His double-walled city was adorned by huge mud-brick palaces with elaborate hanging gardens, a great processional way, and a huge ziggurat. It was to Babylon that a large contingent of Jews were taken as captives after Nebuchadnezzar's armies sacked Jerusalem. This event is immortalized in Psalm 137:1: "By the waters of Babylon we sat down and wept."

The Babylonian Empire did not long survive the death of Nebuchadnezzar in 556 B.C. The armies of Cyrus of Persia took Babylon in 539 B.C. The eastern Mediterranean world came under the sway of empires much larger than ever before. These were the centuries of classical Greece, when Rome began to emerge as a major power, when the basic foundations of Western civilization were laid. They came from a Mediterranean world that had been evolving economically, politically, and socially for thousands of years. What had begun as an adaptation to the realities of living in arid, but fertile flood plain environments had developed into a web of economic and political interdependency that was far larger than anything the world had seen before—the remote forerunner of the vast global economic system of today. As we shall see in Chapter 10, by the time the Roman Empire dominated the Mediterranean 2000 years ago, new trade routes and markets as far east as India and China were linked to the western Asian world.

CHAPTER 10

Egypt and Africa

A.D. 1950 –

A.D. 1 –

15,000 B.P. –

50,000 B.P. –

100,000 B.P. –

500,000 B.P. –

1.0 Million –

2.5 Million –

Egypt and the Nile Valley were part of the Mediterranean world, yet they were also linked to African societies far upstream. This chapter describes ancient Egyptian civilization and the African kingdoms that became part of a much wider commercial world in later times.

By 5000 B.C., a patchwork of simple village farming communities lay along both banks of the Nile River, from the delta of Lower Egypt to the First Cataract at Aswan and even further upstream. The river itself formed a natural highway between settlements near and far, the prevailing north winds allowing even sailing boats to stem the sluggish current. The villages soon became a patchwork of small kingdoms, each clustered under the rule of local leaders. Within two thousand years, these small polities had become a unified state, at the time the largest literate civilization in the world.

PREDYNASTIC EGYPT: ANCIENT MONOPOLY?

Most explanations for the origin of the state focus on population growth and competition for land and natural resources. In Egypt's case, state formation took place where population densities were still relatively low and there was plenty of vacant land, so neither of these factors played a significant role.

Egyptologist Barry Kemp believes that the village farmers of 4000 B.C. had strong ties to their ancestral lands, expressed in deeply symbolic terms. At first dozens of small communities, each with their own patchwork of

D I S C O V E R Y

Giovanni Belzoni the Mummy Hunter

"Nearly overcome, I . . . contrived to sit; but when my weight bore on the body of an Egyptian, it crushed it like a band-box. . . . I sank altogether among the broken mummies, with a crash of bones, rags, and wooden cases, which raised such a dust as kept me motionless for a quarter of an hour, waiting till it subsided again." Thus did the notorious Giovanni Belzoni, Italian circus performer turned tomb robber, explore ancient Egypt in 1817. Belzoni became a tomb robber by chance when a scheme to mechanize Egyptian agriculture collapsed. He contracted to move a large statue of the pharaoh Rameses II from Thebes to Alexandria. The tall Italian discovered he had a talent for bold discovery. In the course of three hectic years, he opened the great temple at Abu Simbel in Nubia, penetrated the inner chambers of the Pyramid of Kephren at Giza, and discovered the tomb of pharaoh Seti I in the Valley of Kings. Belzoni and his ilk thought nothing of using gunpowder, even of going after rivals with a gun, for everyone was out for spectacular finds and all the loot they could gather. Eventually, he fled Egypt in danger of his life, exhibited his finds in London, then perished trying to find the source of the Niger River in West Africa.

farming land, competed and traded with their neighbors. Kemp likens the behavior and long-term effects to that in a game of Monopoly. In Monopoly, each player maximizes the opportunities thrown out by the dice. In Egypt, both individuals and entire villages took full advantage of favorable locations, of their access to desirable resources, like potting clay, and of chance breaks that came their way. At first the communities, like Monopoly players, were basically equal, but, inevitably some one, or some hamlet, gained an unforeseen advantage, perhaps from trading expertise, or by unusually high crop yields. Equilibrium gave way to a seemingly inevitable momentum, where some communities acquired more wealth, more power, than their neighbors—the prehistoric equivalent of building Monopoly hotels on Park Place. Their victory was inevitable, as they established a monopoly over local trade, food surpluses, and so on, which overrode any threat posed by other political or economic players.

In predynastic times, there were probably hundreds of such "games" in progress. As time went on, the number of players grew fewer, but the stakes were higher as increasingly large chiefdoms vied for economic power and political dominance. Just like Monopoly, players changed over time, some acquiring great power, then losing it as charismatic individuals died or trading opportunities changed. Kemp points out that Egypt had more than enough fertile land and resources to enable such games to play out over many generations. Surplus resources like grain or toolmaking stone were the foundation of power. But he believes the Egyptians also had a genius for weaving a distinctive ideology that imbued leadership and authority with elaborate symbols and rituals. These ideologies became a powerful factor in promoting unification.

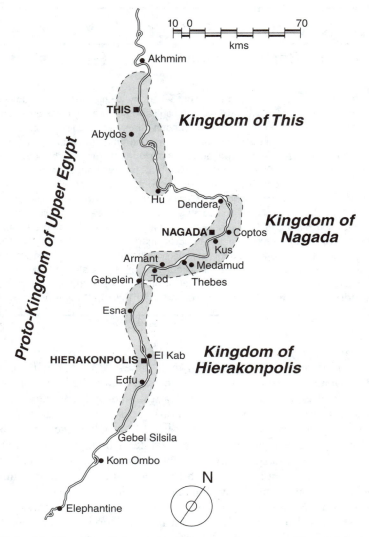

Figure 10.1   Map Showing Predynastic Kingdoms Along the Upper Nile in about 3300 B.C. This is a gross simplification of a complex, ever-changing political situation.

Archaeological excavations and surveys hint at a rapid, but complex consolidation of political power in fewer and fewer hands. By 3500 B.C., three predynastic kingdoms dominated the Nile: **Hierakonpolis, Nagada,** and **This** in Upper Egypt. These little-known kingdoms were the nucleus of a unified Egypt (Figure 10.1).

Archaeology and myth combine for a hypothetical scenario for unification: By 3500 B.C., the kingdoms of Upper Egypt may have had direct contact with southern Arabia and Southwest Asia, bypassing Lower Egypt. Mesopotamian cylinder seals have come from Upper Egyptian sites, and gold

Figure 10.2   THE NARMER PALETTE, A SLATE SLAB CARVED ON BOTH SIDES WITH SCENES COMMEMORATING KING NARMER (MENES), WHOM LEGEND CREDITS WITH UNIFYING UPPER AND LOWER EGYPT   He appears on the palette wearing the white and red crowns of these two regions, presiding over the conquest of the Delta. The central design of entwined beasts (*right*) symbolizes harmony, balancing images of conquest above and below.

was obtained from mines in the eastern desert. Conflict ensued, with the politically most-developed center, Hierakonpolis, emerging victorious. The rulers of Hierakonpolis finally embarked on a campaign of military conquest, which eventually engulfed all of Egypt between the Mediterranean and Aswan.

By 3100 B.C., a semblance of political unity joined Upper and Lower Egypt in the symbolic linking of the gods Horus and Seth depicted in later Egyptian art (Figure 10.2). As these events unfolded, a new state came into being, founded not only on physical, but on a symbolic geography, a harmony achieved by balanced opposites, of which Horus and Seth are but one manifestation. For thousands of years, the Egyptians were concerned with the potential of a world torn between potential chaos and order. They believed that disorder, disequilibrium, could be contained by the rule of kings and by the benign force of the power of the sun. Thus, the Egyptians' intellectual view of the universe coincided with the structure of political power.

Unification was the culmination of local social and political developments that resulted from centuries of gradual change in economic and social life. Predynastic villages were autonomous units, each with its local deities. During the fourth millennium B.C., the larger villages became the focal points of different territories, which in dynastic times became the *nomes,* or provinces, through which the pharaohs administered Egypt. The nomarchs (provincial leaders) were responsible for the gradual coalescence of Egypt into larger political and social units. Their deeds are recorded on ceremonial palettes that were used for moistening eye powder. Some of these palettes show alliances of local leaders dismantling conquered villages. Others commemorate the administrative skills of leaders who brought their villages through drought years by skillful management. The unification of Egypt was a gradual process of both voluntary and involuntary amalgamation. Voluntary unification resulted from common needs and economic advantage. Perhaps it was only in the final stages of unification that military force came into play to bring larger and larger political units under single rulers.

However the process of unification unfolded, there can be no question that unification was the pivotal, and fundamental concept upon which the institutions of ancient Egyptian civilization rested. Unification brought order from political chaos, serenity and rightness to a confused world. The king's task as shepherd of the people was to preserve *ma'at,* "rightness," derived in considerable part from unification.

The Egyptians themselves identified the first pharaoh (the word means "Great House") as Narmer (or Menes). The famous Narmer palette (see Figure 10.3) depicts the semblance of political unity achieved by this king and his successors, as a new state came into being, based on the symbolic balance of the forces of good and evil, unification and fragmentation. The Egyptians believed that only the rule of kings and the benign force of the sun could contain disorder. In reality, unification took several centuries to achieve through a process of deft political alliance and continual warfare.

DYNASTIC EGYPTIAN CIVILIZATION (c. 3000 to 30 B.C.)

Egyptologists conventionally divide ancient Egyptian civilization into four broad periods: Archaic Egypt and the Old Kingdom, the Middle Kingdom, the New Kingdom, and the Late Period. The first three were separated by two intermediate periods that were interludes of political change and instability (see Table 10.1).

Archaic Egypt and the "Great Culture" (3000 to 2575 B.C.)

The Archaic Period comprised the first four-and-a-half centuries of Egyptian civilization, a long period of consolidation when the pharaohs assumed the role of divine kings. They and their high officials invented Egypt's royal tradition, converting it into powerful architectural statements and artistic styles that endured for centuries. Just like Mesoamerican lords (Chapters 12 and 13), the pharaohs made a great play of their rare public appearances, devel-

Table 10.1 ANCIENT EGYPTIAN CIVILIZATION

Years B.C/B.P	Period	Characteristics
30 B.C.	Roman occupation	Egypt an imperial province of Rome
332 to 30	Ptolemaic period	The Ptolemies bring Greek influence to Egypt, beginning with conquest of Egypt by Alexander the Great in 332 B.C.
1070 to 332	Late period	Gradual decline in pharaonic authority, culminating in Persian rule (525 to 404 and 343 to 332 B.C.)
1530 to 1070 B.C.	New Kingdom	Great imperial period of Egyptian history, with pharaohs buried in Valley of Kings; pharaohs include Rameses II, Seti I, and Tutankhamun, as well as Akhenaten, the heretic ruler
1640 to 1530 B.C.	Second intermediate period	Hyksos rulers in the delta
2134 to 2040 B.C.	Middle Kingdom	Thebes achieves prominence, also the priesthood of Amun
2040 to 1640 B.C.	First intermediate period	Political chaos and disunity
2575 to 2134 B.C.	Old Kingdom	Despotic pharaohs build the pyramids and favor conspicuous funerary monuments; institutions, economic strategies, and artistic traditions of ancient Egypt established
2920 to 2575 B.C.	Archaic period	Consolidation of state
3100 B.C.	Unification of Egypt under Narmer-Menes	

oping spectacular settings for major ritual events and festivals. They also created a centralized bureaucracy that directed labor, administered food storage, and collected taxes. At the center of the state lay the concept of a great ruler on earth, who symbolized the triumph of order over chaos. In Egypt, the terms *father, king,* and *god* were metaphors for one another and for a form of political power based on social inequality that was considered part of the natural order established by the gods at the creation.

These four centuries saw the birth of Egypt's "Great Culture," a distinctive ideology that systematized Egyptian civilization over wide areas at the expense of local religious cults. Such an ideology was essential in a society where only a minority could read and write. Scribes held enormous power in all early civilizations, and Egypt was no exception. "Be a scribe. . . . You will go forth in white clothes, honored, with courtiers saluting you," a young man is advised. Writing was power, the key to controlling the labor of thousands of people.

Old Kingdom (c. 2575 to 2134 B.C.)

The Old Kingdom saw society shaped in an image in which the well-being of the people depended on the ruler supported by their labors. Some Old Kingdom pharaohs had reputations as cruel despots, notably Khufu and Khephren, who built the pyramid tombs of Giza, extending the state's resources to the limit. A new image of kingship developed after the death of the pharaoh Djoser in 2649 B.C. The king was now absorbed into the mythic symbol of the sun. The sun god became a heavenly monarch, the pharaoh the deity's representative on earth. On his death, an Old Kingdom pharaoh "went to his double," joining the sun god in heaven. Thus it was that Djoser and his successors lavished enormous expenditure on their sepulchers—at first earthen mounds, then pyramids that became symbolic ladders to heaven, their sloping sides the rays of the sun widening after bursting through a gap in the clouds.

The court cemeteries and pyramid complexes of the Old Kingdom pharaohs extend over a 22-mile (35 km) stretch of the western desert edge, mostly slightly north of **Memphis.** In about 2528 B.C., Snefru's son and successor Khufu built the Great Pyramid of **Giza,** one of the spectacular wonders of ancient Africa and one of the Seven Wonders of the Ancient World (Figures 1.2, 10.3). It covers 13.1 acres (5.3 ha) and is 481 feet (146 m) high. Well over 2 million limestone blocks, some weighing 15 tons apiece, went into its construction. A long causeway linked each pyramid in the Giza complex to a royal mortuary temple. These were austere buildings that housed statues of the king. The nearby sepulchers vested these temples with great authority, for they associated the ruler with what was, in effect, a powerful ancestor cult that linked them to their predecessors and to the gods.

We do not know why the pharaohs suddenly embarked on this orgy of pyramid construction, with all the accompanying demands that it made on the fledgling state. Their construction, like other major Egyptian public works, was a triumph of bureaucratic organization, of organizing and transporting food and building materials. Then officials marshaled skilled artisans and village laborers to quarry, dig, and drag stone into place. What is staggering is the efficient management overview, achieved without computers, deploying and supporting thousands of villagers for short periods of a time as they fulfilled their annual tax-by-labor obligations to the state.

Perhaps, as Kurt Mendelssohn has argued, the pyramids were built as a means of linking the people to their guardian, the king, and to the sun god, the source of human life and of bountiful harvests. The relationship between the king and his subjects was both reciprocal and spiritual. The pharaoh was a divine king, whose person was served by annual labor. In short, pyramid building created public works that helped define the authority of the ruler and

Figure 10.3   THE SPHINX AT GIZA BUILT BY THE OLD KINGDOM PHARAOH KHEPHREN IN ABOUT 2500 B.C. Human-headed lions (sphinxes) were important symbols of royal power.

make his subjects dependent upon him. Every flood season, when agriculture was at a standstill, the pharaohs organized thousands of peasants into construction teams. The permanent (year-round) labor force comprised relatively few people, mainly skilled artisans, the fruit of whose work was placed in position on the main structure once a year. As far as is known, the peasants worked off tax obligations. Their loyalty to the divine pharaoh provided the motivation for the work. Mendelssohn believes the construction of the pyramids was a practical administrative device designed to organize and institutionalize the state by trading redistributed food for labor. As construction proceeded from one generation to the next, the villagers became dependent on the central administration for food for three months a year, food obtained from surpluses contributed by the villages themselves in the form of taxation. After a while the pyramids fulfilled their purpose, and the state-directed labor forces could be diverted to other, less conspicuous state works. A new form of state organization had been created, one that both fostered and exploited the interdependence of Egyptian villages.

Old Kingdom Egypt was the first state of its size in history. The pharaohs ruled by their own word, following no written laws, unlike the legislators of Mesopotamian city-states. The pharaoh had power over the Nile flood, rainfall, and all people, including foreigners. He was a god, respected by all people as a tangible divinity whose being was the personification of *Ma'at*, or "rightness." *Ma'at* was far more than just rightness; it was a "right order" and stood for order and justice. *Ma'at* was pharaonic status and eternity itself—the very embodiment of the Egyptian state. As the embodiment of *Ma'at,* the pharaoh pronounced the law, regulated by a massive background of precedent set by earlier pharaohs.

A massive, hereditary bureaucracy effectively ruled the kingdom, with rows of officials forming veritable dynasties. Their records tell us that much official energy was devoted to tax collection, harvest yields, and administration of irrigation. An army of 20,000 men, many of them mercenaries, was maintained at the height of Egypt's prosperity. The Egyptian empire was a literate one; that is, trained scribes were an integral part of the state government.

Old Kingdom Egypt was a time of powerful, confident rulers, of a virile state governed by a privileged class of royal relatives and high officials. Their talents created a civilization that was for the benefit of a tiny minority. It was for this privileged elite, headed by a divine king, that Egyptian merchants traded for the famed cedars of Lebanon, mined turquoise and copper in Sinai, and sought ivory, semiprecious stones, and mercenaries for Egypt's armies from Nubia.

A prolonged drought cycle after 2250 undermined the Old Kingdom rulers' absolute powers. Three hundred years of repeated famines led to anarchy and a diminution of pharaonic authority (see Table 10.1).

Middle Kingdom (2040 to 1640 B.C.)

In about 2134 B.C., the city of **Thebes** in Upper Egypt achieved supremacy and reunited Egypt under a series of energetic pharaohs. Middle Kingdom rulers were less despotic, more approachable, and less likely to see themselves as gods. They had learned lessons from the past and relied heavily on an efficient bureaucracy to stockpile food supplies and increase agricultural production (Figure 10.4). At the same time, the Theban pharaohs expanded overseas trade, busying themselves with remodeling society into a highly centralized, regimented whole. They tried to turn the Nile Valley into an organized oasis. The experiment failed, as the scale of the task was beyond the state's resources. Again, Egypt fragmented into component parts, as succession disputes engulfed the Theban court. By the 17th century B.C., Lower Egypt was under the control of Hyksos kings, nomadic rulers from Asia. This Second Intermediate Period was a turning point in Egyptian history, for the Hyksos brought new ideas to a civilization that was slowly stagnating in its isolated homeland. They introduced more sophisticated bronze technology, the horse-drawn chariot, and new weapons of war. All these innovations kept Egypt up to date and ensured that subsequent pharaohs would play a leading role in the wider eastern Mediterranean world.

New Kingdom (1530 to 1075 B.C.)

The New Kingdom began when a series of Theban rulers fought and finally conquered the Hyksos. An able pharaoh named Ahmose the Liberator turned Egypt into an efficiently run military state, tolerating no rivals and rewarding his soldiers with gifts of land, while retaining economic power and wealth in his own hands. Ahmose set the tone for the greatest era in Egyptian history.

Figure 10.4   MODELS OF A BOAT AND AN ESTATE GRANARY BELONGING TO A MIDDLE KINGDOM COURTIER NAMED MEKETRE   He rides in his boat sitting under a canopy. On his estate, laborers fill bins with wheat as scribes in a neighboring office record the amounts being stored.

Now the king became a national hero, a military leader who sat on a throne midway between the Asiatic world in the north and the black Nubian king-doms of the south (see below). He was an imperial ruler, a skilled general, the

Figure 10.5   Temple of Amun at Karnak

leader of a great power. As we saw in Chapter 9, Egypt now became a major player in the shifting sands of eastern Mediterranean politics, competing with the Hittites and Mitanni for control of lucrative trade routes and sea ports. New Kingdom pharaohs financed their kingdom with Nubian gold, turning the lands beyond the First Cataract into a lucrative colony.

Thebes was now capital of Egypt, the "Estate of Amun," the sun god. The Temple of Amun at Karnak, built mostly between the 16th and 14th centuries B.C., was the heart of the sacred capital (Figure 10.5). Amun was the "king of the gods," a solar deity who conceived the pharaohs, then protected them in life and death. The "Estate of Amun" extended to the western bank of the Nile opposite Thebes, where the pharaohs erected an elaborate city of the dead. They themselves were buried in secret, rock-cut tombs in the arid Valley of Kings. Their sepulchers became models of the caverns of the underworld traversed by the night-sun.

The New Kingdom witnessed a brief period of religious unorthodoxy in 1353 B.C., when a heretic pharaoh, Akhenaten, turned away from Amun to a purer form of sun worship, based on the solar disk Aten. Akhenaten went so far as to found a new royal capital at El-Amarna downstream of Thebes, on land associated with no established deity. The capital was abandoned, leaving a priceless archaeological legacy—a unique archive of New Kingdom society that archaeologists have excavated at intervals for over a century.

In 1333 B.C., eight-year-old Tutankhamun succeeded to the throne. He presided over a troubled kingdom, so his advisers took the only course open to them. They restored the old spiritual order, reverting to the dynastic traditions of the early pharaohs. Tutankhamun himself ruled for a mere 10 years,

Figure 10.6   THE ANTECHAMBER OF TUTANKHAMUN'S TOMB, WITH HIS ROYAL CHARIOTS IN THE FOREGROUND (*LEFT*) AND FUNERARY BEDS TO THE RIGHT

but achieved in death an immortality that transcends that of all other pharaohs, simply because Howard Carter and Lord Carnarvon found his intact tomb in the Valley of Kings (Figure 10.6).

The Rameside pharaohs of 1307 to 1196 B.C. labored hard to elevate Egypt to its former imperial glory. Rameses II (1290 to 1224 B.C.) campaigned far into Syria, financing his military campaigns and an orgy of temple building with Nubian gold. He met his match at the Battle of Kadesh in Syria, where the Hittites fought his army to a standstill. From that moment on, Egypt lost political influence in southwestern Asia, and began a slow, at first barely perceptible, decline.

Late Period (1070 to 30 B.C.)

With the death of Rameses III in 1070 B.C., Egypt entered a period of political weakness, during which local rulers exercised varying control over the Nile. The pharaohs were threatened by Nubian rulers from the south, who controlled Egypt for a time in the eighth century B.C. Assyrians, Persians, and Greeks all ruled over the Nile for varying periods of time until Rome incorporated the world's longest-lived civilization into its empire in 30 B.C. The Greeks brought much of Egyptian lore and learning into the mainstream of emerging Greek civilization, ensuring that ancient Egypt contributed to the roots of Western civilization.

EGYPT AND AFROCENTRISM

The ancient Greeks and Romans believed that Egypt was the fountain of all civilization. While archaeological discoveries have shown that urban civilization developed in both Egypt and Mesopotamia at the same time, most scholars believe that civilization developed in isolation along the Nile, in a fertile, if unpredictable river valley that was a world unto its own.

Some African-American historians of the so-called **Afrocentrism** school disagree, for they believe that the institutions of Western civilization were born in tropical Africa and that ancient Egypt was a black African civilization. These arguments, which first surfaced in the 1950s, have reached a high level of sophistication in linguist Martin Bernal's celebrated "Black Athena" theory. Bernal presents archaeological, historical, and linguistic evidence to place ancient Egypt at the core of Western civilization. Egyptologists are almost unanimous in demolishing his arguments on the grounds they do not stand in the face of scientific data. For example, Afrocentrists claim that the ancient Egyptians were black-skinned tropical Africans. In fact, both tomb paintings and biological data point to a generally Mediterranean population, but one that became increasingly cosmopolitan in later centuries, as Egypt enjoyed closer contacts with other lands, including tropical Africa.

NUBIA: THE LAND OF KUSH (3000 to 633 B.C.)

If ancient Egypt was indeed a civilization unto itself, what connections did it enjoy with the people of the Nile Valley living south of the First Cataract at Aswan? The arid country that lay upstream was **Nubia,** the Land of **Kush,** famous to the ancient Egyptians for its gold, ivory, and slaves. Nubia straddled the Middle Nile, a narrow strip of fertile land that extended far upstream into modern-day Sudan as far as the borders of highland Ethiopia. The most fertile valley lands lie along the Dongola Reach between the Third and Fourth Cataracts. It was here that some of the earliest complex Nubian societies developed, among groups who had been herders and farmers since before 4000 B.C.

Old Kingdom pharaohs sent their armies to subdue Nubia and boasted of lucrative cattle raids. Egyptian prospectors journeyed far into the desert in search of fine rocks and semiprecious stones. The Middle Kingdom kings were more ambitious, for they discovered Nubian gold. In 1900 B.C. pharaoh Amenemhet fortified strategic reaches with 10 strongholds, most of them at strategic points where trade routes intersected with the river. This trade lay in the hands of the Nubian chieftains of **Kerma** in the heart of the Dongola Reach, a small town with palaces and temples, fortified with elaborate defenses and four gates. Kerma's rulers enjoyed great wealth and were buried under large burial mounds surrounded with as many as 400 sacrificial victims (Figure 10.7). All this wealth came from trade connections with people living in the desert and farther upstream, and with the Egyptians far downstream. But the New Kingdom pharaohs, who wanted this wealth for themselves, marched on Kush in 1500 B.C. and made it a colony. Nubia now changed from

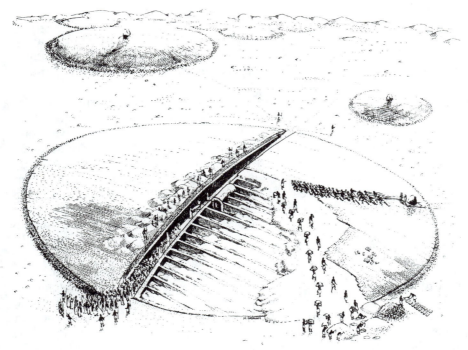

Figure 10.7 A Royal Tomb at Kerma, Nubia—Laborers Rush to Complete the Mound as the Burial Takes Place

a country of village farmers and chiefdoms into something resembling a vast plantation state, worked for the benefit of absentee landlords to provide commodities of all types at the cheapest possible cost.

The economic and political shock waves that rolled over the eastern Mediterranean after 1200 B.C. not only overthrew the Hittites and weakened Egypt (Chapter 9) but also loosened the pharaohs' hold on Nubia. After four centuries of confusion, Nubian civilization achieved new heights. The rulers of the new Kush espoused ancient Egyptian religious beliefs and assumed the powers and ideology of the pharaohs. Their wealth came from the Egyptian export trade, from gold, ivory, and many other commodities.

Between 730 and 663 B.C. Nubian monarchs not only ruled over Kush, they presided over Egypt itself. King Piye marched north in 730, honored the sun god Amun at Thebes, then subdued rebellious rulers in the delta far downstream. Piye was content to rule Egypt from Kush, but his successors transferred their court to Thebes, as the servant became the master, the conquered the conquerors. The Nubian pharaohs did much to restore art and religion, but they were inexperienced in foreign affairs, which led to their downfall. In 663 B.C., King Assurbanipal of Assyria sacked Thebes and the ruler of the day fled to the safety of Kush. In 591, an Egyptian army marched upstream and "waded in Kushite blood." King Aspelta fled far upstream to Meroe, some 300 miles (482 km) upstream, where Nubian monarchs ruled in peace for more than 800 years.

MEROE AND AKSUM

The move to **Meroe** came when the focus of Nubian trade was shifting away from the eastern Mediterranean to the Red Sea and Indian Ocean. This new commercial world linked the Red Sea, the Persian Gulf states, India, and ultimately Southeast Asia and China into a vast web.

The island of Socotra off northeast Africa and the mysterious Land of Punt on the coast of the southern Red Sea were spice-rich lands where Africans rubbed shoulders with Arabians, Indians with Egyptians. Well-traveled trade routes linked Red Sea coasts with the Nile and the eastern Mediterranean coastline, traversed by laden asses, and, increasingly, by camels, aptly named the "ship of the desert" by the Arabians who first domesticated them as early as 2500 B.C. By the third century B.C., camel breeders dominated the overland caravan trade and brought prosperity to Meroe.

Meroe (593 B.C. to A.D. 330)

Meroe lies on the east bank of the Nile, some 124 miles (200 km) north of Khartoum. Its rulers administered a string of villages and towns along the river from Lower Nubia to Sennar on the Blue Nile, controlling the gold, ivory, and slave trade with Egypt. The city also lay astride bustling caravan routes that linked the river with the Red Sea and extended far to the west, along the southern margins of the Sahara (Figure 10.8).

Figure 10.8   GENERAL VIEW OF MEROE, SHOWING PYRAMIDS AND SLAG HEAPS   Two thousand years ago Meroe lay amidst fertile grasslands; it is now desert, partly as a result of overgrazing and excessive tree cutting for charcoal burning by the city's inhabitants.

Some 24 kings and queens ruled over Meroe between 593 and 220 B.C. These black-skinned rulers were the descendants of the great pharaoh Piye and his successors. They preserved many of the conservative standards of ancient Egyptian civilization, but with a distinctive African slant. For centuries, they administered a complex, exploitative economic enterprise for their own benefit, controlling trade through a network of carefully policed trade routes and by force.

Ironworking was big business at Meroe, for iron ore was plentiful nearby. Huge slag heaps overlooked the temples and palaces of the city, accumulated over centuries of manufacture that began as early as the seventh century B.C. Iron-tipped tools and weapons gave Meroitic armies strategic advantages over their desert neighbors.

Meroe reached the height of its prosperity during the first century A.D., when it maintained regular trading contacts with the Roman Empire. A century later, the city was in decline, finally overthrown by the armies of King Ezana of the kingdom of Aksum in the nearby Ethiopian highlands between A.D. 325 and 350.

Aksum (A.D. 100 to 1000)

Aksum had prospered off the Red Sea trade, an African kingdom, whose rulers adopted many ideas from south Arabia in the five centuries before Christ (Figure 10.9). Its highland homeland was a fertile, if unpredictable environment, where irrigated cereal crops, among them a native grass called teff, flourished, providing large food surpluses in good years. By the first century A.D., Aksum was a powerful kingdom, in regular contact with Rome, handling all manner of exotic luxuries and commodities through its port at Adulis on the Red Sea. Adulis became so important that Aksum soon overshadowed Meroe, as the Nile trade declined.

The archaeology of Aksum is still little known, but its rulers lived in imposing multistory palaces and were buried under tall columns up to 108 feet (33 m) high, carved to represent such buildings (Figure 10.10). At about the time he overthrew Meroe, King Ezana abandoned the religion of his forefathers and adopted Christianity, which had reached his domains through Aksum's widespread trading connections.

Christianity flourishes in Ethiopia to this day, but Aksum faltered as Islam acquired increasing influence over the Red Sea trade in the seventh century A.D. At the height of its powers, Aksum was a potent symbol of a new, much more international world, which sprang from the ruins of the Roman empire and linked Asia and Africa with lasting ties.

ANCIENT AFRICAN KINGDOMS

The new trade networks of the Indian Ocean and Red Sea, and the development of long-distance caravan routes across the Sahara Desert had an indelible effect on African history, linking tropical African kingdoms with a much

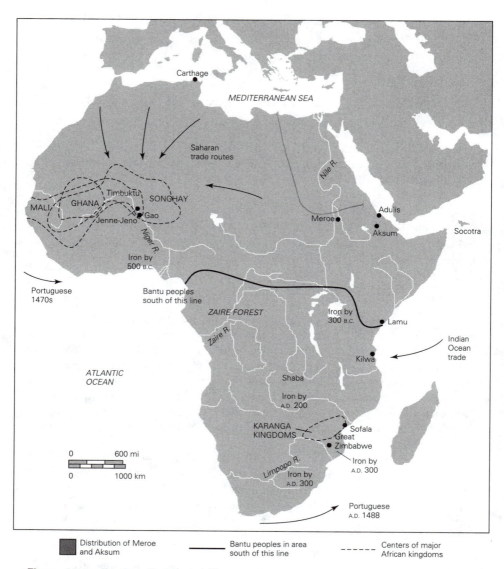

Figure 10.9 AFRICAN STATES AND KINGDOMS

larger foreign world. The cultural isolation of sub-Saharan Africa finally broke down during the early Christian era. The insatiable demands of its neighbors for copper, gold, ivory, and slaves brought Africans in touch with Mediterranean and Indian Ocean trading systems.

The camel revolutionized contacts across the desert. Camels are perfectly adapted to desert travel, so much so that North African merchants could organize regular caravans that crossed the Sahara from the Mediterranean to

Figure 10.10 A ROYAL STELA AT AKSUM, ETHIOPIA

tropical West Africa. African gold and ivory eventually became important sources of medieval European wealth.

No one knows when mariners discovered the cycles of the Indian Ocean monsoon winds. The northeast monsoon brings sailors to Africa in winter. Then, in summer, the northwest monsoon returns them to their destination. These cycles are so regular that a sailing vessel can travel from India to Arabia or East Africa and back within 12 months. The monsoon winds were known to Egyptian and Greek navigators by A.D. 100, by which time the Indian Ocean was part of the vast trading networks that linked China with the Southeast Asian and Mediterranean worlds. There was an insatiable demand for African ivory, gold, silver, iron, and slaves in Arabia and India.

Arabian dhows, downwind sailing vessels, brought cargoes of Indian cotton, strings of cheap glass beads, Chinese porcelain, and other exotic goods to the East African coast. There they traded them for ivory and other raw materials brought to coastal ports and towns like Manda, Lamu, and Kilwa. From the coast, small parties of traders traveled far into the interior, along intervillage paths, developing trading contacts and relationships that were to endure for many centuries. By A.D. 300, isolated strings of Indian glass beads were worn by villagers in the heart of central Africa, more than 600 miles (965 km) from the Indian Ocean.

The Spread of Iron (c. 500 B.C. to A.D. 250)

The Saharan trade brought iron and ironworking south of the desert for the first time, as early as the fifth century B.C. More a utilitarian than a decorative metal, and ideal for tropical forest clearance and agriculture, iron spread rapidly through sub-Saharan Africa as agricultural economies took hold for the first time. Farmers had settled in the great East African lakes region by the last few centuries B.C. and to the banks of the Zambezi and Limpopo Rivers in the early Christian era. The newcomers absorbed, eliminated, or pushed out the indigenous foragers. Today, forager populations survive only in areas that are too arid for farming, such as the Kalahari Desert in southern Africa.

The Kingdoms of Ghana, Mali, and Songhay (c. A.D. 800 to 1550)

Throughout the first millennium A.D., the Saharan gold trade continued to expand gradually, reflected by larger settlements south of the desert. Islamic conquerors took control of the Saharan trade at the end of the first millennium A.D., a development that brought literate and much-traveled Arab geographers to the lands south of the Sahara. There, the geographer al-Bakri described the Kingdom of Ghana as being so rich in gold that "it is said that the king owns a nugget as large as a big stone."

The Kingdom of **Ghana** straddled the northern borders of the gold-bearing river valleys of the upper Niger and Senegal. No one knows when it first came into being, but the kingdom was described by Arab writers in the eighth century A.D. The Ghanians prospered from the gold, ivory, and salt trade. They also exported kola nuts (used as a stimulant) and slaves. In return they, and their successors, received cloth, leather goods, glass beads, and weapons. The King of Ghana probably presided over a loosely knit alliance of minor chiefs and small towns and had little real power.

Ghana dissolved into its constituent chiefdoms during the 11th century. Two centuries of incessant squabbling ensued, until the Kingdom of **Mali** came into being at the hands of an able ruler named Sundiata. Sundiata came to power in about 1230 and founded his new capital at Mali on the Niger River. A century later, Mali extended over much of sub-Saharan West Africa. The fame of the Mali kings spread all over the Islamic world (Figure 10.11). The city of Timbuktu on the fringes of the western Sahara became not only a famous caravan center but a celebrated place of Islamic scholarship. All this

Figure 10.11   THE ISLAMIC MOSQUE AT JENNE, MALI, ON THE SOUTHERN FRINGES OF THE SAHARA DESERT   Islam was a strong influence on West African kingdoms.

prosperity was based on the gold and ivory trade. Malian gold underpinned not only much of the Islamic world, but the treasuries of European kings, too. Before Columbus sailed to the New World, Mali and its lesser neighbors provided no less than two thirds of Europe's gold.

Mali's Islamic rulers governed with supreme powers granted by Allah and ruled their conquered provinces with carefully selected religious appointees, or even through clever slaves, chosen for their loyalty and political acumen. Islam provided a reservoir of thoroughly trained, literate administrators who believed that political stability resulted from efficient government and sound trading practices. So confident was the Malian king Mansa Musa that he left his kingdom and crossed the Sahara on a long pilgrimage to Mecca in 1324. He and his wealthy entourage spent so freely in Cairo that the price of gold was depressed for several years.

About a year later, Mansa Musa brought the great trading center at Gao on the Niger River under his control. The leaders of Gao resented Malian control and threw off its yoke in 1340, founding a rival kingdom, **Songhay**. The new state prospered as a series of able rulers expanded their domains. Most famous among them was Sonni Ali, who expanded Songhay's frontiers far into the Sahara and deep into Mali country between 1464 and 1494, monopolizing much of the gold and ivory trade at the same time.

Songhay was at the height of its powers when Columbus landed in the New World. When it invaded the Americas, Europe acquired new sources for precious metals that trebled the amount of gold and silver circulating in

Europe in half a century. The annual output from America was 10 times that of the rest of the world. The Saharan gold trade declined sharply. Cities like Gao and Timbuktu, as well as the Kingdom of Songhay, crumbled into relative obscurity. By 1550, Songhay had collapsed, as the center of political power moved south into the tropical forests and coastal regions that are now Ghana, Nigeria, and the Ivory Coast, where European ships traded for gold, ivory, and slaves.

Great Zimbabwe (A.D. 1100 to 1500)

The staple commodity of the Indian Ocean trade was elephant ivory. African ivory is softer and more easily carved than the brittle tusk of the Indian elephant. Tusks fed a flourishing market for Hindu bridal ornaments throughout India. This ancient commerce was well established by the late first millennium A.D., and it continued to prosper long after the discovery of the Americas. By A.D. 1100 a string of small Islamic towns flourished along the coast from Somalia in the north to Kilwa in southern Tanzania in the south. They formed a distinctive coastal civilization that was based entirely on the Indian Ocean trade. From places like the islands of **Kilwa** and Zanzibar, small caravans set off for the interior, carrying bundles of cotton, glass beads, and thousands of seashells from Indian Ocean beaches. These latter were prized as ornaments in the far interior. This trade was very one-sided in strict monetary terms, for the glass beads, cheap cloth, and other luxuries perceived as prestigious in the African interior were worth a fraction of the gold dust, copper ingots, ivory, and slaves that fueled the maritime trade of an entire ocean.

Much East African gold came from the highlands between the Zambezi and Limpopo Rivers in southern Africa. The coastal traders bartered with the **Karanga** peoples of the interior plateau, who were farmers and cattle herders organized into several powerful kingdoms headed by hereditary rulers. These chiefs acquired political power by controlling sources of copper, gold, and ivory and by redistributing imports from the coast to their subjects. Karanga chiefs were also important spiritual leaders, who acted as intermediaries between the people and their ancestral spirits.

One such chief built an imposing stone capital at **Great Zimbabwe** (Figure 10.12). His Great Enclosure with massive free-standing masonry walls lay in the shadow of a low hill at the head of a valley that brought moist winds and mist up from the distant Indian Ocean. It was here that the chief and his priests performed rain-making ceremonies and interceded with the ancestors. Here, too, the chief traded with occasional parties of visiting coastal traders, probably men who were part Arabian, part African. There is no evidence that the Zimbabwe chiefs embraced Islam. Zimbabwe was the center of a truly indigenous African kingdom.

At least five stages of occupation have been recognized at Zimbabwe, the earliest dating to the fourth century A.D. The first settlement was a humble village, the four remaining occupations the work of Karanga peoples who built progressively more complicated stone enclosures and retaining walls. The hey-

Figure 10.12   THE ELLIPTICAL BUILDING AT GREAT ZIMBABWE, ZIMBABWE

day of Zimbabwe was between 1350 and 1450, just before Europeans arrived on the coast. The site was abandoned sometime after 1450, when the local grazing grass and farming land became depleted.

All these indigenous African kingdoms developed in response to economic and political opportunities from outside. But their political, social, and economic institutions were always adapted to local conditions and were logical developments of earlier farming cultures.

After the 15th century A.D., Africa was exploited not only for its raw materials, but for its slaves. The tentacles of the international slave trade touched not only African coasts, but reached into the deepest strongholds of the interior. It was not until the 19th century that Victorian explorers, in pursuit of elusive geographical prizes like the source of the Nile, revealed to a horrified world the full extent of the slave trade and its catastrophic effect on African society.

CHAPTER 11

South, Southeast, and East Asia

A.D. 1950 —

A.D. 1 —

15,000 B.P. —

50,000 B.P. —

100,000 B.P. —

500,000 B.P. —

1.0 Million —

2.5 Million —

The world's earliest civilizations developed in the Nile Valley and western Asia. Within 15 centuries, Egypt, the eastern Mediterranean, Mesopotamia, and the Iranian highlands were linked in a loosely structured and ever-changing economic system. States rose and fell, rulers achieved supreme power, only to see their domains collapse like a house of cards, armies battled over strategic ports and control of vital materials, but the web of interconnectedness adjusted and remained intact. Soon the tentacles of these economic contacts extended far to the east, into southern Asia and far beyond. In Chapter 9, we saw how the emphasis of long-distance trade shifted southward into the Red Sea and Indian Ocean region after the decline of Ancient Egypt in about 1000 B.C. This chapter retraces chronological steps and describes how state-organized societies developed in South and Southeast Asia and China (Figure 11.1).

SOUTH ASIA: THE HARAPPAN CIVILIZATION (c. 2700 to 1700 B.C.)

The Indus River, on the banks of which south Asian civilization began, rises in the snow-clad Himalayas of southern Tibet and descends 1000 miles (c. 1600 km) through Kashmir before debouching onto the Pakistani plains. Here, as in Mesopotamia and the Nile valley, fertile flood plain soils played an important role in the development of state-organized society. Between June and September each year, the spring runoff from the distant mountains reaches the plains, inundating thousands

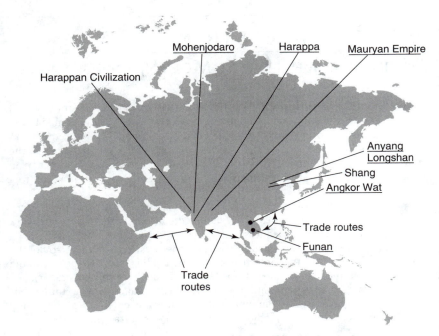

Figure 11.1 Map of Asian Sites and Societies in Chapter 11

of acres of good farming land and depositing rich flood-borne silts as a natural fertilizer, on soil soft enough to be cultivated without the aid of metal artifacts.

Hundreds of village settlements flourished across the Indus valley plains by 3000 B.C. Many of them were small fortified towns with carefully laid-out streets, built above the highest flood level but as close to the river as possible. The next 500 years saw irrigation canals and flood embankments transform the Indus valley environment into an artificial landscape. The obvious leaders for these new communities were the chieftains, traders, priests, and kin leaders, who acted as intermediaries between the people and their gods. Theirs was a philosophy that humans were part of an ordered cosmos that could be maintained by unremitting toil and a subordination of individual ambition to the common good. No one knows when this primordial philosophy developed, but it is probably as old as farming itself, always a risky undertaking in subtropical lands. By 2700 B.C., the most successful leaders of larger settlements presided over hierarchies of cities, towns, and villages.

The early stages of the **Harappan civilization** date to between 3200 and 2600 B.C. The people lived in small villages covering only a few acres, and there are no signs of social ranking. Their environment was like that of Mesopotamia, low-lying, hot, and with fertile soils but no metals. Thus, its inhabitants could not flourish in isolation. Long before the rise of Harappan civilization in the valley, the peoples of the lowlands interacted constantly with their neighbors to the north and west, especially in the highlands of

D I S C O V E R Y

MORTIMER WHEELER AT MOHENJODARO

In 1950, the famed excavator Sir Mortimer Wheeler assembled a team of young archaeologists, students, and local laborers to work on a confusion of mud bricks that projected out of a weathered citadel mound at Mohenjodaro on the banks of the Indus River, in Pakistan. The laborers removed foot after foot of sand, the few bricks grew into many, "until the stark walls of a huge platform began to emerge from the hillside. The aspect was of a fortress, towering grim and forbidding above the plain . . . ."

Wheeler puzzled over the mass of brickwork. A grid of narrow passages, signs of a timber superstructure, a carefully designed platform with an approach way. The enormous structure looked less and less like a fortress, but what was it? Suddenly a light went on in his brain. The narrow passages were air ducts to dry the floor of the timber barn that once housed the city's grain, accessible only from the site away from the teeming streets. The "fortress" was the municipal granary.

Later investigators have questioned Wheeler's granary interpretation, but his massive excavations at Harappa and Mohenjodaro produced a compelling portrait of a long-forgotten, indigenous south Asian civilization.

---

southern Baluchistan in western Pakistan. Metals, semiprecious stones, and timber came from the highlands, where people depended for their subsistence on dry agriculture and sheep herding. Over the millennia, the relationship between lowlands and highlands was fostered not only by regular exchange of foods and other commodities but also by seasonal population movements that brought enormous herds of goats and sheep down from mountain summer pastures in Baluchistan to the lowlands during the harsh winters in the west. This symbiosis between Baluchistan and the Indus may have been a major catalyst in the rise of complex societies in both areas, a symbiosis that was vital not only in the Indus Valley but in distant Mesopotamia as well.

Early Harappan society was in sharp contrast to the complex, sometimes urban society that developed in the lowlands after about 2600 B.C. The transition from egalitarian to ranked society was an indigenous one, with a short period of explosive growth over a period of one or two centuries ending about 2500 B.C. This contrasts dramatically with the long period of increasing social, political, and economic complexity in Egypt and Mesopotamia.

Archaeologist Gregory Possehl believes that this growth may have coincided with a major shift in Sumerian trade patterns. After 2600 B.C., Mesopotamian city-states reorganized their trade in luxuries and raw materials and obtained many of their needs by sea from three foreign states—**Dilmun,** on the island of Bahrein in the Persian Gulf; **Magan,** a port further east; and **Meluhha,** even farther away, where ivory, oils, furniture, gold, silver, and carnelian, among other commodities, were to be obtained. The Sumerians exchanged these goods for wool, cloth, leather, oil, cereals, and cedarwood.

Possehl believes Meluhha to be the Indus Valley region. In about 2350 B.C., King Sargon of Agade in Mesopotamia boasted that ships from all these locations were moored at his city. There are even records of villages of Meluhhans near **Lagash** and elsewhere in Mesopotamia. This was a highly organized mercantile trade conducted by specialized merchants, a trade quite different from that of the exchange networks on the highlands far inland.

The sea trade increased the volume of Sumerian imports and exports dramatically. One shipment of 13,000 pounds (5900 kg) of copper is recorded. The entire enterprise was very different from the basically noncommercial exchange systems of the Iranian Plateau. The trade was under Mesopotamian control, much of it conducted through Dilmun and, in Possehl's view, it had a major impact on the growth of Harappan civilization. Interestingly, its beginnings coincide with the growth of urban centers in both Mesopotamia and the Indus Valley. However, many scholars believe overseas trade was less important than sometimes claimed and that Harappan civilization was an entirely indigenous development.

Mature Harappan Civilization

Mature Harappan civilization developed and flourished over a vast area of just under half a million square miles, a region considerably larger than modern Pakistan. The Indus and Saraswati Valleys were the cultural focus of the Harappan civilization, but they were only one part of a much larger, very varied civilization, whose influences and ties extended over the lowlands of Punjab and Sind, and from the highlands of Baluchistan to the deserts of Rajastan, and from the Himalayan foothills to near Bombay. The age-old relationship between highland Baluchistan and the Indus plains placed the Harappans within a larger cultural system, as did their maritime links with the Persian Gulf.

The Harappan civilization was different from that of the predominantly urban Sumerians in Mesopotamia, covering a core area of more than 300,000 square miles (777,000 sq. km). Gregory Possehl makes an analogy with Egypt, where the Upper and Lower Nile were part of the same civilization, but there were always administrative, cultural, and social differences between the two regions. These were major regional subdivisions of the Harappan civilization, linked by common symbolism and religious beliefs, the foundations of a cultural tradition that endured, albeit in modified form, for many centuries.

Like the Sumerians, the Harappans adopted the city as a means of organizing and controlling their civilization. We know of at least five major Harappan cities. The best known are **Harappa,** after which the civilization is named, and **Mohenjodaro.** Harappa and Mohenjodaro were built on artificial mounds above the floods at the cost of Herculean efforts. Mohenjodaro is by far the largest of the Harappan cities, six times the area of Harappa, and was rebuilt at least nine times, sometimes because of disastrous inundations. Widely accepted population estimates, based on densities of modern, somewhat similar settlements, place some 35,000 to 40,000 people at Mohenjodaro, 23,500 at Harappa.

Figure 11.2   THE GREAT CITADEL AT HARAPPA, PAKISTAN

The two cities are so similar that they might have been designed by the same architect. A high citadel lies at the west end of each city, dominating the streets below. Here lived the rulers, protected by great fortifications and flood works (Figure 11.2). Mohenjodaro's towering citadel rises 40 feet (12 m) above the plain and is protected by massive flood embankments and a vast perimeter wall with towers. The public buildings on the summit include a pillared hall almost 90 feet (27 m) square, perhaps the precinct where the rulers gave audience to petitioners and visiting officials. There are no spectacular temples or richly adorned shrines.

The rulers of each city looked down on a complex network of at least partially planned streets (Figure 11.3). The more spacious dwellings, perhaps those of the nobility and merchants, were laid out around a central courtyard where guests may have been received, where food was prepared, and where servants probably worked. Staircases and thick ground walls indicate that some houses had two or even three stories. There were also groups of single-rowed tenements or workshops at both Harappa and Mohenjodaro where the

Figure 11.3   A Street at Mohenjodaro, Pakistan

poorest people lived, many of them presumably laborers. Some areas of Harappa and Mohenjodaro served as bazaars, complete with shops.

We do not know the names of the rulers who controlled the major cities like Harappa and Mohenjodaro. The anonymity of the Harappan leaders extends even to their appearance (Figure 11.4). These were no bombastic rulers, boasting of their achievements on grandiose palace walls. Thus far, the evidence of archaeology reveals leadership by rulers, perhaps merchants, ritual specialists, or people who controlled key resources or large areas of land. They seem not to have led ostentatious lives; there was a complete lack of priestly pomp or lavish public display. There is nothing of the ardent militarism of the Assyrian kings or of the slavish glorification of the pharaohs.

One reason we know so little about Harappan leaders is that their script still has not been deciphered. Almost 400 different pictographic symbols have been identified from their seals. Linguists do not even agree on the language in the script, but they know it is a mixture of sounds and concepts, just like Egyptian hieroglyphs. Harappan seals depict gods, like a three-headed figure who sits in the yogic posture and wears a horned headdress. He is surrounded by a tiger, elephant, rhinoceros, water buffalo, and deer. Some Harappan experts think the deity was a forerunner of the great god Shiva in his role of Lord of the Beasts. Many Harappan seals depict cattle, which may be symbols of Shiva, who was worshiped in several forms. To judge from later beliefs, he may have had a dual role, serving as a fertility god as well as a tamer or

Figure 11.4 A BEARDED
MAN FROM MOHENJODARO

destroyer of wild beasts. In part he may symbolize the unpredictable dangers
of flood and famine that could threaten a village or a city. If the evidence of
figurines and seals is to be believed, the symbolism of early Indus religion
bears remarkable similarities to that of modern Hinduism.

SOUTH ASIA AFTER THE HARAPPANS (1700 to 180 B.C.)

The Harappan civilization reached its peak in about 2000 B.C. Three centuries
later, Harappa and Mohenjodaro were in decline and soon abandoned. Their
populations dispersed into smaller settlements over an enormous area. The
reasons for this change are still little understood, but may be due to a variety
of factors, among them possible flooding along the Indus, shifts in patterns of
Mesopotamian trade, and changes in subsistence farming. One fundamental
cause may have been major geological disturbances near the source of the all-
important Saraswati River, which caused it to dry up and some tributaries to
divert to new courses, thereby catastrophically disrupting farming life along
its banks.

Other changes followed soon afterward. By 1500 B.C., rice cultivation had
taken hold in the Ganges Basin to the east, opening up a new environment for
farming where conditions were unsuitable for wheat and barley cultivation.
By 800 B.C., an indigenous iron technology was in full use throughout the subcontinent. Iron tools accelerated rice cultivation on the Ganges Plain. Two

centuries later 16 major kingdoms were concentrated around urban centers in the Ganges Plain.

City life in the Ganges Valley marked the beginning of the classic period of South Asian civilization. The new cities became economic powerhouses and centers of great intellectual and religious ferment. Brahmanism was the dominant religion during the early first millennium, a form of Hinduism that placed great emphasis on ritual and sacrifice. But philosophers of the sixth century B.C., like Buddha and Makhali Gosala, challenged Brahmanism with revolutionary doctrines that militated against sacrifice. Buddhism, with its teachings of personal spiritual development, spread rapidly, becoming the dominant religion in the north within five centuries.

Meanwhile, outside powers eyed the fabled riches of the subcontinent. King Darius of Persia invaded the northwest in 516 B.C. and incorporated the Indus Valley into the Persian Empire. Two centuries later, Alexander the Great ventured to the Indus River and brought Greek culture to the area. The great ruler Chandragupta Maurya of Magadha benefited from the power vacuum following Alexander the Great's conquests and carved out the **Mauryan empire,** which extended from Nepal and the northwest deep into the Deccan (see Figure 11.1). His grandson Asoka presided over the empire at its height between 269 and 232 B.C., seeking to unify its diverse people by a well-defined moral and ethical code based on Buddhist principles. As the Mauryan empire came to an end in 185 B.C., South Asia had become part of a vast trading network that linked the Mediterranean world to all parts of the Indian Ocean, and indirectly, to new sources of raw materials many sea miles to the east.

THE ORIGINS OF CHINESE CIVILIZATION (2600 to 1100 B.C.)

In Chapter 6, we described the origins of Chinese agriculture and the gradual elaboration of local society that resulted from cereal and rice cultivation. By 3000 B.C., China was a patchwork of kingdoms large and small, ruled by chieftains buried in considerable splendor. The origins of Chinese civilization in its traditional northern homeland are known only from legend. Such legends tell us that the celebrated ruler Huang Di founded civilization in the north in about 2698 B.C. This legendary warlord set the tone for centuries of the repressive, harsh government that was the hallmark of early Chinese civilization. About 2200 B.C., a Xia ruler named Yu the Great gained power through his military prowess and his knowledge of flood control, by which he could protect the valley people from catastrophic inundations.

What exactly do these legends mean? Who were the **Xia** and their successors, the **Shang?** In all probability they were dynasties of local rulers who achieved lasting prominence among their many neighbors after generations of bitter strife. Every chieftain lived in a walled town and enjoyed much the same level of material prosperity, but each ruler came from a different lineage and was related to his competitors by intricate and closely woven allegiances and kin ties. Each dynasty assumed political dominance in the north in turn, but for all these political changes, Shang civilization itself continued more or less untouched, a loosely unified confederacy of competing small kingdoms that quarreled and warred incessantly.

Royal Capitals

The archaeological record reveals that Shang-type remains are stratified on top of Longshan occupation levels at many places in northern China, and they represent a dramatic increase in the complexity of material culture and social organization. The same trends toward increasing complexity are thought to have occurred elsewhere in China at approximately the same time, for literate states may have emerged in the south and east as well. In form they probably resembled the Shang closely, but few details of the others are known. It seems likely that the Shang dynasty was dominant from approximately 1766 to 1122 B.C. but that other states continued to grow at the same time. The larger area of Chinese civilization ultimately extended from the north into the middle and lower courses of the Huang Ho and Yangtze rivers. In this account, we concentrate on northern Chinese civilization simply because more is known about the archaeology of the Shang than about any other early Chinese state.

Shang rulers lived in at least seven capitals, situated near the middle reaches of the Huang Ho River in the modern provinces of Henan, Shandong, and Anhui (Figure 11.5). The sites of all these towns are still uncertain, but in approximately 1557 B.C. the Shang kings moved their capital to a place named **Ao**, which archaeologists have found under the modern industrial city of Zhengzhou, some 95 miles (153 km) south of Anyang, close to the Huang Ho River. The diggers have found traces of a vast precinct surrounded by an earthen wall more than 33 feet (9.9 m) high, enclosing an area of 2 square miles (5.18 sq. km). It would have taken 10,000 workers laboring 330 days a year for no fewer than 18 years to erect the fortifications alone. This walled compound housed the rulers, the temples, and the nobles. The residential quarters and craft workshops lay outside the Shang walls. These include two bronze factories, one of them covering more than an acre.

The capital moved to the **Anyang** area in approximately 1400 B.C., where it remained until the fall of the Shang more than 250 years later. This new royal domain was known as Yin and may have encompassed a network of compounds, palaces, villages, and cemeteries extending over an area some 120 square miles (310 sq. km) on the northern bank of the Huang Ho River. The core of this "capital" was near the hamlet of **Xiao-tun**, 1.5 miles (2.4 km) northwest of the modern city of Anyang. Years of excavations at Xiao-tun have revealed 53 rectangular foundations of stamped earth up to

Figure 11.5 SHANG ORACLE BONES, USED FOR DIVINATION BY EARLY CHINESE RULERS
A heated point was applied to the ox shoulder blade, which cracked. The priest then
"read" the cracks and recorded the findings.

120 feet (36 m) long, 65 feet (19.5 m) wide, and as much as 5 feet (1.5 m)
high, many of them associated with sacrificial burials of both animals and
humans. One group of 15 foundations on the north side of the excavated
area supported timber houses with mud and stick walls, devoid of sacrificial victims. These are believed to be the royal residences that housed
extended families of nobles living in large halls and smaller rooms closed
off with doors.

Royal Burials

The Shang rulers at first buried their dead in a cemetery just more than a mile northeast of Anyang. Eleven royal graves from this cemetery were excavated during the 1930s. They were furnished on a lavish scale and date to between 1500 and 1200 B.C. The best-known grave is in the shape of a crosslike pit approximately 33 feet (9.9 m) deep with slightly sloping walls. Four ramps lead from the surface to each side of the pit. The coffin of the ruler, which was placed inside a wooden chamber erected in the burial pit, was accompanied by superb bronze vessels and shell, bone, and stone ornaments. One ceremonial halberd has an engraved jade blade set in a bronze shaft adorned with dragons and inlaid with malachite. The rulers were accompanied in death by slaves and sacrificial victims buried both in the chamber itself and on the approach ramps. Many were decapitated, so their bodies were found in one place and their heads in another.

The Shang kings surrounded their sepulchers with hundreds of lesser burials. No fewer than 1221 small graves have been dug up nearby, many of them burials of between 2 and 11 people in a single tomb. In 1976 archaeologists uncovered nearly 200 of these graves. Most of them contained decapitated, dismembered, or mutilated bodies. Some of the victims had been bound before death. These can only have been sacrificial offerings consecrated when the kings and their relatives died.

Bronzeworking

The Shang people are justly famous for their bronzework, best known to us from ceremonial artifacts found in royal tombs. The prestigious metal was not

Figure 11.6   SHANG CEREMONIAL BRONZES

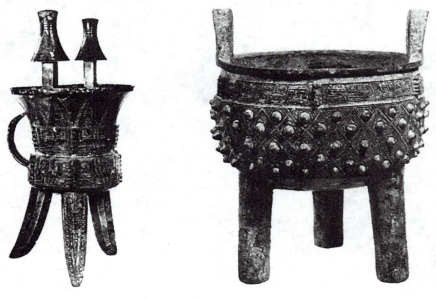

gold, which was in short supply, but bronze. Most Shang bronzeworks are food or drinking vessels, some are weapons, a few are musical instruments, and many are chariot and horse fittings. Bronzeworking was the guarded monopoly of the rulers, a complex art that the Chinese developed quite independently from the West before 2000 B.C. Their smiths produced some of the most sophisticated and elegant bronze objects ever crafted (Figure 11.6). Their elaborate display pieces were copies of clay prototypes carefully sculpted around a baked clay core and encased in a segmented mold. Once the clay version was completed, the baked outer mold was removed, the model broken away from the core, and the two parts reassembled to receive the molten bronze. This complex technique remained in use for at least five centuries.

Shang Warriors

Every early Chinese ruler stayed in power by virtue of a strong army. Shang society was organized on what might be called military lines, so that the royal standing army could be supplemented with thousands of conscripts on very short notice. The kings frequently were at war, protecting their frontiers, suppressing rebellious rivals, or raiding for sacrificial victims. In a sense, every early Chinese state was an armed garrison that could call on armies of more than 10,000 men. The secret was a sophisticated, permanent military establishment and a kin organization through which people were obligated to serve the king when called on. The same basic organization persisted long after the fall of the Shang dynasty in 1100 B.C.

Most surviving Shang weapons come from sacrificial chariot burials, such as the one excavated near Anyang in 1973. The archaeologists did not uncover the wooden chariot itself but a cast of the wooden parts preserved in the soil (Figure 11.7). They brushed away the surrounding soil with great care until they reached the hardened particles of fine sand that had replaced the wooden structure of the buried chariot. They were able to photograph not only the "ghost" of the chariot but also the skeletons of the two horses. The charioteer had been killed at the funeral and his body placed behind the vehicle. The charioteer rode on a wicker and leather car measuring between 3 and 4 feet (0.9 and 1.2 m) across and borne on a stout axle and two spoked wheels with large hubs adorned with bronze caps. In all probability, the nailless chariot was held together with sinew lashings, adorned with bronze and turquoise ornaments, and perhaps painted in bright colors.

THE WAR LORDS (1100 to 221 B.C.)

The Shang dynasty fell in about 1100 B.C. at the hands of the neighboring **Zhou.** The conquerors did not create a new civilization; rather, they took over the existing network of towns and officials and incorporated them into their

Figure 11.7   SHANG CHARIOT BURIAL FROM THE SHANG ROYAL CEMETERY NEAR ANYANG   The wooden parts of the chariot were excavated by following discolorations in the soil left by rotting wood.

own state organization, thus shifting the focus of political and economic power to the south and west, away from Anyang into the fertile Wei Valley near the modern city of S'ian. By this time, the influence of what may loosely be called Shang civilization extended far beyond the north, into the rice-growing areas of the south and along the eastern coasts. The Zhou divided their domains into various almost independent provinces, which warred with one another for centuries. It was not until 221 B.C. that the great emperor Shihuangdi unified China into a single empire (Figure 11.8). His Han Dynasty successors traded with the Western world overland through the celebrated Great Silk Road across Central Asia, and with newly powerful states in Southeast Asia.

Figure 11.8   A Chariot and Charioteer Fabricated in Gilded Cast-Bronze with Silver Inlay, at One-third Life Size   From the tomb of Emperor Shihuangdi, first emperor of China.

SOUTHEAST ASIAN CIVILIZATION (A.D. 1 to 1500)

After 500 B.C., there are signs of major cultural and social change throughout Southeast Asia, which coincide with the introduction of iron technology between about 600 and 400 B.C. The new metallurgy was grafted onto existing bronze technology, but it is uncertain whether ironworking was introduced from India, where forging (smelting in a small furnace) was used, or from China, where sophisticated casting methods were commonplace, involving molten iron at very high temperatures. Larger communities developed, usually centers for craft production. The appearance of larger settlements may have coincided with both irrigation and the advent of plowing, which greatly magnified food production and produced much larger crop surpluses.

Over a period of several centuries, far more complex societies developed, especially in fertile river valleys, societies whose leaders controlled maritime and inland trade over large areas. A growing exposure to artifacts, technologies, and ideas from China and India developed alongside these major changes, as powerful leaders surrounded themselves with all the panoply of public ceremony, ritual feasting, and ostentation.

The Rise of Mandalas

By about A.D. 1, the sea trading networks of Southeast Asia were part of a much larger commercial universe. Indian seafarers dominated the seaways of the Bay of Bengal, penetrating deep into the numerous islands and channels of Southeast Asia. The traders themselves were an entirely maritime people, called *Mwani,* or "barbarians," by the Chinese of the time. They spoke polyglot tongues and were of many lands, some Malays, some Indians, true wanderers who ventured as far east as the South China Sea. The Gulf of Tonkin and South China were served by *Jiwet,* Chinese mariners who brought luxuries to the coast, whence they were transported overland to the imperial capital.

As voyaging increased, especially from southern India to Southeast Asia, a strong cultural influence came to be felt. The chieftains who represented the people of the tribes acted as intermediaries between the foreigners and the indigenous people. Inevitably, the chieftains learned a new way of seeing society and the world. The authority and powers needed to expand and maintain the commerce were not part of the kin-linked society in which the chieftains had lived all their lives. In time, they became familiar with the Brahman and Buddhist conceptions of divine kingship. In a few centuries, kingdoms appeared, run according to Hindu or Buddhist ideas of social order.

These Southeast Asian kingdoms were in a constant state of political flux and had no fixed boundaries. The currency of political life was external, but always fluid, alliances developed between neighboring rulers. Everything revolved around the principal overlord, whose ability to cement alliances and deal with potential enemies dictated his relationships with his rivals. Some experts use a Sanskrit word, **mandala**, an Indian political doctrine that describes the relationships between rulers whose territories were thought of as circles. It is as if they were concertinas, which expanded and contracted as different polities interacted with one another. Each society focused on its own center and its own religious ruler and his retinue. The personal and spiritual qualities of each leader were important variables in a complex, ever-changing political equation.

Divine kingship revolutionized social and political organization in Southeast Asia. Mandalas flourished in riverine and lowland areas, along the lower Mekong, and in the middle Mekong Valley, including the celebrated Tonle Sap plains, the homeland of Khmer-speaking peoples. (Khmer is an Austroasiatic language of considerable antiquity.) There were also mandalas on the Khorat plateau, along the central Vietnamese coastal plain, and in the Red River area, the latter under Chinese control.

The Chinese called the Mekong region **"Funan,"** which meant "the port of a thousand rivers," but the term has little real historical meaning. According to Chinese records, the ports of the delta handled bronze, silver, gold, and spices, even horses bought by sea from central Asia. Most accounts of Funan extol its rich trade in gold, silver, bronze, and spices. They tell of the Funan people, who built a drainage and irrigation system that rapidly transformed much of the delta from barren swamps into rich agricultural land. The development of these fields took the communal efforts of hundreds of people living off the fish that teemed in the bayous of the delta. Most Funans lived in large lake cities fortified with great earthworks and moats swarming with crocodiles. Each major settlement was a port connected to the ocean and its neighbors by a network of artificial canals.

Funan prospered greatly from the third to sixth centuries. Large numbers of Chinese merchants and Indian artisans settled in the cities. They brought new skills with them that the local people copied. In the sixth century many more Indian Brahmans arrived in Funan. They brought the cult of the god Shiva. He appeared in the temples in the form of a *linga,* a phallic emblem of masculine creative power. Where rulers were worshipers of Shiva, the royal linga stood in a temple on the hill that symbolized the center of the capital.

By the sixth century A.D., the center of economic and political gravity had shifted inland, to the middle Mekong and the Tonle Sap. The latter is the central basin of Cambodia, fed by numerous rivers, its fluctuating water levels supporting many acres of fertile soil. The environment was so bountiful that it supported dense urban populations and generated large food surpluses, sufficient to support a wealthy civilization.

The Angkor Mandala (A.D. 802 to 1430)

The overlords of the Tonle Sap all shared one ambition: to rule as large an area as possible. The earlier kings were unable to hold the kingdom together until a dynamic Khmer monarch named Jayavarman II came to power in A.D. 802. Jayavarman II taught his subjects to worship him as a god. All resources were devoted to the preservation of the cult of the god-king. Everyone, whether noble, high priest, or commoner, was expected to subordinate his or her ambitions to the need to perpetuate the existence of the king on earth and his identity with the god in this life and the next. Jayavarman conquered his competitors, reigned for 45 years, and founded a dynasty that prospered for 600 years. He united the Khmer kingdoms into a colorful, spectacular empire that reached the height of its prosperity between A.D. 900 and 1200, shortly after his death.

Jayavarman II presented himself as the reincarnation of Shiva on earth, as the *varman,* the protector. His high priests were invariably energetic, imposing nobles, who supervised every aspect of Khmer life, from agriculture to warfare and the rituals of the state religion. The custom of building a new majestic and holy temple to house the royal linga of each king was the most important of all the religious rituals. As a result, most of the 30 monarchs who followed Jayavarman II left massive religious edifices to commemorate their reigns. These they built on temple mountains or artificial mounds in the center of their capitals, the hub of the Khmer universe, and area known as *Angkor.*

King Suryavarman, a Khmer monarch of the 12th century, built an extraordinary shrine, which is a spectacle of beauty, wonder, and magnificence, the largest religious building in the world. Angkor Wat is 5000 feet by 4000 feet across (1500 by 1200 m). The central block measures 717 feet (215 m) by 620 feet (186 m) and rises more than 200 feet (60 m) above the forest. It dwarfs even the largest Sumerian *ziggurat* and makes Mohenjodaro's citadel look like a village shrine (Figure 11.9).

Every detail of this extraordinary building reproduces part of the heavenly world in a terrestrial mode. The Khmer believed that the world consists of a central continent known as *Jambudvipa,* with the cosmic mountain *Meru* rising

Figure 11.9   ANGKOR WAT, CAMBODIA

from its center. The gods lived at the summit of Meru, represented at Angkor Wat by the highest tower. The remaining four towers depict Meru's lesser peaks; the enclosure wall, the mountain at the edge of the world; and the surrounding moat, the ocean beyond. Angkor Wat was the culminating attempt of the Khmer to reproduce a monument to the Hindu gods: Shiva, the creator; Vishnu, the preserver of the universe; and Brahma, who raised the earth.

Angkor Wat taxed the resources of the kingdom severely. The result of the Khmer rulers' megalomaniacal orgy was a totally centripetal and macabre religious utopia in which every product, every person's labor, and every thought was directed to embellishing the hub of the universe and the men who enjoyed it. The impression of prosperity and stability was illusory—a society where the ruler's power depended on granting of favors, on his successful patronizing of the major aristocratic families. No stable bureaucracy with appointed officials ran the state. The king sat at the center of an unstable mandala, its boundaries defined only by the loyalties of the aristocrats who ruled the outlying provinces.

The endless construction projects and the sheer cost of maintaining public buildings of every kind slowly beggared this totally centripetal mandala. Angkor dissolved by the mid to late 15th century, as the arrival of Islam, then European explorers, changed the course of Southeast Asian history.

CHAPTER 12

Lowland Mesoamerica

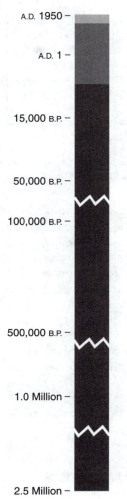

A.D. 1950 –

A.D. 1 –

15,000 B.P. –

50,000 B.P. –

100,000 B.P. –

500,000 B.P. –

1.0 Million –

2.5 Million –

Intricate calendars, great ceremonial centers and superb architecture, mysterious glyphs and spectacular shamanistic rituals: the colorful Maya civilization fascinates archaeologist and layperson alike. Exotic, and, until recently little understood, the Maya epitomize the ancient traditions of civilization in Central America. A search for its origins takes us back nearly four millennia to the village farming communities that flourished in Mesoamerica when Egyptian civilization was at its height and the Shang state dominated northern China. This chapter describes the origins and growth of Maya, and other, lowland civilizations in Central America. Chapter 13 surveys the peoples of the highlands, who interacted constantly with their lowland neighbors.

BEGINNINGS: PRECLASSIC PEOPLES IN THE LOWLANDS (2000 B.C. to A.D. 300)

Two great mountain chains form the backbones of highland Mesoamerica, running down the coastlines until they reach the east-west volcanic chain that forms the Mesa Central, the central plateau (Figure 12.1). The inland basin of the Valley of Mexico with its five lakes forms the heart of the plateau, for thousands of years the center of political and economic life in highland Mesoamerica. The highland regions of southern Mesoamerica are mountainous, with the highland plateau of Oaxaca offering some of the rare flat terrain in the region. Even further south, great mountain ranges enclose the highland plateau where modern Guatemala City lies. The peoples of the Basin of Mexico and the

D I S C O V E R Y

JOHN LLOYD STEPHENS AT COPAN

By any standards, New York lawyer turned traveler John Lloyd Stephens was a remarkable man. In 1839, he and Scottish artist Frederick Catherwood journeyed deep into the Mesoamerican rain forest, following rumors of vanished civilizations and great ruins masked by primordial jungle. They came first to the tiny village of Copán, where "around them lay the dark outlines of ruins shrouded by the brooding forest. The only sound that disturbed the quiet of this buried city was the noise of monkeys moving around among the tops of the trees." While Catherwood drew the intricate hieroglyphs on the Maya stelae, Stephens tried to buy the ancient city of Copán for $50, so he could transport it block by block to New York. The deal fell through when he found he could not float the antiquities downstream.

Stephens and Catherwood visited Palenque, Uxmal, Chichén Itzá, and other sites. They were the first to recognize the Maya as the builders of these great sites. Stephens wrote: "These cities ... are not the works of people who have passed away ... but of the same great race ... which still clings around their ruins." All subsequent research into the Maya and into ancient Mesoamerican civilization has been based on his work. (Quotations from John Lloyd Stephens, *Incidents of Travel in Chiapas and Yucatán* [New York, Harpers, 1841]; pp. 74 and 224).

southern highlands enjoyed a cool climate with most rainfall falling between June and November, sufficient to allow a single crop a year. The more southerly plateaus were still fertile, but warmer.

To the north, the serried mountains of the highlands give way to the low-lying limestone peninsula of the Yucatán, the so-called Maya lowlands. Highland climatic conditions contrasted dramatically with those in the lowlands, where conditions are hot and humid throughout the year. The southern two thirds of the Yucatán make up the Petén, hilly limestone formations covered with dense tropical forest intersected with lakes and swamps. The limestone plains of the northern Yucatán are much drier, with a drainage pattern based on underground water channels. The shores of the Gulf of Mexico are low lying and hot: the low coastal plains of Veracruz and Tabasco, the Yucatán Peninsula, and the heavily forested coastal strip along the Gulf of Honduras.

By 2000 B.C., sedentary villages were common throughout Mesoamerica, dispersed in small communities across highly diverse agricultural environments in both lowlands and highlands. The very diversity of the Mesoamerican environment with its widely distributed food resources and raw materials made everyone dependent on their neighbors, on communities living in very different surroundings. From the earliest times, barter networks linked village to village, lowland groups to people living on the semiarid highlands or in the Basin of Mexico. The same exchange networks also spread compelling ideologies, which were to form the symbolic foundation of ancient Mesoamerican civilization.

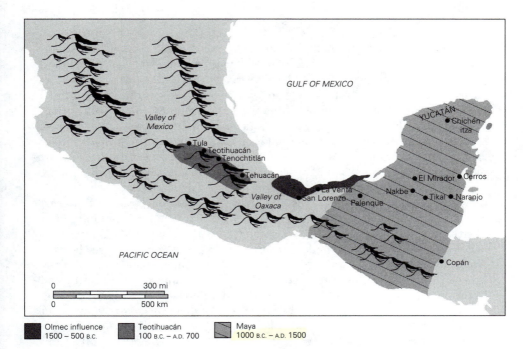

Figure 12.1 MAP SHOWING SITES IN CHAPTERS 12 AND 13

Therein lies a crux of Mesoamerican civilization: the constant interactions and exchanges of both commodities and ideas between people living in dramatically contrasting environments, often within only a few hundred miles of one another.

The first signs of political and social complexity appear in many parts of highland and lowland Mesoamerica between about 2000 and 1000 B.C., during the so-called **Preclassic,** or **Formative,** era. In many regions, small, but often powerful, chiefdoms headed by a chief and a small nobility appeared. A similar pattern of greater social and political complexity appeared in Mesopotamia, Egypt, China, and other areas where early state-organized societies evolved. In Mesoamerica, as elsewhere, the new social complexity can be identified by differences in house designs, by the appearance of small shrines, and through prestigious trade goods such as fish spines and sea shells from the Gulf Coast used in bloodletting and other religious ceremonies. Here, as in other areas, control of trade in exotic, prestigious objects and knowledge of distant lands were vital to the ideology of chiefdoms. Such objects, and the ideology associated with them, symbolized and legitimized the authority of leaders to control both human and natural resources.

There was no one region where this emerging sociopolitical complexity occurred first. Rather, it was a development that took hold more or less simultaneously in many regions of Mesoamerica, not in isolation, but with each region interacting with others. The most famous of these early societies was the Olmec.

The Olmec (1500 B.C. to 500 B.C.)

The **Olmec** occupied a revered place in the legend and lore of later Mesoamerican civilizations. Maya priests recognized the great cultural legacy they owed to these little-known ancestral Mesoamericans. Earlier scholars thought in terms of a "mother civilization," of an Olmec state that was the ancestor of all later Mesoamerican civilizations. Today, we know that "Olmec" was a series of chiefdoms along the Gulf Coast of Veracruz and Tabasco, which may have exercised some influence over adjacent areas of Chiapas and central Mexico in early preclassic times. Olmec society flourished during a period when art motifs, religious symbols, and ritual beliefs were shared between developing chiefdoms in many regions as a result of regular contacts between the leaders of widely separated communities and through day-to-day trade. Olmec art and artifacts have been found over an area 20 times that of the Gulf Coast heartland. Olmec-like artifacts have come from Cuello in the Maya lowlands, and with pre-Maya burials under the city of Copán (for both sites, see below). Archaeologist Arthur Demarest has called this phenomenon a "lattice of interaction," over many centuries, that produced the complex and sophisticated traditions of Mesoamerican civilization that developed in later centuries.

Olmec peoples lived along the Mexican south Gulf Coast from about 1500 to 500 B.C., Their homeland is low lying, tropical, and humid, with fertile soils. The swamps, lakes, and rivers are rich in fish, birds, and other animals, creatures that formed an important part of a new and remarkably sophisticated art style that was to leave a permanent imprint on Mesoamerican life. The origins of the Olmec are a complete mystery, but their culture undoubtedly has strong local roots.

Some of the earliest Olmec settlement comes from a platform at **San Lorenzo**, in the midst of frequently inundated woodland plains. The first village occupation shows few distinctive Olmec traits, but by 1250 B.C., the people of San Lorenzo were farming both dry gardens and fields located on river levees, which produced exceptional crop yields. Soon, San Lorenzo's leaders were erecting ridges and earthen mounds around their platform, on which they built pyramids and possibly ball courts. A century later, magnificent monumental carvings adorned San Lorenzo, apparently portraits of rulers that were often mutilated by the Olmec themselves, perhaps when they died (Figure 12.2). The people of San Lorenzo traded obsidian and semiprecious stones with many parts of Mesoamerica until their center fell into decline after 900 B.C. and was superseded by La Venta, the most famous Olmec site, nearer the Gulf of Mexico.

Was Olmec society a large, homogeneous state, or a series of smaller kingdoms linked together by king, religious, and trading connections? Current opinion favors the second alternative, arguing that originally village land was owned communally by large kin groups. Over many generations, certain families probably acquired control of the most fertile lands, over prime fishing and waterfowl hunting preserves. They became the dominant elite in Olmec society. To give symbolic and ritual expression to their new-found power, the new elite built awe-inspiring artificial mountains and strategically placed open spaces, designed to give an impression of overwhelming power. It was here

Figure 12.2 Colossal Olmec Head from San Lorenzo, with Parrot-like Glyph on the Headdress

that the rulers performed carefully staged public rituals and displays designed to confirm supreme authority. Those who ruled over these settings adorned their precincts with colossal statues of themselves.

Nowhere are these buildings and sculptures more spectacular than at **La Venta,** built on a small island in the middle of a swamp. A rectangular earthen mound 393 feet long by 229 feet wide and 105 feet high (120 m by 70 m by 32 m) dominates the island. Long, low mounds surround a rectangular plaza in front of the large mound, faced by walls and terraced mounds at the other end of the plaza. Vast monumental stone sculptures litter the site, including some Olmec heads bearing expressions of contempt and savagery (see Figure 12.2), perhaps portraits of actual rulers. Thronelike blocks depict a seated figure, perhaps a ruler, emerging from a deep niche carved into stone (Figure 12.3). The sides bear stylized depictions of jaguars, perhaps symbolizing the mythic origins of the rulers among such animals. For about 400 years, La Venta people traded ceremonial jade and serpentine from as far away as Costa Rica, during a time when Olmec ideas of kingship and religious ideology spread far across the lowlands and highlands. Then, sometime around 400 B.C., La Venta was destroyed, its finest monuments intentionally defaced.

Figure 12.3   An Olmec Altar at La Venta Depicts a Lord Sitting Below a Schematic Jaguar Pelt   He emerges from a niche or cave holding a rope that binds prisoners carved on either side of the throne.

One of the most important institutions to come into being in Olmec society was kingship, known to us only from distinctive art styles centered on a mysterious half-jaguar, half-human figure. Olmec lords may have grafted the ancient ideology of the jaguar onto an emerging institution of kingship, where the ruler was a shaman-king, with awesome supernatural powers. The Olmec rain god may have been a half-human, half-animal figure with snarling jaguar teeth, but it was only one of many combinations of mythical beasts that came from the hallucinogenic mind as opposed to the forest itself. Olmec artists grafted eagles' feathers and claws onto serpents and other beasts to form mythical creatures, perhaps one of them the "Feathered Serpent," Quetzalcoatl, the most enduring of all Mesoamerican deities and central to highland civilization for many centuries.

By the time the classic Mesoamerican civilizations of highlands and lowlands arose, dynasties of lords had been ruling Mesoamerica along well-established lines for nearly 1000 years.

The Origins of Maya Civilization: Cuello (before 1000 to after 400 B.C.)

The roots of ancient Maya civilization lie in much earlier cultural traditions in the Mesoamerican lowlands. Boston University archaeologist Norman Hammond was able to trace the roots of Maya culture back to the second millennium B.C., at the Cuello site in northern Belize.

Cuello is a small Maya ceremonial center, today comprising an acre-square, 12-foot (3.6 m)-high platform with a low pyramid. Hammond excavated layer after layer of occupation, until he excavated a pole-framed, palm-thatched house set on a lime-plaster platform dating to about 1000 B.C. The Cuello people maintained the same basic plaza layout for many centuries, making it larger and larger until about 400 B.C. At this point, the villagers converted their ceremonial precinct with its wood and thatch temples into a large public arena. They filled the square with rubble to create a raised platform covering more than an acre. Hammond unearthed the fragmentary skeletons of more than 30 sacrificial victims in the rubble, some with hacked-off skulls and limbs, others sitting in a circle around two young men. Six carved bone tubes buried with the victims bore the interlacing, woven mat motif symbolic of later Mayan kingship. Such mats were royal thrones. The appearance of the motif here may document the appearance of a Maya elite by 400 B.C.

Nakbé and El Mirador (c. 1000 to 300 B.C.)

The **Nakbé** ruins lie 215 miles (346 km) from Guatemala City, and 8 1/2 miles (13.6 km) from the early Mayan city at **El Mirador,** which covers 6 square miles (15.5 sq. km). The two settlements were once linked by a causeway, but smaller Nakbé was occupied much earlier, by about 1000 B.C. Between 650 and 450 B.C., Nakbe's leaders built huge platforms over their earlier ceremonial structures, raising pyramids with blank facades atop them. The pyramids themselves were crowned with three small temples clustered at the top of a steep stairway bounded with panels and masks. Nakbé's temple facades reflect the emerging notion of Ch'ul Ahau, divine kingship, in Maya society. In lavish public ceremonies, important lords donned the masks of gods, symbolizing their role as living gods.

Nakbé reached the height of its powers around 300 B.C., but subsided into complete political and economic obscurity within a few generations, as its neighbor, El Mirador, rose to prominence.

El Mirador enjoyed more reliable water supplies than its neighbor, also a better defensive position. Between 150 B.C. and A.D. 50, the city grew to cover about 6 square miles (16 sq. km). Brigham Young University archaeologists have uncovered at least 200 buildings, including a great complex of pyramids, temples, and plazas. The Danta pyramid at the eastern end of the site rises from a natural hill more than 210 feet (70 m) high. A little over a mile (2 km) west rises the Tigre complex, a pyramid 182 feet (55 m) high surrounded by a plaza and smaller buildings (Figure 12.4). El Mirador is yielding some of the earliest examples of Maya writing, inscribed on potsherds, and occasionally on stucco sculpture. A raised road connected El Mirador with another important preclassic center, Calakmul, 24 miles (38 km) to the northeast.

This stupendous and still little-known city collapsed suddenly in the early Christian era. The dynamics of this collapse are little understood, but are mirrored at other preclassic Maya communities where the institution of kingship rose and was then abandoned.

Figure 12.4   RECONSTRUCTION OF THE CEREMONIAL PRECINCT AT EL MIRADOR

KINGSHIP, GLYPHS, AND POLITICAL CYCLES

Kingship was at the heart of lowland Maya civilization. Maya rulers linked their actions to those of the gods and ancestors, sometimes legitimizing their descent by claiming it reenacted mythical events. In a real sense, Maya history was linked to the present and to the Otherworld, and to the legendary Olmec of the remote past. Society was embedded in a matrix of sacred space and time.

Maya kingship unfolded within an intensely sacred setting, artificial land-scapes where complex ceremonies took place throughout the year, and on longer cycles of time. Thus, the calendar was vital to Maya life, for the complex geography of sacred time was just as important as that of space for determining political strategies and social moves (Figure 12.5). At the heart of Maya life lay both the calendar and the elaborate hieroglyphic script used, among other things, to calculate the passage of time and regular religious observances.

Maya Script

The decipherment of Maya script ranks among the greatest scientific achievements of the 20th century. For generations, most Mayanists assumed the intricate glyphs were used to record the calendar and that the ancient Maya lords were peaceful astronomer-priests. But in 1952 Russian epigrapher Yuri Knosorov demonstrated that Maya script was a phonetic and syllabic hieroglyphic script, just like Egyptian writing. Twenty years later, a group of scholars succeeded in assembling the dynastic histories of Maya lords at several

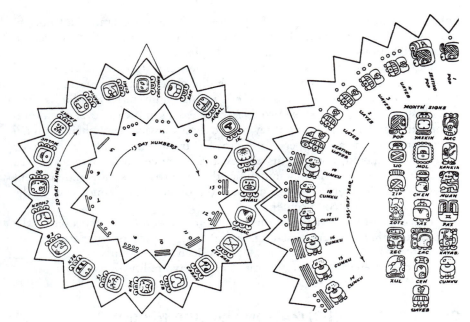

Figure 12.5   THE MAYA CALENDAR, SHOWING THE TWO INTERLOCKING CYCLES   The left wheel is the 260-day *tzolkin,* the sacred calendar with 13 numbers (*inner wheel*) and 20 day names (*outer wheel*). The right-hand wheel is the *haab,* the secular cycle, with 18 months of 20 days each.

important centers like Palenque and Tikal. More than 15 years of rapid-fire, intensive teamwork have since resulted in the partial decipherment of Maya script, although many difficulties await resolution.

Unlike Egyptian or Sumerian script, the Maya archive is limited in scope and confined to inscriptions on clay pots, monumental inscriptions on buildings and stelae, and only four codices (deer-skin documents) that survived the Spanish Conquest. These are public statements of royal accessions, triumphant military campaigns and important ceremonies. They are the political propaganda of Maya lords, the "politically correct" literature of a nobility intent on justifying their deeds, their ancestry. Of the everyday literature of the Maya, we know nothing. But the surviving texts tell us Maya rulers were not peaceful astronomers, but bloodthirsty lords presiding over a patchwork of competing city-states. Decipherment has revealed Maya civilization as a constantly shifting quicksand of diplomatic marriages, political alliances, and brutal conquests. The account of Maya civilization that follows is based on both archaeology and deciphered glyphs.

Political Cycles

Archaeologist Joyce Marcus has observed a remarkable similarity in the ways in which Mesoamerican states rose, reached their peak, then collapsed. She notes a consistent scenario both in the lowlands and highlands, not only in Maya civilization, but with the great city of Teotihuacán and also Toltec and Aztec civilizations in the highlands (see Chapter 13).

This scenario unfolds as follows: First, a new city-state, say Maya Tikal or Teotihuacán, expands its territory through diplomacy, political marriages, and military conquest. The new state reached its maximum territorial limits early in its history. Then, once some provinces reached a significant level of cultural complexity and development, they would break away from their nominal master and become an independent polity. Far from being weakened, the core state still prospered, investing its energy and resources in its own local area rather than in expansion. But sometimes the old provinces, now independent states, would ally themselves against their old overlord and conquer it, so the old state became a second center.

This cycle of rise, expansion on the margins, fissioning, then decline at the expense of others repeated itself again and again, to the point that it can be considered a consistent pattern of Mesoamerican civilization.

Marcus's scenario is well documented in Maya political history.

CLASSIC MAYA CIVILIZATION (A.D. 300 to 900)

Even as El Mirador collapsed, perhaps because its trading connections faltered, two other centers, Tikal and Uaxactun, stepped into the resulting political and economic vacuum. The two centers were less than 12 miles (20 km) apart, too close for bitter rivals to coexist. But their rivalry coincided with the blossoming of Classic Maya civilization.

The Rise of Tikal and Uaxactun (c. 200 B.C. to A.D. 900)

Tikal began life as a small farming village in about 600 B.C., but soon developed into a much larger community. As El Mirador collapsed, the rulers of Tikal built an elaborate complex of more than 100 buildings, monumental structures, pyramids, and royal burial vaults now known as the North Acropolis (Figure 12.6). This lay on the north side of the Great Plaza, which formed the heart of all Maya centers. Now grass-covered, the plaza was originally plastered, an imposing setting for public ceremonies conducted on the surrounding pyramids, symbolic mountains topped by small temples, whose doorways served as gateways to the Otherworld. Over many centuries, successive lords erected new temples and pyramids in the central area. For the first time, one temple bears the portraits of a ruler standing on a woven mat symbolizing kingship. At the same time, Tikal's public art reveals a major shift away from depictions of gods and the cosmos toward portraits of individual rulers.

The continuity of Maya kingship depended on smooth transitions from one generation to the next, on maintaining alliances between factions among the nobility, and on good relationships with neighbors. Deciphered glyphs record

Figure 12.6 THE CENTRAL AREA OF TIKAL

the founding of an enduring Tikal dynasty by a ruler named Yax-Moch-Xoc
(A.D. 219–238). Thirty-nine lords inherited Tikal's throne from this founding
ancestor and maintained dynastic continuity for more than 600 years.

Uaxactun also flourished under another powerful royal dynasty. The
city's monuments, and those of Tikal, soon depict rulers with sacrificial victims cowering at their feet, noble prisoners taken in hand-to-hand combat for
later sacrifice in public rituals. These portraits signal a crucial development in
Maya history—an increasing preoccupation with warfare and campaigns of
conquest. Maya lords now turned from mere raiding of neighbors for sacrificial victims to serious conquest. In these new strategies, they were influenced
by ideas permeating the lowlands from the distant city of Teotihuacán in the
highlands (Chapter 13), where militaristic rituals associated with the rain god
Tlaloc and the planet Venus celebrated new philosophies of war and conquest
as means of achieving political ends.

Inevitably, matters came to a head between the expanding Tikal and Uaxactun, when Lord Great-Jaguar-Paw assumed the throne of Tikal. This formidable warrior defeated the armies of Uaxactun on January 16, A.D. 378.
Great-Jaguar-Paw was not content with prisoners. He ordered Uaxactun
sacked and installed his general Smoking Frog as ruler, to form a new ruling
dynasty. Tikal's rulers continued to prosper in later centuries, eventually presiding over a multicenter kingdom acquired through conquest and diplomatic
marriage. At the height of its powers in the early sixth century, Tikal's territory covered 965 square miles (2500 sq. km), with an estimated population of
more than 360,000 people, a kingdom with an area somewhat larger than

most Sumerian city-states in Mesopotamia 3000 years earlier. But several out-lying kingdoms, among them Calakmul and Dos Pilos, split off from Tikal and became independent domains.

Calakmul (Preclassic Times to A.D. 800)

Once split off from Tikal, **Calakmul** became a major player in the Maya world. A 12-year program of mapping and excavation has revealed a major city that ruled over at least six secondary centers equidistant from the central capital, linked to it by raised earth- or stone-packed roads. Such roads have been known to connect different parts of large Maya cities, but it is only recently that they have been traced over longer distances. These road systems may account for Calakmul's importance as a regional capital in the Maya low-lands, one of three or four states that dominated Maya civilization during the late classic period.

Palenque (A.D. 431 to 799)

Important Maya centers competed ferociously for people, resources, and terri-tory. The overall political situation was in a state of constant flux, as lord vied with lord in a maze of ever-changing diplomatic alliances and short-lived mil-itary campaigns. **Palenque,** famous for its magnificent buildings, was among the most successful centers. Two Palenque lords, Pacal ("Shield"), and his older son, Chan-Bahlum ("Snake-Jaguar"), who ruled in the seventh century, stand out for their vision and wisdom. Palenque's dynastic history had begun on March 11, 431, when Bahlum-Kuk ("Jaguar Quetzal") became ruler. Epig-raphers have reconstructed a dynasty of 12 kings and some minor interrup-tions, ending sometime after 799. But the heyday of Palenque was during Pacal's long reign of 67 years.

Under Pacal's stewardship, Palenque became a masterpiece of Maya architecture. Lying in the foothills of the Sierra of Chiapas, Palenque is a com-pact center by Maya standards, dominated by Pacal's Temple of the Inscrip-tions, built, so glyphs tell us, in A.D. 692 (Figure 12.7). The temple rests on a stepped pyramid rising 75 feet (23 m) above the plaza. A densely wooded hill supports the back of the pyramid. In 1952, Mexican archaeologist Alberto Ruz Lhuillier noticed some holes in a large slab forming part of the temple floor. He lifted the slab and uncovered a rubble-filled stairway leading to the heart of the pyramid. After four months of arduous clearance work, Ruz uncovered the steep stairs, which made a U-turn in the middle. The skeletons of six young male sacrificial victims lay at the foot by a triangular slab sealing a vaulted doorway. Behind it lay a burial chamber 30 feet by 13 feet (9.1 by 3.9 m). A vaulted ceiling soared 21 feet (6.4 m) overhead. The sepulcher lay 80 feet (23.4 m) below the floor of the temple and 5 feet (1.5 m) below the plaza ground surface. Figures of Otherworld figures adorned the chamber walls. Most of the floor area was taken up with a massive, carved stone slab, 10 inches (25.4 cm) thick, weighing about 5 tons (Figure 12.7). Ruz lifted the

Figure 12.7   Tomb of the Maya Ruler Pacal at Palenque, who Died in A.D. 683   The lid of his tomb commemorates his genealogy.

sarcophagus lid with great difficulty and gazed on the skeleton of a tall man covered with jade ornaments. A magnificent jade mosaic mask covered the ruler's head.

When Ruz originally uncovered the tomb, he had no means of identifying its occupant. But the decipherment of Maya script has enabled epigraphers to identify the owner as Pacal himself, who was born in 603, ascended to the throne in 615, and died in 683 at the age of 80. The sarcophagus is a remarkable commentary on Maya kingship. Pacal's genealogy appears in the metaphor of an orchard of fruit trees, an orchard of the ancestral dead. Each ancestor rises with a fruit tree, the earliest in the southeast corner, Pacal's mother and father in the north and south sides. On the lid, the king's artists depict the Sun Lord falling down the trunk of the World Tree into the waiting jaws of the Otherworld. They also included the resurrection as well, a half-skeletal monster carrying a sacrificial bowl bearing the glyph of the sun. Like the sun, Pacal would rise again in the east after his journey through the Otherworld.

The great Palenque dynasty flourished during a period of Maya history that has been called one of warring states. Just as in China, small state vied with small state in a constant quest for economic and political power. But the Maya lords lacked the organization and military logistics to control wide areas and garrison conquered cities, so the diplomatic and military landscape changed constantly, even when large regional states like those of Tikal and Calakmul were dominant. After A.D. 770, signs of political stress become more common, as minor nobles and others took advantage of the constant instability to carve out their own independent domains, often on the periphery of large states. This stress is well documented at the city of Copán in modern-day Honduras.

Copán (earlier than A.D. 435 to 800)

Copán's pyramids and plazas cover 30 acres (12 ha), rising from the vast open spaces of the Great and Middle Plazas to an elaborate complex of raised, enclosed courtyards, pyramids, and temples known to archaeologists as the Acropolis (Figure 12.8). Here successive rulers built their architectural statements atop those of their predecessors in an archaeological jigsaw puzzle of the first magnitude. After years of work, archaeology and epigraphy have written at least the outlines of a city founded in pre-Maya times and deeply involved in the events of the late classic period.

Long-term field surveys have documented dramatic population changes through the long history of the city. The surveys extend over an area of 9 square miles (24 sq. km) and have mapped more than 3400 house mounds, roads, farming terraces, and other features. They show how between A.D. 550 and 700 the Copán state expanded rapidly, with most of the population concentrated in the core and immediate periphery zones. Between 700 and 850, the Copán Valley reached its greatest sociopolitical complexity, with a rapid

Figure 12.8 ARTIST TATIANA PROSKOURIAKOFF'S RECONSTRUCTION OF COPÁN

population increase to between 18,000 and 20,000 people. These figures, calculated from site size, suggest the local population was doubling every 80 to 100 years, with about 80 percent of the people living within the core and immediate periphery. But now people were farming foothill areas, as the population density of the urban core reached over 8000 people per 0.3 square mile (1 sq. km), with the periphery housing about 500 people per 0.3 square mile (1 sq. km). Eighty-two percent of the population lived in relatively humble dwellings, an indication of the extreme stratification of Copán society.

The earliest inscription at the site dates to December 11, A.D. 435, and was the work of ruler Yax-Ku'k-Mo' ("Blue Quetzal Macaw"). For four centuries, Blue Quetzal Macaw's successors formed a powerful dynasty at Copán and became a major force in the Maya world. But on May 3, 738, in an interesting example of Joyce Marcus's scenario, the subordinate ruler of neighboring Quirigua turned on his master, captured, and sacrificed him. But Copán seems to have maintained a measure of independence and survived. In 749, a new ruler, Smoke Shell, ascended to the throne of the once-great city. He embarked on an ambitious campaign of rehabilitation, even marrying a princess from distant Palenque. He also embarked on a building frenzy, which culminated in the Temple of the Hieroglyphic Stairway, built in 755, one of the oldest and most sacred of Copán's precincts (Figure 12.9). By this time, the city was top heavy with privilege-hungry nobles and rife with political intrigue. Collapse was imminent.

Maya civilization reached its peak in about A.D. 600. But the lowlands were never unified politically during the classic period. What the Maya elite did share was a set of highly complex traditions and a network of contacts between rulers that transcended the local interests of individual kingdoms and considerable local diversity. Only when a few aggressive and exceptionally talented leaders appeared did several centers coalesce into multi-center states such as arch-rivals Tikal and Calakmul. The central institution of Maya civilization was kingship, for it was the concept that unified society as a whole. Maya kings lived and carried out their deeds in the context of a history they recorded in building projects at Tikal, Palenque, and elsewhere. Maya elites lived out their lives in the context of the kings that ruled them, and, in turn, thousands of commoners lived their lives with respect to the nobility.

CERÉN: LIVES OF COMMONERS

We would know little of the lives of commoners, but for a fortunate archaeological discovery. A humble Maya village at Cerén in San Salvador was buried under feet of volcanic ash by an unexpected eruption in the sixth century A.D. The people fled for their lives, leaving their possessions behind them. Payson Sheets and a team of Salvadoran archaeologists have located several houses using ground-penetrating radar. Each Cerén household had a thatched dwelling for eating, sleeping, and other activities, as well as a storehouse, kitchen, and sometimes other structures. The villagers stored grain in clay vessels with tight lids, suspending corn cobs and chilis from the roof. They kept

Figure 12.9
Tatiana Proskour-iakoff's Rendering of the Hieroglyphic Stairway, Copán
More than 2200 glyphs provide an elegant statement of the Maya kings' supernatural path, in a brilliant piece of archaeological detective work. Portraits on the stairs depict Copán's lords as warriors carrying shields, with inscriptions recounting their deeds. At the base of the stairway stands a figure, perhaps Smoke Shell himself, where an altar forms the base of the stairway, in the form of an inverted head of the rain god Tlaloc.

many implements, including sharp-bladed stone knives in the rafters out of the way of children. The excavations have revealed three public buildings, also the nearby fields where the maize plants were doubled over, the ears still attached to the stalk, a "storage" technique still used in parts of Central America today. Judging from the mature maize, the eruption came at the end of the growing season, in August.

THE CLASSIC MAYA COLLAPSE (A.D. 900)

By A.D. 800, Maya populations in the Petén heartland were declining sharply, and both monument carving and major construction soon came to an end. Everywhere, villages and towns were exploiting every possible acre of cultivable land to feed a rapidly growing population. A century later, Maya civilization in southern lowlands suddenly and inexplicably collapsed.

Everyone studying this catastrophe agrees that many factors led to the collapse. Using computer simulations to study population densities and the potential for agricultural production in the southern highlands, University of

Arizona archaeologist Patrick Culbert has shown that population densities in some parts of the lowlands rose to as high as 518 people per square mile (200 per sq. km) during the late Classic period over an area so large that it was impossible for people to adapt to bad times by moving to new land or emigrating. Culbert theorizes that the magnitude of the population loss during the two centuries after A.D. 800 was such that social malfunction alone cannot account for it.

Failure of the agricultural base must have been an important component in the collapse equation. This may have been caused by prolonged drought cycles, revealed in core borings and pollen samples from lake beds. As populations rose, agricultural activity intensified, with much of the lowlands covered with terrace and raised-field systems. To feed dense urban populations on a permanent basis required a level of management and social changes that the Maya could not achieve, especially when so many people were involved in construction projects and, apparently, in military activity. A rapidly expanding population was dependent on an agricultural system that made no allowance for long-term problems such as drought. As Maya agricultural productivity fell, disease may have reached epidemic proportions, and population densities plummeted, making recovery impossible. So the Maya took the only option remaining to them: they abandoned their great cities and dispersed into small villages.

The Copán surveys have documented the dramatic changes in Maya society that resulted from the collapse of this great city. Copán's ruling dynasty ended in A.D. 810, just as serious urban depopulation began. The urban core and periphery zones lost about half their population after 850, while the rural population increased by almost 20 percent. Small regional settlements replaced the scattered villages of earlier times, a response to cumulative deforestation, overexploitation of even marginal agricultural soils, and uncontrolled soil erosion near the capital. By 1150, the Copán Valley population had fallen to between 5000 and 8000 people.

Endemic warfare may also have been a powerful factor in the collapse. At **Dos Pilos** in northern Guatemala, 65 miles (105 km) from Tikal, Arthur Demarest uncovered evidence for civil war and prolonged conflict. Founded by a renegade noble from Tikal in A.D. 645, Dos Pilos' later rulers expanded their domains through conquest, eventually controlling more than 1500 square miles (3884 sq. km) of territory by the mid-eighth century. Dos Pilos now controlled major jade and obsidian trade routes. Its lords lavished wealth on ornate palaces and a pyramid topped by three temples. Hieroglyphs found with "Ruler 2's" grave (A.D. 698–726) under a small temple tell of carefully contrived diplomatic alliances, political marriages, and military campaigns.

By A.D. 761, Dos Pilos had overextended itself, despite frantic attempts to maintain its domains. Nearby Tamrindo attacked its neighbor and killed "Ruler 4," despite desperate resistance from his people. The invaders tore down the royal palace and robbed temple facades to build crude fortification walls with wooden palisades to surround the central precinct. The people clustered inside in a small village of timber huts, while the nobles fled to build a new center at **Aquateca.** The new center lay atop a steep cliff above a deep chasm, protected on three sides by natural features, the entire complex surrounded by massive defense walls. The Aquatecans held out for another half century, despite constant attacks. By the early ninth century, Demarest believes that warfare became so endemic that the survivors of Dos Pilos even built defensive walls around their fields to protect their dwindling crops. In a last desperate stand, they dug three moats, one 460 feet (140 m) long, across a peninsula in Lake Petexbatun, creating an island fortress. The bedrock from the canals became defensive walls and a walled wharf for a canoe landing. Even this outpost did not last long, for the inhabitants abandoned it in the 800s.

The Maya collapse affected a large area of the southern lowlands between the early 9th and early 10th centuries. Great centers were abandoned, monumental inscriptions and public buildings ceased, and populations declined rapidly. Within a century, vast areas of the southern lowlands were abandoned, never to be resettled.

POSTCLASSIC MAYA CIVILIZATION (A.D. 900 to 1517)

Despite the collapse in the southern lowlands, Maya religious and social orders still endured in the more open country of the northern Yucatan. Just as Tikal and other famous cities collapsed, northern centers like **Chichén Itzá** in the northeast came into prominence during the postclassic period.

Chichén Itzá itself has never been fully mapped, so its area and exact population remain a mystery. The city's central core is well known, its central plaza dominated by the Castillo, the Temple of Kukulcán (Quetzalcoatl), a square, stepped pyramid about 75 feet (23 m) tall, crowned with a temple, with stairways on all four sides (Figure 12.10). The Temple of the Warriors lies west of the Castillo, an inner temple with sculpted pillars masked by a later more elaborate structure. The mosaics, carved facades, and sculpted serpents and warriors on the later temple show Toltec influence from the highlands. During its heyday, this great city maintained contacts with the Maya of the Gulf Coast lowlands, and through them with the Valley of Oaxaca and the highlands.

Postclassic Maya civilization was marked by as much volatility as that of earlier years. Political infighting and ecological problems may have been part of the cause. As Chichén Itzá collapsed in the 13th century, the city of **Mayapan** moved into the economic and political vacuum and dominated the northern Maya world. Mayapan lies in the center of the northern Yucatan, a densely populated, walled city with about 12,000 inhabitants built near a series of natural wells. It was a trading center, dependent on an expanding waterborne trade in bulk goods like cacao, salt, and obsidian. Her confeder-

Figure 12.10   THE
CASTILLO AT CHICHÉN
ITZÁ

acy fell apart in the mid-15th century. Three quarters of a century later, in
1519, Spaniard Hernan Cortés and his conquistadors landed on the Gulf lowlands, to change the face of Mesoamerica forever. His objective was not the
lowland Maya, but the gold-rich kingdom of the Mexica in the distant highlands, described in the next chapter.

C H A P T E R 1 3

Highland Mesoamerica

Throughout the long history of Mesoamerican civilization, lowlands and highlands were linked inextricably to one another. This chapter describes the highland Mesoamerican civilizations, which culminated in the complex, rapidly changing world of the Aztecs, disrupted catastrophically by the Spanish conquest of A.D. 1519 (see Figure 12.1).

THE RISE OF HIGHLAND CIVILIZATION (2000 to 500 B.C.)

Many of the foundations of highland Mesoamerican civilization were laid in two areas: the Valley of Oaxaca and the Valley of Mexico.

The Valley of Oaxaca

The warm, semiarid Valley of Oaxaca is the homeland of the modern-day Zapotec people. By 2000 B.C., maize and bean agriculture supported dozens of small villages and hamlets of 50 to 75 people. In time, some of these settlements grew to considerable size, with as many as 500 inhabitants, some of them nonfarming artisans and priests. The earliest farming villages lie on the valley floors, where water supplies were more plentiful. As local population densities rose, the Oaxacans expanded onto slopes and into more arid lands. Eventually, argues Kent Flannery, the economic power generated by these rising farming populations gave highland areas like this an edge over their neighbors.

The evolution of larger settlements in Oaxaca and elsewhere was closely connected with the development of long-distance trade. Simple barter networks of earlier times evolved into sophisticated regional trading organizations in which Oaxacan and other village leaders controlled monopolies over sources of obsidian and its distribution. Soon magnetite mirrors (important in Olmec ritual), tropical feathers, and ceramics were traded widely between highlands and lowlands. The influence of the lowlands was felt most strongly in Oaxaca, where Olmec pottery and other ritual objects appear between

D I S C O V E R Y

BERNAL DIAZ AND TENOCHTITLAN

"And when we saw all those cities and villages built in the water, and other great towns on dry land, and that straight and level causeway leading to Mexico, we were astounded. These great towns and pyramids and buildings rising from the water, all made of stone, seemed like an enchanted vision. . . . Indeed some of our soldiers asked whether it was not all a dream . . . ." Spanish conquistador Bernal Diaz was one of the 600 soldiers and adventurers who accompanied Hernan Cortés on his hazardous march from the Gulf Coast to the heart of the Aztec empire. He was an impressionable youth when he gazed out over the Valley of Mexico in 1519 and saw the Aztec capital, Tenochtitlán, stretched out before him. Half a century later he wrote: "I stood looking at it, and thought that no land like it would ever be discovered in the whole world, because at that time Peru was neither known nor thought of." Then he added: "All that I then saw has been destroyed." Cortés reduced Tenochtitlán to rubble in a brutal siege in 1521, founding Mexico City on its ruins. Aztec civilization collapsed. Thousands of Indians perished from smallpox and other exotic diseases introduced by the conquistadors. But Diaz knew he had witnessed a unique moment in history, a sight of a well-ordered preindustrial city at the height of its powers. His memories of his first sighting of the Aztec capital were as fresh in his seventies as they were when he glimpsed the Valley of Mexico for the first time. (Quotations from J.M. Cohen, *The Conquest of New Spain* [Baltimore: Pelican Books, 1963], pp. 214–215).

1150 and 650 B.C. Many of them bear the distinctive human-jaguar motif of the lowlands, which had an important place in Olmec ideology (Chapter 12).

In 1300 B.C., the largest settlement in the Valley of Oaxaca was **San José Mogote,** which lay at the junction of three side valleys, a village of thatched houses with about 150 inhabitants, sharing one lime-plastered public building. During the next century, San José Mogote grew rapidly into a community of 400 to 600 people living in rectangular houses with clay floors, plastered and white-washed walls, and thatched roofs over an area of about 50 acres (20 ha). Public buildings then appeared in larger Oaxacan settlements, built on adobe and earth platforms. Fragments of conch shell trumpets and turtle shell drums come from these structures. Clay figurines of masked, costumed dancers lie in San José Mogote's ceremonial buildings (Figure 13.1). There are marine fish spines, too, almost certainly used in personal bloodletting ceremonies performed before the gods. By 400 B.C., there were at least seven small chiefdoms in the Valley of Oaxaca.

The basic Mesoamerican pattern of civilization came into being over more than 1000 years in the highlands. In the Valley of Mexico, in Oaxaca, and elsewhere, a larger center was ruled by an elite and served by a rural population living in lesser villages scattered throughout the surrounding countryside.

Figure 13.1 Four Masked and Costumed Dancers from San José Mogote, Valley of Oaxaca, Placed Deliberately to make a Scene, Early Evidence of Ceremonial Activity in the Community

By 50 B.C., at least some of the centers, like Monte Albán in the Valley of Oaxaca, achieved considerable size and complexity. The new highland elites presided over hierarchies of priests and officials and had the ability to command the labor of hundreds, if not thousands, of farmers to build and maintain temples, pyramids, and palaces. They controlled large food surpluses, which supported a growing population of nonfarmers, merchants, and artisans. Their political power rested on their ability to coerce others, on well-established notions of social inequality, and, above all, on a complex, and often publicly reenacted, social contract between rulers and their subjects. The people saw their leaders as intermediaries between the living and the ancestors, between their plane of existence and the spiritual world. An elaborate calendar and, soon, writing, regulated every aspect of ceremonial and daily life, and helped generations of rulers presiding over many kingdoms to legitimize their dynastic origins and their relationship to the gods. Highland civilization, with its carefully regulated agriculture, marketplaces, and lucrative trade monopolies, was to flourish for 2000 years.

MONTE ALBAN (500 B.C. to A.D. 750)

Two major city-states dominated the Mesoamerican highlands in the early first millennium A.D., at the time when classic Maya civilization flourished in the lowlands: Monte Albán in the Valley of Oaxaca, and Teotihuacán in the Valley of Mexico.

Monte Albán was founded in about 900 B.C. on a hill overlooking three arms of the Valley of Oaxaca 1300 feet (400 m) below (Figure 13.2). The new

Figure 13.2 MONTE ALBÁN, VALLEY OF OAXACA

settlement grew rapidly, soon boasting of more than 5000 inhabitants. The chosen hill commands a spectacular view and a unique setting, but did not make economic sense as a site for a major ceremonial center, lying as it does far from fertile agricultural lands in the valley below. Perhaps nearby San José Mogote's leaders simply chose an imposing site overlooking their domains as a symbol of their power and political domination. In any event, Monte Albán soon assumed great importance, becoming a major state by 150 B.C. Between 200 and 350 B.C., more than 16,000 people lived in the city, the population rising to a peak of 30,000 during the late classic period, between A.D. 500 to 700. Here, again, the Marcus model of rapid expansion, then growth in the center before decline (Chapter 12) may hold true.

Between 300 and 100 B.C., Zapotec rulers laid out the Main Plaza atop the artificially flattened hilltop. Monte Albán became an elaborate complex of palaces, temples, and plazas, some of which served as ritual settings, others as markets. The city straddled three hills, with at least 15 residential subdivisions, each with their own plazas. Most inhabitants lived in small houses erected on stone-faced terraces built against the steep terrain. Years of archaeological excavation and survey have mapped more than 2000 houses, and an enormous ceremonial precinct centered around the paved Main Plaza. This ritual ward evolved over more than 1000 years of continuous rebuilding and modification, which had the effect of progressively isolating the plaza and those who lived around it from the rest of the city. The Late Classic plaza of A.D. 500 to 720 was 975 feet long and 480 feet across (300 by 150 m), bounded on its north and south sides by 37-foot (12 m)-high platform mounds with staircases leading to buildings atop them (see Figure 13.2). The rulers and their families lived in a complex of buildings on the north platform, which also served as the formal settings for meetings with high officials, and with emissaries from other states such as Teotihuacán.

Monte Albán reached the height of its power after 200 B.C., when it rivaled another expanding state, Teotihuacán to the north. The two great cities coexisted peacefully and traded with one another for centuries. Parts of Monte Albán were still occupied until the Spanish conquest.

VALLEY OF MEXICO: TEOTIHUACÁN (200 B.C. to A.D. 750)

As early as 600 B.C., a series of chiefdoms ruled over the Valley of Mexico. Five centuries later, two of them, Cuicuilco in the west, and Teotihuacán to the east were vying for leadership of the Valley. At that moment, nature intervened with a major volcanic eruption, that buried and destroyed Cuicuilco completely, leaving Teotihuacán the master of the Valley of Mexico and adjacent parts of the central highlands.

Teotihuacán grew rapidly during the ensuing centuries, as thousands of people moved from outlying communities into the metropolis. Whether they moved voluntarily or as a result of conquest and compulsory resettlement is unknown. At least 80,000 people lived in the city by A.D. 100. Like Monte Albán, Teotihuacán may have grown from constant military conquest, in another example of the Marcus model of initial rapid expansion. Between A.D. 200 and 750, Teotihuacán's population grew to more than 150,000 people, making it similar in size to all but the very largest cities of contemporary western Asia and China.

Archaeologist René Millon's map of the city reveals an enormous community that grew over many generations according to a long-term master plan. Over more than eight centuries, the Teotihuacanos built 600 pyramids, 500 workshop areas, a great marketplace, 2000 apartment complexes, and precinct plazas, all laid out on a grid plan anchored by the 3-mile (5 km) long Street of the Dead, which bisects the city on a north-south axis, oriented exactly 15.5 degrees east of north, an orientation established by astronomical observation (Figure 13.3).

The Teotihuacán map suggests that the city was grouped into wards based on both kin ties and more-commercial considerations. Most people lived in standardized, walled residential compounds up to 200 feet (60 m) on each side, connected by narrow alleyways and compounds. Some of these barrios (neighborhoods) were home to craftspeople like obsidian workers or potters. There were also military quarters. Foreigners from the Valley of Oaxaca, also lowland Veracruz, lived in their own neighborhoods. More important priests and artisans lived in dwellings built around small courtyards. Prominent nobles occupied elaborate palaces with central, sunken courts.

At the very core of Teotihuacán's being was the Sacred Cave under the 210 (64 m) high Pyramid of the Sun, an entryway to the Underworld. The

Figure 13.3 Teotihuacán, Showing the Pyramid of the Sun (*Back Left*) and the Avenue of the Dead, with the Pyramid of the Moon in the Foreground

cave was the focus of the powerful creation myth perpetuated by the city's leaders. A sight line from the mouth of the cavern to the western horizon may have associated such astronomical phenomena as the setting sun to specific dates in the local calendar. Teotihuacán's first, and very able, leaders used this cave and the creation myth associated with it as the catalyst for putting their city on the political and religious map. They laid out their entire city as a symbolic landscape commemorating the creation and their principal gods. Their architects laid out the Avenue of the Dead perpendicular to the Sacred Cave and built a small pyramid dedicated to what scholars call "the Great Goddess," associated with the Sun, on the site of the present Pyramid of the Moon, framing it with a sacred mountain on the horizon. They then constructed a Pyramid of the Sun on the site of the Sacred Cave, dedicated to the Great Goddess and to a deity of fire, rain, and wind.

The broad avenue extends southward for 2 miles (3.2 km), where it intersects an east-west avenue, thereby dividing the city into four quadrants. The huge, square enclosure known as the Ciudadela, with sides over 1300 feet (400 m), long lies at the intersection. Here lies the Temple of Quetzalcoatl, the Feathered Serpent, a six-level pyramid adorned with tiers of inset rectangular panels placed over a sloping wall (Figure 13.4). The architects took Teotihuacán's centuries-old symbolism of the Sacred Cave as a passageway and built it into the Temple of the Feathered Serpent. The facade is thought to depict the moment of creation, when opposed serpents, one representing lush greenness and peace, the other desert, fire and war, cavort in the primordial

Figure 13.4   Temple of Quetzalcoatl, Teotihuacán

ocean, painted blue in the background. The Temple of Quetzalcoatl was built to the accompaniment of at least 200 human sacrifices, young warriors with their hands tied behind their backs sacrificed in groups of 18 individuals, the number of 20-day months in the year.

A powerful cult of sacred war and human sacrifice, sometimes called "Star Wars," became associated with the Feathered Serpent, the Storm God, and the cyclical movements of the planet Venus. The beliefs associated with this "Star Wars" cult spread widely in Mesoamerica and had a profound effect on Maya civilization (Chapter 12). The Ciudadela lay at the very center of Teotihuacán, at the crossroads of the city, and the symbolic center of the cosmos, the axis around which the universe revolved.

Teotihuacán was a unique city, covering at least 8 square miles (20.7 sq. km), and a major place of pilgrimage, a sacred city of the greatest symbolic importance. Its prosperity came from trade, especially in the green obsidian found nearby, which Teotihuacán's merchants exchanged for all manner of tropical products, including bird feathers, shells, and fish spines from the lowlands. Food supplies came from the intensive cultivation of valley soils, and from acres of swamp gardens built up in the shallow waters of the nearby lakes. This was a brightly colored city, a landscape painted in every hue, the houses adorned with polished whitewash, which still sticks to wall fragments. But above all, the great city spoke a powerful symbolic language, which comes down to us in architecture, art, and ceramics. Its leaders perpetuated an origin myth that had their great city as the place where the cosmos and the present cycle of time began. Every ritual within Teotihuacán's precincts fostered the belief that its people were honored and responsible for maintaining the cosmos. A cult of war and sacrifice governed by an eight-year cycle ensured the well-being of the cosmos, the city, and its inhabitants. Teotihuacán's armies were formidable in battle, their victories the source of the prisoners sacrificed to the gods.

To be a Teotihuacano was to be honored, for one dwelt at the very center of the world. But this honor carried important obligations to the city, the lords, and the gods. Every citizen served the state, through artisanship, through laboring on public works, and by serving in Teotihuacán's armies. These obligations were fulfilled through the ties of kinship that underlay every household, every apartment compound, every royal palace, linking everyone in the great city in the common enterprise of maintaining the cosmos. On occasion, the government attempted planned resettlement of city dwellers on adjacent, underutilized lands, where agricultural production could be maximized, especially on irrigable lands near the lakes. But most people still lived in the city, the heart of a large, loosely knit state about the size of the island of Sicily in the Mediterranean, some 10,000 square miles (25,900 sq. km).

Teotihuacán's rulers controlled the destinies of about half a million people, but its main impact on lowland and highland Mesoamerica was economic, ideological, and cultural rather than political. Its power came from conquest and trade, and, above all, from a carefully nurtured ideology that made the great city the place of creation, the very cradle of civilization. So successful was this religious propaganda that a ruined Teotihuacán was still deeply revered by the Aztecs and other highland peoples at the time of the Spanish conquest seven centuries later.

After about A.D. 650, Teotihuacán's ideology became increasingly militaristic, at a time when the state may have become more oppressive. The city's enormous population combined with uneven exploitation of the Valley of Mexico's resources may have created serious economic problems that threatened to undermine the state. The end, when it came, was cataclysmic. The Ciudadela was attacked in about A.D. 750, its temples and palaces burned and razed. The destruction was part of a systematic desanctification of Teotihuacán both politically and ritually, to prevent new rulers from rising from the ashes. No one knows who the agents of total destruction were, but Teotihuacán and its state vanished from history, only to be remembered in legend as the place where the Toltec and Aztec world of later times began.

THE TOLTECS (A.D. 650 to 1200)

Teotihuacán had acted as a magnet to the rural populations of the highlands for many centuries. When the great city collapsed, her inhabitants moved outward as other central Mexican cities expanded into the political vacuum left by her conquerors. Political authority passed rapidly from one growing city to the next. Eventually, one group achieved a semblance of dominance: the Toltecs.

Early Toltec history is confusing at best, but, like other highland peoples, they were composed of various tribal groups, among them the Nahua-speaking Tolteca-Chichimeca, apparently semicivilized people from the fringes of Mesoamerica. (Nahuatl was the common language of the Aztec empire at the Spanish Conquest.) A ruler named Topiltzin Quetzalcoatl, born in the year 1 Reed (A.D. 935 or 947) moved the Toltec capital to Tollan, "the Place of Reeds," (the archaeologists' **Tula**) in its heyday a city of some 30,000 to 60,000 people, far smaller than Teotihuacán. Here bitter strife broke out between the followers of the peace-loving Topiltzin Quetzalcoatl and those of his warlike rival Tezcatlipoca, "Smoking Mirror," god of warriors and of life itself. The Tezcatlipoca faction prevailed by trickery and humiliation. Topiltzin and his followers fled Tula and eventually arrived on the shores of the Gulf of Mexico. There, according to one account, the ruler set himself on fire decked out in his ceremonial regalia. As his ashes rose to heaven, he turned into the Morning Star. The Spanish conquistadors learned another version of the legend in which Topiltzin Quetzalcoatl fashioned a raft of serpents and sailed over the eastern horizon, vowing to return in the year 1 Reed, of which you will read more below.

In the years following Topiltzin Quetzalcoatl's departure, the Toltec state reached its greatest extent, controlling much of central Mexico from coast to coast. By A.D. 900, Tula was a prosperous town of artisans that soon grew into a city of as many as 40,000 people covering 5.4 square miles (16 sq. km). By A.D. 1000, the Toltec lords had laid out their capital on a grid pattern with a wide central plaza and ceremonial center bordered by imposing pyramids and at least two ball courts. Four colossal warriors carrying spearthrowers and incense bags support the roof of a temple atop a pyramid (Figure 13.5). A grim "Serpent Wall," 131 feet (40 m) long runs along the north side of the pyramid, bearing friezes of serpents consuming skeletal humans. Everything points to a now militaristic society, obsessed with human sacrifice.

Tula's temples, pyramids, and ball courts were torn to the ground in about 1200, when the Toltec empire fell apart.

AZTEC CIVILIZATION (A.D. 1200 to 1519)

During the next century, a political vacuum existed in the Valley of Mexico, where a series of moderate-sized city-states prospered and competed. Into this settled and competitive world stepped a small and obscure group, the Azteca, or Mexica. Within a mere two centuries, these insignificant players on the highland stage presided over the mightiest pre-Columbian empire in the Americas.

The Aztecs' history as they tell it, reads like a rags-to-riches novel. They claimed they came from Aztlan, an island on a lake west or northwest of Mexico, migrating into the Valley under the guidance of their tribal god Huitzilopochtli, "Hummingbird on the Left," who was soon reborn as the Sun God himself. This was the official version perpetuated by official Aztec

Figure 13.5 Colossal Warriors Atop Pyramid B at Tula

historians and recorded by the Spaniards. Such migration legends were common in ancient Mesoamerica and should not be taken at face value. The Aztecs had certainly settled in the Valley by the 13th century, but they were unwelcome arrivals in the densely settled valley. Eventually they settled on some swampy islands in the marshes of the largest lake in the Valley, where they founded twin capitals, Tenochtitlán and Tlatelolco, sometime after 1325. Fierce and ruthless warriors, the Aztecs became mercenaries for the lord Tezozomoc of the expanding Tepanec kingdom in 1367. The Aztecs shared in the spoils of his expanding domains, soon adopting the institutions and empire building strategies of their employer.

After Tezozomoc's death in 1426, an Aztec ruler named Itzcoatl and his exceptionally able adviser Tlacaelel attacked the Tepanecs and crushed them in one of the great battles of Aztec history. The Aztecs became the masters of the Valley of Mexico and set out to rewrite society and history itself. The great Tlacaelel ordered all the historical codices of the Aztecs' rivals to be burnt, creating a mythic, visionary history of the Mexica in their place. The Aztecs were now the chosen of the Sun God Huitzilopochtli, the true heirs of the ancient Toltecs, great warriors destined to take prisoners in battle to nourish the sun in its daily journey across the heavens. A series of brilliant and ruthless leaders embarked on aggressive campaigns of conquest, destined to fulfil

Aztec destiny. The greatest Aztec ruler was Ahuitzotl (1486–1502), the sixth *tlatoani,* or "speaker." His armies marched far beyond the Valley, to the borders of Guatemala. Just like Teotihuacán and Tikal, the initial conquests rapidly delineated the broad outlines of their domains.

The Aztec empire covered both highlands and lowlands and affected the lives of over 5 million people. Brilliant strategist and able administrator, Ahuitzotl was a single-minded militarist, who believed fervently in his divine mission to nourish the Sun God. Twenty thousand prisoners are said to have perished in 1487 when he inaugurated a rebuilt Great Temple of Huitzilopochtli and the Rain God Tlaloc in the central precincts of Tenochtitlán.

Tenochtitlán

In its late-15th-century heyday, **Tenochtitlán** was a sophisticated and cosmopolitan city with a social, political, and economic organization flexible enough to integrate large numbers of outsiders, merchants, pilgrims, foreigners, and thousands of laborers into its already large permanent population. The Aztec capital reflected a society that depended on military strength and on its ability to organize large numbers of people to achieve its end. Thousands of acres of carefully planned swamp gardens (*chinampas*) that intersected with canals provided food for the large urban population.

The city originally consisted of two autonomous communities, Tenochtitlán and Tlatelolco, each with their own ceremonial precincts. By 1519, Tenochtitlán was the center of religious and secular power, while the main market was at Tlatelolco. The capital was divided into four quarters, which intersected at the foot of the stairway up the Great Temple of Huitzilopochtli and Tlaloc within the central walled plaza. The rectangular plaza was about 500 yards (457 m) square, large enough to accommodate nearly 10,000 people during major public ceremonies (Figure 13.6).

Thanks to recent excavations by Eduardo Matos Moctezuma, we know that the Great Temple stood on the north side of the plaza, a stepped pyramid with two stairways and two shrines, dedicated to Huitzilopochtli and Tlaloc respectively. Huitzilopochtli's red chapel lay to the right, Tlaloc's blue shrine to the left. Moctezuma unearthed no less than six earlier phases of the temple, the second dating to about 1390 and virtually complete. Moctezuma points out that the great pyramid depicts the four celestial levels of the Aztec cosmos, the original ground surface being the earthly plane of existence. It was from this point that the four cardinal directions of the Aztec world radiated, each associated with colors, different personifications of gods and goddesses. From here a vertical channel led to the heavens above and the Underworld below.

Tenochtitlán was the symbolic center of the universe, a city set in a circle of water, Aztlan itself, the mythic island surrounded by water. The greatest festivals of the Aztec world unfolded at the great pyramid, ceremonies marked by rows of brightly dressed prisoners climbing the steep stairway to their death. The victim was stretched out over the sacrificial stone. In seconds, a priest with a obsidian knife broke open his chest and ripped out his still-

Figure 13.6   Artist's Reconstruction of the Central Precincts of Tenochtitlán, with the Great Temple of Huitzilopochtli at Left

beating heart, dashing it against the sacrificial stone. The corpse rolled down
the steep pyramid into the hands of butchers at the foot, who dismembered
the body and set the skull on the great skull rack nearby (Figure 13.7). Despite
a reputation for cannibalism, most experts believe the Mexica consumed only
small amounts on ritual occasions, perhaps as acts of spiritual renewal.

The World of the Fifth Sun

The Aztecs were militaristic, but every deed, every moment of living, was filled
with symbolic meaning and governed by ritual. They inherited the cyclical
view of time, established by the movements of the heavenly bodies, which had
lain at the core of Mesoamerican civilization for millennia. Their 365-day secular calendar measured the passing of seasons and market days. A ritual calendar on a 260-day cycle consisted of 20 "weeks" of 13 days each. Each
week, each day, had a patron deity, all of them with specific good and evil
qualities. Once every 52 years, the two calendars coincided, a moment at
which time was thought to expire until rekindled by the priests lighting a
sacred fire in a sacrificial victim's chest. Then a new cycle began amidst general rejoicing.

Aztec creation legends spoke of four suns preceding their own world, that
of the Fifth Sun. A cataclysmic flood destroyed the world of the Fourth Sun.
Primordial waters covered the earth. The gods gathered at the sacred city,
Teotihuacán, where they took counsel. Two gods were chosen to represent the
Sun and Moon. They did penance for four days, then immolated themselves in
a great fire in the presence of the other gods. They emerged as the Sun and
Moon, blown on their cyclical courses by the wind god Ehecatl. Thus was
born the world of the Fifth Sun, but a world doomed to inevitable, cyclical

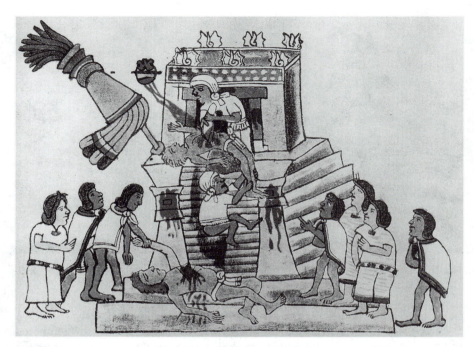

Figure 13.7   AZTEC HUMAN SACRIFICE   A victim's heart is torn out at the Temple of Huitzilopochtli.

extinction. A strong sense of fatalism underlay Aztec existence, but they believed they could ensure the continuity of life by nourishing the sun with the magic elixir of human hearts. This was the reason why human sacrifice was so prevalent in Mesoamerican society, as a means of returning food and energy from living people to the earth, the sky, and the waters. Feeding the sun was warrior's business, for they were the chosen people of the sun, destined to conquer, or to suffer the "Flowery Death" (death on the sacrificial stone) when captured in battle. From birth, in formal orations, in schools, through art, architecture, poetry, even in dress codes, the Aztecs were told theirs was a divine quest—to carve out an empire in the name of Huitzilopochtli.

The Aztec State

The Aztec empire was a mosaic of ever-changing alliances, cemented together by an elaborate tribute-gathering machine, and controlled by a tiny group of rulers, the lord of Tenochtitlán being principal among them. Everything was run for the benefit of a growing elite, who maintained their power by ruthless and efficient taxation campaigns, political marriages, and the constant threat of military force. Tribute was assessed on conquered cities and taken in many forms, as raw materials like gold dust, metal artifacts, or tropical bird feathers for ceremonial mantles and headdresses (Figure 13.8). Fine ornaments, even capes, were assessed from communities specializing in such products. Twenty-six cities did nothing but provide firewood for one royal palace alone. Expert

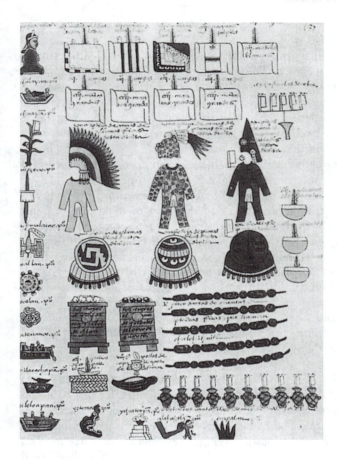

Figure 13.8 AZTEC TRIBUTE An inventory, preserved in the *Codex Mendoza,* an account of Aztec society compiled after the Spanish Conquest for the Viceroy of New Spain, lists, among other items from the province of Tochtepec: "1600 rich mantles, 800 striped red, white, and green mantles, 400 warrior's tunics and shorts. ..." The tribute included colored bird feathers, cacao, and tree gum.

smiths made musical instruments like bells, and alloyed copper to bring out shimmering gold and silver hues. Both color and sound were central parts of Mesoamerican ideology, commemorating the sun and moon, the sounds of rain, thunder, and rattlesnakes, helping bring symbolic order to the world.

Both settlement data and other archaeological data suggest that the Aztec empire was less centralized, both as a society and an economy, than its great predecessor, Teotihuacán. To what extent it originated through decision making at the top, as opposed to market dynamics such as supply and demand is still unknown.

Under the highly visible and much touted imperial veneer lay a complex foundation of small kingdoms, towns, and villages, all integrated into local economies. Many of them existed before the Aztec state, or even earlier; civilizations came into being and continued after the Spanish Conquest. At the same time, the economic and political patterns of the empire were highly variable, both regionally and socially, in everything from land tenure to craft specialization, patterns of urbanization to merchants and markets. This intricate social mosaic, only now being revealed by a new generation of archaeological research, lay behind a facade of seeming political and economic uniformity and centralization.

Tribute and trade went together, for the Aztec empire depended heavily on professional merchants, *pochteca*. The Aztec merchants formed a closely knit class of their own, serving as the eyes and ears of the state, and sometimes achieving great wealth. Tenochtitlán's great market at Tlatelolco was the hub of the Aztec world, attended, so the Spanish chroniclers record, by at least 20,000 people a day, and 50,000 on market days. There were gold and silver merchants, dealers in slaves and tropical feathers, sellers of capes and chocolate, every kind of merchandise imaginable. The market was supervised closely by officials appointed to ensure that fair practices prevailed.

The state itself was run for the benefit of the rulers and the nobility, a privileged class who controlled land and had the right to make use of communal labor. Through birthright, tribute levies, and appointed positions, nobles controlled nearly every strategic resource in the empire, and the trade routes that handled them. An elaborate dress code covered everything from ornaments to cape and sandal styles, regulations designed to restrict the size of the nobility. The tribute and labor of tens of thousands of commoners supported the state. The humble commoners with their coarse capes and work-worn hands supplied a small number of people with an endless supply of food, firewood, water, fine clothing, and a host of luxury goods that came from all over the lowlands and highlands. Only slaves and prisoners were lower in the social hierarchy.

Every Aztec was a member of a *calpulli,* or "big house," a kin-based group of families that claimed descent through the male line from a common ancestor. The four quarters of Tenochtitlán were organized into neighborhoods based on such groups. The *calpulli* served as the intermediary between the individual commoner and the state, paying taxes in labor and tribute, and allocating people to carry out public works. Most important, the *calpulli* held land communally and allocated it to its members. An elected leader maintained special maps showing how the land was being used and dealt with government tribute collectors. The *calpulli* provided a measure of security to every member of society, while providing an efficient device for the state to govern a teeming and diverse urban and rural population and to organize large numbers of people for armies or work projects at short notice. None of the Aztecs' social and political institutions were new. They had been used with ruthless success centuries earlier by the Toltecs and the rulers of Teotihuacán, even if, in the Aztec case, they worked within a more flexible and diverse milieu.

THE SPANISH CONQUEST (A.D. 1517 to 1521)

The Aztec empire was at its height when the aggressive and militaristic ruler Ahuitzotl died in 1501. The following year, Moctezuma Xocoyotzin ("the Younger") was elected to the throne, a complex man, said to be a good soldier, but given to introspection. When reports reached Tenochtitlán in 1517 of mountains moving on the Gulf of Mexico, of white-bearded visitors from over the eastern horizon to the Maya of the distant Yucatán, Moctezuma became obsessed with ancient Toltec legends, with the departure of Topiltzin Quetzalcoatl, who had sailed over the eastern horizon vowing to return in the year 1 Reed. By grotesque historical coincidence, Hernan Cortés landed in Vera Cruz in the year 1 Reed (1519), convincing Moctezuma that Topiltzin Quetzalcoatl had returned to claim his kingdom.

The story of the Spanish conquest that followed unfolds like a Greek tragedy. The conquest pitted an isolated, battle-hardened expeditionary force of about 600 men against a brave, driven people who were convinced, like their illustrious predecessors, that every act of war was imbued with deep symbolism. The Aztecs had long used war to feed the relentless appetite of the gods and to keep a loose patchwork of vassal states in order. With a skilled enemy exploiting their uneasy allies, they found themselves on their own. All they could do was to defend themselves desperately against a puzzling foe quite unlike any adversary they had encountered. This small and determined band of gold-hungry adventurers were accustomed to long and arduous military campaigns, and it was inevitable that they would prevail.

Ten years passed before the whole of Mexico (New Spain) was under secure Spanish control. Tens of thousands of people died in bloody encounters, hundreds of thousands more from exotic diseases like influenza and smallpox introduced by the newcomers. Instead of the divine benevolence of Quetzalcoatl, the conquerors brought suffering, death, exotic diseases, and slavery. More than 3000 years of Mesoamerican civilization passed rapidly into centuries of historical obscurity.

CHAPTER 14

Andean Civilizations

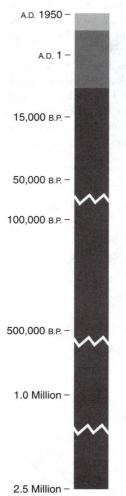

A.D. 1950 —

A.D. 1 —

15,000 B.P. —

50,000 B.P. —

100,000 B.P. —

500,000 B.P. —

1.0 Million —

2.5 Million —

In its late-15th-century heyday, the vast Inca empire, known as **Tawantinsuyu** ("The Land of the Four Quarters"), extended from high-altitude mountain valleys in the Andes through dry highland plains to foothills to tropical rain forests and to coastal deserts, some of the driest landscape on earth (Figure 14.1). This chapter describes the development of Andean civilization, which culminated in the Inca empire.

Over many centuries, two "poles" of Andean civilization developed, the one along the north coast of what is now Peru, the other in the south-central Andes. Only the Inca succeeded in joining the two into one vast empire. The northern pole was centered on the bleak and effectively rainless Peruvian desert plain, which extends south nearly 350 miles (550 km) along the coast as far as Collasuyu, reaching a width of up to 62 miles (100 km) in the area of the Lambayeque River. Some 40 rivers and streams fueled by mountain runoff flow across the plain, but they can only be used for irrigation in areas where the surrounding desert is low enough.

The southern pole embraced the high plains of the Lake Titicaca Basin, highland Bolivia and parts of Argentina and northern Chile in the south-central Andes. Much of this region was too dry and cold to sustain dense human populations. The northern end of the Lake Titicaca Basin was somewhat warmer and better watered, making both alpaca and llama herding and potato and quinoa agriculture possible.

Andean civilization pursued many different evolutionary pathways, which came together in a remarkable mosaic of states and empires, in large part as a result of widely held spiritual beliefs and by constant interchange

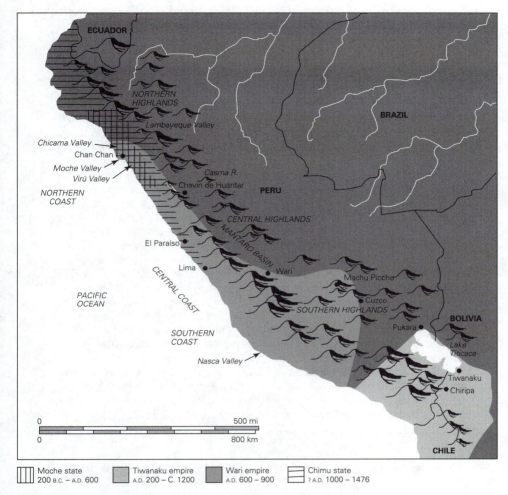

Figure 14.1   Map Showing Archaeological Sites in Chapter 14

between the coast and the highlands and between neighboring valleys and large population centers. Tawantinsuyu itself was a unique political synthesis sewn together by the Inca lords of the Andes in the centuries just before European contact. It was the culmination of centuries of increasing social complexity throughout the Andean area.

THE MARITIME FOUNDATIONS OF ANDEAN CIVILIZATION

The rugged central Andean mountains are second only to the Himalayas in height, but only 10 percent of their rainfall descends the Pacific watershed. The foothill slopes and plains at the western foot of the mountains are man-

D I S C O V E R Y

HIRAM BINGHAM AT MACHU PICCHU

The year was 1911. American explorer Hiram Bingham was high in the Andes, struggling along precipitous, densely forested paths, slipping ankle deep in mud at every corner. Bingham was searching for Vilcabamba, the last refuge of the Inca ruler Manca Inca when he fled from the Spaniards in 1537. With a local farmer as a guide, he and his men climbed in places on all fours, high above the tumbling Urubamba River. Suddenly, he emerged into the open, high atop a mountain ridge. Bingham climbed a granite stairway leading to a plaza with two temples. He wandered through "a maze of beautiful granite houses . . . covered with trees and moss and the growth of centuries." He wandered for hours among "walls of white granite . . . carefully cut and exquisitely fitted together." Stone terraces climbed like giant staircases up the hillside. A twisting path led to ruined houses built with fine Inca stonework. A granite stairway led Bingham to a plaza with two temples, one containing a large altar stone. "The sight held me spellbound," declared Bingham. On this mountain ridge, the Incas had built Machu Picchu, a settlement in such a remote, inaccessible setting that Bingham claimed it was the "lost city of the Incas." For three years, Bingham worked at Machu Picchu, clearing, excavating, and mapping houses and temples.

Machu Picchu is one of the most spectacular archaeological sites in the world, but was never a lost city, for the local farmers were well aware of its existence. Bingham himself believed he had found Vilcabamba, but in 1964 explorer Gene Savoy identified the remote Inca settlement of Espiritu Pampa in the forested Pamaconas Valley as Manca Inca's last capital. (Quotations from Hiram Bingham, *Lost City of the Incas* [New York: Athenaeum, 1964]; p. 212.)

tled by one of the world's driest deserts, which extends virtually from the equator to 30 degrees south, much of it along the Peruvian coast. At the opposite extreme, the richest fishery in the Americas hugs the Pacific shore, yielding millions of small schooling fish such as anchovies. These easily netted shoals support millions of people today, and they supported dense prehistoric populations. In contrast, the cultivation of this dry landscape requires controlling the runoff from the Andes with large irrigation systems that use long canals built by the coordinated labors of hundreds of people. Only 10 percent of this desert can be farmed, so its inhabitants rely heavily on the bounty of the Pacific, including the enormous shoals of easily netted anchovies. Surprisingly, perhaps, this apparently inhospitable desert was a major center of complex early states, which traded with neighbors in the highlands and built large ceremonial centers.

In the 1970s, archaeologist Michael Moseley proposed what he called the "maritime foundations of Andean civilization" hypothesis. He argued that the unique maritime resources of the Pacific coast provided sufficient calories to support rapidly growing, sedentary populations, which clustered in large communities. In addition, the same food source produced sufficient surplus to free up time and people to erect large public monuments and temples, work organized by the leaders of newly complex coastal societies. This scenario runs contrary to conventional archaeological thinking, which regards agriculture as the economic basis for state-organized societies. In the Andes, argued Moseley, it was fishing. For thousands of years, coastal populations rose, and their rise preadapted them to later circumstances, under which they would adopt large-scale irrigation and maize agriculture.

Several critiques of the maritime foundations hypothesis have appeared, all of them based on the assumption that large coastal settlements could not have been supported by maritime resources alone. Most of these critiques have tended to ignore the potential of anchovies. Overall, the maritime foundations hypothesis has stood the test of time well, provided it is seen as a component in a much broader evolutionary process, which also took place inland, in the highlands, and in areas where the width of the coastal shelf precluded extensive anchovy fishing.

Richard Burger argues that changing dietary patterns in the highlands, where agriculture became increasingly important, would have created a demand among farmers for lowland products—salt, fish, and seaweed. Seaweed is rich in marine iodine and could have been an important medicine in the highlands, used to combat endemic goiter and other conditions. By the same token, carbohydrate foods like white potatoes that could not be grown on the coast have been found in sites in the Pacific lowlands. Thus, the formation of states in both lowlands and highlands may have been fostered by continuous interchange between coast and interior.

Michael Moseley believes that the reliance on maritime resources led to a preadaptation in the form of large, densely concentrated populations, whose leaders were able to organize the labor forces needed not only for building large ceremonial centers but also for transforming river valleys with sizable irrigation schemes. Under this scenario, irrigation farming was in the hands of a well-defined group of authority figures, who took advantage of existing simple technology and local populations to create new economies. This transformation, based as it was on trade, maize agriculture, and a maritime diet, acted as a "kick" for radical changes in Andean society. But the transformation was based on ancient fishing traditions, which can be documented thousands of years earlier at early coastal villages.

COASTAL FOUNDATIONS (2500 to 900 B.C.)

Agriculture remained a secondary activity until comparatively recently in the lowlands. Despite this, sedentary villages of several hundred people flourished along the north coast between 2500 and 1800 B.C. This "Initial Period" of Andean civilization was a critical millennium, for new concerns both with the cosmos and with religion permeated the Andes. The new beliefs manifested themselves in a wave of monumental construction in both lowlands and highlands, notably of U-shaped ceremonial structures.

Figure 14.2   El Paraíso, Peru

El Paraíso, built close to the mouth of the Chillón River near Lima in about 1800 B.C., is the oldest of these U-shaped ceremonial complexes and the closest one to the Pacific (Figure 14.2). This vast site consists of at least six huge square buildings constructed of roughly shaped stone blocks cemented with unfired clay. The people painted the polished clay-faced outer walls in brilliant hues. Each complex consisted of a square building surrounded by tiers of platforms reached by stone and clay staircases. The largest is more than 830 feet (250 m) long and 166 feet (50 m) wide, standing more than 30 feet (10 m) above the plain. The rooms apparently were covered with matting roofs supported by willow posts. Perhaps as many as 100,000 tons of rock excavated from the nearby hills were needed to build the El Paraíso buildings. There are few signs of occupation around them, though, as if they were shrines and public precincts rather than residential quarters. The two largest mounds of collapsed masonry lie parallel to one another, defining a vast, elongated patio covering more than 6 acres (2.5 ha).

What is most surprising is that these huge structures were erected by people from dozens of scattered villages. For reasons not yet understood, they united in a building project that channeled most of their surplus energies into a vast monumental center, a place where few people lived but where everyone apparently congregated for major public ceremonies.

El Paraíso's U-shaped layout coincides with the florescence of similarly shaped ceremonial centers in the interior, at a time when coastal people began to consume much larger amounts of root crops, to make pottery, and to shift their settlements inland to river valleys. Some scholars believe that this move coincided with the introduction of large-scale canal irrigation. Perhaps the spread of U-shaped ceremonial centers reflects a radical restructuring of society that accompanied major economic change.

What does this mean in ritual terms? In many parts of the Americas the ritual manipulation of smoke and water served as a way of bridging stratified layers of air, earth, and bodies of water in the cosmos. The early ceremonial centers of the coast and highlands may reflect an ancient tradition of using these substances to maintain communication with the cosmos.

THE EARLY HORIZON AND CHAVÍN DE HUANTAR
(900 to 200 B.C.)

In 1943, archaeologist Julio Tello identified a distinctive art style in stone, ceramics, and precious metals over a wide area of highland Peru, a style he named Chavín after a famous prehistoric ceremonial center at Chavín de Huántar in central Peru. Tello's research led to a long-held belief among Peruvianists that the widespread Chavín art style was a "mother culture" for all later Andean civilizations, somewhat equivalent to the Olmec phenomenon in Mesoamerican prehistory. This became a distinctive "Early Horizon" in Peruvian prehistory, dating to about 900 B.C., when there was a great expansion of indigenous religious belief by conquest, trade, and colonization when—civilization began.

Chavín de Huántar is testimony to an elaborate, well-developed iconography. The temple area is terraced with an impressive truncated pyramid on the uppermost level (Figure 14.3a). The 32-foot (10 m) high pyramid appears solid but is in fact hollow, a honeycomb of stone passages and rooms. The galleries are ventilated by special rectangular tubes. The temple housed a remarkable carving of a jaguarlike human with hair in the form of serpents, the famous "Lanzón," which may have served as an axis joining the heavens, and earth, and the Underworld (Figure 14.3b). The deity seems to be acting as an arbiter of balance and order. The entire center was a place of mediation with the heavens and the Underworld. Chavín's priests and religious functionaries served as intermediaries between the living and the supernatural. In this shamanlike role, they transformed themselves into supernatural jaguars and crested eagles.

Chavín art reflects these transformations. Jaguar motifs predominate; humans, gods, and animals have jaguarlike fangs or limbs; snakes flow from the bodies of many figures (see Figure 1.10). The art is both grotesque and slightly sinister. Many figures were carved in stone, others in clay or bone, their nostrils dripping with mucus from ingesting hallucinogenic substances. The principal god may have been a nature deity, associated with thunder and other powerful meteorological phenomena of the nearby high mountains.

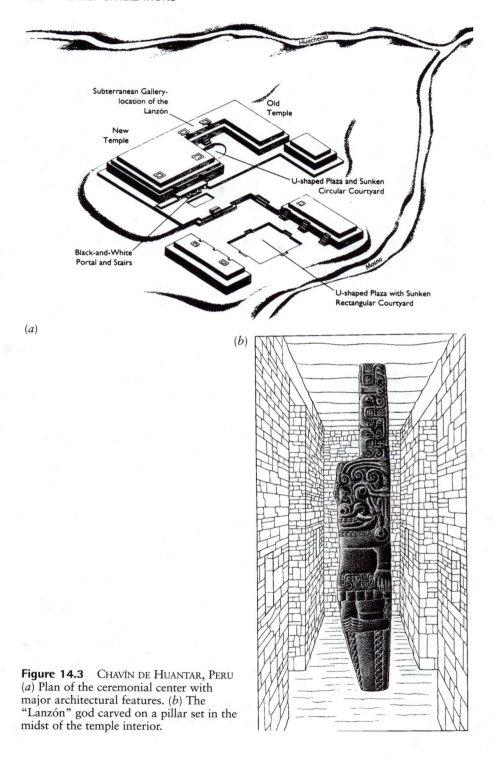

(a)

(b)

Figure 14.3   CHAVÍN DE HUANTAR, PERU
(a) Plan of the ceremonial center with
major architectural features. *(b)* The
"Lanzón" god carved on a pillar set in the
midst of the temple interior.

Conceivably, theorizes Richard Burger, Chavín de Huántar was a four-stage artificial mountain, where rituals surrounded the circulation of water. Under these beliefs, the earth floated on a vast ocean. From there, water circulated through mountains to the Milky Way in the heavens, where it became rain to water human fields before flowing back into the ocean. Peruvian archaeologist Luis Lumbreras has replicated the deep roaring sound of water flowing through the elaborate stone-lined tunnels and canals of the great shrine. He believes that the roar of the water would have echoed through the temple during the rainy season, a symbolic link between the rain-giving mountains, the temple, and the layers of the cosmos.

With its tangled animal and human motifs, Chavín art has all the flamboyance and exotic touches of the tropical forest. The animals depicted—cayman, jaguar, and snake—are all forest animals. The art may have originated in the tropical forests to the east of the Andes, but the Early Horizon Chavín temple has a U shape with a sunken central plaza, an architectural design documented centuries earlier at other coastal and highland sites.

Chavín represents a coalescence of traits and ideas from both the coast and the forest that formed a flamboyant cultural manifestation over a local area of the highlands. The Early Horizon may have been a long period of cultural change and political adjustment.

THE INITIAL PERIOD

The Initial Period saw the development of distinctive coastal and highland societies at either end of the Andean world, on the North Coast and on the shores of Lake Titicaca far to the south.

The Coast (after 1800 B.C.)

After 1800 B.C., a set of interacting polities developed in the Moche, Casma, Chillón, and other river valleys where irrigation agriculture flourished. Centuries before, communication networks had arisen that linked not only neighboring coastal river valleys but lowlands and highlands as well. These trade routes, which straddled all manner of environmental zones, helped spread technology, ideology, pottery making, and architectural styles over large areas, giving a superficial sense of unity that was reflected in the widespread use of common art motifs.

By this time, people had moved from the coast inland. The subsistence base changed from fishing to large-scale irrigation agriculture. Even the first farmers probably made some limited use of canals to water their riverside gardens. However, the new works were on a far larger scale, spurred by the availability of an army of workers fed by abundant Pacific fish; by the presence of gentle, cultivable slopes inland; and by the expertise of the local people in farming cotton, gourds, and many lesser crops such as squashes and beans.

At first, each family may have worked together to irrigate its own sloping gardens, but gradually each community grew so much that essential irrigation works could be handled only by cooperative effort. Organized irrigation perhaps began as many minor cooperative works between individual families and neighboring villages. These simple projects eventually evolved over many centuries into elaborate public works that embraced entire inland valleys, controlled by a corporate authority who held a monopoly over both the water and the land it irrigated.

Lake Titicaca Basin: Chiripa and Pukara (1000 B.C. to A.D. 100)

As Chavín de Huántar rose to prominence in the northern highlands, a separate Early Horizon tradition of complex society developed around Lake Titicaca far to the south. The plains landscape of the basin was gradually transformed by ever more intensive agriculture and herding.

At **Chiripa** on the southern shore of the lake, farming and herding were integrated into much earlier hunter-gatherer traditions. Chiripa itself remained a small village until about 1000 B.C., when a platform mound was built in the community, then modified many times over the centuries. Eventually, carved stone plaques set into the walls depicted serpents, animals, and humans, the earliest appearance of a stone carving tradition that persisted along the shores of the lake for many centuries. Sixteen rectangular buildings surrounded the court. Many features of the Chiripa shrine, especially the stepped doorways, sunken courts, and niche-like windows, are ancestral to the later Tiwanaku architectural tradition, which used the same devices for its ceremonial architecture. The religious beliefs associated with this architecture have been grouped under the "Yaya-Mama Religious tradition," which flourished for many centuries.

Another major center flourished at **Pukara,** 47 miles (75 km) northwest of Lake Titicaca, with a large residential area and an imposing ceremonial complex on a stone-faced terrace, complete with rectangular sunken court and one-room structures on three sides. Judging from the distribution of Pukara pottery styles, the kingdom's power was confined to the northern Titicaca Basin, but ceramics and other artifacts from as far afield as the north coast reflect widespread trade connections. Tiwanaku, then a smaller center than in later centuries, presided over the southern shores of the lake between 400 B.C. and A.D. 100. There is no evidence that Pukara incorporated its southern neighbor.

From the Initial Period onward, the Andean region witnessed an extraordinary array of state-organized societies that displayed a remarkable diversity of culture, art, organization, and religious belief. At the same time, there were broad similarities in cosmology and culture that distinguish these societies from states elsewhere in the prehistoric world.

THE MOCHE STATE (200 B.C. to A.D. 700)

By 200 B.C., the Moche state had begun in northern coastal Peru, flourishing for 800 years. Its origins lay in the Chicama and Moche valleys, with great ceremonial centers and huge irrigation works.

Figure 14.4   A Lord of Sipán
WEARING FULL REGALIA

The spectacular discovery of undisturbed Moche tombs near the village of **Sipán** about 420 miles (680 km) northwest of Lima has revolutionized our knowledge of Moche's elite. Peruvian archaeologist Walter Alva has excavated three unlooted royal burials. The sepulchers contained plank coffins holding the extended skeletons of men wearing gold nose and ear ornaments, gold and turquoise bead bracelets, and copper sandals. A ceremonial rattle, crescent-shaped knives, scepters, spears, and exotic seashells surrounded each body (Figures 14.4 and 14.5).

Comparing the objects found in the tomb with people depicted in Moche art, Christopher Donnan has identified the man as a warrior-priest. Such individuals are depicted on Moche pots presiding over sacrifices of

Figure 14.5 Artist's Reconstruction of Tomb 1 at Sipán, Showing the Lord in his Regalia Set in his Coffin, also Male and Female attendants   Once the coffins were in place, a low-beamed roof was set in place, too low for someone to stand inside the chamber. A seated body with crossed legs watched over the burial chamber from a small niche in the south wall, about 3 feet (1 m) above the roof.

prisoners of war (Figure 14.6). Apparently, Moche warriors went to war specifically to take captives. They would strip them of their armor and weapons, then lead them in front of the Warrior-Priest. Then the prisoner's throat was cut and the Warrior-Priest and others drank the blood of the slain victim while the corpse was dismembered. On pot after pot, the Warrior-Priest wears a crescent-shaped headdress atop a conical helmet, exactly the regalia found in the Sipán tombs. Such men were a priesthood of nobles living in different parts of the kingdom, who enacted the Sacrifice Ceremony at prescribed times.

Moche society consisted of farmers and fisherfolk as well as skilled artisans and priests, who are depicted on pots with felinelike fangs set in their mouths and wearing puma-skin headdresses. A few expert craft potters created superb modeled vessels with striking portraits of arrogant, handsome men who can only have been the leaders of Moche society (Figure 14.7). The potters modeled warriors, too, complete with shields and war clubs, well-padded helmets, and colorful cotton uniforms. Moche burials show that some members of society were much richer than others, lying in graves filled with as many as 50 vessels or with weapons or staffs of rank. We do not know exactly how Moche society was organized, but we can assume that the ruler wielded

Figure 14.6 A MOCHE LORD PRESIDES OVER A PARADE OF PRISONERS WHO ARE BEING SACRIFICED A frieze from a painted pot "unrolled" photographically.

authority over a hierarchical state of warriors, priest-doctors, artisans, and the mass of the agricultural population. For instance, there was at least one Moche-style settlement in each subject valley.

By this time the coastal people were expert metalworkers. They had discovered the properties of gold ore and extracted it by panning in stream beds rather than by mining. Soon they had developed ways of hammering it into fine sheets and had learned how to emboss it to make raised designs (Figure 14.8). They also had worked out the technique of annealing, making it possible to soften the metal and then hammer it into more elaborate forms, and they joined sheets with fine solder. The smiths used gold as a setting for turquoise and shell ornaments, crafted crowns, circlets, necklaces, pins, and tweezers.

Figure 14.7 A MOCHE PORTRAIT HEAD

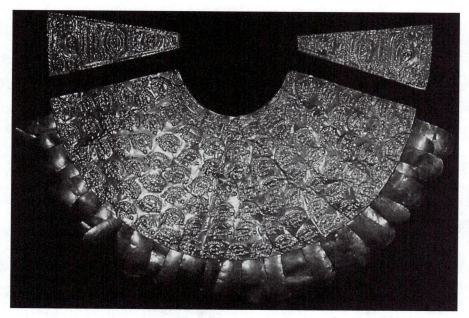

Figure 14.8 MOCHE HAMMERED-GOLD BREASTPLATE

The Moche was a multivalley state that may have consisted of a series of satellite centers that ruled over individual valleys but owed allegiance to the great centers of the Moche Valley. At one time the Moche Valley presided over the coast as far south as the Nepeña Valley. Where possible, the Moche extended their ambitious irrigation systems to link several neighboring river valleys and then constructed lesser copies of their capital as a basis for secure administration of their new domains.

Like all Andean coastal societies, the Moche lived at the mercy of droughts and El Niños. Michael Moseley believes that a series of natural disasters struck Moche domains in the late sixth century. The first may have been a devastating drought cycle between A.D. 564 and 594, identified from the growth rings deep in mountain glaciers between **Cuzco** and Lake Titicaca. Crop yields in some valleys may have fallen as much as 20 percent. Some time between 650 and 700, a great earthquake struck the Andes, choking rivers with debris from landslides. Within a half century Moche civilization collapsed.

THE MIDDLE HORIZON: TIWANAKU AND WARI (A.D. 600 to 1000)

The Middle Horizon flourished between A.D. 600 and 1000 in the southern highlands. This period saw the beginnings of monumental building at a highland site—Tiwanaku—that would influence much of the Peruvian world.

Tiwanaku

Between A.D. 600 and 1000, the wealthiest highland districts lay at the southern end of the central Andes, in the high flat country surrounding Lake Titicaca. This was fine llama country. The local people maintained enormous herds of these beasts of burden and were also expert irrigation farmers. The *altiplano* supported the densest population in the highlands, and almost inevitably, the Titicaca region became an economic and demographic pole to the prosperous northern coast.

By A.D. 450 **Tiwanaku,** on the eastern side of the lake, was becoming a major population center as well as an economic and religious focus for the region. The arid lands on which the site lies were irrigated and supported a population of perhaps 20,000 around the monumental structures near the center of the site. By A.D. 600 Tiwanaku was acquiring much of its prosperity from trade around the lake's southern shores. Copper working probably developed independently of the well-established copper technology on the northern coast.

Tiwanaku was not only an economic force; it was a religious one as well. The great enclosure of Kalasasaya is dominated by a large earth platform faced with stones (Figure 14.9). Nearby, a rectangular enclosure is bounded with a row of upright stones, and there is a doorway carved with an anthropomorphic god, believed to be the staff god, sometimes called Viracocha.

The striking Tiwanaku art style is related to earlier iconography found at Pukara. So powerful was the iconography and, presumably, the political and economic forces behind Tiwanaku that there was a serious political vacuum in the south after A.D. 1200, when Tiwanaku inexplicably collapsed into obscurity.

Figure 14.9   A GREAT SUNKEN COURT AT TIWANAKU, BOLIVIA

Wari

Wari in the Ayacucho Valley is a highland urban and ceremonial center that stands on a hill. It is associated with huge stone walls and many dwellings that cover several square miles. The Wari art styles show also some Pukara influence, especially in anthropomorphic, feline, eagle, and serpent beings depicted on ceramic vessels. Like their southern neighbors, the Wari people seem to have revered a Viracocha-like being. By A.D. 800, their domains extended from Moche country in the Lambayeque Valley on the northern coast to south of Nasca territory, down the Moquequa Valley of the south-central Andes and into the highlands south of Cuzco. They were expert traders, who probably expanded their domain through conquest, commercial enterprise, and perhaps religious conversion. Storehouses and roads probably were maintained by the state. As with the Inca of later centuries, the state controlled food supplies and labor.

Wari itself was abandoned in the ninth century A.D., but its art styles persisted on the coast for at least two more centuries. Both Wari and Tiwanaku were a turning point in Peruvian prehistory, a stage when small regional states became integrated into much larger political units. There was constant and often intensive interaction between two poles of Andean civilization in the highlands and lowlands, each with quite different food resources and products. This interaction, long a feature of Andean life, was to intensify in the centuries that lay ahead.

THE LATE INTERMEDIATE PREIOD: SICÁN AND CHIMU (A.D. 700 to 1460)

The highland states traded regularly with several emerging polities on the coast, each of them founded on extensive irrigation systems. The decline of Moche in the Lambayeque Valley had left somewhat of a vacuum, filled by the **Sicán** culture after A.D. 700. Sicán reached its peak between A.D. 900 and 1100, centered on the Lambayeque Valley and remarkable for its magnificent gold work. Between A.D. 1050 and 1100, an El Niño caused widespread flooding and disruption. In 1375, an expanding Chimu state overthrew Sicán and absorbed its domains into a new empire.

The Moche Valley had long been densely cultivated, but the **Chimu** people now embarked on much more ambitious irrigation schemes; they built large storage reservoirs and terraced hundreds of miles of hillside to control the flow of water down steep slopes. So effective were these irrigation techniques that the Chimu controlled more than 12 river valleys with at least 125,000 cultivable acres, all of it farmed with hoes or digging sticks.

The focus of the Chimu state was **Chan Chan**, a huge complex of walled compounds lying near the Pacific at the mouth of the Moche Valley. Chan Chan covers nearly 4 square miles (10.3 sq. km), the central part consisting of nine large enclosures laid out in a sort of broken rectangle. Each enclosure probably functioned as the palace for the current ruler of Chan

Figure 14.10   Chan Chan, the Chimu Capital, Showing a Royal Compound

Chan, who probably built himself a new headquarters near those of his predecessors (Figure 14.10). The adobe walls of these compounds once stood as high as 33 feet (9.9 m) and covered areas as large as 670 by 2000 feet (201 by 600 m). The walls were not constructed to defend the rulers but to provide privacy and some shelter from the ocean winds. Each enclosure had its own water supply, a burial platform, and lavishly decorated residential rooms roofed with cane frames covered with earth and grass. The same enclosure that served as a palace during life became the ruler's burial place in death. The common people lived in tracts of small adobe and reed-mat houses on the western side of the city. Similar dwellings can be seen on the coast to this day.

Oral traditions tell us that the Chimu rulers practiced the institution of split inheritance, whereby each ruler inherited no material possessions to finance his reign. Split inheritance (described further below) was to play a major role in Inca civilization (also described below). Chimu rulers had access to and control of a huge labor pool. They employed laborers to expand and maintain irrigation works, and they served as military levies to acquire new lands and expand the tax base.

Rulers soon learned the value of officially maintained roadways that enabled them to move their armies from one place to the next with rapid dispatch. They constructed roads that connected each valley in their domain with the capital. These were the roads that carried gold ornaments and fine hammered vessels to Chan Chan and textiles and fine, black-painted vessels throughout the empire. All revenues and tribute passed along the official roadways, as did newly conquered peoples being resettled in some area far from their original homeland. This draconian resettlement tactic was so successful that the Inca adopted it. The ruler then would install his own appointee in the new lands, in a compound palace that was a smaller version of Chan Chan itself.

The Chimu Empire (**Chimor**) extended far south, at least to Casma and perhaps reaching to the vicinity of modern Lima, for the main focus of civilization lay on the northern Peruvian littoral, where the soils were fertile and large-scale irrigation was a practical reality.

For all its wide-ranging military activities and material wealth, Chimor was vulnerable to attack from outside. The massive irrigation works of the northern river valleys were easily disrupted by an aggressive conqueror, for no leader, however powerful, could hope to fortify the entire frontier of the empire. The Chimu were vulnerable to prolonged drought, too, for the storage capacity of their great irrigation works was sufficient to carry them over only one or two lean seasons. Perhaps, too, the irrigated desert soils became too saline for agriculture, so that crop yields fell drastically when population densities were rising sharply. Since the Chimu depended on a highly specialized agricultural system, once that system was disrupted—whether by natural or artificial causes—military conquest and control of the irrigation network were easy, especially for aggressive and skillful conquerors such as the Inca, who conquered the Chimu in the 1460s.

THE LATE HORIZON: THE INCA STATE (A.D. 1476 to 1534)

The Late Horizon of Peruvian archaeology was also the shortest, dating from A.D. 1476 to 1534 and the period of the Inca Empire. The Inca were born into an intensely competitive world, their homeland lying to the northwest of the Titicaca basin in the area around Cuzco. They were a small-scale farming society living in small villages, organized in kin groups known as *ayllu,* groups claiming a common ancestry and also owning land in common.

The later Inca rulers clothed their origins in a glorious panoply of heroic deeds. It is likely, however, that the Inca were a fractious, constantly quarreling petty chiefdom. The chronicles of early conquest reflect the constant bickering of village headmen, and the earliest Inca rulers were probably petty war leaders (*sinchi*), elected officials whose success was measured by their victories and booty. To stay in office, they had to be politically and militarily adept so that they could both defeat and appease their many potential rivals. The official Inca histories speak of at least eight Inca rulers between 1200 and 1438, but these genealogies are hardly reliable.

During the 14th century, the Inca flourished in this competitive atmosphere because their leaders were expert politicians as well as warriors. A leader named Viracocha Inca rose to power at the beginning of the 15th century. Unlike his raiding predecessors, however, he turned to permanent conquest and soon presided over a small kingdom centered in Cuzco. Viracocha Inca became the living god, the first in a series of constant religious changes that kept the new kingdom under tight control.

Around 1438, a brilliant warrior named Cusi Inca Yupanqui was crowned Inca (the term "Inca" can refer to both the ruler and the people) after a memorable victory over the neighboring Chanca tribe. He immediately took the name Pachakuti ("He Who Remakes the World") and set about transforming the Inca state. In particular, he and his henchmen developed a form of royal ancestor cult. This in itself was not especially significant since Pachakuti simply reworked an age-old Andean tradition, but the law of split inheritance that went along with it had a lasting and profound significance. A dead ruler was mummified. His palace, servants, and possessions were still considered his property and were maintained by all his male descendants *except* his successor, normally one of his sons. The deceased was not considered dead, however. His mummy attended great ceremonies and would even visit the houses of the living (Figure 14.11). Those entrusted to look after the king ate and talked with him, just as if he was still alive. This element of continuity made the royal mummies some of the holiest artifacts in the empire. Dead rulers were visible links with the gods, the very embodiment of the Inca state and of the fertility of nature.

Meanwhile, the ascending ruler was rich in prestige but poor in possessions. The new king had to acquire wealth so he could both live in royal splendor and provide for his mummy in the future—and the only wealth in the highland kingdom was taxable labor. Therefore, every adult in Inca country had to render a certain amount of labor to the state each year after providing for the basic subsistence needs of his own ayllu. This *mit'a* system repaired bridges and roads, cultivated state-owned lands, manned the armies, and carried out public works. It was a reciprocal system. The state, or those benefiting from the work, had to feed and entertain those doing it. Since the Inca rulers needed land to provide food for those who worked for them and the earlier kings owned most of the land near Cuzco, the only way a new ruler could obtain his own royal estates was by expansion into new territory. The conquest had to be permanent, the conquered territory had to be controlled and taxed, and the ruler's subjects had to be convinced of the value of a policy of long-term conquest.

Figure 14.11   INCA ANCESTOR WORSHIP   A drawing by seventeenth-century native Andean chronicler Felipe Guaman Poma de Ayala.

A highly complicated set of benefits, economic incentives, rewards, and justifications fueled and nourished the Inca conquests. Inca rulers turned into brilliant propagandists, reminding everyone that they were gods and that the welfare of all depended on the prosperity of all rulers, past and present, and on constant military conquest. There were initial economic advantages, too, in the form of better protection against famine. Also, the rulers were careful to reward prowess in battle. Nobles were promoted to new posts and awarded insignia that brought their lifestyle ever closer to that of the king, and even a brave warrior could become a member of the secondary nobility.

The Incas' successful ideology provided them with a crucial advantage over their neighbors. Within a decade of Pachakuti's accession they were masters of the southern highlands. Their army had become an invincible juggernaut. In less than a century the tiny kingdom taken over by Pachakuti had become a vast empire. Topa Inca (1471–1493) extended the Inca Empire into Ecuador, northern Argentina, parts of Bolivia, and Chile. Another king, Wayna Capac, ruled for 32 years after Topa Inca and pushed the empire deeper into Ecuador.

Tawantinsuyu, the empire, was divided into four large provinces known as *suyu* (quarters), each subdivided into smaller provinces, some of them coinciding with older, conquered kingdoms. All the really important government posts were held by Inca nobles. The Inca rulers realized, however, that the essence of efficient government in such varied topography was efficient communications, so the road builders commandeered a vast network of age-old highways from the states they conquered. They linked them in a coordinated

Figure 14.12   INCA ARCHITECTURE WAS BASED ON CLOSELY FITTED STONE BLOCKS They were moved by human hands as Andean llamas could only carry loads of about 100 pounds (45 kg).

system with regular rest houses so that they could move armies, trade goods, and messengers from one end of the kingdom to the other in short order.

At the time of the Spanish conquest, the Inca controlled the lives of as many as 6 million people, most of them living in small villages dispersed around larger centers. Inca political and religious power was based on major ritual locations like Cuzco in the Andes, where the ceremonial precincts were built of carefully fitted stones (Figure 14.12). The Inca ruler held court in Cuzco, surrounded by plotting factions and ever-changing political tides. One villain was the very institution of split inheritance that fueled Inca military conquest. Every ruler faced increasingly complex governance problems as a result. The need for more and more conquests caused great military, economic, and administrative stress. The logistics of long-distance military campaigns were horrendous, and the soldiers had to be fed from state-owned land, not royal estates. Moreover, although their tactics were well adapted to open country, where their armies were invincible, the rulers eventually had to start fighting in forest country, where they fared badly.

Meanwhile the empire had grown so large that communication became an increasingly lengthier process, compounded by the great diversity of people living within the Inca domain (Figure 14.13). Under its glittering facade, *Tawantinsuyu* was becoming a rotten apple. In the end, the Inca Empire was overthrown not by

Figure 14.13   MACHU PICCHU, AN INCA SETTLEMENT HIGH IN THE ANDES

Peruvians but by a tiny band of foreigners with firearms who could exploit the inherent vulnerability of such a hierarchical, conforming society.

THE SPANISH CONQUEST (1532 to 1534)

This vulnerability came home to roost in 1532, when a small party of rapacious Spanish conquistadors landed in northern Peru. When Francisco Pizarro arrived, the Inca state was in some political chaos, its people already decimated by smallpox and other diseases introduced by the first conquistadors. Inca Wayna Capac had died in an epidemic in A.D. 1525. The empire was plunged into a civil war between his son Huascar and another son, Atahuallpa, half brother to Huascar. Atahuallpa eventually prevailed, but as he moved south from Ecuador to consolidate his territory, he learned that Pizarro had landed in Peru.

The Spaniards had vowed to make Peru part of Spain and were bent on plunder and conquest. Pizarro arrived in the guise of a diplomat, captured Atahuallpa by treachery, ransomed him for a huge quantity of gold, and then brutally murdered him. A year later the Spaniards captured the Inca capital with a tiny army. Despite pockets of resistance, the world's last preindustrial state collapsed.

Epilogue

Our journey through the long millennia of prehistory ends on the very threshold of modern times. It ends with the so-called Age of Discovery that saw European explorers sailing ever further from their homelands in search of gold and spices, to serve God, or simply out of compelling curiosity.

Western Europe was born 3000 years ago. For thousands of years it had been a geographical outpost of Asia, on the fringes of civilizations and empires based in the Near East and Mediterranean lands. Twenty-five centuries ago, Europe became a western peninsula with a consciousness and identity all its own. This consciousness was born of Greek civilization, and matured still further in much later European victories against Huns, Turks, and Moors. It was a Christian enclave, driven by doctrines that encouraged a deep sense that the individual was as important as the state. A growing sense of individualism and adventure bred an intense curiosity about the outside world. What peoples lived south of the endless sands of the Sahara Desert? Were there distant lands beyond the boundless horizons of the western ocean?

During the 1420s and 1430s, Henry the Navigator, Prince of Portugal, organized annual voyages of exploration southward from Europe deep into tropical latitudes. His captains coasted down the west coast of Africa and rounded the great western bulge in 1433. Then, in 1488, Bartolemeu Dias rounded the southern tip of Africa. He came in contact with the **Khoi Khoi,** simple cattle herders who appeared to wander aimlessly with their herds. The Khoi Khoi made a profound impression on the Western mind, for they appeared more primitive in their customs than any other people on earth. For centuries, the Khoi Khoi were thought of as half-apes, half-humans, lower on the Great Chain of Being than other human beings. They vanished a mere 70 years after European settlement at the Cape of Good Hope in 1652, their herding adaptation destroyed by encroaching white farmers.

Dias was followed by Vasco da Gama in 1497, who sailed up the east African coast to what is now Kenya, then followed the trade winds to India. Thus, Europeans found an alternative route to the rich gold and spice markets of south and southeast Asia. They sailed along ancient seaborne routes that linked Africa, with its seemingly inexhaustible exports of gold, ivory, and slaves, with markets that had an insatiable demand for such commodities. In the centuries that followed, Africa was exploited for human and material wealth not only by European nations, but by Islam. The burgeoning international slave trade decimated African populations far from the continent's familiar coastlines. European explorers did not penetrate the far interior until the 19th century, by which time Africa was already part of a vast and complex world economic system.

As Dias and da Gama explored African shores, so did Christopher Columbus sail west to the "Indies" in 1492. He thought he was at the threshold of Asia. In fact he revealed a New World teeming with new species of animals and plants and a great diversity of American Indian societies. As we have seen, the great civilizations of Mexico and Peru collapsed rapidly in the face of the conquistadors, while epidemics of smallpox and other exotic diseases decimated Native American populations within a few generations of the first European visitors wherever they appeared.

With the rounding of the Cape of Good Hope and the discovery of the Americas, the final chapter of human prehistory began, a complex and long drawn-out clash between increasingly elaborate Western civilization and a myriad of non-Western societies in all parts of the world. The basic scenario was relived again and again. A small party of European explorers would arrive, as did Captain James Cook in Tahiti and New Zealand, or French voyager Marion du Fresne in Tasmania, Australia. Almost invariably the first encounter was a fleeting kaleidoscope of curiosity, sometimes horrified fascination, and often romantic excitement. Sometimes spears were thrown and muskets fired. At others there was friendly trading of furs for cheap glass beads and other trinkets. Almost invariably, however, there was total incomprehension on both sides.

Sometimes the people thought that their strange visitors were gods, as did Moctezuma with Hernan Cortés at the gates of Tenochtitlán. An elderly Maori chief in New Zealand told a 19th-century official that the priests had told him the whites were spirits with eyes in the backs of their heads, an apparent reference to Cook's oarsmen facing the stern in their boats. All too soon, and wherever they appeared, the strangers proved not to be gods, but to be only too human—aggressive, warlike, and acquisitive.

At first the contacts were brief ones. But soon Europeans came in larger numbers to trade for furs, to refit their ships, or to search for gold. Then the missionaries arrived, seeking to convert the heathen and to save their souls. Australia became a dumping ground for convicts, many of whom escaped and brutalized Australian Aboriginal groups. In many places the early visitors were followed by a flood of colonists, often impoverished, land-hungry farmers from Europe who sought a better life in the fertile soils of the African interior, British Columbia, New Zealand, or Tasmania.

These were permanent residents, people with iron tools and firearms in search of new homes and lush acreage. They competed with the indigenous populations for prime land, elbowing them aside, sometimes hunting them down, or often acquiring large farms through shady land sales or illegal treaties. Almost inevitably, the indigenous population lost their land, territory that had often been vested in the same kin groups for centuries, if not millennia. They had few options open to them, except to retreat onto remote, marginal lands where they preserved a shadow of their former culture and lifeway, if they were able to survive at all. The only alternative was to assimilate themselves into the newcomers' society, where they almost always lived on the margins, often employed as agricultural laborers or domestic servants.

The spread of Western civilization around the world has accelerated dramatically since the Industrial Revolution of the late 18th century. This revolution was another catalyst in human history, which created industrial societies driven not by human hands but by fossil fuels. It fostered insatiable demands for raw materials of all kinds, gave birth to the steamship and the railroad, and led to large-scale human migrations from Europe to America, from Asia to all parts of the Pacific and North America on an unprecedented scale. The mass population movements of recent times have had catastrophic effects on non-Western societies large and small.

Today, there are no parts of the world where traditional lifeways survive untouched by modern civilization. There are a handful of groups deep in the Amazon Basin and in highland New Guinea who have still not come into sustained contact with industrial civilization. These are endangered societies, as rain forests are felled and landscapes modified beyond recognition by the insatiable maw of industrial civilization. To all intents and purposes, however, the ancient world, which began over 2.5 million years ago in Africa, has vanished into near-oblivion except insofar as we know it from modern scientific research.

Guide to Further Reading

The references that follow have been selected as ways of exploring the topics covered in this book in more detail. The emphasis is on general works, all of which contain comprehensive bibliographies that summarize the specialist literature. For more detailed information, please consult one of the major summaries listed here or ask a specialist. The emphasis here is on English-language sources, simply because most readers are English-speaking.

GENERAL WORKS AND JOURNALS

Two major college textbooks offer more comprehensive summaries of world prehistory. My *People of the Earth,* 9th ed. (New York: Addison Wesley Longman, 1998)) is a much-expanded version of this book. Robert Wenke's *Patterns in Prehistory,* 4th ed. (New York: Oxford University Press, 1994) has an authoritative evolutionary perspective. John Gowlett's, *Ascent to Civilization* (New York: Random House, 1992) is an excellent guide for the Stone Age. The best atlas of archaeology for the general reader is Chris Scarre (Ed.), *Past Worlds: The Times Atlas of Archaeology* (London: Times Books, 1988). The same author's *Timelines* (London: Dorling Kindersley, 1993) is a magnificently illustrated chronological guide to human history from the earliest times to A.D. 1500. Brian Fagan (Ed.) *The Oxford Companion to Archaeology* (New York: Oxford University Press, 1996) is a reference book that tells you everything you ever wanted to know about archaeology—and more.

Dozens of local, national, and international journals cover the subject matter of this book, most of them aimed at specialists. Among those carrying popular articles are *National Geographic Magazine, Natural History, Smithsonian,* and *Scientific American. Archaeology* is a lively magazine for enthusiast and professional archaeologist alike. *Antiquity, The Journal of World Prehistory,* and *World Archaeology* carry articles of wide interest to serious archaeologists and informed lay people. American archaeologists rely heavily on *American Antiquity* and *American Anthropologist.* Old World archaeologists often publish in *The Journal of the Royal Anthropological Institute* and the *Proceedings of the Prehistoric Society,* while the latest hominid discoveries often appear in *Nature* or *Science. The Journal of Field Archaeology* is of high technical value and often contains definitive field reports.

Chapter 1: The Study of Human Prehistory

The history of archaeology is widely accessible through the National Geographic Society's *The Adventure of Archaeology* (Washington, DC: National Geographic Society, 1985), also through Paul Bahn (Ed.), *The Cambridge Illustrated History of Archaeology* (Cambridge: Cambridge University Press, 1996). For American archaeology, see Gordon Willey and Jeremy Sabloff's, *A History of American Archaeology*, 2d ed. (New York: W.H. Freeman, 1994). Popular books on science and archaeology include: Brian Fagan, *Time Detectives* (New York: Simon & Schuster, 1995) and the National Geographic Society's *In the Unknown* (Washington DC: National Geographic Society, 1997). Archaeological theory enjoys an enormous literature. Bruce Trigger's *History of Archaeological Interpretation* (Cambridge: Cambridge University Press, 1989) is definitive. Lewis Binford's *In Pursuit of the Past* (New York: Thames and Hudson, 1983) and David Meltzer, Don Fowler, and Jeremy Sabloff (Eds.), *American Archaeology Past and Future* (Washington DC: Smithsonian Institution Press, 1986) are useful assessments.

Method and theory in archaeology are well covered in a series of widely available college textbooks. These include the companion volume to this work, my *Archaeology: A Brief Introduction*, 6th ed. (New York: Addison Wesley Longman, 1997) and a more comprehensive treatment: *In the Beginning*, 9th ed. (New York: Addison Wesley Longman, 1994). Robert Sharer and Wendy Ashmore, *Archaeology: Discovering the Past*, 3d ed. (Mountain View, CA: Mayfield, 1994) is another useful book. Paul Bahn and Colin Renfrew, *Archaeology*, 2d ed. (New York: Thames and Hudson, 1996), is a magisterial handbook of archaeological method and theory that is an essential reference book for any serious student of the past. Lastly, Robert Layton (Ed.), *Who Needs the Past?* 2d ed. (London: Routledge, 1994) contains essays on the relationship between indigenous peoples' values and archaeology.

Chapter 2: Human Origins

The literature is enormous and sometimes polemical. Roger Lewin's, *Bones of Contention* (New York: Simon & Schuster, 1987) offers an excellent historical survey for the lay reader. The same author's *Human Evolution*, 3d ed. (Oxford: Blackwell Scientific Publications, 1993) gives an excellent summary of what we know about human evolution. Donald Johanson and Maitland Edey's, *Lucy: The Beginnings of Humankind* (New York: Simon & Schuster, 1981) is an excellent popular account of the Hadar finds. Donald Johanson, Lenora Johanson, and Blake Edgar's, *Ancestors: In Search of Human Origins* (New York: Villard Books, 1994) covers the main developments of human evolution in a book written to accompany a television series entitled *Ancestors*. Ian Tattersall's, *The Fossil Trail: How We Know What We Think We Know About Human Evolution.* (New York: Oxford University Press, 1996) is a closely argued account of human origins for a general audience. At a more technical level, Robert Foley's *Humans Before Humanity* (Oxford: Blackwell,

1995) discusses the ecological background to human origins. Steven Mithen's, *Prehistory of the Mind* (London: Thames and Hudson, 1997) is a brilliant essay on the evolution of human intelligence for a general audience. Nicholas Toth and K.D. Schick's, "The First Million Years: The Archaeology of Proto-human Culture," in *Advances in Archaeological Method and Theory 9* (1986): 1–96, is an excellent summary of recent thinking on the archaeology of human origins. Richard Klein's, *The Human Career* (Chicago: University of Chicago Press, 1989) is an advanced textbook. For scavenging research, see Robert Blumenschine and John Cavallo's, "Scavenging and Human Evolution," *Scientific American* 257 (1992) (10): 90–96.

Chapter 3: African Exodus

There are few general summaries of the long millennia covered by this chapter. My *The Journey from Eden* (New York: Thames and Hudson, 1990) is a more recent popular account of the origins of modern humans, which also discusses earlier developments. See also the relevant portions of Steven Mithen's *The Prehistory of the Mind,* already cited, also Philip Lieberman's, *Uniquely Human: The Evolution of Speech, Thought, and Selfless Behavior.* (Cambridge, MA: Harvard University Press, 1991). Clive Gamble's, *The Palaeolithic Settlement of Europe* (Cambridge, England: Cambridge University Press, 1986) is an excellent overall summary of developments in this and Chapter 4. More specialist contributions include J. Desmond Clark and Jack Harris's "Fire and Its Roles in Early Hominid Lifeways," in *African Archaeological Review* 3 (1985): 3–28. Robert Foley's "Hominid Species and Stone-Tool Assemblages: How Are They Related?" in *Antiquity* 61 (1987): 380–392, is a provocative essay on the relationship between stone tools and biological evolution. For bamboo and archaic humans, see Geoffrey Pope's "Bamboo and Human Evolution," *Natural History* 10 (89): 49–56. A popular account of modern humans origins is Christopher Stringer and Robin McKie's *African Exodus: The Origins of Modern Humanity* (New York: Henry Holt, 1997). Chris Stringer and Paul Mellars (Eds.) *The Human Revolution,* 2 vols. (Edinburgh: Edinburgh University Press, 1989, 1990) provides specialist essays on the controversies surrounding the subject, including an important article by Gunter Braüer on archaic *Homo sapiens* in Africa. See also: M.H. Nitecki and V. Nitecki (Eds.), *Origins of Anatomically Modern Humans* (New York: Plenum Press, 1994). Anthony Marks's "The Middle to Upper Palaeolithic Transition in the Levant," in *Advances in World Archaeology* 2 (1983): 51–98, covers the technological changeover associated with modern humans. See also Roger Lewin's *The Origin of Modern Humans* (New York: Scientific American Library, 1993). Chris Stringer and Clive Gamble's *The Search for the Neanderthals* (London: Thames and Hudson, 1993) and Erik Trinkaus and Pat Shipman's *The Neanderthals: Changing the Image of Mankind* (New York: Alfred Knopf, 1992) are excellent popular accounts of these archaic humans.

Chapter 4: Diaspora

The Journey from Eden, already cited, carries a basic summary of the material in this chapter, which can be amplified from numerous references of both a general and more specialist nature. Australia and New Guinea are well summarized by J. Peter White and James O'Connell's *A Prehistory of Australia, New Guinea, and Sahul* (Sydney: Academic Press, 1982). However, this is somewhat outdated by new discoveries, well summarized by Jim Allen in "When Did Humans First Colonize Australia?" *Search* 20, 5 (1989): 149–154. See also: David Frankel, *Remains to be Seen: Archaeological Insights into Australian Prehistory* (Melbourne: Longman Cheshire). The Cro-Magnons have been described by many popular authors. Randall White, *Dark Caves and Bright Visions* (New York: American Museum of Natural History, 1986) is a useful summary, especially when amplified by Paul Bahn and Jean Vertut, *Images of the Ice Age* (New York: Viking, 1988), which is an invaluable analysis of Stone Age art. Clive Gamble, *Timewalkers: The Prehistory of Global Colonization* (Stroud, Glos: Alan Sutton, 1994) offers a broad and provocative view of the topics in this chapter. Olga Soffer and Clive Gamble (Eds.), *The World in 18,000 B.P.* (Edinburgh: Edinburgh University Press, 1991) contains useful articles on the late Ice Age, as does Soffer's edited *The Pleistocene Old World* (New York: Plenum Press, 1985). The same author's monograph *The Upper Palaeolithic of the Central Russian Plains* (New York: Academic Press, 1985) describes Mezhirich in detail. For the controversies surrounding the first settlement of the Americas and the Clovis people, see Brian Fagan, *The Great Journey* (New York: Thames and Hudson, 1987). Some recent essays on the same subject appear in Tom Dillehay and David Meltzer (Eds.), *The First Americans: Search and Research* (Boca Raton, FL: CRC Press, 1991). See also David Meltzer, *The Search for the First Americans* (Washington, DC: Smithsonian Institution Press, 1994).

Chapter 5: The Origins of Food Production

For forager archaeology and the issue of social complexity among them, see R.L. Bettinger, "Archaeological Approaches to Hunter-Gatherers," *Annual Review of Archaeology* 16 (1987): 121–142. *A Pleistocene Revolution,* edited by Paul Martin and Richard Klein, (Tucson: University of Arizona Press, 1984), summarizes evidence for extinction of big game in many parts of the world. Douglas Price and James Brown edited *Complexity among Prehistoric Hunter-Gatherers* (Orlando, FL: Academic Press, 1985), which contains valuable essays on the issue of social complexity. Douglas Price's "The Mesolithic of Western Europe," in the *Journal of World Prehistory* 1 (3) (1987): 225–305 describes complex hunter-gatherers in Europe, while Stuart Struever and Felicia Holton's, *Koster: Americans in Search of Their Past* (New York: Anchor Books, 1979) is a popular account of that famous site. Further descriptions of Archaic cultures in North America, and of the Chumash Indians of California, can be found in my *Ancient North America* (New York: Thames and Hudson, 2d ed., 1995). Also: Stuart Fidel, *Prehistory of the Americas.* 2d ed. (Cambridge: Cambridge University Press, 1992).

The classic theories surrounding the origins of agriculture are gathered in Stuart Struever's anthology *Prehistoric Agriculture* (Garden City, NY: Natural History Press, 1971). Bruce D. Smith's *The Emergence of Agriculture* (New York: W.H. Freeman, 1994) summarizes what we know of early agriculture and animal domestication throughout the world, as well as the remarkable results being obtained from AMS radiocarbon dating of grain. Mark Cohen's *Health and the Rise of Civilization* (New Haven, CT: Yale University Press, 1988) is an essay on paleopathology and early farming. Kent Flannery's *Guilá Naquitz* (Orlando, FL: Academic Press, 1986) is an exemplary monograph, which is essential reading, if for nothing else, for its hypothetical dialogues, which contain a multitude of wisdoms about archaeology and archaeologists. David Harris and Gordon Hillman edited *Farming and Foraging* (Oxford: Clarendon Press, 1989), which contains excellent articles on early agriculture and processes of plant domestication.

Chapter 6: The Earliest Farmers

Andrew Moore's "The Development of Neolithic Societies in the Near East," in *Advances in World Archaeology* 4 (1985): 1–70, contains much of value on Abu Hureyra and is authoritative. European agriculture: Graham Barker, *Prehistoric Farming in Europe* (Cambridge, England: Cambridge University Press, 1985). Richard I. Ford's (Ed.), *Prehistoric Food Production in North America* (Ann Arbor: University of Michigan Museum of Anthropology, 1985) offers insights into the origins of maize and other crops. Europe: I.J. Thorpe, *The Origins of Agriculture in Europe* (London: Routledge, 1996) and Barry Cunliffe (Ed.) *The Oxford Illustrated Prehistory of Europe* (Oxford: Oxford University Press, 1996). Early farming in Asia: Gina Barnes's *China, Korea, and Japan.* (London: Thames and Hudson, 1993) summarizes Chinese evidence, while Charles Higham's *The Archaeology of Mainland Southeast Asia* (Cambridge, England: Cambridge University Press, 1989) is comprehensive and authoritative. The Americas: see Bruce Smith, *The Emergence of Agriculture*, already cited above. See also S. H. Wills, *Early Prehistoric Agriculture in the Southwest* (Santa Fe, NM: School of American Research Press, 1989), which covers the introduction of maize.

Chapter 7: Chiefs and Chiefdoms

For Pacific voyaging, the interested reader can do no better than to start with Geoffrey Irwin's *The Prehistoric Exploration and Colonization of the Pacific.* (Cambridge, England: Cambridge University Press, 1992). This remarkable study is based not only on archaeology and computer simulations, but on the author's own voyages. Peter Bellwood's *Man's Settlement of the Pacific.* (Oxford: Oxford University Press, 1979) and *The Polynesians* (New York: Thames and Hudson, 1979) summarize the first colonization of the Pacific Islands. Patrick V. Kirch's *The Evolution of the Polynesian Chiefdoms* (New York: Cambridge University Press, 1984) describes complex societies in the

Pacific. New Zealand archaeology: Janet Davidson, *The Prehistory of New Zealand* (Auckland: Longman Paul, 1984). Southwestern archaeology is well analyzed by Linda Cordell, *The Prehistory of the Southwest* (Orlando, FL: Academic Press, 1984). For the Eastern Woodlands, see an excellent summary by Bruce Smith, "The Archaeology of the Southeastern United States: From Dalton to de Soto, 10,500 to 500 B.P.," in *Advances in World Archaeology 5* (1986): 1–92. Also Judith Bense, *Archaeology of the Southeastern United States.* (San Diego Academic Press, 1994). Cahokia and the Mississippian receive thorough examination in Timothy R. Pauketat and Thomas E. Emerson's (Eds.) *Cahokia: Domination and Ideology in the Mississippian World.* (Lincoln, NE: University of Nebraska Press, 1997).

Chapter 8: State–Organized Societies

The literature is enormous. Charles Redman, in *The Rise of Civilization: From Early Farmers to Urban Society in the Ancient Near East* (San Francisco: W. H. Freeman, 1978), critiques theories up to the late 1970s. Christopher Scarre and Brian Fagan's *Ancient Civilizations* (New York: Addison Wesley Longman, 1996) summarizes the world's early civilizations for beginning readers. See also Kent Flannery's, "The Cultural Evolution of Civilizations," in the *Annual Review of Ecology and Systematics* (1972): 399–426, which is good on ecological and systems approaches. Elizabeth Brumfiel's "Aztec State Making: Ecology, Structure, and the Origin of the State," *American Anthropologist* 85 (2) (1983): 261–284 discusses social approaches. Norman Yoffee's "Too Many Chiefs? Or Safe Texts for the 90s," in Andrew Sherratt and Norman Yoffee's (Eds.) *Archaeological Theory—Who Sets the Agenda?* (Cambridge: Cambridge University Press, 1990) reflects much current thinking. Writing: Andrew Robinson's *The Story of Writing.* (London: Thames and Hudson, 1995) is a lavishly illustrated essay for beginners.

Chapter 9: Mesopotamia and the Eastern Mediterranean World

Two books summarize the Sumerians admirably. Samuel Kramer's *The Sumerians* (Chicago: University of Chicago Press, 1963) is a well-deserved popular classic. Harriett Crawford's *Sumer and the Sumerians* (Cambridge, England: Cambridge University Press, 1991) is an up-to-date synthesis. Nicholas Postgate's *Early Mesopotamia: Economy and Society at the Dawn of History* (London: Kegan Paul, 1993) is also definitive. See also: Seton Lloyd's *The Archaeology of Mesopotamia.* 2d ed. (London: Thames and Hudson, 1983) and Hans J. Nissen's *The Early History of the Ancient Near East, 9000 to 2000 B.C.* (Chicago: University of Chicago Press, 1988). The Hittites: J.G. MacQueen, *The Hittites.* 3d ed. (New York: Thames and Hudson, 1996). For later events, see K.W. Whitelaw and R.B. Coote's *The Emergence of Israel in Historical Perspective* (Sheffield, England: Almond Press, 1987). The Assyrians are described in Nicholas Postgate's *The First Empires* (Oxford: Phaidon,

1977). The Minoans and Mycenaeans: Oliver Dickinson, *The Aegean Bronze Age*. (Cambridge, England: Cambridge University Press, 1994); Sinclair Hood, *The Minoans* (New York: Thames and Hudson, 1973); Lord William Taylour, *The Mycenaeans*, 2d ed. (New York: Thames and Hudson, 1990).

Chapter 10: Egypt and Africa

The ancient Egyptians have attracted an enormous literature. Three volumes provide a good general summary. Cyril Aldred's *The Egyptians*, 3d ed. (New York: Thames and Hudson, 1998) is a concise account, while Barry Kemp's *Ancient Egypt: The Anatomy of a Civilization* (London: Routledge, 1989) is destined to become a classic. Nicholas Reeves's *The Complete Tutankhamun* (New York: Thames and Hudson, 1990) is a magnificent tour of the golden pharaoh's sepulcher. Nubia is little known to anyone but specialists, but the following are useful starting points: William Adams's *Nubia: Corridor to Africa* (London: Alan Lane, 1977) is a comprehensive, if outdated, monograph that is still useful. David O'Connor's *Ancient Nubia: Egypt's Rival in Africa* (Philadelphia: University of Pennsylvania Museum, 1993) offers an update. Meroe: Peter Shinnie's *Meroe* (London: Thames and Hudson, 1967) is still the best source for an overview. Aksum is summarized by Roland Oliver's *The African Experience* (London: Weidenfeld and Nicholson, 1991), which also provides a summary of early African history. Graham Connah's *African Civilizations* (Cambridge, England: Cambridge University Press, 1987) is a superb account of early African kingdoms, including Nubia, Meroe, and Aksum. Nehemiah Levetzion's *Ancient Ghana and Mali* (London: Methuen, 1971) and Peter Garlake's *Great Zimbabwe* (New York: Thames and Hudson, 1973) provide beginning summaries.

Chapter 11: South, Southeast, and East Asia

Mortimer Wheeler's *The Indus Civilization*, 2d ed. (Cambridge, England: Cambridge University Press, 1962) is still a major source on the Harappan Civilization. Gregory Possehl's (Ed.), *The Harappan Civilization* (London: Aris and Phillips, 1982) and *Harappan Civilization: A Recent Perspective* (New Delhi, India: Oxford and IBH Publishing, 1993) provide updates, as does Bridget and Raymond Allchin's *The Rise of Civilization in India and Pakistan* (Cambridge, England: Cambridge University Press, 1983). Raymond Allchin's *The Archaeology of Historic South Asia* (Cambridge, England: Cambridge University Press, 1995) covers the Mauryan and later societies. Chinese prehistory is well summarized by K-C Chang in *The Archaeology of Ancient China*, 4th ed. (New Haven, CT: Yale University Press, 1986), and the same author's *Shang Civilization* (New Haven, CT: Yale University Press, 1980) is authoritative. *The Origins of Chinese Civilization*, edited by David Keightley (Berkeley and Los Angeles: University of California Press, 1983), contains much useful material. Gina Barnes's *China, Korea, and Japan* (London:

Thames and Hudson, 1993) is an up-to-date summary in English. Paul Wheatley's "Urban Genesis in Mainland Southeast Asia," in R.B. Smith and W. Watson (eds.), *Early Southeast Asia* (Oxford, England: Oxford University Press, 1979), pp. 288–303, deals with the origins of Southeast Asian civilization. For Southeast Asia generally, see Charles Higham, *The Archaeology of Mainland Southeast Asia* (Cambridge, England: Cambridge University Press, 1989).

Chapters 12 and 13: Mesoamerican Civilizations

A good starting point is *The Early Mesoamerican Village,* edited by Kent Flannery (New York: Academic Press, 1976), which also contains a rich foundation of wisdom about archaeology generally, as well as valuable information on early complexity in the Valley of Oaxaca. For the Olmec, see Michael Coe and Richard Diehl's *In the Land of the Olmec* (Austin: University of Texas Press, 1980), also Nick Saunders's *People of the Jaguar* (London: Souvenir Press, 1989) is excellent on jaguar cults. Joyce Marcus and Kent Flannery's *The Zapotec Civilization* (London: Thames and Hudson, 1996) is a richly illustrated account of Monte Albán and the origins of civilization in the Valley of Oaxaca. Teotihuacán is well described in René Millon, R.B. Drewitt, and George Cowgill's *Urbanization at Teotihuacán* (Austin: University of Texas Press, 1974), while William Saunders, Jeffrey Parsons, and Robert Santley's *The Basin of Mexico* (New York: Academic Press, 1979) describes the comprehensive archaeological surveys carried out in this highland region.

The Maya literature is rich and often contradictory. Linda Schele and David Freidel's *A Forest of Kings* (New York: Morrow, 1990) is a popular synthesis of Maya history based on both archaeology and glyphs, which is seminal. Their *Maya Cosmos* (New York: Morrow, 1993) discusses Maya astronomy and world views. Norman Hammond's *Ancient Maya Civilization* (New Brunswick, NJ: Rutgers University Press, 1982) and Jeremy A. Sabloff's *The New Archaeology and the Ancient Maya* (New York: Scientific American Library, 1990) are useful summaries, while the latter's *The Cities of Ancient Mexico* (New York: Thames and Hudson, 1989) provides a guide to major Mesoamerican sites. Michael Coe's *The Maya,* 5th ed. (New York: Thames and Hudson, 1993) is another widely read summary. A recent popular account is T. Patrick Culbert's *Maya Civilization* (Washington, DC: Smithsonian Institution Press, 1994).

The Toltecs are summarized by Richard Diehl in *Tula, the Toltec Capital of Ancient Mexico* (New York: Thames and Hudson, 1983). The Aztecs are analyzed by Geoffrey W. Conrad and Arthur A. Demarest, *Religion and Empire* (Cambridge, England: Cambridge University Press, 1984), their civilization is described in Richard Townsend's *The Aztecs* (London: Thames and Hudson, 1992). Inga Clendinnen's *Aztecs: An Interpretation* (Cambridge, Eng.: Cambridge University Press, 1991) is a valuable analysis of Aztec history, which is especially good on sources. For the Spanish Conquest, see Charles Dibble and Arthur Anderson's *The Florentine Codex* (Salt Lake City: University of Utah Press, 12 vols., 1950–1975).

Chapter 14: Andean Civilizations

Michael Moseley's *The Incas and Their Ancestors* (New York: Thames and Hudson, 1992) is an excellent summary of Andean archaeology for the general reader. *Peruvian Prehistory,* edited by Richard Keatinge (Cambridge, England: Cambridge University Press, 1988) contains useful essays covering the general subject. See also: Jonathan Haas. S. Pozorski, and T. Pozorski, eds., *The Origins and Development of the Andean State* (Cambridge: Cambridge University Press, 1987), a somewhat technical edited volume. *Early Ceremonial Architecture in the Andes,* edited by Christopher Donnan (Washington, DC: Dumbarton Oaks, 1985), brings together articles on early architecture on the coast and in the highlands. Richard Burger's *The Prehistoric Occupation of Chavín de Huántar* (Berkeley: University of California Publications in Anthropology, 1984) describes excavations at this most important of sites. Nick Saunders's *People of the Jaguar,* already cited, gives a valuable analysis of Chavín iconography. Lawrence Sullivan's monumental excursion into traditional Latin American religions, *Icanchu's Drum* (New York: Macmillan, 1988) is essential for any student of Andean archaeology. The Moche are well described by Christopher Donnan and Donna McClelland, in *The Burial Theme in Moche Iconography* (Washington DC: Dumbarton Oaks, 1987). Christopher Donnan and Walter Alva's *Royal Tombs of Sipán* (Los Angeles: Fowler Museum of Cultural History, UCLA, 1994) is the definitive account of one of the most spectacular finds of this century. Tiwanaku: Alan Kolata, *Tiwanaku* (Oxford, England: Blackwell, 1993). See also the same author's "The Agricultural Foundations of the Tiwanaku State," *American Antiquity* 51 (4) (1986): 748–762. For information on Huari, William Isbell and Katharina Schreiber, "Was Huari a State?" *American Antiquity* 43 (1978): 372–389. Chimu: Michael Moseley and C. Kent Day (Eds.), *Chan Chan: Andean Desert City* (Albuquerque: University of New Mexico Press, 1982).

The best starting point for the Inca civilization is Conrad and Demarest's *Religion and Empire,* already cited. John Rowe's *Inca Culture at the Time of the Spanish Conquest* (Washington, DC: Smithsonian Institution Handbook of South American Indians, vol. 2, 1946) is still a definitive account. John Hemming's *The Conquest of the Incas* (Baltimore: Pelican Books, 1983) describes Pizarro's ravages.

Epilogue

Three books cover the closing centuries of prehistory from different perspectives. John Bodley's *Victims of Progress,* 2d ed. (Menlo Park, CA: Cummings, 1982) is a widely consulted college textbook. My *Clash of Cultures,* 2d ed. (Walnut Creek, CA: AltaMira Press, 1997) describes contact between Westerners and a series of non-Western societies for a general audience. Eric Wolf's *Europe and the People Without History* (Berkeley and Los Angeles: University of California Press, 1984) is the authoritative account, with a strong anthropological bias.

Glossary of Technical Terms

Accelerator Mass Spectrometry (AMS) Dating A method of radiocarbon dating, which counts actual C14 atoms. Requires very small samples and can be used to date items as small as individual seeds.

Andes (Andean) Term used by archaeologists to refer to those areas of Peru and adjacent countries where state-organized societies developed.

Anthropoid The taxonomic suborder of apes, humans, and monkeys.

Arboreal Tree-living.

Archaeological culture The material remains of a human culture preserved at a specific space and time at several archaeological sites.

Archaeology The study of the human past using the surviving material remains of human behavior.

Artifact A humanly manufactured or modified object.

Atlatl Throwing stick used by early North American hunters, a spear thrower.

Ayllu Andean kin group claiming descent from a common ancestor.

Band Egalitarian associations of families knit together by close social ties.

Bipedal Walking upright on two feet.

Blade technology A stone tool technology involving the use of preshaped cores and long, parallel-sided blades produced with the aid of a punch. Characteristic of many Upper Paleolithic peoples.

Burin A chisellike stone tool made on a blade used for grooving stone, antler, bone, and wood, also for making rock engravings.

Chiefdom Societies headed by leaders with exceptional entrepreneurial, political, or ritual powers, which are still kin-based.

Civilization *See* State-organized society.

Clan A group of people from many lineages who live in one place and have a common line of descent a kin grouping.

Cognitive archaeology The "archaeology of mind," using archaeological methods to study human motives, ideologies, and intangibles.

Composite tool An artifact made up of more than one component, such as a stone spear point and the shaft.

Context In archaeology, the exact location of a site, artifact, or other archaeological find in time and space.

Cultural ecology The study of the ways in which human societies adapt to, and transform, their environments.

Cultural process The ways in which human cultures change over time.

Cultural system The adaptive mechanism, made up of many parts, that humans use to adapt to their physical and social environment.

Culture The primary nonbiological means by which humans adapt to their natural environment.

Culture as adaptation *See* Cultural ecology.

Culture history Descriptions of human cultures derived from archaeological evidence.

Cuneiform From the Greek word *cuneus,* wedge. Mesopotamian script made by stamping clay tablets with a wedge-shaped stylus. Long used as an international diplomatic script in the ancient eastern Mediterranean world.

Curation Retaining tools for future use.

Dendrochronology Tree-ring dating.

Diffusion The spread of ideas over short or long distances.

Ethnoarchaeology The study of living societies to aid in the interpretation of ancient ones.

Ethnographic analogy Comparison of artifacts and other culture traits from living societies with those of ancient ones.

Ethnographic present A term used to describe prehistoric societies before contact with Europeans. It is not based on reality.

Fertile Crescent A term used to describe the crescent of territory from the Nile Valley through the Iranian highlands to Mesopotamia, where agriculture and civilization first began.

Flotation A method of recovering plant remains by passing them through screens and water.

Fluting A term used to describe the vertical thinning flake removed from the base of Paleo-Indian projectile points in North America with a punch. The thinned base made it easier to mount the point on the shaft.

Food Production Agriculture and animal domestication.

Groove-and-splinter technique Longitudinal grooving of antler and bone to produce long, parallel-sided grooves for making spear points, harpoons, and other artifacts. Used by Upper Paleolithic and Mesolithic peoples.

Ground stone Artifacts manufactured by pecking the surface and edges with a stone, then grinding them smooth, to form sharp working edges. A technique used for axes and adzes employed for felling trees and woodworking.

History The study of the past using written records.

Holocene From the Greek word for "recent." Refers to the millennia since the end of the Pleistocene (Ice Age) about 10,000 B.C.

Hominid Primates of the family Hominidae, which includes modern humans, earlier human subspecies, and their direct ancestors.

Hominoid A primate superfamily that includes apes and hominids.

Inevitable variation Cumulative culture change due to minor differences in learned behavior over time.

Invention New ideas that originate in a human culture by accident or design.

Kiva Sacred ceremonial room built by prehistoric peoples in the American Southwest.

Knuckle walking Specialized way of getting around on four limbs, which uses the backs of the hands for supporting body weight.

Mandala A Hindu conception of the state used in southeast Asian archaeology.

Megalith From the Greek "large stone." A term applied to stone-built graves widespread during early farming times in western Europe, generally in the fifth millennium B.C.

Mesoamerica A term used by archaeologists to refer to those parts of central America where state-organized societies arose.

Microlith From two Greek words for "small stone." Diminutive stone artifacts manufactured on tiny blades and used as barbs and points for spears and later arrows. Characteristic of the late Ice Age and early Holocene societies.

Migration The movement of people from area to another.

Multilinear cultural evolution Cultural evolution along many diverse tracks.

Pleistocene The last geological epoch, sometimes called the Ice Age or Quaternary.

Pongid The family of nonhuman primates closest to humans.

Post-processual archaeology Approaches to the past that examine ideology, motives, and nonenvironmental aspects of culture change.

Potassium-argon dating A radiometric dating method which dates geological strata and early archaeological sites from volcanic rocks. Used to date prehistory from the earliest times up to about 100,000 years ago.

Prehistory Human history before the advent of written records.

Preindustrial civilization *See* State-organized societies. Also, a civilization organized without the use of fossil fuels.

Prestate societies Small-scale societies based on the community, band, or village.

Primordium The very beginning. The starting point of creation myths.

Prosimian The taxonomic suborder that includes femurs, tarsiers, and other so-called pre-monkeys.

Quaternary *See* Pleistocene.

Rachis. A hinge that joins a seed to a plant.

Radiocarbon dating A radiometric dating method based on the decay rates of radiocarbon isotopes. It is highly effective for dating developments over the past 40,000 years.

Settlement pattern The distribution of human settlement on the landscape and within archaeological communities.

Shaman Priest or spirit medium. The word comes from the Siberian Tungus word *saman,* meaning priest.

Sinodonty A distinctive cluster of tooth features associated with Siberian and Native American populations.

Spear thrower A hooked and sometimes weighted stick or equivalent device used for hurling spears.

State-organized society A large-scale society with strongly centralized government and marked social stratification. Synonymous with preindustrial civilizations.

Tribe Clusters of bands linked by formal kin groups.

Urban Revolution V. Gordon Childe's concept of an Urban Revolution was based on the assumption that metallurgy, specialists, and food surpluses caused a revolution in human life and urban civilization.

World prehistory The study of human prehistory from a global perspective.

Glossary of Archaeological Sites and Cultural Terms

This glossary covers major cultural terms and archaeological sites. It does not include names of leaders and other individuals.

Abri Pataud, France A rock shelter used by Upper Paleolithic foragers in southwestern France during the late Ice Age. Famous for its evidence of reindeer hunting.

Abu Hureyra, Syria A village site by the Euphrates River occupied first by foraging groups before 7700 B.C., then by very early farmers. Famous for its excellent botanical evidence for agricultural origins.

Acheulian stone technology A technology based on hand axes, cleaver, and flake artifacts that flourished in Africa, Europe, southwestern Asia, and parts of Southeast Asia between about 1.8 million and 200,000 years ago. Named after the town of St. Acheul in northern France.

Adena culture A culture dating between 500 B.C. and A.D. 400, centered on the Ohio valley and famous for its elaborate earthworks.

Adulis, Ethiopia A Red Sea port associated with the Aksum civilization.

Aksum Ethiopian highland civilization of the first millennium A.D. that traded with the Mediterranean and Indian Ocean worlds.

'Ain Ghazal, Syria Early farming village of the eighth millennium B.C.

Ali Kosh, Iran A farming settlement on the Khuzistan Plains occupied between 8000 B.C. and 6000 B.C.

Atapuerca, Spain Cave system that has yielded fossils of 200,000 year-old humans, probable ancestors of the Neanderthals.

Altamira, Spain Magdalenian painted cave dating to about 15,000 years ago. Famous for its polychrome bison paintings.

Ambrona, Spain An Acheulian butchery site dating to between 200,000 and 400,000 years ago.

Anasazi Major Southwestern cultural tradition centered on the Four Corners region, which reached its greatest efflorescence after A.D. 1100.

Angkor Thom and Angkor Wat, Cambodia Royal capitals and shrines built by the Khmer rulers of Cambodia between A.D. 1000 and 1200.

Anyang, China Central core region of Shang civilization of northern China between 1400 and 1122 B.C.

Ao, China Shang civilization capital in northern China occupied in about 1560 B.C.

Aramis, Ethiopia Site on the Awash River where *Ardipithecus ramidus* was discovered and dated to 4.4 million years.

Archaic Generalized label given to later forager cultures in the Americas, highly diverse and often sophisticated cultures dating from 6000 B.C. into recent times.

Assur, Iraq Assyrian capital on the Tigris River, which was powerful after 900 B.C.

Aquateca, Guatemala Late Classic Maya settlement of the ninth century A.D.

Babylon, Iraq Major early city-state, and later capital of the Babylonian empire under King Nebuchadnezzar in the sixth century B.C.

Bandkeramik complex A cultural label describing the first farmers of central and northwestern Europe of about 6000 B.C. Distinguished on the basis of line-decorated pottery.

Benin, Nigeria A West African forest kingdom with a capital of the same name, which flourished before the 14th century A.D. until recent times.

Boqueirão da Pedra Furada, Brazil A controversial site, claimed to have yielded evidence of early human settlement in Brazil by 40,000 years ago.

Broken Hill *See* Kabwe.

Cahokia, Illinois Major ceremonial center of the Mississippian culture built after A.D. 900.

Calakmul, Guatemala Major Maya political and religious center from Preclassic times to A.D. 800.

Çatalhöyük, Turkey Early farming town that prospered on the obsidian trade between 6000 and 5000 B.C.

Chaco Canyon, New Mexico *See* Chaco Phenomenon.

Chaco Phenomenon Generic name given to the Anasazi sites and associated phenomena of Chaco Canyon, New Mexico, in the 11th and 12th centuries A.D.

Chan Chan, Peru Capital of the Chimu civilization, after A.D. 1000.

Chauvet. *See* Grotte de Chauvet.

Chavín de Huántar, Peru Ceremonial center in Peru's Andes foothills dating to between 900 and 200 B.C. Source of much Andean art and ideology.

Chichén Itza, Mexico Postclassic Mayan center in the northern Yucatan, especially in the thirteenth century A.D.

Chilca, Peru A semipermanent foraging settlement on the Peruvian Coast dating to after 4000 B.C.

Chimu civilization Lowland civilization in Peru's Lambayeque valley, which flourished between c. A.D. 1000 and 1476.

Chimor, Peru The domains of the Chimu civilization.

Chiripa, Peru A ceremonial center near Lake Titicaca founded in 1000 B.C.

Cliff Palace, Mesa Verde, Colorado Major Anasazi pueblo site in Mesa Verde, which reached its greatest extent after A.D. 1200.

Clovis tradition Widespread Paleo-Indian tradition associated with very early settlement throughout North America. Dates to the ninth millennium B.C.

Copán, Guatemala Major Maya center during the mid-first millennium A.D.

Coxcatlán, Mexico A rock shelter in the Tehuacán Valley that yielded desiccated maize cobs dating to about 2000 B.C.

Cro-Magnon, France A rock shelter near Les Eyzies in southwestern France where the first late Ice Age people were found in 1868. The Upper Paleolithic people of western and central Europe are often called Cro-Magnons.

Cuzco Capital of the Inca empire in highland Peru.

Dilmun, Bahrein Important transshipment port between Mesopotamia and the Indus valley in the Persian Gulf as early as 2500 B.C.

Dos Pilos, Guatemala Important Classic Maya center after A.D. 600.

D'uktai Cave, Siberia The best-known site for a widespread very late Ice Age culture in Northeast Siberia, which may have been the ancestor of some early Native American groups. Dates to as early as 18,000 years ago.

East Turkana, Kenya Location where fossil hominids and their sites date to c. 2.5 million to 1.6 million years ago.

El Mirador, Guatemala Preclassic Maya center dating to between 250 and 50 B.C.

El Paraíso, Peru Ceremonial center in Peru's Chillon Valley dating to c. 1800 B.C.

Erech Early Sumerian city-state of about 2800 B.C.

Fort Rock Cave, Oregon A site with possible evidence of human occupation in North America as early as 12,000 B.C.

Funan, Cambodia Prosperous city-state in Southeast Asia between the third and sixth centuries A.D.

Ganj Dareh, Iran A seasonal foraging camp of 8500 B.C. in the Zagros Mountains.

Ghana, Kingdom of West African state on the southern fringes of the Sahara Desert, that controlled much of the West African gold trade as early as the eighth century A.D.

Giza, Egypt Major pyramid site of Old Kingdom Egypt dating to c. 2600 B.C.

Great Zimbabwe, Zimbabwe Major religious and trading center and Karanga chiefdom between about A.D. 100 and 1500.

Grotte de Chauvet, France. Painted late Ice Age cave with remarkable depictions of lions, rhinoceroses, and other animals, dating to as early as 31,000 B.C.

Guilá Naquitz, Mexico A cave occupied by a small band of foragers between 8370 and 6670 B.C. Important for the study of early bean and squash cultivation.

Hadar, Ethiopia Location where many specimens of *Australopithecus afarensis* have been found, dating to about 3 million years ago.

Harappa, Pakistan Major city of the Harappan civilization, c. 2500 B.C.

Harappan civilization Indigenous Indian civilization of the Indus valley of what is now Pakistan, c. 2700 to 1700 B.C.

Hatti Hittite kingdom centered on Anatolia in the second millennium B.C.

Hidden Mammoth site, Alaska A hunting camp in central Alaska dating to about 9700 B.C.

Hierankonpolis, Egypt Ancient Egyptian town, center of an important Predynastic kingdom.

Hittites *See* Hatti.

Hohokam A widespread desert farming culture centered on southern Arizona, which flourished from about 300 B.C. to A.D. 1500.

Hopewell tradition A widespread religious and burial cult centered on Illinois and the eastern United States, which flourished from 200 B.C. to A.D. 400.

Huon Peninsula, New Guinea Site where 40,000-year-old ground stone axes offer early evidence of human settlement on the island.

Jarmo, Iran Early farming village in the Zagros Mountains occupied before 5000 B.C.

Jericho, Jordan Biblical city and famous archaeological site with evidence of an early fortified town of the eighth millennium B.C. and of farming settlements as early as 7800 B.C.

Kabwe (Broken Hill), Zambia Site in Central Africa where a robust form of early *Homo sapiens* was discovered. Exact age unknown.

Kanesh, Turkey Hittite settlement founded in the seventeenth century B.C. famous in later centuries for its Assyrian trading quarter.

Karanga Generic name given to the Shona-speaking peoples of Zimbabwe.

Kerma Nubian kingdom of the third millennium B.C.

Khoi Khoi Pastoral cattle herders of the southernmost tip of Africa, encountered by Portuguese explorers in the 15th century A.D.

Kilwa, Tanzania East African coastal trading port, which was a major transhipment point for African gold and ivory after A.D. 1200.

Kish Early Sumerian city-state of about 2800 B.C. and later.

Kalambo Falls, Zambia Lake bed site where Acheulian occupation levels over 200,000 years old were found.

Knossos, Crete Palace of Minos at Knossos was a major center of Minoan civilization. The site was occupied from before 2000 B.C. to about A.D. 1400.

Koobi Fora, Kenya Location of some of the earliest traces of stone manufacture in the world, some 2.5 million years ago.

Koster, Illinois A stratified site in the Illinois River valley of the North American Midwest inhabited from about 7500 B.C. to A.D. 1200 by foragers, then maize farmers.

Koto Toro, Chad *Australopithecus afarensis* site south of the central Sahara dating to about 3.0 to 3.5 million years ago.

Kush An African state in the Sudan, which flourished along the Nile River after 900 B.C.

La Ferrassie, France A rock shelter near Les Eyzies in southwestern France, where evidence of Neanderthal burials was found.

Laetoli, Tanzania Site where hominid footprints were preserved in hardened volcanic ash 3.75 million years ago.

Lagash, Iraq Major Sumerian city-state of the third millennium B.C.

La Madeleine, France *See* Magdalenian.

Langebaan Lagoon, South Africa Site where 117,000 year-old footprints of an anatomically modern human are preserved in a fossilized sand dune.

Lapita culture A cultural tradition in the southwestern Pacific, responsible for colonizing much of the offshore Pacific after 2000 B.C.

Lascaux, France Major site of Magdalenian cave painting in southwestern France dating to about 15,000 years ago.

La Venta, Mexico Olmec ceremonial center dating to after 900 B.C.

Le Tuc d'Audoubert, France A Magdalenian ceremonial site famous for its clay bison figures.

Machu Picchu, Peru Inca settlement high in the Andes occupied during and after the Spanish conquest.

Magan Persian Gulf transshipment port between Mesopotamia and the Indus Valley.

Magdalenian culture Late Ice Age culture with sophisticated technology and art tradition found in southwestern France, parts of central Europe, and northern Spain. Flourished between 15,000 and 12,000 years ago. Named after the La Madeleine rock shelter, Les Eyzies, Dordogne.

Mali, Kingdom of West African state that succeeded Ghana in about A.D. 1200 and became internationally famous for its gold during the next century.

Maori people New Zealand's indigenous inhabitants, with ancestry in Polynesia dating back to at least A.D. 1000.

Mauryan Empire, India Early Indian empire centered on the Ganges River during the mid-first millennium B.C.

Maya civilization Major lowland Mesoamerican civilization from about 1000 B.C. until the fifteenth century A.D., with the Classic period ending in about A.D. 900.

Mayapan Postclassic Maya center ruled by the Cocom family after the 13th century A.D.

Meadowcroft Rock Shelter, Pennsylvania A long occupied rock shelter, with possible evidence of human occupation as early as 12,000 B.C.

Meer, Belgium A Stone Age camp of 6000 B.C., used by stoneworkers.

Meluhha Important Persian Gulf transhipment port for the Indus civilization. Location unknown.

Memphis, Egypt Capital of Old Kingdom Egypt, 3100 to 2181 B.C.

Merimda Beni Salama, Egypt A farming settlement in the Egyptian delta dating to about 4500 B.C.

Meroe, Sudan Royal capital of the kingdom of that name on the Nile River from about 500 B.C. to A.D. 400. A major trading center.

Mesa, Alaska A forager camp site in the Brooks Range of northern Alaska, occupied in about 9700 B.C.

Mesa Verde, Colorado A series of canyons in Colorado famous for their multiroom Anasazi pueblos of the 13th and 14th centuries A.D.

Mezhirich, Ukraine Late Ice Age forager camp with elaborate mammoth bone houses on the Ukraine's Dnieper River, dating to about 17,000 years ago.

Minoan civilization Bronze Age kingdom centered on Crete, which reached its height between 1900 and 1400 B.C.

Mississippian culture A maize and bean farming culture in the midwestern and southeastern United States dating from A.D. 900 to 1500, remarkable for its large ceremonial centers, elaborate religious beliefs, and powerful chiefdoms.

Mitanni Bronze Age state of the 2nd millennium B.C., east of the Euphrates River. Contemporary with the Hittites.

Moche civilization Coastal Peruvian civilization centered on the Chicama and Moche valleys, dating from 200 B.C. to A.D. 600.

Mogollon Southwestern cultural tradition of about 300 B.C. to c. A.D. 1100. A highland farming culture without major population centers.

Mohenjodaro, Pakistan Major city of the Harappan civilization (see Harappan civilization).

Monte Albán, Mexico Major city and state in the Valley of Oaxaca during the first millennium A.D.

Monte Verde, Chile A streamside forager site in northern Chile dating to about 10,000 B.C.

Mound City, Ohio A Hopewell mound complex covering 13 acres (5.26 ha) in the Ohio River valley.

Moundville, Alabama Major Mississippian town and ceremonial center after A.D. 900.

Mousterian technology Stone tool technology associated with Neanderthal peoples of Europe, Eurasia, and the Near East after about 100,000 years ago. Based on carefully prepared disk cores. Named after the French village of Le Moustier.

Mycenae, Greece Citadel of Mycenaean kings, c. 1500 B.C.

Mycenaean civilization Bronze Age civilization on mainland Greece, which reached its height between 1500 and 1200 B.C.

Nagada, Egypt Predynastic Egyptian kingdom in Upper Egypt dating to the fourth millennium B.C.

Nakbé, Guatemala Early Maya ceremonial center of 600 to 400 B.C.

Nineveh, Iraq Capital of Assyrian Empire under King Assurbanipal, c. 630 B.C.

Nubia "The Land of Kush," which lay upstream of Ancient Egypt in the present-day Sudan.

Oldowan The earliest known human stone tool technology, based on simple flakes and choppers, which appeared about 2.5 million years ago and remained in use for nearly a million years. Named after Olduvai Gorge.

Olduvai Gorge, Tanzania A site where stratified early hominid archaeological sites are associated with long dried up Lower and Middle Pleistocene lakes dated to between 1.75 million and 100,000 years ago.

Olmec Lowland Mesoamerican art style and series of cultures, which formed one of the foundations of later civilizations in the region. c. 1500 to 500 B.C.

Palenque, Guatemala Mayan city and ceremonial center ruled by the Shield Dynasty for many centuries, and powerful in the seventh century A.D.

Paleo-Indian Generalized label given to the earliest forager cultures in North America. Approximate time span from before 12,000 to 6000 B.C.

Paloma, Peru A large foraging settlement with limited agriculture on the Peruvian Coast, dating to after 4000 B.C.

Panalauca Cave, Peru A site which has yielded evidence of early quinoa cultivation and lama herding, dating to about 2500 B.C.

Phoenicians Expert traders who controlled much Mediterranean trade after 500 B.C. Founders of the city of Carthage in North Africa, they became hated rivals of Rome.

Preclassic The early stages of Maya civilization, c. 300 B.C. to A.D. 250. Sometimes called the Formative.

Pueblo Bonito, New Mexico A major Anasazi pueblo in Chaco Canyon, occupied in the 12th century A.D.

Pukara, Peru Center of a small kingdom in the north Lake Titicaca Basin in the early first millennium A.D.

Pylos, Greece Mycenaean palace famous for its archives of clay tablets, dating to c. 1500 B.C.

Sahul Australia, New Guinea, and surrounding the continental shelf during the late Ice Age.

San José Mogote, Mexico Important Valley of Oaxaca farming village of the second millennium B.C.

San Lorenzo, Mexico Major Olmec center dating to c. 1250 B.C.

San Marcos Cave, Mexico Important Tehuacán Valley site for the early history of maize.

Santorini, Greece Island some 70 miles (113 km) north of Crete, site of a violent eruption in the fifteenth century B.C.

Schoningen, Germany Stone Age archaeological site. About 400,000 years old, which yielded the earliest known wooden spears.

Sea Peoples Traders and pirates, who dominated much of the eastern Mediterranean for 300 years after 1200 B.C.

Shang civilization Early civilization centered on the Huang Ho River of northern China dating to c. 1766 to 1122 B.C.

Sicán, Peru Coastal Andean culture c. A.D. 700 to 1375.

Sipán, Peru Major ceremonial center of the Moche people, celebrated for its spectacular royal burials and dating to about A.D. 400.

Snaketown, Arizona Major Hohokam settlement near the Gila River, which was an important ceremonial center.

Songhay, Kingdom of West African state, which succeeded Mali after A.D. 1450 and collapsed after 1500, partly because of the new supplies of gold that reached Europe from the Americas.

Southern Cult A term given to a series of artistic motifs and associated religious beliefs of the Mississippian culture found over a wide area of the Midwest and southeastern United States.

Sunda Continental shelf of Southeast Asia during the late Ice Age.

Taima Taima, Venezuela A site with possible evidence of early human occupation in the 12,000 B.C. range.

Tawantinsuyu Inca name for their empire, "The Land of the Four Quarters."

Tehuacán Valley, Mexico A dry valley in Mexico where some of the earliest evidence for maize cultivation has been discovered.

Tenochtitlán, Mexico Capital of the Aztec civilization from about A.D. 1325 to 1521, estimated to have had a maximum population of about 250,000 people.

Teotihuacán, Mexico Major city in the Valley of Mexico, that flourished from about 200 B.C. to A.D. 750.

Thebes Capital of Middle and New Kingdom Egypt after 1520 B.C. and a major center of the worship of the sun god Amun.

This, Egypt Predynastic Egyptian kingdom in Upper Egypt in the fourth millennium B.C.

Tikal, Guatemala Classic Maya city, which reached the height of its power in A.D. 200 to 600.

Tiwanaku, Bolivia Highland Andean state near Lake Titicaca, which traded with a wide region, dating to between A.D. 200 and 1000.

Torralba, Spain *See* Ambrona.

Trinil, Java, Indonesia Gravel deposits up to 1.8 million years old, which have yielded the fossil remains of *Homo erectus*.

Trois Frères, France Magdalenian painted cave, famous for its sorcerer figures.

Tula, Mexico Capital center of the Toltec civilization, c. A.D. 900 to 1160.

Uaxactun Classic Maya city in the Mesoamerican lowlands defeated by its neighbor Tikal in A.D. 378.

'Ubaid culture Early farming culture of about 5000 B.C. in southern Iraq.

Ugarit, Syria Major port and commercial kingdom in the northern Levant during the Bronze Age, c. 1200 B.C. and later.

Uluburun, Turkey Bronze Age shipwreck site off southern Turkey, dating to the 14th century B.C.

Ur (Ur-of-the-Chaldees), Iraq Biblical Calah, Ur was a major city of the Sumerian civilization in the third millennium B.C.

Uruk, Iraq The world's first city, flourishing from 4500 B.C. for more than 2000 years.

Valsequillo, Mexico A site where mastodon bones and artifacts date to about 12,000 B.C.

Verkhene-Trotiskaya, Siberia The earliest known D'uktai site in Siberia, dating to about 18,000 years ago.

Wallacea Sulawesi and Timor, Southeast Asia, during the late Ice Age.

Wari, Peru Major highland Andean kingdom centered on a urban and ceremonial center of that name, c. 800 A.D.

Willandra Lakes, Australia Shell middens and camp sites dating from 37,000 to about 26,000 years ago.

Xia Early dynasty of northern Chinese rulers dating to before 1700 B.C., known from both archaeological evidence and legend.

Xiao-tun, China Capital of Shang civilization, 1400 to 1122 B.C., located in the Anyang region of northern China.

Yangshao, China A widespread farming culture in the Huang Ho River Valley of northern China after 5000 B.C.

Zhou An important Chinese dynasty that ruled over much of northern China after 1122 B.C.

Zhoukoudian, China Cave site famous for its *Homo erectus* fossils dating to as early as 500,000 years ago.

Zimbabwe *See* Great Zimbabwe.

Photo Credits

Page 5: Ancient Art & Architecture Collection. Page 7: Superstock. Page 13: British Museum. Page 28: Gordon Hillman. Page 34: Theya Molleson, Natural History Museum. Page 46(T): Transvaal Museum Museum, South Africa. Page 46(B): Alun R. Hughes and Phillip V. Tobias/University of the Witwatersrand, Johannesburg. Page 47: © 1994 Tim D. White/Brill/Atlanta. Page 48: Institute of Human Origins/Don Johanson. Page 49: John Reader/Photo Reserachers. Page 51: Institute of Human Origins. Page 52: National Museums of Kenya. Page 67: Ian Everard. Page 69: Cambridge Museum of Archaeology and Anthropology. Page 73: F. Clark Howell. Page 76: © Javier Trueba/Madrid Scientific Films. Page 77: David L. Brill/Atlanta. Page 81(T): Giovanni Caselli. Page 99: Peabody Museum, Harvard University. Page 102(A): Musee de l'Homme. Page 102(B): Topham/The Image Works. Page 102(C): Musee de l"Homme. Page 104: Jean Vertut. Page 106: Giovanni Caselli. Page 113: Arizona State Museum. Page 119: Center for American Archaeology, Kampsville IL. Page 122: Peter Howorth/Chrome Imagery. Page 128: Royal Anthropological Institute, London. Audrey I. Richards © 1935. Page 135(T): S. von Herbenstain. Page 138: Andrew Moore. Page 141: Michael Holford. Page 146: Henle/Monkmeyer. Page 151: R.S. Peaody Foundation for Archaeology, Andover, MA. Page 153: John W. Rick. Page 157: Ashmolean Museum, Oxford. Page 160: Granger. Page 161: British Library: Page 165: Teiwes, Arizona State Museum. Page 167: Granitsas/The Image Works. Page 170: Field Museum of Natural History, Chicago. Neg. 90925. Page 171: Van Bucher/Photo Researchers. Page 173: Cahokia Mounds State Historic Site, painting by Lloyd K. Townsend. Page 175: Museum of the American Indian, Heye Foundation/Art Resource, New York. Page 190: Metropolitan Museum of Art. Page 192: © British Museum. Page 194: Kenneth Garrett/National Geographic Society Image Collection. Page 201: British Museum. Page 204: Robert Harding Picture Library. Page 205: University of Pennsylvania Museum. Page 208: © Institute of Nautical Archaeology/Frey. Page 210: Fotoarchiv Hirmer Verlag, Munich. Page 211: Fotoarchiv Hirmer Verlag, Munich. Page 212: Ira Block/Image Bank. Page 213: Ira Block/Image Bank. Page 219 (both): Giraudon/Art Resource, New York. Page 223: John Ross/Robert Harding Picture Library. Page 225 (both): The Metropolitan Museum of Art, Museum Excavations, 1919-1920. Edward S. Harkness and Rogers Funds, 1920. (20.3.5). Page 226: Fotoarchiv Hirmer Verlag, Munich. Page 227: Metropolitan Museum of Art. Page 229: Ancient Nubia: Egypt's Rival in Africa by David O'Connor. (Philadelphia: The University Museum, University of Pennsylvania). Page 230: P.L. Shinnie. Page 233: Werner Forman Archive/Art Resource, New York. Page 235: Angel Martinez Bermejo/Sygma. Page 237: Granger. Page 242: The Winchester Excavations Committee, Winchester, England. Page 243: Roger-Viollet Documentation Generale Photographique, Paris. Page 244: Scala/Art Resource, New York. Page 247: Peabody Museum Harvard University. Photo by Hillel Burger. (neg. N28172). Page 248: Smithsonian Institution. Page 250: China Friendship Society. Page 251: An Keren/New China Pictures/Eastfoto. Page 254: Granger. Page 259: Werner Forman Archive/Art Resource, New York. Page 260: Mary Ellen Miller. Page 262: Rutlege, El Mirador Project. Page 265: © Robert Frerck/Odyssey/Frerck/Chicago. Page 267: Robert Frerck/Odyssey/Chicago. Page 268: © President and Fellows of Harvard College 1978, Peabody Museum Harvard University. Photo by Hillel Burger. Page 270: © President and Fellows of Harvard College 1978, Peabody Museum Harvard University. Photo by Hillel Burger. Page 273: Alper/Stock Boston. Page 276: From Robert D. Drennan, "Contextual Analysis of Ritual Paraphenalia in Formative Oaxaca," in Kent V. Flannery, ed., The Early Mesoamerican Village (New York: Academic Press), 1976. Reprinted by permission of the author and publishers. Page 277: © Robert Frerck/Odyssey/Frerck/Chicago. Page 279: Robert Frerck/Odyssey/Chicago. Page 280: Lesley Newhart. Page 283: Lesley Newhart. Page 285: American Museum of Natural History. Page 286: Codex Magliabecchi (facsimile)/British Museum. Photography by John Freeman. Page 287: The Bodelian Library Oxford. Codex Mendoza MS Arch Selden A.1 folio 46. Page 294: Jeffrey Quilter. Page 299: UCLA Fowler Museum of Cultural History/Photography by Susan Einstein. Page 300: UCLA Fowler Museum of Cultural History/Painting by Percy Fiestas. Page 301(B): Peabody Museum Harvard University. Photo by David de Harpoort, 1958. Page 302: Boltin Picture Library. Page 303: ©Saunders/Werner Forman Archive/Art Resource, New York. Page 305: M. Moseley/Anthro-Photo. Page 308: Werner Forman Archive/© Saunders/Art Resource, New York. Page 309: George Holton/Photo Researchers.

Index

Abri Pataud, France, 99
Abu Hureyra, Syria, 33, 34, 125, 134, 137–138, 156
Accelerator mass spectrometry (AMS) radiocarbon dating, 124, 126
Acheulian technology, 71–73
Adams, Robert, 184–185, 187
Adaptation
    culture as, 27–32
    by primates, 40–43
Adaptive radiation, 52–53
Adena culture, 169
Aeschylus, 14
Africa
    ancient kingdoms of, 231–237
    early farming in, 140–141
    Homo erectus and, 62, 65–69, 71
    human exodus and, 62–88
    See also specific places
Afrocentrism, 228
Age of Discovery, 158
Age of Humanity, 38
Agricultural (Neolithic New Stone Age) Revolution, 115, 117, 123
Agriculture
    domestication of animals and, 133–134, 135
    earliest farmers and, 132–153
    early
        in Africa, 140–141
        in the Americas, 148–153, 163–165
        in Asia, 136–140, 145–148, 198
        in Egypt, 140–141
        in Europe, 142–145
        in Mesopotamia, 198
        in Southwest Asia, 136–140
    experimental harvesting and, 28
    irrigation, 165, 184–185, 306
    maize and, 149–152, 163–164, 172
    theories of farming origins and, 121–124
    See also Farming; Food production
Ahmose the Liberator (king of Egypt), 224–226
Ahuitzotl (Aztec ruler), 284, 288
'Ain Ghazal, Syria, 138
Akhenaten (king of Egypt), 226
Akkadian kingdom, 206
Aksum, Ethiopia, 231, 233
al-Bakri, 234

Alexander the Great (king of Macedonia), 245
Ali Kosh, Iran, 140
Altamira, Spain, 93, 103
Alva, Walter, 17, 299
Ambrona, Spain, 73
Amenemhet (king of Egypt), 228
American Southwest
    chiefdoms and, 163–168
    human occupation of, 163–168
Americas
    early agriculture in, 148–153, 163–165
    Mississippian culture in, 33, 171–176
    settlement of, 109–114
    See also American Southwest; Andean civilizations; Mesoamerica; North America; *specific places*
Amun, 226, 229
Anasazi, 164, 166–168
Andean civilizations, 290–310
    coastal foundations of, 293–295
    early farming in, 152–153
    Early Horizon of, 295–297
    Inca state and, 181, 306–310
    Initial Period of, 297–298
    Late Horizon of, 306–310
    maritime foundations of, 291–293
    Middle Horizon of, 302–306
    Moche state and, 17–18, 32, 186–187, 191, 192, 298–302
    Spanish conquest and, 292, 309, 310
Angkor Mandala, 253–254
Angkor Wat, Cambodia, 253–254
Animals, domestication of, 133–134, 135
Anthantnama, 14
Anthropoids, 40
Anyang, China, 246, 249, 250
Ao, China, 246
Aquateca, 272
Aramis, Ethiopia, 45, 47
Arboreal locomotion, 48–49
Archaeological context, 18
Archaeology, 6–8
    cognitive, 32
    context of, 18
    defined, 7
    of early humans, 56–58
    ethnoarchaeology and, 23